A PILGRIM IN A PILGRIM CHURCH

A Pilgrim in a Pilgrim Church

MEMOIRS OF A CATHOLIC ARCHBISHOP

Rembert G. Weakland, OSB

WILLIAM B. EERDMANS PUBLISHING COMPANY
GRAND RAPIDS, MICHIGAN / CAMBRIDGE, U.K.

Published 2009 by

Wm. B. Eerdmans Publishing Co.

2140 Oak Industrial Drive N.E., Grand Rapids, Michigan 49505 /

P.O. Box 163, Cambridge CB3 9PU U.K.

www.eerdmans.com

Printed in the United States of America

15 14 13 12 11 10 09   7 6 5 4 3 2 1

Library of Congress Cataloging-in-Publication Data

Weakland, Rembert.

A pilgrim in a pilgrim church: memoirs of a Catholic archbishop /

Rembert G. Weakland.

p.   cm.

Includes bibliographical references and index.

ISBN 978-0-8028-6382-9 (cloth: alk. paper)

1. Weakland, Rembert. 2. Bishops — Wisconsin —

Milwaukee — Biography. I. Title.

BX4705.W3815A3   2009

282.092 — dc22

[B]

2009012119

Excerpts from Geoffrey Chaucer's *Canterbury Tales* appearing in this volume are from the original text edited by A. C. Cawley, Everyman's Library (New York: Alfred A. Knopf, 1968).

Quotations from the modern English prose version are from THE CANTERBURY TALES by Geoffrey Chaucer, translated by David Wright, copyright © 1964 by David Wright. Used by permission of Vintage Books, a division of Random House, Inc.

To the ecumenical and interfaith community in Milwaukee,

to the faithful of the Archdiocese of Milwaukee,

but especially to its priests;

in gratitude.

Contents

FOREWORD   ix

PROLOGUE: Broken and Re-glued   3
Milwaukee, Wisconsin (May 2002)

PART I

1. Inheriting Coal Dust in the Veins   23
Patton, Pennsylvania (1927-1940)

2. Thirsting for Knowledge   41
St. Vincent, Latrobe, Pennsylvania (1940-1948)

3. Absorbing New Worlds   63
Rome (1948-1951)

4. Experiencing a Second Novitiate   76
New York–Milan (1952-1957)

5. Transitioning from Old Church to New   91
St. Vincent (1957-1963)

6. Testing Challenges of Leadership   111
St. Vincent (1963-1967)

Contents

PART II

7. Adjusting to the Eternal City   127
   Rome (1967-1973)

8. Traveling the World Over   160
   (1967-1973)

9. Applying the Wisdom Learned   190
   (1973-1976)

10. Ministering in the Last Years of Pope Paul VI   210
    Rome (1973-1977)

PART III

11. Learning to Be an Archbishop   235
    Milwaukee (1977-1983)

12. Drafting "Economic Justice for All"   273
    (1981-1986)

13. Sorting Out Positions   293
    Milwaukee-Rome (1983-1988)

14. Balancing Conflicting Models of Church   326
    Milwaukee (1989-1996)

15. Struggling toward the Finish Line   369
    Milwaukee (1996-2002)

EPILOGUE: Final Reflections   417

ACKNOWLEDGMENTS   424

INDEX   427

Foreword

In spring 2002, on a visit to Milwaukee, I sat down to dinner with Archbishop Rembert Weakland. The storm over clerical sexual abuse was blowing full force. As editor of Commonweal, I wanted to hear the views of a seasoned churchman on the scandal that was tearing the Catholic Church apart. However many facts he might willingly share — or not — in an interview with a journalist, I anticipated an informed assessment from a man deeply familiar with the ins and outs of the Vatican and of the Catholic Church in the United States.

Archbishop Weakland readily acknowledged the gravity of the scandal, conveying in some detail his own long-standing effort to resolve cases of clerical sexual abuse of minors in the Archdiocese of Milwaukee. Though he was following the canonical procedures set down in church law, he told me that his efforts to dismiss these priests were regularly rebuffed by Vatican officials. The archbishop was also troubled by the failure of some bishops to take matters in hand during earlier exposés of clerical abuse cases. While some adopted the guidelines proposed by the United States Conference of Catholic Bishops or devised their own, others did little or nothing to deal with their clergy abusers. All of these distinctions were lost in the revelations that emerged in early 2002 about the Archdiocese of Boston, and then many other locales. Everywhere Catholic dioceses were under siege, and all bishops were under suspicion.

The dilemma the archbishop described was troubling, and it was not his dilemma alone. If a knowledgeable Vatican insider like Weakland had not succeeded in convincing Rome, what could ordinary bishops do with priests who had abused children and yet could not be dismissed from the clergy? Moving them from parish to parish, even after what was purported to be successful treatment, led to repeat offenses; isolating them from children proved practically impossible and therefore was no guarantee of safety. On the civil rather than canonical side of the law much might have been done — as we now see — but local police and prosecutors were often reluctant, in Milwaukee as elsewhere, to bring child abuse cases to a courtroom — even if parents were to agree to the notoriety of a public forum. As Weakland describes these scenarios in this memoir, psychological and pastoral issues weighed heavily in how a bishop assessed and dealt with conflicting charges and denials. But in 2002, all nuance was lost in a cascade of accusations.

Not long after our dinner conversation, Weakland himself was caught in a media storm. The offense was not child abuse, but, given the context of the time, his own transgression delivered another jolt to the church and more grist for the scandal mills. The prologue to *Pilgrim in a Pilgrim Church* gives a dramatic account of the end of his ecclesiastical career in a blaze of TV cameras and a penitential rite at Milwaukee's St. John's Cathedral. Full of remorse, he begged forgiveness from his flock for an adult homosexual relationship from years earlier that had ended in demands for money, a confidentiality agreement, and the use of diocesan funds to forestall a public trial. The Vatican immediately accepted Weakland's resignation, and his career ended. He seemed to disappear.

In meetings over the years, I had admired Weakland's considered and thoughtful reflections on issues polarizing the church; he was knowledgeable and straightforward. On reading news accounts of the far from clear charges and of his apology, I wrote a brief comment in *Commonweal*. "His intelligence and balance have always seemed to me a true gift to the church. It saddens me greatly that on the eve of his retirement, a two-decades-old encounter — perhaps an indiscretion, perhaps a grave sin — with an adult male should be publicized so as to destroy the reputation of a great churchman." Somewhat against the tide of opinion, I lamented what seemed to be a concerted effort to exploit this homosexual relationship by taking advantage of media interest in the sex abuse scandal: "It is a tragedy that legitimate concern about the sexual abuse of children by priests is turning into a sexual witch hunt."

Six years after these events, I had a phone call from Eerdmans' Jon Pott, who asked if I would read and offer an assessment of a manuscript from Rembert Weakland. Rumors had had him working on a memoir; apparently he had finished it. A very long manuscript soon arrived. I read it, absorbed and fascinated by the story he had to tell. Small-town boy from Pennsylvania — smart, hard-working, musically gifted — grows up in poverty, raised by a widowed mother with six children. St. Vincent's Archabbey in Latrobe offers him a high school education; he becomes a monk, an accomplished pianist, and a teacher. Studies at St. Anselm's, the Benedictine college in Rome, are followed by courses at the Juilliard School of Music in New York and at Columbia University, and by eye-opening work in a Manhattan parish. Finally, he returns to St. Vincent's and is elected abbot. All by the age of thirty-six!

This quintessentially American story of rising from poverty continues on to become a quintessentially Catholic story of ecclesiastical advancement in Rome: Weakland is elected abbot primate of the Benedictine order, launches on an unprecedented series of visits to monasteries around the world, adapts the fifteen-hundred-year-old monastic order to the needs of the Vatican II church, and becomes a confidant of Pope Paul VI. Finally, he takes on the very unmonastic and lonely task (for a monk) of serving as Archbishop of Milwaukee and a leader in the U.S. Catholic church.

"Great history," I reported back to Jon Pott.

When he subsequently asked if I would work with Archbishop Weakland to revise and cut the manuscript, I hesitated. I am not a book editor; five thousand words is generally my outer editing limit. And though I am a cradle Catholic, I am not particularly attuned to the culture of the Catholic clergy. And I feel little confidence in dealing with the topic of homosexuality, thanks in good measure to its often closeted nature. How could I help with a memoir in which this was a core issue, apparently obscure for many years to the author himself? I suppose I was prompted finally to say yes because I am a great admirer of the Benedictines who educated me and set me on the path summed up in the title of another book, *The Love of Learning and the Desire for God*, by Jean LeClercq, OSB. And, I have made clear, I was and am an admirer of Rembert Weakland.

But *Pilgrim in a Pilgrim Church* is more than a history of ecclesiastical life in the late twentieth century. It is also a remarkable memoir. The person of Rembert Weakland comes through: intellectually serious, musically accomplished, religiously astute, and pastorally energetic. He is a man of deep Catholic conviction unafraid to follow and express his well-tutored intuitions on what the faith requires not only of him but also of his episcopal peers in Rome and the United States. While he served as abbot primate, his commitment to the Benedictine tradition led to turf wars and struggles with curial officials that found their way to the desk of Paul VI. The pope, acquainted with the Benedictines and sympathetic to their autonomous form of governance, helped Weakland resolve these issues in the order's favor; a firm friendship was established.

Returning to the United States in the late seventies, Weakland brought the Benedictine tradition of consultation of the community to his pastoral work in Milwaukee. So too, as chair of the U.S. Bishops Committee commissioned to write a pastoral on economic life, he held far-ranging hearings and conversations with people from every walk of life. The publication of "Economic Justice for All," along with the pastoral on peace and war, chaired by Cardinal Joseph Bernardin of Chicago, implemented a new consultative pastoral style in the U.S. Catholic Church. In Milwaukee, the same pattern prevailed with clergy and laity, especially women who participated in his hearings on the role of women in the church and on abortion. As Archbishop of Milwaukee, Weakland found his relations with Pope John Paul II less congenial than they had been with Paul VI. Renovations to the cathedral, appointment of auxiliaries, and a variety of issues, personal and parochial, led to direct confrontations with the pope and curial officials that few Catholics would imagine possible, some of these disputes petty in the extreme.

Weakland's departure from public life in 2002 created a gap in the U.S. church's leadership. Though Weakland was widely regarded as liberal, and even a bit radical by many Catholic and secular commentators, his temperament, knowledge, and long experience offered critical balance in a church increasingly polarized by internal disagreements and public disputes.

The penitential service in St. John's Cathedral was not the end of Weakland's story. We now have in *Pilgrim in a Pilgrim Church* a robust account of what leadership in the Catholic Church today requires and entails. Indeed, it is easy to imagine that without that abrupt end to a distinguished career, Weakland might never have pursued the self-scrutiny and reassessment that have produced this candid and absorbing memoir. Though Weakland maintains a certain episcopal reserve, *Pilgrim in a Pilgrim Church* is unlikely to be duplicated in its breadth, detail, or frankness by any Catholic prelate.

As Weakland writes in the prologue, immediately after the penitential service, feeling shamed and humiliated, he wanted nothing more than to hide, to avoid people and steer clear of public life. In time, steady sympathy from friends, parishioners, and Catholics in Milwaukee as well as around the country drew him to reconsider his situation and his prospects and to come to terms with his homosexuality. He says, "I felt a new freedom, a sense of being liberated for the first time. I could begin to come to terms with my life as a whole in a spirit of truth and sincerity that had eluded me till then. For at least two decades, I felt I was walking an ecclesiastical tightrope, trying to be true to myself but also loyal to the institution that had nurtured and sustained me for many decades. The tension between being myself and trying to be a bishop in an image I found outmoded ceased."

Close observers of the U.S. Catholic Church would agree that bishops long regarded as princes of the church have fallen from grace and fallen hard. The clerical abuse scandal is hardly the only challenge they have faced over the last few decades. Weakland's account of his years as archabbot in Rome and as archbishop of Milwaukee amply portrays the spiritual, ecclesiastical, and administrative struggles church leaders live with every day. Even more, Pilgrim Weakland amply demonstrates the persistent effort required of a follower of Christ to be a member and servant of his church. The end of an ecclesiastical career turns out to have been the beginning of a new spiritual journey.

MARGARET O'BRIEN STEINFELS

Now preye I to hem alle that herkne this litel tretys or rede, that if ther be any thyng in it that liketh hem, that therof they thanken oure Lord Jhesu Crist, of whom procedeth al wit and al goodnesse. And if ther be any thyng that displese hem, I preye hem also that they arrette it to the defaute of myn unkonnynge, and nat to my wyl, that wolde ful fayn have seyd bettre if I hadde had konnynge. For oure book seith, "Al that is writen is writen for oure doctrine," and that is myn entente. Wherfore I biseke yow mekely, for the mercy of God, that ye preye for me that Crist have mercy on me and foryeve me my giltes . . . and graunte me grace of verray penitence, confessioun and satisfaccioun to doon in this present lyf, thurgh the benigne grace of hym that is kyng of kynges and preest over alle preestes, that boghte us with the precious blood of his herte; so that I may been oon of hem at the day of doom that shulle be saved. Qui cum patre et Spiritu Sancto vivit et regnat Deus per omnia secula. Amen.

Chaucer: Valediction, *The Canterbury Tales*

(Now I beseech all who are listening to or reading this little treatise, if there is anything in it that pleases them, they should thank Our Lord Jesus Christ from Whom proceeds all wisdom and all goodness. If there be anything that displeases them, I ask them to attribute it to a lack of my ability and not to my will. I would very gladly have spoken better if I had had the skill. For our Book says, "All that is written is written for our instruction" and that is my intention. Therefore, I humbly beseech you, for God's mercy, that you intercede for me that Christ have mercy on me and forgive me my guilt . . . and grant me the grace of true repentance, confession, and satisfaction in this present life, through the merciful grace of Him who is King of Kings and Priest over all Priests, Who ransomed us with the precious blood of His heart; so that I may be one of those who shall be saved on the day of judgment. Qui cum Patre et Spiritu Sancto vivit et regnat, Deus, per omnia secula. Amen.)

Broken and Re-glued

Milwaukee, Wisconsin (May 2002)

In the early evening of May 31, 2002, I sat in my office, the office of the archbishop of Milwaukee, knowing it would be the last time. Much had happened in this room, many decisions made, many interviews given, many troubled people seen. With curiosity I looked out at the crowd that was gathering and the TV vans and cameras filling the parking lot. Then I looked around the room, at the books, the statues, the paintings. I was leaving the bronze statue of Pope Paul VI and the painting of Pope John Paul II for my successor. My desk stood between them. In my heart I knew that my twenty-five years as archbishop had been good years that could not be taken from me.

I was about to face the faithful of the Catholic Church of Milwaukee to make a necessary public apology, impelled by my concept of church as a community of loving, sustaining, forgiving believers. I went over and over in my mind every word of what I planned to say, wanting to take full responsibility for my actions and not blaming others. This penitential ceremony would give me an opportunity to apologize and to seek not so much God's forgiveness, having done so long before, but that of the community. In this penitential service, we were re-enacting a mode of public penance common in the early Church and continued in the monastic tradition. My mind kept going back to the monastic Chapter of Faults and the vision of gentle Abbot Alfred Koch who, each year on Ash Wednesday, in the presence of the whole community, with patent meekness and humility admitted his failings of the previous year.

Sitting in that familiar space preparing myself, I prayed some psalms, concentrating as best I could. Slowly and in rhythm with my breathing, I repeated versions of the "Jesus prayer": an invocation like "Loving Savior" or "Lord Jesus" while inhaling; a long pause; and then the petition "Be with me" or "Sustain me" while exhaling. I asked for the strength to able to stand before the clergy and people of the archdiocese with sincerity and confidence and offer my apology and make my plea for forgiveness.

I come before you today to apologize and beg forgiveness.

I know — and I am sure you do too — that the Church to be authentic must be a community that heals. But I also know — and you do too — that there is no healing unless it is based on truth. In my remarks I will do my best.

I apologize to all the faithful of this archdiocese which I love so much, to all its people and clergy, for the scandal that has occurred because of my sinfulness.

Long ago I placed that sinfulness in God's loving and forgiving heart, but now and into the future I worry about those whose faith may be shaken by my acts.

The early Church was wise to declare that God can use imperfect instruments to build the Kingdom and that the effectiveness of the sacraments does not depend on the holiness of the minister. For me that thought brings some, though meager consolation. It does not in any way diminish my need to beg forgiveness of all of you.

I acknowledge and fully accept my responsibility for the inappropriate nature of my relationship with Mr. Paul Marcoux. I apologize for any harm done him. At that time, 1979, I did not understand that responsibility in the same way as I do now. I have come to see and understand the way in which the power of the Roman collar can work in such relationships and even more so, a bishop's miter.

There is an understandable concern about the money paid out in the settlement agreement of 1998. I understood the settlement agreement in question as compensation for Paul Marcoux because of the claim that I had interfered with his ability to earn income. Rather than spend the money litigating this claim, I agreed to an out-of-court settlement. In hindsight I can see why it has the appearance of "hush money." Perhaps I should have handled the situation differently. If I had done so, there would still have been sizeable costs to the Church, but at least it would have been out in the open.

One of my fears in not accepting the settlement was the prospect of scandal and embarrassment to myself and to the Church. For that lack of courage, I apologize.

This money did not come from the Stewardship Appeal or from any diocesan funds designated for charitable or pastoral work. In my mind, the money I had given the archdiocese was more than the settlement amount. To my continued embarrassment, I now am told that is not true. In my remaining years I will continue to contribute to the archdiocese whatever I can and, of course, the archdiocese will receive whatever effects I own on my death.

People who are concerned about me ask how I feel at this moment. The best nouns to describe those feelings would be remorse, contrition, shame, and emptiness. This final word reminds me of an insight from St. Therese of Lisieux. She once wrote that she wanted to go to God empty-handed. I think I know now personally what she meant by that phrase. I have learned how frail my own human nature is, how in need of God's loving embrace I am. Empty-handed for me now means a willingness to accept my humanity totally, just as Christ accepted that same human nature out of love. But for me it also means to be fully receptive to whatever God wants to place in those hands, to be ready with empty hands to receive new life.

But I am also aware much self-pity and pride remain. I must leave that pride behind. Each day I will try to leave room for God to enter into my life more and more. Ultimately I understand that the humanity God so loved and sought to redeem, including my own humanity, will be transformed by his loving embrace and grace.

Again I apologize to all of you. You have been so extraordinarily loving and caring to me during these years and now during this crisis for me and for you. I want to take this occasion to say how very grateful I am to all of you for the zeal and vitality of faith you have demonstrated during the time I have been privileged to minister here. I also thank the groups of professionals who have contributed their skills and insights to that vitality. I thank all of you for the wonderful support shown me through the years and at this moment. In the future I count on your prayers and I hope for your forgiveness.

This penitential rite with its somber prayers of repentance and its power to offer reconciliation confirmed for me once again that ritual in times of crisis is one of the great gifts of the Catholic tradition. My "confession" and remorse could be given heartfelt public expression before people who had been so trusting of me.

How had my life as archbishop ended in a penitential service? How had matters reached this end? I had been given a privileged life. My monastery had provided me with a superb education and the best possible monastic training. The Benedictine abbots of the world had elected me abbot primate. Pope Paul VI had named me archbishop of Milwaukee. In church circles I had found a place as a serious and forward looking leader. Slowly but surely the people of Milwaukee had come to accept and befriend me. The U.S. Catholic bishops had trusted me to carry out difficult and time-consuming tasks. Now this world was crumbling about me.

*   *   *

From 1945, when I joined the monks at St. Vincent Archabbey in Latrobe, Pennsylvania, until 1977, the Benedictine ideal had fed me, intellectually and spiritually; I thrived in the community. Two sustaining forces, daily monastic prayers and living in community, continually fostered my celibate commitment. With my appointment as archbishop of Milwaukee in 1977 that routine was gone and my inner journey disrupted. As a bishop my identity was totally transformed and I had to begin my priestly and spiritual journey anew.

An episcopal appointment had never entered my mind. I would never have joined a monastery if I had nurtured such ambitions. But when Pope Paul VI asked it of me, I could not say no. He had been kind and generous to me during my ten years in Rome as head of the Benedictines. Though harboring many doubts, I resolved to do my very best and took up my post in Milwaukee.

Two drastic changes followed in short order. After I was less than a year in Milwaukee, Pope Paul passed away (August 6, 1978). A month later, my mother, the strongest influence in my life, joined him in death. The loss of my monastic community, my mother, and the friendship of Paul VI made my first years in Milwaukee very difficult — difficulties made more complex by changes in Rome. Cardinal Karl Wojtyła's election, after the untimely death of Pope John Paul I, did not surprise me and my first reactions were positive. I soon found, though, that I was off to a bad start with the new pontiff over remarks of mine that offended some in Milwaukee's large Polish community. Then, complaints about my decisions in the arch-diocese reached his desk with regular frequency. The full account of these first years in Milwaukee and my recurrent difficulties with the new pope and members of his curia will come later in the story; I mention them here because they added to the challenge of my finding my way as a bishop and to the disturbing sense that I was on my own in how I would fulfill that new role.

During these months of loneliness, isolation, and vulnerability, I struck up a friendship with Paul Marcoux, who was then in his early thir-ties. We shared an interest in the theology of Father Bernard Lonergan, SJ, and a love of music; he had a fine baritone voice. At the time, I judged him to be mature and understanding, though he was perhaps a bit adrift. As far as I know he had never finished his undergraduate degree in music; he worked in a factory in nearby Waukesha.

I first met Marcoux at public events, chatting after lectures, after con-certs, or in casual encounters. By this time of my life I had accepted my ho-mosexual orientation, an awareness I had suppressed since my teens but that came back belatedly in my forties. Later I will write about the shock of discovering that I might be sexually attractive to others with correspond-ing challenges to my vow of celibacy. In any case, what started as an ac-quaintance with Marcoux became a friendship and soon turned into a kind of idealized, even romantic, infatuation on my part. When in the sum-mer of 1979 he asked me to share an evening meal, I accepted. That eve-ning ended in sexual touches that he later would call "date rape." Our spo-radic relationship continued for some months while I kept closing my eyes to its conflict with my vow of celibacy, to the sinfulness of it all, and to the inevitable disillusionment. Over time, it became clear that rather than friendship what Marcoux wanted from me was large sums of money for "Christodrama," a form of psychodrama based on Gospel stories that in-volved participants in role-playing. I was critical of the project: Paul had no degree in psychology or counseling and showed little ability to handle money. Still to show my support, I contributed $14,000 to the project, in ef-fect, my life savings, but I made it clear that I had no more personal funds and could not be of further financial help.

When he quit his job in Waukesha and insisted that I give him money, I began to come to my senses. My hope had been to share my deeper inter-ests and aspirations; he undoubtedly had his own expectations. He needed financial security in order to pursue his personal goals, especially the de-velopment of Christodrama. With the sage help of a patient priest-confessor from among the Jesuits and of a psychologist, I came to realize that I had mistaken Marcoux's makeup and needs and that this relationship was no answer to my loneliness. Although there were moments when I thought it could continue without any sexual component, I realized the constant danger to my celibate commitment and the need to break off the relationship.

He then started to send threatening letters demanding large sums of money; I sought out an independent lawyer who called it extortion. The Milwaukee district attorney agreed with that assessment and suggested two options. I could open a legal case against Marcoux and face whatever publicity that might involve, or I could refrain from bringing charges and there would be no record in the D.A.'s files. I decided to drop the matter. My lawyer advised me to consult the authorities in Rome, but it was the last thing in the world I wanted to do. Since my relations with the new pontificate had not been positive, I could not expect a sympathetic hearing. Nonetheless, not settling the issue then and there was undoubtedly a major mistake.

On August 24, 1980, in an attempt to close the issue, I wrote Marcoux a letter explaining why our friendship could go nowhere. My mother had advised me never to put anything in writing that I did not want the whole world to read. Wise woman, what foresight she had! Though I hesitated to commit my feelings to paper, I recklessly did so out of a sense of pastoral duty and with trust in Marcoux's loyalty. I wanted to admit my deep affection for him, without denying my worry about his insistence that I give him money for his Christodrama project. More than anything, however, I wanted him to realize that my vows as a Benedictine monk were sacred to me, even if that did not make sense to him. I pointed out these hindrances to any true friendship, knowing this would displease him.

> During the last months I have come to know how strained I was, tense, pensive, without much joy. I couldn't pray at all. I just did not seem to be honest with God. I felt I was fleeing from Him, from facing Him. I know what the trouble was: I was letting your conscience take over for me and I couldn't live with it. I felt like the world's worst hypocrite. So gradually I came back to the importance of celibacy in my life — not just a physical celibacy but the freedom the celibate commitment gives. I knew I would have to face up to it and take seriously that commitment I first made thirty-four years ago. I found my task as priest-archbishop almost unbearable these

months and I came to realize that I was at a crossroads — and I knew I had to get the courage to decide. There is no other way for me to live, Paul. Ridicule me if you must — I am expecting it. Say I am seeking escapes, but I must be me.... I have to be free and unencumbered, if I want to give total service to His Church. There is no other way for me....

Sometime after that, Marcoux moved to Madison and I lost track of him. In subsequent years, I would hear from monks in one or another European Benedictine monastery that a guest, Mr. Paul Marcoux, claiming to be a close friend of mine, sent his regards. Once Marcoux wrote me a short letter with the plea that "we just be good friends again." (Friends told me he was having trouble marketing his Christodrama project among the bishops and had been told a word of support from me would be very helpful.)

The Marcoux encounter left me unraveled. I still yearned for a relationship, a friendship in which someone would understand and accept me as I was. Somewhat on the rebound, I was caught up over the next few years in an effort to find an intimate relationship with another. Finally I came to realize that seeking such a relationship as a monk and bishop was sinful and given my late sexual awakening an adolescent response. Very slowly I began to come to terms with my loneliness. I took steps that made me more positive about my life and mission, allowing me to become the kind of bishop I felt I could and should be. It took time to understand what spiritual writers had always said, namely, that there is a hole, a deep void, an unfulfilled yearning that all humans possess — some sensing it more than others — and into that emptiness and loneliness no other person can really reach; it would be too much to expect of any creature. That void comes from a yearning for the transcendent and will be filled with nothing else. Human love can only be an image, a sign, of the fulfillment that comes from the Divine. St. Augustine wrote that our hearts will be restless till they rest in God. I vowed to accept this spiritual restlessness, working around it, not expecting it to go away, but eager to use it to relate more compassionately to others who deeply feel that same void.

Almost two decades later, my letter to Marcoux came back to haunt me. In the fall of 1997, Matt Flynn, the diocesan lawyer, came to tell me that he had been approached by a lawyer acting on Marcoux's behalf, asking for damages for sexual abuse that he claimed happened in 1979 when he was in his early thirties. In a few days, I had to leave for Rome to participate in a synod of bishops. During those meetings in late November and early December, I was in frequent phone contact with the lawyers back home. Eventually the first demand was dropped because Marcoux's lawyers were convinced that the statute of limitation had expired. Marcoux's next proposal was to sell me the letter I had written in August 1980 for a million dollars; again it was extortion and I totally rejected it.

The synod in Rome ended and I returned home to my busy bishop's schedule. Some months later the archdiocesan lawyer again heard from the Montreal lawyer representing Marcoux. This time the threat of a lawsuit took a different approach, namely, that I had interfered in Marcoux's professional life, preventing him from making a livelihood because of my negative attitudes toward him and Christodrama. Again, he demanded a million dollars. The legal brief was lengthy and cited locations all over Europe and the United States where such interference was said to have taken place. There was no way I could recall when or how I had responded in the last twenty years to other bishops or professionals who may have been interested in bringing Christodrama to their dioceses. I could well have responded critically without any thought that this would be the basis for a future lawsuit against me. I had never confronted such a situation. A part of the proposed settlement was to include, among other elements, absolutely no concession on my part of any abuse, the end of Marcoux's demands for money, and his retrieval and destruction of all copies of my 1980 letter. Deep within me I knew that this was impossible. I strongly suspected that the *Milwaukee Journal Sentinel* and others had copies of the letter and he could not retrieve them. Later events have not caused me to change my assumption.

Agreeing to the settlement was not an easy decision. For hours, I sat on the calming enclosed patio of my house weighing the options. The hope of bringing an end to a burden that had weighed on me for decades was tempting. Saving my good name certainly played an important role in my thinking. But would it be the end? Legal counsel advised settlement because the cost of fighting such a case would be very high, probably exceeding half a million dollars, given the number of depositions that would have to be taken all over the world.

I toyed with the possibility of asking Rome to accept my resignation so I could fight the case. But I had no stomach for a public trial. In a culture such as ours where the intimate aspects of people's private lives have become everyone's daily entertainment, I felt that the whole matter would be exaggerated out of proportion. Although I felt sure of being vindicated on the abuse charge, I knew I would lose my reputation. Neither was I certain of winning against Marcoux's charge that I had interfered with his chance of making a livelihood. Given the current attitudes toward Catholic bishops in the United States, a jury might have awarded even higher damages than he was demanding. Would the settlement allow me to finish my term as archbishop at the age of seventy-five? That could only happen if the confidentiality of the settlement were iron-tight, but I harbored the suspicion that such confidentiality had already been breached by circulation of my letter of 1980.

After much prayer and reflection, I sent the archdiocesan lawyer to Montreal to begin negotiating a settlement. I had decided that if the bargaining between the lawyers could bring the sum below half a million dollars, I would agree to an out-of-court settlement. Any sum above that would have to go to the Archdiocesan Finance Council as required by church law; a public lawsuit might then follow. $450,000 was agreed upon. All copies of the 1980 letter were to be destroyed and the matter closed. The archdiocesan comptroller assured me that the building fund from which the archdiocese had been paying all such settlements had sufficient funds to cover that amount. (I did not ask then what properties were last sold and what moneys were deposited in that account.)

The settlement agreement, a rather tight one legal counsel assured me, was signed. But the matter continued to weigh heavily on my heart. Did I do what was right, or was I only protecting my own hide? Over and over again, I have asked myself why I did not take the matter to Rome, but at the time, throwing myself on the mercy of the pope and the curia did not seem a real alternative. I was convinced that there were no clear and just processes whereby a bishop could defend himself. The treatment received in Rome by bishops in similar difficulties was not promising; the procedures were clouded in secrecy. These cases were decided as the pope and his staff thought best.

There was another way I felt hemmed in, held hostage by the Church; it went back to another of my monastic vows. As a monk, I had found my vow of poverty liberating. My personal needs were taken care of by the monastery in a way that was more than adequate. But when at the age of fifty I became a bishop that vow was suspended by church law. For the first time in my life, I had to apply for a social security number and pay income tax. The archdiocese now took care of my needs, and they did so generously: my salary was a thousand dollars a month. Out of that I had to take care of clothing, toiletries, books, music, vacations, and contributions to charities and other causes that I wanted to support. All other income — royalties from my writings, honoraria for lectures or other public functions, Mass stipends, etc. — went either to my monastery or to archdiocesan bodies. As a result, my savings were meager and I could never have come up with the sum needed for the Marcoux settlement.

Though this financial setup was meant to free me from worries about money, it also had a controlling effect that comes with dependency and the fear that one's well-being could be left to the whim of others. Over my twenty-five years as archbishop, that monthly sum increased at the same rate as all the other diocesan salaries, so that by the time the lawsuit came I was receiving around $3,000 a month. I had managed to put a minimum amount in an IRA, but never had monies sufficient for purchasing anything substantial of my own.

Though this sounds like a complaint, it is not meant to be. The Church has been good to me; I have never wanted for anything; I have been able to contribute to all the causes I love. But the fact was that as a bishop there was no way for me to take care of an extraordinary personal need. I had to fall back on my dependency on the Church. This bothered me.

As I was making the settlement decision, all of this weighed on my mind. Furthermore, I was used to agreeing to settlements as a means of solving such problems. All I had to do was ask the archdiocesan comptroller if there were sufficient funds in the account from which we were paying out settlements. Without asking where this money came from, I agreed to the settlement with Marcoux.

These few pages about the settlement have been very hard for me to write. I have tried to be honest in describing what was going through my mind then, how I lived through the events, and how the decisions were made. Nonetheless, I am troubled still by my own reactions. The lawyers, archdiocesan and personal, responding to the U.S. district attorney's inquiry about the source of the settlement payment and its legality, agreed that the phrasing was correct: "I understood the settlement agreement in question as compensation for Paul Marcoux because of the claim that I had interfered with his ability to earn income." An investigation by the federal attorney confirmed that there was nothing illegal in the payment; but the loss of the money still bothered me.

But as the reader well knows the matter did not end with the 1997 settlement.

*   *   *

On the morning of May 23, 2002, a week before the public apology, I was alone in the archbishop's house on the grounds of St. Francis Seminary in Milwaukee. Having passed a restless night, I rose early, went to the chapel, and knelt before the Blessed Sacrament. The votive light before the tabernacle played over the stark figures on the chapel's icons, making them seem to dance. I lit the small votive candle suspended in front of the icon of Mary and Child, figures painted on wood in golden and deep red tones against a dark, somber, green background. A gift to me from the Benedictine nuns of Bosnia-Herzegovina, I treasured it and hoped the example of their courage would strengthen me. Taking out my worn volume of the Liturgy of the Hours, I remembered my novice master of fifty years before saying: "If you keep the Divine Office each day, in times of stress and anxiety it will keep you." I would like to say I prayed calmly and confidently that morning, but that would not be true. I was too distracted.

Slowly I made my way up the stairs to a small sitting room and flicked on ABC's "Good Morning America." I had been warned the day before by members of the press that there would be a story. The teaser announced a scandal involving a Roman Catholic archbishop. Paul Marcoux appeared on the screen publicly accusing me of "date rape." This had taken place, he said, in 1979 when he was in his early thirties. He also said that there was a 1998 confidential settlement between himself and the Archdiocese of Milwaukee for $450,000. As I looked at his image on the screen, I realized I would have passed him unrecognized on the street. I was another man then, as was he.

Looking at my watch and realizing that Washington, D.C., was an hour ahead of Milwaukee, I immediately phoned Archbishop Gabriel Montalvo, apostolic nuncio and the pope's representative in the United States, to inform him of the broadcast. "Of course," he said, "you are going to deny it." I admit to a slight and fleeting temptation to deny anything had ever happened. Then it would have ended up being as a case of "he-said/he-said." But I could not bring myself to such dishonesty. Furthermore, the explanation for the $450,000 settlement would sound absurd. I said to Archbishop Montalvo: "I will deny that any abuse took place, but will not say that nothing ever happened between us."

Rome was wired and my resignation as archbishop of Milwaukee was made effective immediately. I had actually submitted my resignation two months earlier on April 2, my seventy-fifth birthday, as required by church law. In fact, so that the event would sink clearly into my mind as a moment of dramatic change, I mailed it myself from the downtown post office in Milwaukee. A response came back within three weeks: the resignation was accepted *nunc pro tunc,* i.e., it was accepted but would be effective whenever the Roman authorities decided. I was to stay in office till a successor was named.

I had pleaded in my letter to be permitted to retire immediately, though foolishly I gave no reason for this urgency. The press kept hinting that a scandalous story would soon appear. I was tired and dispirited. Knowing that it takes months, sometimes a year, before a successor is appointed, I should have given cogent reasons for rapid action, but I had hesitated, hoping the delay would not be too long. On May 23, my worst fears had been realized.

Did this public revelation on television come as a total surprise? Not really. There had been hints before that the press knew of the settlement. For several years, I was convinced that the editors of the *Milwaukee Journal Sentinel* had a copy of the 1980 letter to Marcoux ending any involvement with him. More recently, I had received several unsigned memos from insiders at the newspaper telling me an "exposé" was coming. A week before May 23, I received a strange and unsettling phone call from a former employee of the archdiocese relaying a message from a reporter with whom I had had a very rocky relationship. This intermediary said that the story of the Marcoux affair and the settlement would be broken on ABC's "Good Morning America" within the next few days. Why was this information being relayed to me and why in this oblique fashion? I would like to have interpreted the warning as a kindness so I would be prepared, but my immediate reaction was to see it as a form of vindictiveness.

In these same weeks, several celebrations in honor of my twenty-five years as bishop and imminent retirement had been planned throughout the archdiocese. I cancelled my appearance in Kenosha on May 21 expecting the announcement that morning. When nothing happened, I decided to preside and preach at a similar service at St. Anthony's in Pewaukee on the evening of May 22. Large numbers of cameras from the major TV affiliates alerted me that D-Day was approaching. It was no wonder I did not sleep well that night. For some time, I had reason to expect that something would happen; till then I felt held hostage. Yes, I was forewarned, but never enough to anticipate the anxiety and bewilderment I suffered when it actually came.

The most difficult task before me after the story on "Good Morning

America" was to call my brother and sisters and explain to them in as succinctly as possible what was happening. I could not lighten their burden or
mitigate their shock, but only beg for as much understanding as they
could muster at that moment and with the little knowledge they had.

Though I needed time to assess what was happening to me, I also
knew decisions had to be made quickly for the good of clergy and people.
The days that followed were full of meetings with staff and lawyers. A hur-
ried press release had to be drawn up.

I felt I could say with all sincerity that, from my point of view, this was
not a case of "date rape." Yet given the tenor of the times and the large
number of cases of clerical sexual abuse of minors that had come to light, I
knew my situation would be reported by some members of the media as if
it belonged in that category. (Time was to show that I was right in that assumption.) I tried to keep a level head and determine as best I could what
my next response should be. One thing was clear: I did not want trial by
press or TV and talk-radio. I would not be drawn into those forums,
though many invitations were offered to respond to Marcoux. I feared being caught up in the kind of media coverage that seeks to make public entertainment out of personal failings to satisfy prurient curiosity.

Between May 23 and May 31, I read very few newspapers and watched
no TV reports. I needed time for prayer and reflection. I knew a short press
release would not be a sufficient response for the clergy and laity of the
archdiocese. More was needed. A press conference was suggested, but it
did not seem to be the proper setting in which to apologize and ask forgiveness. I was concerned about the scandal these revelations brought to
people I knew and loved, and so a candid, public apology in a solemn and
prayerful atmosphere had to be my response. I made my "confession" and
apology, as recounted in the opening page of this chapter. The responses I
received from many in the archdiocese were encouraging and affirming.
Slowly letters began to pour in from all around the country, almost all of
them supportive and forgiving.

*   *   *

After the apology and penitential service on the evening of May 31, my first
reaction was to creep into myself and remain there as in a cocoon, to hide
away in some forgotten hermitage till Christ, in his safe and secure arms,
would come to carry me, like Lazarus, across the barriers of death and
place me in his Father's bosom (Luke 16:19-31). Shame was the best word to

describe my feelings. I felt anxious in venturing out in public, fearing everyone would look at me, as if I wore a scarlet letter. I knew this sense of shame could foster a paralysis, so I did my best to move beyond it. Certain convictions helped me do that.

Long before, I had given up the notion of dividing people into good and evil and had come to see everyone as a mixture, the good being more often the dominant force. In looking at my whole life and not wanting to isolate one moment of it, I tried to balance the good and the bad and felt, for the most part, the good had really dominated. I would not let myself be categorized as a bad person — weak, perhaps, but not bad. It had seemed to me that there was in the American religious tradition a kind of false "Calvinism" that sought to put people into such categories. I long ago had rejected this tendency — it was not the way Jesus treated sinners in the Gospels. I would learn to accept the good I did in life as well as the bad and not minimize that good.

Second, I made up my mind not to let anger take hold of me. As a religious superior, I had dealt with too many people who permitted their lives to be ruled by an anger that harmed only themselves. I had often said to others, and now had to say to myself: anger destroys the person who is angry and does no harm to the person who is the object of the anger. Anger can also become the source of actions that are later regretted. I can honestly say that I did not let anger take hold at that moment. In my own mind I decided not to blame anyone but myself and reiterated my desire to take full responsibility for my own actions. But I also decided to hold my head high.

More than anything else, however, I had preached often to others and now to myself that our God is a God of love and second chances. If I preached this to others and acted as the faith-community's minister in dispensing such pardon to them, then I had to believe that God's love for me was not diminished. At the beginning, I was full of shame, but I hoped a salutary shame, not a negative, debilitating sense of worthlessness. I believed that God uses imperfect instruments, not perfect ones, to build the Kingdom. In my own weakness I sensed a new strength and became a better pastor because of it, certainly a more compassionate one.

I kept asking myself what God wanted of me next, how I could use this humiliation for a better understanding of what the Church is all about. I asked how I should grow spiritually because of and through these events. I stood naked before the world and felt that life was starting over for me. The fact that I had retired made this all the more evident. It was a beginning, not an ending. Our God is a God of the future, I would say to myself.

The story is not yet totally narrated. It still lacks an ending. It is in God's eyes but a new phase, a new calling.

God's love and providential care for me became visible through the human care and concern of so many others. Being imbued with the sacramental principle that God works through others and through signs and symbols, I sensed deeply the action of the Divine presence in the many letters, e-mails, and phone calls I received. If anything, I became convinced that my healing came about because others were acting as healers to me. The outpouring of love surprised me — I do not know why. Most of those who wrote just wanted to affirm my goodness and my worth in a moment when I doubted it. Many women in particular reached out to me at that time. I was humbled when, over time, many people, especially women, came forward with contributions so that the archdiocese was totally reimbursed and suffered no financial loss. With the exception of the abbot primate of the Benedictines, I did not hear from any authorities in Rome nor receive any sign of support from anyone there.

Music had been an integral part of my life from childhood and my chief means of emotional expression. Now music served many roles — release of anger, soothing of spirit, and an ever-present sign of transcendence.

It may seem strange, but I felt a new freedom, a sense of being liberated for the first time. I could begin to come to terms with my life as a whole in a spirit of truth and sincerity that had eluded me till then. For at least two decades, I felt I was walking an ecclesiastical tightrope, trying to be true to myself but also loyal to the institution that had nurtured and sustained me for many decades. The tension between being myself and trying to be a bishop in an image I found outmoded ceased.

On another level, I wondered if I could now talk openly of my sexual orientation without fear. It had become public knowledge that my orientation was homosexual. There was nothing more to hide; no one could do anything more to me. I was free.

Naturally I wished I had had a more realistic introduction to sexuality in my early formation. My life had been too sheltered, but I do not blame anyone for the lack of sexual maturity. When I was growing up, I doubt if one would have found in most Catholic families, schools, or seminaries clear and adequate instruction about sexual matters.

One evening after I had moved to my new apartment, some of us retired priests, all in our seventies and eighties, were sitting around after supper discussing the formation we had received in sexuality and celibacy. All agreed that the accent had been placed entirely on purity. In

Catholic high schools the question was how far one could go in petting before committing a mortal sin. In the seminary, dating was out of the question and the only criterion seemed to be a prohibition on masturbation. As long as one did not masturbate, one could be ordained a priest. Nothing was ever said to us about falling in love and how to handle oneself when one did. Sexual desire was seen as something negative, almost evil in itself. Neither the extreme pain of loneliness nor the joys of falling in love were ever discussed.

Throughout my adult life the question of my sexual orientation had been a question I did not want to face. This fact must also be a part of my tale. Since my teen years hiding it had become a way of life; I feared even admitting it to myself. But eventually I did and now I had to accept that this fact was public information. Through prayer and reflection I had arrived at certain convictions. For example, I did not let this awareness reduce my sense of worth as a person. I had rejected as unhelpful, even harmful, the statement of the Congregation for the Doctrine of the Faith in 1986 that this orientation made me "objectively disordered." Since this orientation was not voluntarily acquired, such language was insignificant to me. Either God created me that way or permitted forces beyond my control to make me that way, so I felt no diminution in God's love. I did not see myself as a person defined by my sexuality.

In fact, I worried that the use of such language could provoke a new form of "theology of contempt," the Augustinian teaching that had been used to explain why the Jewish people were meant to suffer and would always be second-class citizens. Throughout history it had created a mindset among some Christians that made it laudatory to commit acts of violence against them. To say that homosexuals are to be treated with respect even though they are objectively disordered is demeaning, a new form of double-talk. It would be much more helpful and truthful simply to say that we know almost nothing about the causes of human sexuality and for now leave the question at that. Moreover, I was convinced that we have to cease putting labels on people, especially pejorative ones.

A few negative letters and e-mails I received on the subject were especially vicious and threatening. I confess that one of the reasons I feared going to public gatherings was because of the publicity surrounding my sexual orientation, especially in the light of the hostility toward me on talk-radio in Milwaukee. Gradually that fear has diminished.

In addition, I was never sure that sexual attraction was so clearly black or white. Experience had demonstrated to me that some extremely homophobic men often were hiding tendencies which they did not want to ac-knowledge. There is so much gray in this area. From my own experience, with a remarkable mother and my supportive sisters, and with so many women who have been very close to me and whom I love dearly, I shy away from sexual absolutes. We all have witnessed same-sex bonding that un-doubtedly, even if on a subconscious level, had sexual overtones but that was nurturing and enriching. I wonder if all of this is not just a sign of the boundless nature of God's love for us humans, in whose image and likeness we are created. I simply decided that our God's love is without bounds and cannot be encapsulated in any form of human sexuality.

I decided to continue living in Milwaukee in retirement since I had spent the last quarter of a century of my life in that city and most of my friends lived there. My support groups were in Milwaukee. This city had become home to me.

Everyone kept asking me what I intended to do with my time in retire-ment. It was then I decided to write the story of how my life had unfolded, partly for my own sake, partly to be able to share with others. I write be-cause I am internally propelled to share with those I love and served for so many years a fuller story than I was able to tell in May 2002 when I apolo-gized publicly to them. Most of all, this need is rooted in a religious moti-vation. It is embedded in my concept of the Church's nature as a commu-nion of believers on a faith journey, a communion of saints (few in number) and of sinners (most of us). My story affects everyone else's story and thus, at least in part, belongs to them.

*   *   *

These are the points I meditated on through the month of June 2002 as I gradually moved from the archbishop's residence that I had loved so much to new quarters at the Cousins Center. About twenty retired priests lived there, and I would not be lacking for company at daily Mass and at meals.

My piano is a fine 1906 Mason and Hamlin that was redone when I came to Milwaukee. There was no question about the piano: it would go with me. Unbelievable as it might seem, the movers, in taking the piano from the old house to my new little apartment at Cousins Center, dropped it! I went at once to inspect the damage. There the piano lay in pieces; the old glue had not held and the piano had broken apart. Now it had to be to-tally re-assembled and re-glued, re-strung and re-voiced. It had to be made whole again.

Was this accident a symbol of my own life at age seventy-five? I too had to be glued back together by God's love. God had to re-string me. I knew I had to say my "yes" to this redoing and let God's love take hold of me totally. I decided that it was important not just to survive but to come out reconstructed and whole again. I decided to see 2002 as a fresh beginning; it was my chance to come to the end of life's journey in God's way, not mine.

My last night in the bishop's house was June 24. That night I lived out of my suitcase because early the next morning my priest secretary, the most efficient and generous Father Len Van Vlaenderen, was to drive me from Milwaukee to Pennsylvania, where two of my sisters still lived near my hometown. The trip provided an important breathing space — a chance to look back on my early life and at the blessings received and to look forward to a totally different and still uncertain future.

PART I

Whan that Aprill with his shoures soote
The droghte of March hath perced to the roote,
And bathed every veyne in swich licour
Of which vertu engendred is the flour;
Whan Zephirus eek with his sweete breeth
Inspired hath in every holt and heeth
The tendre croppes, and the yonge sonne
Hath in the Ram his halve cours yronne,
And smale foweles maken melodye,
That slepen al the nyght with open ye
(So priketh hem nature in hir corages);
Thanne longen folk to goon on pilgrimages,
And palmeres for to seken straunge strondes,
To ferne halwes, kowthe in sondry londes.

Chaucer: Prologue, *The Canterbury Tales*

(When the sweet showers of April have pierced the dryness of March to its root and soaked every vein in moisture whose quickening force engenders the flower; when Zephyr with his sweet breath has given life to tender shoots in each wood and field; when the young sun has run his half-course in the sign of the Ram; when, nature prompting their instincts, small birds who sleep through the night with one eye open make their music — then people long to go on pilgrimages, and pious wanderers to visit strange lands and far-off shrines in different countries.)

CHAPTER 1

Inheriting Coal Dust in the Veins

Patton, Pennsylvania (1927-1940)

Father Len dropped me off at my sister Barbara's condo in Hollidaysburg, Pennsylvania, outside of Altoona. From there it would be easy to visit Patton, where I was born and grew up. Nestled in an Appalachian valley, the small town was founded in 1893 as a hub for the offices of the surrounding soft-coal mining companies. And it was a small town: the 1920 census reported 3,628 inhabitants. Yet, Patton boasted a hotel and moviehouse — the only ones for many miles around — in addition to its twelve churches and twelve bars. The biggest church was St. Mary's on the hill, the parish that played a special role in my family's life: the Weaklands were all baptized there. I learned my first lesson in ecumenism at St. Mary's when each year the pastor would ask a few altar boys to take candles around to the other churches as a Christmas gift.

Most of our friends and neighbors were Protestant and no one ever said we Catholic kids could not associate with them, although we were not permitted to attend the summer revival meetings held in tents outside the town to hear the famous preachers and gawk at renowned faith-healers, like Katherine Cullman. Nor were we permitted to make fun of any of their religious manifestations, not even the Holy Rollers or the snake handlers. There was one well-liked Jewish family, but the town was essentially white and Christian. The only African-Americans we ever saw were the few young black men who came to suction out the outhouses of homes without indoor plumbing. We kids followed behind in amazement, staring at their black skin beaded with sweat and covered with white lime.

My father and grandfather owned the Palmer House Hotel at the town's main intersection. There my mother gave birth to me on April 2, 1927, and carried me up to St. Mary's Church herself — so she told me — on Sunday, April 10, to be baptized and given the name George Samuel after my maternal and paternal grandfathers. The name Rembert, by which most people know me, was given in 1946 when I pronounced my first vows as a Benedictine monk. I was child number four in a family of six children, preceded by two sisters and a brother, and followed by two more sisters. I was the last born in the hotel since soon after my birth we moved to a normal house. Apparently my mother did not feel that raising kids in a hotel was a good idea.

In 1929, a financial crisis closed the Patton Bank and marked the beginning of the Depression with its catastrophic effects on Patton and all the surrounding towns. That same year a disastrous fire almost totally destroyed the Palmer House Hotel, causing financial ruin for the family and forcing us to move to the Flats, a poorer part of town. The fire took its toll on my father by first killing his spirit. Mom said he spent much time with his friends in the few unheated rooms of the burnt-out hotel, drinking and lamenting. It was a bout with pneumonia that brought him down on April 3, 1932, the day before his thirty-fifth birthday and the day after my fifth, leaving a wife and six children, the oldest nine, the youngest six months.

That fifth birthday is one of my first clear memories. Like any kid, I looked forward to being the center of attention for a few hours that day. Instead, something seemed wrong: no one was around, no one seemed excited about my birthday, no signs of festivities were evident. My mother had deposited my younger sister and me in the home of strangers where, in the evening, she came to hold me a bit and lay me down to sleep. Next day we two were brought back to our own home in the Flats where everyone was upstairs in my parents' bedroom. Despondent and unhappy, I could hear the murmur of soft voices. We two kids were quietly ushered into the room.

Every detail of the events that followed, every aspect of the room, everyone's actions are still vivid in my mind. My father, Basil Francis Weakland, coughing deeply, lay dying, struggling to stay alive. Although the curtains were drawn and it was dark in the room, I remember how every piece of furniture was arranged, how the candles on the bedstand that kept sentinel by the crucifix flickered and cast odd-shaped shadows on the wall, how the priest had withdrawn to the side, how Dr. Cooper kept busy doing something that was not helping. Finally the coughing changed to the dread sound of a death rattle and my mother, sobbing, fell on the body of my dying father.

Later relatives criticized her for permitting the younger kids to witness this scene. Yet the memory of it has caused me no sleepless nights. Although not truly understanding the significance of it all, I was always glad to have been physically present at a moment that was to affect our futures so profoundly.

Although the church services left no traces in my memory, the interment at the cemetery did, perhaps because the burial ceremonies did frighten me. My father was given a military funeral, which was punctuated by deafening bursts of gunfire over the open grave followed by eerie echoes from a distant hill; a bugle near the coffin mournfully sounded *Taps* and, after an aching pause, the subdued echo came back. All this was so perplexing and strange that I hid behind my mother's skirt till it was finished and a military man came over and stiffly gave her the triangularly folded flag that had covered my father's casket.

*   *   *

How I wish I had known my father better! In May of 1917, at the age of twenty and after two years of college, he joined the Marines and was soon shipped to the Dominican Republic. His rise in rank was rapid; within three years he was a captain in charge of the city of La Vega and its surroundings. When my father came home on furlough in February 1922, he married my mother and took her back to the Dominican Republic. He resigned his commission in January 1923, and they both returned to the States for the birth of my sister Betty, their first child.

My recollections of my father are few but precious — being carried on his shoulders (as perilous as it seemed to me at that age since he was 6' 4½"), being encouraged to jump and then caught in his strong arms, being taught by him how to pee standing up by the commode, being carried to the doctors in those same strong arms after tramping on a broken milk bottle that went through my foot.

On rainy days my mother would allow us to go to the attic and take out some things from my father's trunk. Photos from the Dominican Republic that showed him in full dress uniform standing guard over the tomb of Columbus were especially fascinating. Among the curiosities was a white envelope containing a picture of me as a smiling baby with a head of spit curls. My dad had made my mother cut them off, but she had saved them and they were still in that envelope. It often made me wonder if my mother had really wanted another girl.

Those who knew my father well always spoke highly of him. His two brothers, Edgar and Adrian, and his half-brother John (my godfather) all lived into their nineties and became images of what my father must have been like — gentle, bright, inquisitive, and talented. Once when I was in my late teens, I was introduced to Father Thomas Wolf, the ninety-year-old pastor of a parish a few miles from Patton. On hearing my name, he asked if I was Baz Weakland's son, and spoke in glowing terms of my dad, saying he had been my father's confessor for years. That my dad had his own confessor impressed me and indicated that he took religion seriously. His brothers often told me that Baz should have left the small town and gone on to more challenging work where his talents would have been fulfilled.

How often it has come to me that much of my life was spent seeking the father-figure that had been there so briefly, but I was grateful to have Weakland blood in my veins. My father was the epitome of the Weakland male figures going back to the original John Weakland, who in 1757 married Susan Cunningham in Hagerstown, Maryland, made his way to the mountain parts of Western Pennsylvania, and established a temporary homestead among the Indians. The family legend is that the Weaklands, devout and fervent Catholics, had sailed from England to the Maryland colony in 1641 as indentured servants, working for a Thomas Cornwallis for five years to pay off their indebtedness. The legends further claim that they were not originally English but Dutch and that the name had been anglicized, a fact that accounted for the many spellings of it that can be found in official documents.

John and Susan had three sons and a daughter who settled permanently in Western Pennsylvania and my direct line goes back to their oldest son John (1758-1854) and his wife Catherine Jackson (1769-1861). They were a sturdy pair, both living into their nineties. This John Weakland was a legendary figure in the history of Western Pennsylvania, his memory being especially commemorated in the history of the Catholic Church in that region. He farmed and hunted, traded with the Indians, and then sold his wares in Baltimore. Once a year a priest would come north and circuit ride through that area, saying Mass in the different homes and solemnizing the baptisms and weddings already performed by the patriarch of the Weakland family since they had not waited for the priest to come. We would say it was a lay domestic church. The patriarchs must have been reading the Bible regularly for the Sunday family prayer meeting because the boys were given names like Samuel, Aaron, Levi, Zephoniah. The historical descriptions of John Weakland fit my father perfectly — over six-feet tall, calm and peaceful, strong and fearless.

From the Weakland side of the family I inherited a frontier spirit of tenacity and forthrightness that was embedded in this fascinating older Catholic tradition. The Weaklands had come to America to practice their faith freely and had left the Maryland colony toward the end of the seventeenth century when that freedom was in danger; then they kept that faith alive in the mountains of Pennsylvania without the strength of the organized church they had known in Europe. Moreover, the men were as active in the faith as the women. Since the Weaklands had arrived in the New World before the Revolutionary War and had fought in it, they considered themselves fully American with no need to prove it, unlike Catholic immigrants of the nineteenth century. To be able to trace one's ancestors back to older Catholic roots was exciting for a youngster my age.

*   *   *

If you were to open the desk drawer in my study today, you would find a double-edged safety razor and next to it a small handsome golden pen-and-pencil set. When, in my early teens, my sisters teased me relentlessly about the peach-fuzz that was growing on my chin, Mom let me take my dad's razor out of the trunk, use it, and keep it. It lies in the desk drawer as a personal sacramental, a way of bringing my father to mind. The pen-and-pencil set was a gift to my mother from my father at their wedding. After her death in 1978, my sisters passed it on to me; it, too, serves as a personal sacramental, bringing a vision of my mother as a teacher since in every way she was the best teacher I ever knew, both in school and out of school.

My mother's family name was Kane, a family that emigrated to the United States from County Tyrone in Northern Ireland about 1849, during the potato famine. They ultimately settled in Patton at the end of that century. My mother, Mary Delilah Eulalia, the oldest child of George Kane and Myrtena Buck, was born there in 1897. After graduating from high school, she went to Normal School to prepare to be a teacher. Until her marriage in 1922, she taught all grade levels in small rural schools around Patton, sometimes teaching all eight grades in one classroom with its potbellied stove in the middle. Although she gave up teaching to take care of the family, she never lost her intense love of learning. After my father's death, life was difficult. Pictures from that period show her looking very shy, almost ashamed of our poverty.

After my dad's death, we moved to an even poorer section of town, a dilapidated wooden structure with no furnace, just a potbellied stove in the living room and a coal stove in the kitchen, and no hot water heater. Though this was a double house, I have only vague recollections of the families who came and went. Only their side of the house, however, was excavated to form a hard clay-floored cellar to which both families had access. Since we had no refrigerator, we kept food there in the hot months. On Saturdays Mom would fire up the kitchen stove and heat bucket after bucket of hot water, dump it at intervals into the tin tub in the middle of the kitchen, and call each one of us in by seniority to take our baths. It was while soaking in that tin tub on Saturday afternoons that I heard my first operas broadcast from the Metropolitan Opera House in New York. Before the opera began I would read the account of the plot, listen carefully to Milton Cross as he announced the names of the singers, and then just bathe in the beauty of it all.

Louvers in the ceiling allowed the stove heat to rise to the second floor, upstairs, but little warmth ever reached there. During the winter, Mom would place bricks in the stove's oven and, when hot, wrap them in flannel and place them in our beds. Then, we undressed behind the stove in the living room and, in our long underwear, make a wild dash for the beds upstairs. We made an even wilder dash in the morning to dress downstairs behind that stove. My older brother and I shared a room and bed and, being bigger, he always got the warm brick. That bed had no springs, just slats and ropes and a thin mattress. The winters were severe in Patton, with piles of snow and the thermometer often falling below zero. After we went to bed, Mom would crawl under the house to cut off the water supply and drain the pipes so they would not freeze and burst. This process was reversed in the morning. If the weather became even more severe — ten below zero was not uncommon — she slept on the couch in the living room to keep the fire stoked through the night. Until we boys were old enough to handle an axe, she chopped the wood for the two stoves and hauled the coal up from the basement.

Our house was situated less than fifty yards from the railroad tracks and so we lived with the constant rumbling of trains in the background. A small creek called Chest Creek, polluted by sulfur that seeped into it from abandoned coal mines, ran on the other side of the railroad tracks. Our house was rat infested and often Mom, when she crawled under the house, had to scare them away. Rat traps were everywhere, especially in the clay cellar; once a trapped rat was running around wild down there. Mom put on a raincoat, went down with a clothes-line pole, cornered and killed it. Years later, when she was old and seemed so fragile and petite, I had a hard time reconciling that image with what she had to put up with after my father's death.

The first serious decision she had to make was whether to place us in foster homes, as some urged her, or to try to make it on her own. I preserve a vivid image of her at the kitchen table talking to us about this decision, crying, pounding the table, and forcefully asserting that no one would ever break up the family and take us away from her. Instead, we went on relief.

At that time, the monthly relief check was thirty-eight dollars. Rent was eight plus coal and electricity cost, which left less than thirty dollars a month to take care of food and clothing for seven people. New clothes were a rarity; I wore hand-me-downs from my brother and later my uncles. A few years later, when I was already in St. Mary's grade school, those of us on relief also obtained clothing made by a project supported by the WPA (Works Progress Administration). We had to go to the fire hall and stand in line for hours with all the other kids on relief to be measured. My brother and I received new brown corduroy knickers. In school those of us on relief were now marked publicly, and, being exceptionally sensitive to the teasing of the other kids, I came to resent being poor.

We had our share of illnesses. I always had a sore throat and was susceptible to colds. Not a one of us played the "too-sick-to-go-to-school-or-church" card lightly with Mom since that meant staying inside all day, even if one felt cured by noon. We all had measles, mumps, and the usual kids' stuff, but thank God no polio or any of the serious diseases that some kids in town contracted. We had the usual ailments of poor kids, the itch, head lice (that meant having a shaved head for boys or having hair doused with kerosene for girls). Mom searched our beds assiduously for bedbugs, rampant she would say in the town movie house, and would roll the mattresses over every week as a preventative. I am amazed when I think back on those years that we survived as well as we did. Doc Cooper, who had assisted my father at his death, provided all our medical needs without ever charging a penny.

Life also had its joys, simple as they were. We had a radio, and that meant listening to the Lone Ranger, Jack Benny, George Burns and Gracie Allen, and being able to hear great music on the Firestone Hour and the

Met broadcasts. We had no phone; in fact, I was in high school before I ever talked on a phone. We never had a car, and didn't miss one. I never owned a bicycle or even a baseball glove and at the time it didn't seem like such a big deal — lots of kids didn't have bikes.

In the winters most of us ice-skated, a sport I always loved, but shoe skates were too expensive and we used the clamp-ons that rapidly ruined our shoes. Without doubt, keeping shoes that fit was the most problematic part of our clothing since they wore out so fast and soon became too small. We kids all went to school with pieces of cardboard inserted into our shoes to hide the holes where they were worn through. In the hot summers, when there was hardly a breath of air, we swam in Chest Creek, directly below where it had been dammed up to supply the town with water, and we kids all learned to swim. Even though the sulfur in the water seeping from the mines ate the buckles off our suits, it was worth it because it was at the swimming hole where we learned to mingle with all kinds of other kids regardless of their religion. Each of us has many a story to tell about that swimming hole, the characters who swam there, and the near drownings that occurred.

I started at the public school in 1932, the fall after my father died. My mother was courageous in sending me there since in those days it was seen as an act of defiance against church law. The bishops insisted that every Catholic kid be in a Catholic school so they would not fall under the Protestant influence that dominated public school systems. Kindergarten and pre-kindergarten were words and concepts unheard of in Patton. Although I was only five in April and the rule for the Catholic school was that one had to be five before January 1, Mother simply decided that I should be in school. She explained to the pastor that in her mind I was ready for school, needed the discipline it would bring, and that after one year she would enroll me in the Catholic school. So it was to be.

*   *   *

The most important happening for me during those years in that ramshackle house by the railroad tracks was that I learned to play the piano and began to develop an interest in music. We didn't possess much furniture, just the bare essentials brought with us from the Flats, but we did own an old upright piano that was strongly built, weighed a ton, kept its pitch pretty well, and had a remarkably good action and pleasant tone. Grandma Kane had bought it for my mother many years before and it had made the journey from the hotel to all the houses the family lived in. It had still a few more journeys before it. We also possessed a set of ten books called *Modern Music and Musicians* that had been purchased by Grandma for my mother and her sisters that ended in my mother's keep. The last three volumes were devoted to music theory, music history, and the plots of the operas. I devoured those volumes. The seven others contained piano music, with one of them, volume five, being graded from easy to hard with all the musical explanations needed. I began with that volume and worked my way through it when I was about seven. The long winter nights were filled with music.

By happy chance our third-grade sister explained the makeup of all the scales, major and minor, all the key signatures, and how to read music. I just took it for granted that all kids had to learn this material just as they had to learn how to add and subtract. Having read all this material in volume five, I was proud that I was already ahead of the group. This same sister taught us how to decipher Gregorian chant notation and to recognize and interpret all the neumes. Again I took it for granted that every third and fourth grader in the world could distinguish a podatus from a climacus, a torculus from a porrectus, and knew that there were four lines in Gregorian and five in modern music.

No one in school asked about my interest in music then and no one followed up on what we had already learned, but, working on my own, I came to know the contents of the inherited ten volumes, both the piano pieces and the music history and theory in them. It was fun trying to play most of the pieces; some, like the salon pieces in the early volumes, I could sight-read, but others, like those in the final volumes, were really tough. Regrettably there were no sonatas by Mozart or Haydn, just a few Fantasies and Variations, but ten of Beethoven's most famous sonatas were there and later I played opus 110 for the entrance examine at Juilliard and opus 109 as a part of my final recital. There were a few Bach pieces, mostly transcriptions of large organ works, but the *Chromatic Fantasy and Fugue* and the *Italian Concerto* could be found there; years later I played the latter for my final recital at Juilliard. Lots of Chopin, Schumann, and Liszt completed the contents. The music was highly oriented toward the Romantic period, which, consequently, influenced my musical tastes and ideals during those years growing up.

While we were still living in the old house, I made my first communion, and relished the contests for reciting the catechism from beginning to end along with all of those practices and habits that went with growing up in the Catholic faith. Religion was never just another school subject but a form of external habits that were important for life. My mother was a woman of deep faith and we all absorbed that attitude from her, but she did not have the kind of Irish piety that seemed typical in that community nor the accompanying pious talk. Although she didn't push religious practices on us, we were all regular Mass-goers. From first grade on we learned to put a few pennies in the collection each week as an important duty.

When I became a Mass server, it brought relief from a practice I very much disliked. The parish charged pew-rent, i.e., some people paid for a given seat for a year; if a renter found you in the seat, he could claim it and make you look elsewhere. We Weakland kids, having no money to rent a seat, would sit in the back where there were a few open pews available on a first-come first-served basis. Sometimes we tried to figure out who would not be at Mass that Sunday and sneak into their place only to be forced to move before Mass began. Of course, the wealthy people, like the Prindibles, who were owners of the bank and the clay works, had rented three seats in the third row. Since it was their habit to enter the church with special solemnity precisely at the last minute, we servers would wait till they were in place at the 10:00 o'clock High Mass on Sunday before ringing the bell to begin the service. Even so, the pastor wryly would remind us that they received no more of Jesus Christ at communion than the rest of us.

My mother was a remarkable woman. Not only did she raise the six of us on her own, she had a mind of her own. Once she ran, unsuccessfully, for town tax collector. My Grandpa Kane had an avid interest in politics because of his involvement in the coalminers' union. Since we were staunch Democrats, I grew up thinking that only Protestants could be Republicans. Often when my mother would talk about her lost campaign for office, she would elevate her voice perceptibly and add: "It's easy to see that it's a man's world and a woman just doesn't stand a chance." My first lesson in feminism! She also had an independent mind with regard to some of the positions the Church took, an attitude I probably inherited. She felt free to criticize the bishop and the pastor as much as she wanted, but became upset when any Catholic did so publicly. She would be unhappy if a Catholic wrote a letter critical of the Church in the local newspaper, saying we should not expose our faults to Protestants. She possessed a good deal of common sense about religion and a no-nonsense approach to faith that was not too sentimental but also not all in the head.

It was from her that I absorbed my strong opposition to dictators and authoritarian rulers. To me Hitler and Mussolini represented the epitome of evil because they disregarded human dignity and rights. When we prayed together in the evening before bed, Mother insisted we pray for those dictators too, even if we did not want to. We heard nothing of Communism in those days; it simply did not seem to be a threat to us. Although we all knew who the pope was (Pius XI), he was a distant figure with absolutely no influence on our lives in the little town of Patton. I don't remember any pastor or sister in the school ever quoting a pope.

Those who grew up in the Depression were distinctly marked by that experience. We learned to be frugal and to conserve; we learned to eat every mouthful that was on our plate and not complain; we learned not to waste anything; we appreciated the little we had and learned to make do; we learned to share. If later we seemed foolish to the next generation because we went to such lengths to save a few cents, it was because habits of frugality were ingrained in us. We also learned to appreciate the United States and the opportunities it afforded us to move ahead. We carry scars from those experiences, but today they seem to have been for the better. Mother made it clear to us from the beginning that we could and would rise above the poverty we lived in and she tried to make sure we received the tools to eventually be able to do so. She kept her own dignity through it all, and we did too.

*   *   *

Eventually the old house was put up for sale and we had to look for a new home. I was about ten then. One opened up on the other end of town, not far from Grandma and Grandpa Kane's, in a slightly nicer neighborhood. The house even had a furnace and a hot water tank. The problem was that the rent was eleven dollars a month. By that time Mother was working occasionally outside the house, we kids were bringing in a little bit, the relief money was higher, and the new house had a large garden in the back where we could grow our own vegetables. Finally we made the decision to move. It did not mark the end of our dependency on relief, but it was a sign of hope that things might get better.

The move meant making new friends. Most of the kids were Protestant, but that did not seem to bother my mother. Like all ten- and twelve-year-olds, we were curious about everything. We exchanged bits of information, sought out *National Geographic* magazines (one of the tools kids in my day used for sex education), and talked up a storm. Sex was not a forbidden subject, just one about which we knew very little because that subject was unheard of in public and Catholic schools and probably even less in families. Most of us learned what we could from each other. I still recall the day one kid said that his dad told him that playing with oneself would cause a man to go crazy — a common myth that I heard from several sources as I was growing up.

We all had our chores as well. Mine were chopping wood, taking care of the stoves, and, most of all, gardening, which came easily to me. My rows of lettuce were as straight as could be. I learned to stake the tomatoes and the beans, and pick the bugs off them as well. I grew several kinds of lettuce and lots of different kinds of onions. It is evident that I was proud of my gardening. My beefsteak tomatoes brought praise even from our Protestant neighbors.

The Church of God, one of Patton's twelve churches, was located three doors up from us on our side of the street. We called its worshippers the Holy Rollers and on Sunday evening they would sing up a storm. When they were coming to church and during their prayers, Mom forbad us to play cards on the front porch, especially in the summer months when the windows of the church were wide open and they could see us. They did not approve of card-playing and Mom said we should not scandalize or offend them. In those days our Protestant neighbors considered Catholics lax since we drank alcohol, played cards, gambled, and even danced. The blue laws were very much enforced in the state of Pennsylvania when I was a boy.

During these years I became more and more moody, roaming the woods behind the house, picking berries by myself, and immersing myself in reading and music. As the years moved on, my intellectual interests and my excitement about school increased and I soaked up everything available. We possessed few books at home, but those we had I read several times. In retrospect, I probably felt inferior to the other kids in social status and compensated by trying to be superior in my grades.

In seventh grade the class sponsored several hobby-shows where students could bring their favorite collections and pastimes. It had never occurred to me how many kids in the world collected postage stamps, pictures of movie-stars, baseball players, and singers. Instead, using old-fashioned airplane glue, I had built a small village out of wooden matchsticks, with a typical country church in the center, neat rows of miniature houses, stores, trees, flowers, and the like. My brother helped me haul it up to school; I recall the very date: December 1, 1938.

Before we left the house and without my knowledge, Mom gave my brother some piano music and told him to tell sister that I also played the piano and should do so since that was how I really passed my time. The model village attracted some attention but not as much as the piano-playing. I began with Chaminade, continued with Chopin, and ended with Rachmaninoff. The sister in charge brought all the other sisters in the school to her class room to hear me play and then called the pastor in the rectory to come over to the school. The next day my mother was asked to accompany me to school; lots of conversation with the sisters, the pastor, and my mom followed. Finally, the pastor decided that I should have piano lessons and that Sister Leonilla would become my first piano teacher. Mother objected, saying that we had no money to pay for lessons, but the pastor said money was no problem and that they would be free as long as I took them seriously.

In reflecting back on those first lessons, I can see that Sister Leonilla was a marvelous teacher, exacting, at times even fussy, knowing the basics and giving me a wonderful refresher course on everything I had learned on my own, filling in any lacunae and taking me a few steps beyond. For two years she continued to teach me without the question of payment for the lessons ever arising.

In seventh grade I had a distressing musical experience. The kids from several grades were combined for the event, so my brother and I were herded like the others into the same room. We had an "amateur hour," very popular in those days, but this time with a twist: instead of practicing before hand, we had to pull out of a hat a little piece of paper telling us what to do. My paper read: "Sing a song." Singing was not something a kid in seventh grade does willingly, but the sister in charge — probably Mother Pancratia — put a songbook in my hand with the page open at *Taps* and told me to sing it. *Taps* was the worst possible choice since I had never heard it sung with words before and knew it as a bugle call. Even worse, it brought back painful and disturbing memories of my father's funeral. As I started to sing, my voice cracked a few times and then nothing recognizable came out, causing the kids to burst into laughter. Being a very earnest lad, I continued to the end, as far off the mark as my pitch was. Mother Pancratia was also laughing and added: "Well, it is evident that Georgie should stick to piano-playing." Humiliated, I sat down.

That evening at supper my brother could not wait to relate what had

35

happened at the talent show and told the whole story with appropriate embellishments. He noted, for example, that the kid who sat behind him, Sandy Rodgers, yelled out: "He's flatter than a horse turd." That story made the rounds, and every time visitors or relatives would come to the house, I would be asked to play for them. Then some one of the siblings would say: "But don't ask him to sing." It was years later when I entered Juilliard on the graduate level and was taking the entrance exam on sight-singing and dictation that Susan Bloch, one of Juilliard's most creative teachers, recognized my psychological problem. After trying to sing just a few notes of the piece she put in front of me, I froze totally provoking her to say: "Tell me what happened to you and your singing." I repeated to her the story of the famous talent show and my subsequent fear of singing. She was just the right person to begin to free me up and give me the confidence I needed.

*   *   *

When I was still in seventh grade, sister had a heart attack and my mother was asked to take her place. In those days it was rare to have a lay person teaching in a Catholic school; in fact, we often called it the sisters' school because they were the only teachers. Since all of us kids were in school, Mother decided she could raise the family and still teach. Accepting to be hired and given a salary, however, posed a problem: we would then lose our relief money. The pastor cheated and did what I later learned was illegal: he did not pay her a salary but considered her a volunteer. Then regularly, a few times each week in the early morning, we would find baskets of food in abundance — fruit, vegetables, meat, bread, and the like — on the back porch. He had decided to pay my mother in kind.

But having my mother as my teacher in school was not easy: she was most demanding of us Weakland kids, almost severe, and then tried to make up for it by being very loving when we got home. I tried to adjust, knowing she wanted to show no favoritism, but found it a bit artificial. One of her specialties was analyzing and diagramming sentences, a skill that prepared me well for my later Latin classes in high school and college.

At the beginning of the next year, the pastor of St. George, the Slovak parish, asked me to become the organist so Sister Leonilla gave me weekly lessons on both the organ and piano. She taught me the art of pedaling and how to obtain a good legato on the organ by rapidly switching fingers on the keys. To this day her sage advice still rings in my ears: she told me that playing the organ could be harmful for pianists only if they became sloppy about finger articulation and thus permit the fourth and fifth fingers to become weak. In fact, she said that playing the organ can help a pianist obtain a good legato with the fingers only, an important asset in playing Bach and the Baroque repertoire on the piano. She was absolutely right.

St. George's had an antique pipe organ with a straight pedal board, one found many times later in my life, especially in Europe, and I enjoyed playing it. The choir sang mostly well-composed and very melodic Slovak hymns that matched the parts of the Mass they accompanied — later I learned these were called "Sing-Messe." The Slovak hymns at Christmas and Easter were marvelous and I enjoyed being a vital part of the mix. Sister Leonilla taught me what to look for in accompanying a choir so that the organ would assist them and sustain them without dominating.

But the old organ at St. George's was always in need of repair, forcing me to improvise around those stops and keys that did not always sound. Finally, the pastor, judging the old pipe organ beyond repair, decided to buy a Hammond. There was one obstacle, however: the bishop who was coming soon for Confirmation had forbidden any parish to buy an electronic organ. Undaunted, the pastor bought the Hammond anyway, but left the casement of the old pipe organ in place and hid the loudspeakers behind the exposed pipes. He strictly ordered me to "play the Hammond like a pipe organ." I followed orders, used no tremolo or vibrato during the service, put on lots of upper partials, and played only crisp baroque music. At the end of the Confirmation the bishop thanked the pastor for the beautiful ceremony and congratulated him especially on the church's exceptionally fine pipe organ. The bishop proudly asserted that, if a little church like St. George's could afford such an excellent pipe organ, then any church could. I learned one thing from this experience: it is easy to fool bishops! Needless to say, the pastor gave me an extra five bucks for having so expertly deceived the bishop.

Having become an altar boy in fourth grade, I found myself gravitating in those pre-adolescent years toward religious things: I enjoyed serving Mass, perfecting the Latin, never missing a beat carrying the book from one side of the altar to the other, always having the incense ready on time, and being alert to every wish of the pastor. When it was a question of serving a wedding or funeral, the pastor almost always picked me. The boys liked getting out of class for such events and, of course, earned a few pennies that way too. The special events of the year were the midnight Mass on

Christmas and Forty Hours. The whole family attended these ceremonies, especially midnight Mass, and then we would have some milk before opening our presents — and then bed. I remember walking home in the early morning after midnight Mass with the moon glistening on the snow, happy as any young lad could be.

As I look back, I can see that a part of my religious makeup was already visible. I seemed to flow quickly and imperceptibly from an aesthetic experience to a religious one. I did not analyze that connection then, but it is now clear to me there was an intimate connection between these two experiences. One night, lying on the living room floor in the dark and listening to Schubert's *Symphony no. 5,* I really felt that God was present to me in and through the music. Every time I heard that symphony in the following years, I would again relive that experience. It always created within me a calm and fulfilling sense of wonder, of safeness, and of inner spiritual repose. I never tried to explain this to anyone; it was my secret.

In fourth grade I first began to think of becoming a priest. At home it was customary for us to play church, using the piano as an altar because it was situated against the wall like all the altars in those days and because, with the keyboard cover closed, there was space for a glass and for the Necco wafers we used as hosts. As one would have expected in those days, I was always the priest. Sometimes we would have a burial service and one of my sisters would have to lie still as we put candles around her and incensed her, saying all the prayers in an improvised pig-Latin. Liturgy fascinated me. Without being able then to articulate these feelings, I can say now that it was like living for a short period in a world apart. There one could sense God's presence in an aura of holiness. I came away from these ceremonies feeling different than before, more whole and full. I cannot describe that feeling adequately even now, but it was real to me and very much a part of me, very much like the feeling I had when I had played the piano well, exhausted but happy and at peace. Perhaps it also served as an escape from the drudgery of the daily poverty of life around me.

When in the eighth grade and wanting to tell someone about my wish to be a priest, I feared to approach Father Bertrand, the pastor. He was too severe and aloof, although I admired how graciously and kindly he had treated my mother and all of us in our poverty. He would sometimes ask me to copy names into the baptismal book or mow the lawn or do some other easy chore and then pay me exorbitantly with a ten- or twenty-dollar bill. He never treated us as inferior because we were poor but always with the utmost dignity. His intellectual knowledge also impressed me. I was fond of Father Basil, the pastor of St. George's Church, and found him easy to approach, but I decided it would be an offense to Father Bertrand, my pastor, to talk to Father Basil first. So I talked to Sister Leonilla about that desire. She in turn talked to the pastor.

One day in mid-winter during school hours I was told to go over to the rectory because Father Bertrand wanted me to play the piano for the Benedictine pastor of nearby Carrolltown. At the end of my little recital Father Bertrand said: "I am going to send George to St. Vincent next year for high school." I thought at that moment that the decision had been made without me, but that was not true. Sister Leonilla had talked to Father Bertrand, who in turn had talked to my mother and those talks were to continue. Mom held out, saying that I was too young to go away to high school, but the pastor responded with some pretty persuasive arguments. He had insisted that I would never receive a first-rate education in Patton, especially in Latin and Greek; I would receive better musical training at St. Vincent; I could test out my vocation. Finally, Mother left the decision to me, and I selected St. Vincent, the Benedictine high school at Latrobe, some sixty miles away. Again the question of money did not enter into the equation. Father Bertrand assured Mom that the Benedictine community would take care of all that — and they did.

The only one who seemed a bit unhappy was Sister Leonilla, but I never knew why till years later when she told me that it was taken for granted that I would become a Benedictine like Fathers Bertrand and Basil when it was clear that I could even have been a Jesuit! She told me that they were the "Cadillac" of religious orders, and, since I had the talent to be one, it should have been explored. But, for my part, there have never been regrets that this choice was not considered.

Looking forward to graduating from eighth grade in the spring of 1940, I knew the sisters who taught me would remain forever a part of my life. My classmates, too, would never be forgotten because we had come together in a way that often happens in small towns. We got along pretty well — there were never any angry disputes — even if there were rivalries for first prizes and awards. Some of the girls were very pretty, but I do not recall having a crush on anyone. Since I was not much into sports except swimming and ice-skating, some of the boys may have found me a bit of a sissy, but they never said so in my hearing. I certainly was an overachiever, pretty cocky, and a bit of a know-it-all, in fact, probably somewhat obnoxious with my conceitedness and braggadocio. At graduation I won my share of the medals for my grades and contribution to the life of the school.

I was the first in our family to leave home; the others followed after they graduated from high school. This grand exodus must have been hard on Mom, but she never interfered and, I think, secretly admired our independence; after all, it was how she had brought us up and what she had eventually hoped for us. She showed unwavering trust in each one of us. Perhaps, reflecting on what had happened to my father in those years of the Depression and after the fire at the Palmer House Hotel, she felt it was wise that we children move on early in life to new challenges. Each time I have returned to Patton and reflected on my early years, I have marveled at the depth of the sacrifices she made and how very wise she was.

During the summer of 1940, at the ripe age of thirteen, I sent my application to St. Vincent Scholasticate, the section of St. Vincent Prep School intended for those thinking about priesthood and the Benedictine Order. The acceptance letter came back promptly and I prepared through the summer to go away that fall. How far away it seemed then, although it was only sixty miles! Among the novelties I had to face was the purchase of a suit since all the students had to wear a coat to class, and so I worked at the drugstore and the swimming pool and did other odd jobs to earn enough money to buy one.

The week before leaving Father Bertrand called me into his study in the rectory for final instructions. Briefly and without any real explanation he told me to avoid a Father X since he was known to prey sexually on young boys. Other than that he told me to enjoy my studies and gave me a few hints on how to adjust to the new school where he had been headmaster. Finally he told me that as pastor he would have to fill out a form each fall before I returned to school, asking if I had behaved myself and had gone to Mass regularly. He said when I was home not to worry and that he would always fill out the form in glowing terms; he trusted me. In fifteen minutes I was out of his office, still pondering all that he had said. Leaving home frightened me, but it was also exciting, a new journey with many unknowns.

CHAPTER 2

Thirsting for Knowledge

St. Vincent, Latrobe, Pennsylvania (1940-1948)

In my journey back to St. Vincent's in 2002, we approached by the old road so that first the lake appeared and then the monastery building rose out of the hill like a medieval Byzantine cloister on Mount Athos. It was good to come back and spend a few weeks in the shadows of buildings I had once called home.

I arrived at St. Vincent first in the fall of 1940. It had been founded in 1846 by Benedictine monks from Bavaria and had expanded a great deal since then: in addition to the monastery, there were a high school, a college, and a major seminary. The population of all these enterprises numbered over a thousand. St. Vincent boasted of a farm, a gristmill, a private coal mine, a pond to swim in, a lake for ice skating, basketball courts, tennis courts, baseball and football fields, an auditorium with nine-foot pianos and incredible acoustics, and several fabulous organs in its many chapels. The monastic library with its ancient tomes and the college library with its modern periodicals put me in awe of the knowledge at the students' fingertips. How could it all be absorbed? And then, there was a band, a symphony orchestra, and a variety of choirs and choruses. Coming from the little town of Patton, I was overwhelmed by the complexity and diversity of these riches, but knew that I would never suffer boredom or lack challenges, intellectual and religious, in the years I would make this monastery and school my home.

Over the years, each time I returned it was my custom to walk up the hill to the monastic cemetery. Two unending rows of metal crosses embedded in concrete dotted that hill. On each cross was etched simply the name of the monk along with the dates of his birth and death. *In 2002, I returned to this spot with special feelings of attachment and affection. I wish I could write something about each one who influenced me during my formative years, but it would be a very long litany. At each grave as I paused I finished my thoughts with a prayer of gratitude. Recalling those I knew best has helped to restore and heal me.*

In 1940 I settled in easily at St. Vincent. We scholastics, as we were called, occupied our own wing, sleeping in two big dormitories, and studying in two big study-halls. The schedule was tight but not strenuous. We rose about 5:30, attended Mass, had time for meditation, and finally breakfast — made up mostly of big pieces of homemade whole-wheat bread, the wheat grown on the farm and the flour ground in the gristmill. We smothered the bread with lots of butter and jams and drank milk by the gallons. The cooks and those in charge of the food were Benedictine nuns from Bavaria under Mother Leonarda Fritz's capable direction; our meals prepared without frills were always nourishing and abundant.

Younger monks, not yet ordained and still in studies, were appointed our "prefects." They rotated duties each week: one slept in our dormitory in a curtained-off area (we sometimes heard him slip out at 4:00 for Matins in the monastery); one was in charge of recreation; another kept discipline in the study-hall. They may have been young, inexperienced, and just a few years older than we but they were, with very few exceptions, fine persons and good examples to us.

Those high school years were a time of intellectual awakening for me. We attended class with the other Prep students, ordinary lay students — a good system to broaden our perspectives and ease some of the rigidity of the minor seminary program. Moreover, the Prep School's superiors were an enlightened and friendly bunch, professionally trained for their work.

In the early days we studied Latin till it came out our ears. Those who taught us in high school gave us a heavy dose of grammar and vocabulary, but, unfortunately very little understanding of Latin literature. When, in college, we entered seriously into the study of the standard classics, mostly Virgil and Cicero, an appreciation began to grow.

Archabbot Alfred Koch was the abbot when I first came to St. Vincent and was still abbot when I later entered the monastery. *His rotund figure came to mind one day during my visit in 2002 when I walked up to the cemetery and passed the very spot where I had first encountered him in 1940.* One fall evening I saw him sitting out on a bench by the old baseball field talking with some of the scholastics. He asked me, as I joined in the conversation, what class I liked best. Greek was my answer. "Ah, Greek!" he said, and began to recite passage after passage in that language. What a bright man! I was impressed. He liked to debate with us and I recall on another evening he differed with me on the interpretation of Platonic love in Wagner's operas. I didn't know what I was talking about, but that never keeps a high school kid from spouting off. He was patient and ended the argument quoting from memory passages from *Tristan und Isolde* in German. On those rare occasions when he came out to our grounds, I tried to be in the group he joined for conversation. *Naturally on my 2002 visit, I paused longer at the large stone cross around which the archabbots were buried and said a special prayer for him.*

My problem in high school was that I loved every subject, from Greek and languages to math and physics. For the required modern language I picked German because I could practice it every day with the sisters in the kitchen. Wanting to study French on my own, I found a faculty member to tutor my pronunciation. But this barrage of languages was not all we studied. In English literature we had fine and exciting teachers. I thrived in this atmosphere and made good grades. I think back on those four years of high school with deep gratitude for which my family was paying nothing. It was coming to me gratis, thanks to the Benedictine community.

Not all the curriculum was of a traditional kind, in fact, we had something quite "new," not even the kids I saw back in Patton had anything like it. Under the label of "Civics," we studied Catholic social teaching. We learned all about the encyclicals *Rerum novarum* by Leo XIII and *Quadragesimo anno* by Pius XI. Those pages reinforced my growing distrust of dictatorial and totalitarian regimes. Hitler and Mussolini were to me the epitome of dangerous people because they destroyed personal freedom and integrity. I feared those who claimed that much authority over the lives of others and who were accountable to no one. That class, in addition to emphasizing the rights of labor, started to give form to ideas that marked my political thinking for decades to come.

Years later I wrote a short piece with the title "Explaining Myself to Rome" in which I tried to lay out my sentiments in this regard and their sources. As will be described later, it was a period in which tensions between the Church in the United States and Roman officials were growing. In it I explained:

I grew up with just as great a fear of Fascism as I had of Communism. Hitler and Mussolini were diabolical figures to me, examples

43

of how single individuals with uncontrolled power over other human beings could cruelly dehumanize people sacred in the eyes of God, and could justify such abuse for the sake of an ideology. I guess I grew up with a fear of absolute power, unfettered and uncontrolled, held by some people over others. It often surprises me to see that people I know do not share this fear to the same degree, but instead lend their support to dictatorships in Central and South America because such governments may seem anti-Communist. I know this fear also affects my attitude toward church authorities and religious obedience. (*America,* September 21, 1985, 127)

World War II was background to all of my high school years. Although I was too young for the draft, it was evident that the war was going to continue for a long time and we all developed interests that focused on it. Though I had never been in an airplane in my life, I could distinguish all the different bombers and fighters. The war, though a distant possibility, was very real to us.

*   *   *

When information about adolescence and sexual development is broadcast everywhere, it is hard to retrieve the hushed atmosphere in which I came of age. In the early 1940s, sexual matters were wrapped in a cocoon of silence; sexual activities, if there were any, were swathed in obscurity and, if uncovered, made to disappear. Thanks to later novels and movies, boys' boarding schools, of which St. Vincent was a type, have come to have reputations for sexual initiation, seduction, and even cruelty. As I have tried to recover memories of those days, certain events now seem to have a context and vocabulary that simply didn't exist at the time, at least in our world.

Although successful in my studies, I cannot say the same about acquiring a deeper understanding of myself, psychological or sexual. I lived very much in my head, and my only emotional outlet was my music. Looking back, I was almost certainly oblivious about my sexual development and makeup. No one used the phrase "sexual orientation"; there were occasional oblique references to homosexuality in psychology class. I did not understand this as something definitive, but supposed that everyone could be sexually attracted to others regardless of gender. Had it come to that, I would never have accepted to be "classified" as homosexual. In the milieu that prevailed then, this would have meant being ostracized. But it was hardly an issue: confessors never asked and religious superiors rarely mentioned sex at all. Only masturbation was spoken of, and at that gently and without creating anxiety. If there was homosexual activity among my fellow students, I knew nothing about it. Though it is anachronistic to use the term, there were no signs of a "gay subculture" in our small world.

What to make of signs that some now take to signal such a subculture? Such signs as I remember cannot be taken as definitive. Some students were not interested in playing sports; they were referred to as "the sewing circle." Though by today's standards, they might have seemed effeminate, no one would have classified them as gay. In fact, one of the most effeminate of the group later left the monastery, married, and became a leader in Selma during the Civil Rights Movement. And then, some of the older boys took what they called a "duck," i.e., a younger student, usually a freshman or sophomore, who polished shoes, fetched food, and was at the elder's beck and call. In return, a duck received protection when needed and could hang around with the older crowd and seem more sophisticated. Although there may have been sexual undercurrents to this initiation rite, it did not seem so since some of the biggest jocks were involved. I was never anyone's "duck," and, when I became an upper classman, I never thought of looking for one. No one showed signs of being sexually interested in me, and no one made sexual overtures to me.

One event, however, I believe it was at the beginning of our junior year, marked the class profoundly. During recreation, when we were hanging out and chatting, one of the students reported that a priest-teacher was messing around, grabbing students indecently, touching them, etc. I recalled my pastor's, Father Bertrand's, warning about Father X, but this was not he; it was Father Y. I was one among the boys that urged that those involved tell our superior the whole story. They did. The consequences were unsettling. The priest was gone immediately. The superior talked to almost every student in the high school. Some who were involved left right away; some left at the end of the year; some stayed on. I never knew how it was determined who fell into which category, who left voluntarily and who did not. No one mentioned help for those who had been abused. The prevailing view about them was, "They will forget all about it as they grow older." I have often wondered if I had been right in insisting the superior be told since I had not expected that anyone would be expelled. But is that what really happened? No public explanations were ever given. It was a long time before life moved on at its normal pace.

This event and the general way in which sex was treated left me with the notion that one's sexuality and sexual inclinations were like a spigot: one could turn it on and off as one desired. It was all a matter of will. Will-power and self-control were the solution to all sexual desires. My impression was reinforced by the overriding attitude of Catholic culture in which sexuality focused almost exclusively on maintaining chastity. Dating was treated as a very risky undertaking: How close could you go to the edge of the cliff without falling off? How much touching, kissing, necking could go on without committing a mortal sin?

Nevertheless, this experience of seeing our class decimated left me very uneasy. It may have forced me to repress more deeply my own feelings. Only now in writing about this time in my life, do I recall that one of the boys who had been abused quoted a remark by Father Y: "Once he got Weakland to fall, he would be back — more than any of the rest — for more." That must have troubled me so deeply that I buried it deep in my memory; I forgot it until I started in writing these memoirs to reflect again on this period. Looking back, I recognize that my adolescent confusion and uncertainty about sex and sexual orientation led me to bury this remark as having nothing to do with me or my future.

My course of action was clear: I decided then and there to be as "masculine" as I could. I entirely avoided the "sewing circle" crowd, becoming more energetically involved in sports, especially basketball and football. The scholastics were not allowed to play tackle football, only tag ball. I became a better than average punter and a fairly fast runner. I also developed a close friendship with one of my classmates who was a real sportsman, a "jock." We would pass and kick the football for hours on end. He was religiously very conservative, almost pious. He was not a gifted student and had to work hard. (I was really surprised when, after second year of college, he was dropped as a candidate for the novitiate because of what was considered a serious heart condition.)

In all these activities and my studies, I submerged any sexual desires as deeply as I could, not wanting to give the slightest sign of any homosexual orientation, and denying, even to myself that this could be possible. Naturally, I spoke to no one about the matter, afraid of being sent home.

One evening during the following summer, as my mother and I were working in the garden, I took advantage of the moment to bring up the events of the past year. I explained what had happened, especially what had happened to many of my classmates. Mother listened without comment and surprised me with only one remark: "Well, I hope your own first sexual experiences will be beautiful and the outcome of deep love." Though I had not yet made the decision to become a priest and my mother might have thought I might marry some day, the remark struck me as strange at the time. On reflection, I think she was saying something that I had not fully grasped; the abuse may have had repercussions on the victims that I had not fathomed. I did not have the vocabulary or the courage then to talk to her about homosexuality. I still wonder what her reaction might have been, or what she thought my own tendencies were.

During high school I spent three summers back home in Patton. By the last summer of 1943, the rapidly dwindling Weakland family (my mother and two sisters) had moved up the street to live with Grandma Kane, who otherwise would have been alone in her big house. These were quiet and lazy summers. I worked some at the Patton drug store, did some outdoor painting, and lots of organ playing, subbing for organists all over the county who were sick or on vacation. The last summer home, being sixteen, I took and passed the junior lifeguard test, and became a lifeguard at the newly constructed public swimming pool. They were dull and uneventful times and I kept pretty much to myself and my own thoughts. I read, especially novels, and entertained myself with music.

*   *   *

After two years of college, the scholasticate ended and a decision had to be made whether to enter the monastic novitiate or go on to a secular vocation. I began college in the summer of 1944 and those first two years moved on an accelerated schedule because of the war. Though the rostrum of teachers changed, Latin, Greek, English literature, and science remained the curriculum's mainstays. Again, I flourished under outstanding teachers. For the first time, I also began to enjoy history classes; the professor was a medievalist much influenced by the work of Christopher Dawson.

Introduction to psychology was taught by a teacher mediocre at best. Being bored in his class, I took Freud's complete works out of the library, and tried to make my way through them. The superior found out what I was reading (who snitched?) and took them from me. They were placed then in the section of the library we called "hell," the area reserved for forbidden books that could only be taken out with the head librarian's permission and with a written note from the professor teaching the course. Father Maurice Costello, another psychologist on the college faculty, heard this story, went to the superior, and asked if he could tutor me in reading Freud's works. The superior agreed and Father Maurice dutifully met with me each week as we read Freud together until my interest began to wane. I did not know Father Maurice well, but was impressed that he would go out of his way to be of help. His example taught me that one should not be afraid of ideas that at first seem contradictory to one's traditional religious concepts, but to accept the challenge of working out a synthesis. It was no surprise to me when later he was appointed president of the college.

I resolved when I began writing these memoirs not to mention all who taught me but I must say a word about Father Michael Hlavčak who taught Greek on the college level — though he seemed to know every language — and who for two years after the regular courses continued to tutor me. What a memorable experience! We translated six books of the *Iliad* and six books of the *Odyssey* into Latin. (He felt it was too easy to translate them into English. I soon knew every part of a ship in both languages!) Then we spent time with patristic authors, St. Basil and St. John Chrysostom.

Father Michael gave me my love for languages. He had music stands around the room, and on each had placed an open dictionary of a different language. He put a pencil mark beside each word as he looked it up. One of his store of little aphorisms was that if I looked up a word three times and did not know it forever, I was not being attentive. He also had many collections of the classics in English and would compare special passages, selecting not only the most accurate translation but the one he thought best conveyed the original's mood and spirit. Once we got into an argument over how to translate a particular Greek passage. His solution to the argument still amazes me. He selected the editor of the Loeb edition of the work in question to be the arbiter, sent the professor a letter that outlined the two possibilities without saying which solution was his and which mine. When the reply came back preferring mine, Father Michael was delighted that I had won.

An eccentric, he probably would not have been able to endure the pressures of life in the world, but he thrived in a monastic environment. Long after I had entered the monastery and was ordained, I happened to be seated during recreation at a table with Father Michael and a few monks. One said to Father Michael, "If I had spent my whole life in the library studying words, I could speak all those languages too." Father Michael calmly replied: "The difference between you and me is that I did it, you didn't." *At his grave, I prayed, but also smiled a bit in gratitude.*

St. Vincent, Latrobe, Pennsylvania (1940-1948)

*　　*　　*

One of the advantages we scholastics shared during those six years was that we went home only at Thanksgiving, Christmas, and Easter. That gave us weekends to devote to extracurricular activities. For me much of that time was spent in music.

The head of the music department was Father Ralph Bailey. His sparkling, extrovert personality made him the right person for high school bands, choruses, and musicals. Father Ildephonse Wortman began giving me piano lessons. Ildie, as we affectionately called him, was a fine choice. He shared his love for Mozart, a composer he played well and understood even better. His knowledge of piano technique was not well developed, but his feel for the classical repertoire was phenomenal. He was also a philosopher and had me read the works of Jacques Maritain, especially *Art and Scholasticism,* and those of Étienne Gilson. Seeing my interest in French, he gave me some of the works of Jules Combarieu, an earlier French musicologist and historian — works that had never been translated into English — and then helped me to read them. His understanding of Gregorian chant and how it should be sung was unsurpassed. I have never encountered anyone with such a gift. The monks told me that in his last illness, suffering excruciating pain from cancer, he continued to sing Gregorian chant from memory as he waited for the Lord to take him. *At his grave site I paused long in gratitude. I even sang, sotto voce, the "Salve Regina," trying to imagine how Ildie would have wanted it rendered.*

Toward the end of my freshman year in college I fell into a deep crisis of faith. An incompatibility between the need for faith and the discoveries of modern science had hit me: one did not need God as an explanation for the world around us because eventually a natural cause would be found for everything and that explanation would suffice. Now my crisis seems trite to me, but then it was a serious and nagging problem, like an itch that would not go away.

For days I pondered these issues without resolve. Finally, I asked one of the prefects if it might be possible to talk with Father Justin Krellner, one of the holiest and most learned monks in the monastery. Although I had never met Father Justin, I knew that he was a well-known scripture scholar whom everyone respected. There are certain turning points or moments of clarity in life that determine the direction of the future. That meeting with Father Justin was one of them. First, I was impressed that he would spend a few hours listening and responding to the concerns of a college freshman. Second, I was surprised at how seriously and thoughtfully he re-plied to my questions, not showing any sign of irritation or belittling them. Moreover, he was not scandalized or anxious when I said I thought I was losing my faith.

When it was his turn to respond, he talked about a similar struggle go-ing on between scripture and science and that whatever was true in one field had to be reconciled with what was true in the other, since truths could not contradict one another. He tried to show me that the history and tradition of the Catholic Church revealed a continuing tension over how the Church could absorb other truths into its own system wherever they might be found. At times, he said, this took many generations and much suffering, but the Church, in the end, was always richer for the confronta-tion. This had happened in every period of history, he said, but I didn't know enough to follow all his details. He began with the Hellenistic influ-ences apparent in the New Testament, the challenge in the Middle Ages of Aristotelianism and the subsequent Thomistic synthesis, the Renaissance return to the classics and the emphasis on the body and the human, and now the more recent scientific thrust. The solution, he suggested, was not "either/or," a neat split between religion and science, but entailed an ongo-ing struggle to find the synthesis between the two. This was the important task before the Church in our day.

Moreover, he pointed out to me that there are some things one could not put under a microscope — like grace, forgiveness, the Divine indwell-ing, the afterlife. He talked to me about the meaning of redemption and the role of Jesus Christ. It became clear to me that I had not fully under-stood the Incarnation and its significance. Perhaps I had perceived re-demption in too negative a fashion and had not taken into consideration its positive effects; those could only come from Divine initiative. His treat-ment was to give me a powerful challenge rather than a finished solution — just the right approach that then answered my needs. I had entered his room a doubting deist and came out a searching Christian.

The years 1944 and 1945 were intense ones for the development of my inner self and the struggle to find out what religion was going to mean to me in the future. All the answers were not on the table, but I felt at ease; the struggle would be worthwhile and even exciting. I began to pray more ar-dently and more freely. I can say that after that crisis, doubts of faith were not a major problem for me. I accepted the process and the growth that faith involved, that faith would always be a leap for me and perhaps even a struggle. I did not seem to need the security of all the answers, but found the search for the solutions exhilarating. In fact, I came to fear those who felt they had the answers. At times, I sensed they were avoiding facing the new problems that our age had brought forth through scientific discovery.

Strangely enough, a book — probably way over my head — that I came upon in the scholasticate library by accident (or was it?) influenced me even more, François René de Chateaubriand's *The Genius of Christianity.* It fit me like a glove at the time. Its more Romantic approach to religion and the relationship between religion and the aesthetic experience clarified my perspective. Though I did not understand it completely, it opened me for greater affectivity in prayer. I was becoming a Romantic in my tastes and outlook and even in my prayer-life.

*   *   *

Entering novices usually did so in July after completing the second year of college. My class, i.e., the three or four who remained, would only finish that year in August of 1945 so our entrance was postponed to September. This was a big decision for me: to go on or not? My mother had made it clear that I could return home any time I wanted and it would be okay with her. I weighed the possibilities. Should I work to become a concert pianist? Or should I join the Benedictine community and become a monk? The turning point, and a rather dramatic one, came in March of that year. I had played Mozart's *Concerto in D Minor* with the college community orchestra. In those days the musicians' union paid for players from the Pittsburgh Symphony to augment our local orchestras. This usually brought a few professionals to each string section and extras in the brass and woodwinds. It did wonders for the local orchestra. The concert was a huge success.

When the applause ended and I had returned to the dressing room, a clarifying moment came. I had played well. I had enjoyed it. But it was absolutely clear to me that I did not want to make concertizing my life. As a concert pianist I would be an "also-ran," not the best. I feared, too, that it would not totally fulfill me as a person. I still am amazed at how clear-cut that decision was.

Whether or not to enter the monastery was another decision. I weighed all the reasons, negative and positive, for and against. Finally, I decided to enter and I was at peace. What had drawn me to St. Vincent at age thirteen were not the same reasons that led me to enter the Benedictine community at eighteen. Undoubtedly I had left home so young out of attraction to the social and intellectual opportunities. My chief religious motivation at the time was simply my desire to be a priest; St. Vincent seemed to be the first necessary step. What kept me at St. Vincent, in addition to this vague desire to be a priest, was the excitement of the place itself and the opportunities it opened up for a kid from a small town like Patton. Surprisingly enough, it was not a deep knowledge of the Benedictine way of life that brought me to make the decision to enter the monastery — that would only come later. Instead, it was the example of the Benedictines I had met. If that way of life could produce people I had come to know and respect, then I could see myself fitting in there and finding as much fulfillment as any human could expect in this life. This argument by example was a compelling one for me then.

The challenges of a celibate life were not real to me at that time. I had had no personal sexual experiences. I had not fallen in love with anyone and had no relationship that would raise questions in my mind. Perhaps there was an immaturity that prevented me from seeing the reality of a life commitment of celibacy. In any case, although I was forced to consider what was at stake and try my best to understand the sacrifices involved, I knew that there were many years ahead in my course of studies before that decision had to be made for life.

*   *   *

In September, after a few weeks at home, I put aside any idea of a musical career and entered the monastery.

The custom at that time was to give each novice a new name, not one already found in the monastery; Kenan was the name given me. I disliked it because I did not know how to pronounce it. Later that year I had a chance to talk with the novice master about this and he asked me to give him two other possibilities. I submitted Callistus and Rembert. He went to the abbot and my monastic name was changed to Rembert. When, some years later, we were permitted to go back to our baptismal names, I stayed with Rembert, a name I had grown to like and by which I was known.

As I look back now on the novitiate year, I appreciate what a luxury it was to have a full year free from other responsibilities in order to look at the Benedictine way of life from inside, and to see if it suited me. The following year, 1946, was the centennial of the founding of the monastery with numerous celebrations planned. It meant lots of manual work for the novices as we cleaned or painted every corner of the many buildings and chapels. We worked for days in the crypt of the church, which was totally redone to commemorate the anniversary celebration. All the abbots of the United States were coming to help celebrate.

This heavy workload did not impede our regular classes and hours of prayer and spiritual reading. We rose with the community at 3:40 for Matins and Lauds at 4:00. Most mornings we would be in church till about 7:00. There were private Masses to be served, the other canonical hours of prayer to be recited, prime and terce on most days, and then the solemn community Mass with its Gregorian chant propers and ordinaries. Choir rehearsals for the younger members of the community took place later in the day and for us Benedictines formed a regular part of our routine. Some of the monks had excellent voices and carried the rest of us.

Classes and reading filled the time from 8:30 to about 11:00 each morning. The novice master would take us through some passage of the Rule of St. Benedict and its interpretation. Some days he spoke about the liturgy of the season and the day. On other days we studied the history of the Benedictine Order or had a class in the psalms with the Archabbot Alfred Koch, who had a degree in Scripture from the University of Vienna. The archabbot possessed a stunning tenor voice, almost a German Heldentenor. On Christmas and exceptional feast days when he was principal celebrant for the pontifical Mass and I was at the organ, I would have him intone the Gloria so that he could sail up to a high F full throttle and rock the church.

The afternoons were devoted to manual work. We chanted Vespers each day in Latin, followed by spiritual reading and then supper. Recreation lasted till 7:30, and sung Compline brought the day to an end, introducing the grand silence that lasted till breakfast the next morning. Usually we were so tired that by 9:00 we were eager to go to bed.

The novice master was Father Quentin Schaut. I could not have asked for a better choice. His field was English literature, and he had done his studies at Oxford in England. He had been strongly influenced by the English Benedictine tradition, and we were introduced to it at St. Vincent. That tradition had a deep mystical bent that traced its roots back to the medieval period through works like *The Cloud of Unknowing*. Because the English monasteries had developed a strong academic tradition with renowned schools, they had learned to relate their monastic life and its values to their scholarship and teaching. I wish I had paid more attention to his translation of the Rule of Benedict and other monastic literature since he prepared well and gave us every nuance of scholarship then available.

Some found him a bit aloof and his repartees a bit sharp, but not I. Although he was about forty, he tried his best to relate to us, the new generation. His period as novice master was crucial in the history of the monastery. I did not understand at the time how innovative he was but I later came to realize more fully his contribution.

The novitiate began with an eight-day retreat. When it was over, Father Quentin called us in separately for a brief conference. His first words to me were that I was to practice the piano for several hours three days a week. I protested that I had given up music in order to be a monk. He smiled and said the first thing I would learn as a monk was obedience and that I should practice. He added: "Remember, as a monk you do not give up who you are; you just learn to use your talents in a different way." I practiced regularly.

When I visited the line of crosses in the cemetery, I always paused long at Father Quentin's grave. What I knew of monasticism, both theoretical and practical, came from him. One cannot overestimate the influence a novice master has on those he teaches and leads.

Since its foundation in 1846 the monastery of St. Vincent followed the Bavarian tradition that its founder, Abbot Boniface Wimmer, had brought from his own monastery of Metten Abbey in Bavaria. That Bavarian tradition had remained relatively unchanged since the sixteenth century and fit perfectly the Bavarian monasteries with their large schools, florid Baroque churches, love for art and music, and a humane approach to monastic practice and discipline. In later descriptive terms they would have been considered active and not contemplative communities. The work the priest-monks would be engaged in was principally teaching in the schools and administering parishes, especially those closest to the monastery. Wimmer's concept also included a large group of lay brothers who would do the farm work and all the other trades and crafts needed for such a large institution. The division between priests and brothers in practice resulted in two almost totally distinct communities. The brothers did not have a vote in the monastic chapter, had their own prayer life — reciting daily three rosaries and some litanies — and came after the priests in rank and at table.

The monasteries that were the principal centers of monastic reform in the eighteenth century — Solesmes in France, Maredsous in Belgium, Beuron and Maria Laach in Germany — had not yet been founded, and so St. Vincent was not directly affected by these movements. Such reforms placed more emphasis on the liturgy with solemn singing of the Divine Office. St. Vincent was, instead, a beehive of activity that kept a regular, but not fanatical, monastic discipline.

After the founding of Solesmes and Beuron and the greater interest among lay Catholics in monasteries as spiritual oases for retreats and contemplative needs, St. Vincent continued its Bavarian way with its emphasis on schools and assisting in the parishes. This emphasis on work often created tensions and divisions in the community. It seemed there were always some monks calling for a reform — wanting to close the schools, demanding more time for private prayer, crying out for longer hours in choir, seeking more daily solemn liturgies, begging for more silence, striving to reduce outside work, and so on. Even before Wimmer's death in 1887, the movement to introduce Gregorian chant on major feast days and thus forgo a Haydn, Mozart, or Schubert Mass with full orchestra had gained ground. But this movement did not totally succeed until after the First World War.

The monks at St. Vincent had always sung some chant, especially for the Divine Office, but had used the old Ratisbonne edition from Regensburg in Bavaria. In the early 1930s a young monk-musician was sent to Quarr Abbey on the Isle of Wight where Solesmes monks lived in exile. He was to learn the new chant and introduce it at St. Vincent. The story goes that the old monks in anger rebelled against the new and created a scene by tossing the Solesmes books into the middle of the choir. According to the Bavarian tradition, clearly noted in our monastic ceremonial, each antiphon at Vespers was to be intoned by a different monk, starting with the highest-ranking in choir at the time — the abbot, the prior, the subprior, the novice master, and then the oldest monks. To help the monk so designated, I would first play the melody on the organ from the Solesmes edition, only to find that many of the older monks would intone instead the old Ratisbonne version, and this about a dozen years after the old had been abandoned. This experience taught me something about the history of chant and how hard it is to change such cultural heritages. My generation was steeped in the new Solesmes system, and the gracious and loveable nature of monks like Father Ildephonse made the new seem like the best choice.

*   *   *

If I dwell now on what I learned during that novitiate year and the formation in religious life that I received, it is because it is impossible to understand me without knowing something about that Benedictine spirituality in which I was formed. In many ways, I have never lost it, even though I have lived for the last quarter of a century outside of a Benedictine monastery.

Father Quentin seemed to set aside the *Tyrocinium Religiosum,* a spiritual manual from sixteenth-century Bavaria which was still printed by our monastery. Instead, he gave us a host of other works to read and reflect on, most from the English tradition: the famous medieval mystical treatise already mentioned, *The Cloud of Unknowing;* Augustine Baker's *Holy Wisdom* (first published in 1657); Cuthbert Butler's *Benedictine Monachism: Studies in Benedictine Life and Rule* (1919); Abbot Prosper Guéranger's *Liturgical Year* (many English editions were published since it first began to appear in 1841); Abbot Paul Delatte's *The Rule of St. Benedict: A Commentary* (1921); Abbot Columba Marmion's *Christ the Ideal of the Monk* (1922); Justin McCann's *St. Benedict* (1937); and similar works.

One can see that we were being exposed to the best of the English monastic tradition with some of the reformed French tradition and not simply living with the older Bavarian sources from the Baroque period. Although we heard the names of the German monastic reform writers, like Placid and Maurus Wolter and Ildephonse Herwegen, I cannot say that they influenced Father Quentin's thinking or that he quoted from them very often. On special feast days, much to our delight, he would read to us in his semi-serious tone C. S. Lewis's *Screwtape Letters* that had just been published. Slowly but judiciously, he was making an amalgam of the older tradition and the reformed tradition, one that was well-adapted to the circumstances of St. Vincent.

What did I learn from him about monastic life that attracted me to it? The first aspect would have to be Benedict's sacramental approach. St. Benedict saw the monk as on a search for God. Father Quentin often repeated to us that Benedict did not say the important point was finding God, but the continuous search for God. First of all, that search took place daily in the monastic prayer routine. The day was broken up with constant reminders of the presence of God. One had to be listening daily to God's voice. His approach to the long hours of praying in Latin in choir was to have us novices simply relax, note any phrase that struck us, and try to keep that phrase in mind during the rest of the recitation of the hours as a kind of mantra. We even kept booklets with these phrases — all in Latin. I must admit that this worked well when we recited in Latin, but had to be altered when the Office changed to English and the words seemed — all of them — to just jump off the page. So many monks would then say that they did not know they were reciting all those poignant words when they were praying in Latin.

Father Quentin also introduced us to the liturgical year in a way that I, as a Catholic, had never understood it. In fact, I believe that that novitiate year was the best time in my life for living all the details and nuances of the liturgical calendar. He taught us that every feast is really a feast of Christ, of his paschal mystery, that is, of his death and resurrection. Advent that novitiate year was a revelation to me. I had not known how the texts were to change every day as one approached Christmas and how the spirit of waiting was intensified. Each day at Vespers we sang the seven early medieval "O" antiphons, intoned by the archabbot himself in the most solemn of tones.

For the first time in my life Christmas was not anticipated but came after the four-week preparation. The three Masses of Christmas were sung at their proper time. We were tired when it was all over, but I soon began to notice a difference between liturgical tiredness and work tiredness. The first had a good feeling about it. I later came to understand this difference again when I began to attend many Orthodox ceremonies. Among them liturgical tiredness is more common. We Benedictines strove for balance, even in prayer.

Lent, too, was a special occasion in the monastery, as one could take the fasting and extra prayers seriously and participate more fully in what this season intended the Christian to experience. It had been my desire at the beginning of the novitiate to read the Bible from cover to cover. Lent was a wonderful time for extra biblical reading so that I was able to accomplish this feat. It was the only time in my life that I read all the books of the Bible in order. The Triduum leading up to Easter were also special days, but the reformed liturgy for those holy days had not yet been published and so, even in the monastery, they still lacked the depth they were to acquire later. We novices had to work hard during those days, as they were a period of monastic spring house-cleaning so that everything at Easter would be fresh and new.

Liturgy also appealed to my aesthetic instincts. When Benedict in his Rule wrote that only those should intone in choir who could edify the listeners, he could not have guessed the important historical consequences of that remark. For Benedictines, liturgy must be carried out to edify, to build up *(aedificare)* the listener. Thus, it must be done well. There was no doubt that the monastic liturgies at St. Vincent on the great feasts had a quality about them that was unequaled, a spirit of enthusiasm and elan that was felt by all.

When, years later, I came to Milwaukee as bishop, I noticed at once that this diocese had a similar spirit, due I am sure to the long musical and aesthetic tradition that had been a part of its history. I have never had that same experience at pontifical liturgies in Rome, where I always felt — and still do — that I am a part of a large Baroque stage production, where the external appearances are more important than the internal meaning and where there is little sense of a single worshipping community. Liturgy often becomes pageantry. I have found that any two liturgies could be exactly alike in content and in rubrics, but totally dissimilar in the experiences projected. It made me all the more convinced that liturgy is not synonymous with rubrics. Frequently, in visiting other monasteries throughout the world, I would again find this satisfaction and know that I was among Benedictines or those who had learned from Benedictines. Perhaps the most subtle aspect of liturgy that many never learn is timing: giving each moment its proper weight is as important as the rubrics.

Benedictines not only do their liturgies well, but they also understand that the aesthetic atmosphere in which the monks live out their lives will influence how they think and pray. They cultivated, thus, an instinct for art and architecture, and Father Quentin made us very aware of these values. He told us how Cardinal Newman had described Benedictine education as "poetic" in an attempt to capture this aesthetic spirit that pervades a monastery. It was not aestheticism for its own sake, but a part of the monk's search for God.

Another sacramental aspect of the monastic tradition that we had to learn was the way in which Benedict saw the whole of life as an expansion of the Eucharist. Benedict said that the tools of the monastery should be seen as extensions of the vessels of the altar — an idea that has always stayed with me. Everything is sacramental, a place for finding Christ. One can distinguish, thus, between good and evil, but not between secular and sacred. Benedict saw Christ in the abbot, the sick, the guest, the needy. The search for God becomes more explicit in the search for Christ and the place to find Christ becomes everywhere. The intensification of the search might be at the altar, but it never ceases there. This idea was new to me and became a powerful influence in my life as a way of looking at the world and all that is in it.

At first I thought that obedience would be difficult for me. I tended to nip at the heels of those above me, especially if I thought authority had gone to their heads. I had read or heard about blind obedience, about novices forced to do crazy things like watering sticks just because the superior said to do so. My fears, evolved in the 1930s, about authoritarian regimes were still with me. As I understood obedience in the Benedictine tradition, it had to be an imitation of Jesus' obedience to his Father's Will, that it included obedience first to God's Word, then to one's calling, and was not, thus, without bounds and strictures. Perhaps I was fortunate in having so many enlightened superiors and my experiences taught me that they truly had my best interests at heart and wanted to be of help to me, to see me grow in every way and become the person God wanted me to be.

Benedict considered Christ with his disciples gathered around him as an icon of how the abbot should relate to his community; Father Quentin was forceful in pointing out that we monks were all adults and there was no room for infantilism in that image. Moreover, Benedict did not fall into the mistake of making the abbot the only icon of Christ in the monastery. The monks were also to see Christ in the sick, in the guests, in one another. In addition, whenever anything important was to be decided about life in the community, the abbot was to consult the whole body. For all these reasons, I never feared in the monastery the kind of dictatorial, authoritarian approach to governance that I had often associated with religious obedience.

We had very little discussion or tutoring, however, on celibacy. It was never discussed as such nor were there attempts to integrate it into our spirituality. That was typical of the day. I cannot say that the superiors were prudish; they just did not talk about such things. Perhaps, too, celibacy was seen more as a discipline, a sacrifice to be made, a prerequisite for living in community, rather than a subject for teaching.

Finally, I soon understood that the novitiate was a way of learning to live in a community. In those days many of the candidates came from large families and were accustomed to living together in close quarters. The value of community balanced the value of the individual. I learned it was a delicate balance but an important one. There were a lot of monks with idiosyncrasies that could irritate — deeply irritate. Living in community supplied the monastic penance for most of us. In some respects this balance between community and individuals cut against American civil religion where the rights and value of the individual came first and the community was brought into the picture only insofar as it heightened the first. The Rule of Benedict saw the monastery as an organism with different roles for each member so that it could function smoothly for the good of all. All had to feel, however, a connectedness to the community since it became one's home, one's family. It involved a sharing of all things, but for a higher and more spiritual cause. I have always hoped this would be the image of the Church itself, where relationships counted as a mirror of the communion of saints. Although I often found these values conflicting in theory — the individual versus the community — I also found that it was possible though not always easy to find solutions that would preserve both. Just searching for that solution was in itself an important way to keep the values alive.

The novitiate year passed rapidly and it was soon time for first vows on September 23, 1946. Those vows, pronounced before the abbot and community, were specified for three years. They were then designated "simple vows." According to the Rule they were a promise to try to live a monastic way of life through poverty, chastity, and obedience. As I look back on the novitiate year of preparation, I realize what a privilege it was to have had someone like Father Quentin as novice master. He opened my mind to many aspects of life that I would never have known and helped me form a spirituality that has been important to me my whole life long.

*   *   *

After finishing the novitiate we passed on to the clericate. In those days, this second six-year period of training consisted of two years of philosophy and four of theology. I now fell under a different superior, Father Justin Krellner, whom I esteemed so highly. Again, I lucked out: he was an ideal successor to Father Quentin.

In those days all seminarians majored in philosophy as a preparation for theology. For two years we were barraged with that subject, attending seven periods a week, six taught in Latin and one in English, the latter being a summary of the other six. The Latin textbook used was written by a German monk, Joseph Gredt, in the neo-Scholastic Thomistic style: a thesis was presented, all the opposing views were discussed, and then the correct view triumphantly was laid out.

None of my seminary classes were too challenging for me and so I had time to devote to music. Each week I would take the bus into Pittsburgh to study piano with Professor Selmar Janson at Carnegie-Tech University. Janson had been a pupil of Franz Xaver Scharwenka (1850-1924) and Eugen d'Albert (1864-1932), the latter considered by Liszt as one of his most important pupils. Janson also had been the teacher of Earl Wild, a pianist well known then in musical circles for his fabulous technique. Janson worked me hard, scales of every type and shape, in thirds and sixths and then in double thirds and double sixths. He went over some of the pieces I was playing: Chopin Ballads, Nocturnes, and Waltzes, or Mozart and Beethoven Sonatas, and worked on some of the technical difficulties in each. Finally, he challenged me with a new piece — Sergei Rachmaninoff's *Second Piano Concerto*. He came out to the monastery on March 21, 1948, when I played it with the community orchestra, augmented as before with many musicians from the Pittsburgh Symphony Orchestra. I was twenty-one then and played with lots of bravura, verve, and youthful exuberance, not sparing the tendency to Romantic exaggeration. But I got all the notes and then some!

Father Justin had noticed that I was bored with the seminary classes; they were not challenging enough. He was also concerned about the pace I was keeping since I was the major organist for the monastery choir as well. We talked about that pace during the spring months of 1948 and he suggested that I spend most of the summer working on the monastic farm. It was a lazy, wonderful summer for me. After hours of pitching hay, first with a pitchfork and then tossing bails of straw up on the wagon, at the end of the afternoon, covered with itchy hay sticks, I would dive into the monastery pool by the barn and dress in time to run up to accompany Vespers. In the evenings we played volleyball before Compline. By the end of the summer I felt in fine fettle.

Still concerned about my boredom, Father Justin consulted Fathers Quentin, Ralph, and Ildephonse, and then suggested to Archabbot Alfred a plan for my future formation. In mid-summer Abbot Alfred called me into his study for a talk. He began by telling me that the theologians wanted me to major in theology, the linguists in languages, and the musicians in music. He laid out the plan he, together with the other superiors, had come up with. Music would be my major, and I should prepare myself in that field for teaching music in the college. But he did not want me to be deprived of a European education that he felt would be very broadening for me as a person and monk. Although he was Austrian by birth, he had spent many years in Rome and loved that city. Thus, he wanted me to do my theological studies in Rome at the Benedictine College of Sant'Anselmo. There, he informed me, the classes were divided into two sections: the *cursus theologicus* (for students majoring in theology) and the *cursus seminaristicus* (for students seeking ordination). I was to take classes with those majoring in theology, but the exams with those not seeking a degree but just preparing for ordination; nor was I to write the thesis required for a degree. He laughed and said that should put the musicians at ease.

The solution was not to burden me with degree requirements. He wanted me to be exposed to the best theology teachers. I could take advantage of the resources in Rome for studying music. Thursdays in the Roman seminaries were days off, just as at St. Vincent, and on that day I was to find two good music teachers, one for piano, and one for music theory. Finally, he told me to spend the first summer at Solesmes in France to perfect my French and study Gregorian chant; the second in Munich at the Benedictine house of studies to perfect my German and study piano. At both places, Solesmes and Munich, I would find few monks, if any, who could speak English. "Most of all," he added, "I do not want your studies to interfere with your education."

In early October 1948, after a few days at home, I packed my trunk and shipped it to the *Vulcania,* the steamer in New York that would take me on my first trip outside the country. Two monks who were already studying in Rome were returning and I did not have to travel alone. When the day of departure came, we three knelt in the middle of choir for the *itinerarium,* an old monastic prayer for safe travel.

In 2002, as I visited the graves of Quentin and Justin and prayed at the stone cross under which Abbot Alfred was buried, I recalled in vivid detail that brisk autumn day in 1948, the prayers in chapel, the train ride through the night, the boarding of the Vulcania, *the flowers waiting for me on board, and my youthful excitement and awe. My marveling at the wisdom and trust of these three men had not changed; again my heart was overflowing with gratitude.*

CHAPTER 3

Absorbing New Worlds

Rome (1948-1951)

Naples in 1948 was a mixture of natural beauty and bombed-out edifices. On the morning of our arrival, although everyone on the *Vulcania* was up early, the ship idled in the bay until docking at 7:00. The immense natural beauty was enhanced by a kind of sunlight I had never seen before. The odors were just as memorable, some from the garlic wafting out of the kitchens, some from the strong Italian espresso brewing on the streets, and some from the foul debris floating in the harbor. As I walked down the flimsy gangplank, I caught a glimpse of my sister Betty, now a secretary at the U.S. Embassy in Rome — there to meet and help us through customs. The process went smoothly and we were soon on the train to Rome.

In 1948 Rome was still suffering the after-effects of the war, overcrowded with poverty and food shortages everywhere. Even at Sant'Anselmo, the Benedictine college where I lived, food was sparse and the dried pasta, which sat in open bags on the streets, was full of bugs, making it very unappetizing. In my three years in Rome my weight fell from 172 to 142 pounds so that my poor mother cried when she saw me for the first time on my return home. Buildings were cold. In the winter weather there was heat — but only if you sat on the radiator. My feet froze on those elegant Italian marble and terrazzo floors, and I asked my monastery to send me boots with fur lining. To play the organ in the unheated church, I wore gloves with the tips of the fingers cut out. All of this took some getting used to, but in the end, none of it finally mattered:

Italy was gradually returning to normal and there were signs of hope and stability.

It was fascinating to live in a culture with such deep historical and artistic roots undergoing a radical transformation because of the war, but, most of all, I quickly came to love the Italian people. I experienced their charm, warmth, love, and even cynicism more than most students because Betty lived with the Bianchis, an Italian family of Tuscan origin that I visited frequently. Their Italian was remarkably clear and expressive. Most of my confreres came in contact only with Italian clerics or street vendors, store-keepers, and beggars; I had the good fortune of coming to know another part of Rome's population.

Sant'Anselmo was situated on the Aventine hill (one of the famous seven hills of Rome) in a residential area of small villas, each surrounded by high walls topped with barbed-wire and protruding pieces of sharply cut glass. It was the Benedictine graduate school of studies and the residency of the abbot primate (the order's superior), the university's professors, and Benedictine students from all over the world. It was an elegant place, situated in that convenient and tranquil neighborhood with finely designed buildings in matching red brick and extensive gardens nestled among fruit trees. Sant'Anselmo was forty-five minutes by foot from Vatican City, a pleasant walk along the Tiber.

Adjusting to the cultural diversity of the Benedictine students at Sant'Anselmo challenged all of us. I began to appreciate why Archabbot Alfred wanted me to have this chance at such a young age. We were over a hundred in residence: monks from Germany, Austria, England, Ireland, Italy, France, the United States, Canada, Hungary, Brazil, and Belgium. The house's language was Italian, which we all spoke badly; all the classes were taught in Latin. At the beginning, listening to four hours of Latin lectures a day was exhausting, but after a short period of time it became familiar. Since the final tests were oral and in Latin, I found the best way to study was to talk Latin out loud to the walls in my room.

Abbot Bernard Kaelin, a rather naïve but loveable Swiss from Muri-Gries in the Tyrol region of Italy, had been elected abbot primate in September 1947. He was only the third abbot primate in the history of the Benedictine confederation. Benedictines had not looked favorably on Pope Leo's attempt at the end of the nineteenth century to centralize them. They resisted the title abbot general as being too military. This resistance led to a compromise; first the title would be abbot primate instead of abbot general, and then the primate was given very limited jurisdiction so as not to interfere with the powers of each local abbot. Throughout history Benedictine communities prided themselves on their autonomy and independence, expressed by the free election of their abbots and their vow of stability in a given community. This independence was often a sign of strength but at times a source of weakness. In self-defense, some monasteries in the late Middle Ages had joined together into congregations for protection against bishops and powerful princes. The abbots of these monasteries elected one among them as the president of their congregation for a prescribed period of time. In 1893 these congregations, numbering then about twenty with some two hundred participating monasteries, were joined together by Leo XIII into a confederation under the abbot primate. In later years, trying to explain the difference between Benedictines and other religious orders, I would describe the Benedictine confederation as more like the United Nations than an army.

This model was important to me because it guaranteed that the superior who had jurisdiction over me was my own abbot back home, the superior who knew me best. This monastic tradition was the source of my positive attitude toward the concept of subsidiarity in the Catholic Church, which emphasizes the importance of decentralization. The role of the abbot primate was to represent Benedictine interests to the Roman curia and protect the traditions and history of the monasteries — a task I later found could be time-consuming, but important. The primate sought to maintain unity in the entire confederation and promote what was best for all. Finally, it was his task to look after Sant'Anselmo, the Benedictine university in Rome.

*   *   *

When I arrived at Sant'Anselmo in 1948, the monk directly responsible for the students was the thirty-seven-year-old Father Augustin Mayer of Metten Abbey in Bavaria, the monastery that had founded St. Vincent in Latrobe. *My photos of him show him as tall, thin, and emaciated, looking every bit the image of the ascetical monk in old etchings.* Our lives would crisscross many times in the following decades. For many years he was my confessor, and I could not have been happier with his care and concern.

Father Cyprian Vagaggini, professor of systematic theology, had the most pronounced intellectual influence on me during those years. Raised in Belgium by immigrant Italian parents, he was a monk of the monastery of Saint André, famous for its scholarship and its role in liturgical renewal.

He was the most exciting teacher I ever had. Every morning he lectured for an hour in the grand aula in impeccable Latin, describing boarding a bus, paying his fare, being pick-pocketed, leaving the bus, etc., as if the language was a living one. Because his mind worked in a clear and logical fashion, he presented a new subject with an intellectual rigor that was extraordinary. Without my knowing it then, his method was a departure from the traditional theological manuals and pedagogy common in most seminaries. Best of all, he gave us an appreciation for the use of Scripture in theological discourse. Using the most scholarly exegesis and avoiding any kind of proof-texting, he would point out what could be found in the Bible about the theme in question. Then, he would present a chronological survey of the same theme among the writers of the Patristic period. That too was a new approach for me and opened up entirely new vistas. When the students would laugh at the exaggerated typological use of the Old Testament by one of the Fathers, he would agree that it was fine to laugh, but urged us to look to the theological point and not throw out the baby with the bath water. Finally, with that background he would wrestle with St. Thomas's point of view and then turn to modern theological thought. *As I look now at a photo of him, I see the same excitement in the face and eyes that were there when he taught us theology.*

He could be described as a neo-Thomist, or neo-Scholastic, but with a leaning toward the "nouvelle théologie," or new theology, that was just beginning to make its way, especially in French circles. The late 1940s were difficult years for theologians, some of the most searching had been silenced. We students at Sant'Anselmo did not notice this general unrest, but an occasional event called it to our attention.

One day entering the classroom, Father Cyprian was unusually agitated. Someone among the students had denounced him to the Holy Office for his teaching on the fruits of the Holy Spirit — not one of the central doctrines of the Catholic Church. After the customary prayer, he made every student in the aula take out a pen and write each word he dictated. "This," he uttered, "is what I am teaching on this subject. If anyone quotes me and misses even one word, I will deny I ever said it." He then proceeded to dictate his thesis. You could have heard a pin drop. At a certain point, he yelled at one student who was not writing to leave the room and told him not to return. As he left, Cyprian murmured audibly, "That is the kind who would denounce me."

Whenever anyone asked him if another theologian, because of some position he held or taught, was a heretic, Cyprian replied that it was not his task to declare anyone's teaching heresy. He might add, then, that, if he had a chance to talk to the theologian in question, he would ask how he could hold the thesis he did and reconcile it with some other defined doctrine of the church. That is as far as he would go. I was surprised in later years to see how readily some in the Church labeled others heretics and always recalled Cyprian's wise attitude.

During the years of Vatican Council II, Cyprian emerged as a preeminent liturgist, a *peritus*. Later he wrote many books on liturgy. His concern was always that liturgy be based on good theology and not sentimentality or banal taste. Although he did not teach liturgy in my day, it was often a sub-theme in his lectures on dogma. He opened up for me an understanding of how God can act in this world through material and human instruments, through people, signs, and symbols. He never claimed that the Catholic Church had a monopoly on the action of the Spirit, and expressed discomfort if it seemed the Holy Spirit was being encapsulated in a box of human making.

The entire emphasis in our curriculum was on dogmatic theology so that moral theology was of secondary importance. Our professor for that field carefully followed the usual Roman manuals in his teaching and on every issue always took the safest position. When we came to the section on *De sexto* (the sixth commandment), he made us close our books and forbade us to take any notes, lest in rereading we have impure thoughts. The courses in moral theology left me with the conviction that the Church's traditional approach was to set the bar high, perhaps too high in theory, but to mitigate it by counseling compassion in practice. While the Europeans seemed very comfortable with this approach, it made us Americans uneasy. They did not take the Church's teaching with the same rigor as we Americans did, but accepted that there were many exceptions to every rule. Later I found myself uncomfortable with the discrepancy between practice and norm when the bar was set so high and then not observed. Was this approach helpful in our literalist contemporary religious culture? I wondered then and still do. In general, the way we learned moral theology made it seem too separated from human experience so it could easily appear irrelevant.

There was one teaching in these courses that I had trouble understanding and accepting: the character and interpretation of natural law. I had no problem with the idea of *synderesis,* namely, that we humans have an in-built instinct that enables us to distinguish good from evil, right from wrong; nor did I have a problem accepting that there were objective

67

moral norms. But I rejected the elementary "biologism" that in practice underlay this particular view of natural law. Human nature, I would argue, was also rational and this rationality should color and affect a purely biological concept of the human person.

*   *   *

On Thursday, a day without classes, I pursued my music studies. Tito Aprea of the conservatory of Santa Cecilia who became my piano teacher introduced me to Debussy, one of his favorites and one of mine, and increased my Chopin repertoire and my knowledge of the Bach Suites and Partitas. Aprea was less interested in a dazzling repertoire than in imparting a love for all kinds of music. We studied together some early Beethoven Sonatas like opus 2, no. 3, opus 22, opus 26, and opus 28. The piano at Sant'Anselmo on which I practiced was a magnificent nine-foot Bechstein. Under his kind and precise tutelage, my Romantic tastes were becoming more refined; the excellent piano helped.

For music theory I went to Professor Carducci-Augustini of the Pontifical Institute of Musica Sacra who was a composer and a superb master like those of an older Italian tradition. His fee per lesson was one dollar or a pack of American cigarettes (in war-ravished Italy, still in short supply). I would analyze stacks of music, and then compose in the style of that music. Or I would orchestrate the slow movements of several Haydn and Mozart piano sonatas. Or he would give me three parts of a Haydn quartet and have me add the missing viola part. He excelled in counterpoint: we analyzed Palestrina motets and tried to write in that style. Then he had me work through the exercises in Théodore Dubois's *Traité de contrepoint et de fugue.* By the end, he had me write fugues using themes assigned to the contestants in the nineteenth century for the *prix de Rome* contests.

Four of us at Sant'Anselmo were organists and carried the bulk of the playing for services: Berthold from Kornelimünster near Aachen, Sebastian Moore from Downside, Cassian Just from Montserrat, and myself. I usually played for pontifical Masses, Vespers, and Lauds on major feasts. The primate was able to obtain as a permanent choir master a monk of the Solesmes tradition, Dom Derocquettes, from Quarr Abbey on the Isle of Wight, one of the gentlest musicians I have ever met. His one word of wisdom to me was that the vocation of a monk did not involve having a good voice and thus the monastic choir will always be a group of amateurs trying their best to praise God.

Contact with monks from all over the world whetted my appetite for a greater knowledge of cultural expressions. The Italian climate was softening my more Germanic characteristics. People on the streets seemed freer in showing affection than in the States. How often one would see men walking arm-in-arm down the avenue talking very intimately! At night prostitutes, gathered around their small fires, were always visible, even on our Aventine hill. It was not uncommon, as we were returning on foot from a concert or lecture, for a prostitute to yell to attract our attention, offering a clerical discount. If we took instead the steep shortcut up the hill that led to the former gardens of the Dominicans, we always had to keep custody of the eyes; it was common to find copulating couples here and there. Italians are not only more expressive of their affections, but also more openly sexual in their demeanor.

*   *   *

Following Abbot Alfred's program, I spent my two summers immersed in other cultures and languages, the first in France at Solesmes Abbey, the second in Germany. En route to Solesmes, my companions and I went to Chartres. As the bus rolled along the flat countryside, the towers of the cathedral seemed to rise above the horizon. The celebrated stained-glass windows, hidden during the war years, had just been re-installed. The superior of the minor seminary where we were staying took us over to the cathedral, already locked for the night, and led us up a narrow stairwell from the crypt to the body of the church for a short peek. The setting sun cast a warm blue haze over the whole interior. For me it was almost a mystical experience. The next day we saw the building in greater detail; I could have spent my time simply watching the sun create ever-new bluish hues over the interior of the church as it crept higher in the sky and then settled in the west.

I parted from my companions and went on my way to Solesmes. While waiting in the parlor for the guestmaster to come and show me to my cell, the porter gave me the accumulated mail. The first letter I opened was from the prior at St. Vincent, informing me of Father Justin's unexpected and untimely death from a heart attack. He was forty-four years old at the time. It was difficult to describe to the guestmaster how deeply the death of Justin, who counseled me in my crisis of faith, affected me, how broken up I felt.

That summer at Solesmes rests in my mind like a dream of another world. The monks were kind and generous, accepting me wholly into the community's life. It was a privilege to join them in choir, at table, and at recreation. In choir the pace was relaxed and though the chant moved along more rapidly than I had been accustomed to at home or at Sant'Anselmo, it was always smooth and seamless. A few monks had excellent voices that carried the rest of us.

Dom Cardine, later a chant professor at the Pontifical School of Sacred Music in Rome, met with me once a week to introduce me to their paleography studio. With great care he helped me read early tenth-century medieval mnemonic notations and shared the current scientific musicological information about them. Working often in the paleography studio was Michel Huglo, later one of the foremost chant experts in the world. All of this served as necessary background to my later study of Ambrosian chant.

The monks of Solesmes had the reputation of coming from the elite, the nobility of France. One thing was certain: they all spoke excellent French and the table reading was clear and exemplary. I realized that I would learn no Parisian slang that summer! One evening during recreation I was shocked to realize how badly I spoke French. One of the monks was a great mimic. With the encouragement of the others, he finally imitated my French; it was hilarious. I made a resolution that from then on I would try harder not to sound like an American when speaking French. Despite the warm welcome, I felt lonely at times. At Solesmes, unlike Sant'Anselmo, there were no American monks to chat with, and my French was not yet adequate for more serious and personal talk. Though everyone was kind, the natural barrier of linguistic and cultural differences divided me from them.

At one point during my visit, the monks welcomed a special guest, the papal nuncio from Paris, Monsignor Angelo Roncalli, coming for a day of private recollection and prayer. When he arrived, I noted how stout he was. His big black car was a mess, so a few of us helped his chauffeur wash and shine it. As he was leaving, he shook hands and thanked us profusely. Thus, I first saw the man who would be Pope John XXIII.

In early September I received another unexpected note from the prior at St. Vincent, Archabbot Alfred Koch had resigned due to age. His last act was to present my candidacy for solemn vows to the members of the community. He read to them a letter from the rector of Sant'Anselmo highly recommending me, and the monks of St. Vincent unanimously accepted me. On September 8, the community elected Father Denis Strittmatter as Archabbot Alfred's successor. Having a new abbot did not alter my life or change the plan for my education or my progression in monastic life. On September 23, 1946, I had pronounced simple or temporary vows for three years at St. Vincent; now it was time for solemn or final vows. Since September 23 was not a significant feast, the ceremony at Solesmes was postponed till September 29, the feast of St. Michael, the patronal feast of Solesmes. My chart of profession had been written on real parchment by one of the monk-artists at Solesmes and carried the shields of both Solesmes and St. Vincent on the top like bookends at each side of the image of Michael the Archangel. This I signed after reading it at the appropriate moment in the ceremony. The monks went out of their way to make that day very significant and special for me since I was away from my home abbey. It was a great kindness.

These solemn vows were for life, and I confess that I hesitated this time; I was only twenty-two years old. On the other hand, I was a happy monk and saw monastic life as a way of truly being the person God wanted me to be. Yet the vows for life of poverty, chastity, and obedience were a serious undertaking. Again, I had had no sexual experiences that would have made me hesitate. Looking back, I can see that I was probably a bit naïve and immature, but I have no regrets. Poverty had never been a problem, and obedience was easy because I had had such remarkable superiors. My prayer life had not changed much except that it came to me more naturally; I was more relaxed, becoming more and more inclined toward short prayers of praise and thanksgiving and not long litanies full of constant requests and petitions. The summer at Solesmes was ideal for developing an awareness of God's presence during the day.

Father Cyprian in one of his classes had talked about vocations and what he called "co-naturality," i.e., the sense that I could see myself living in that monastic way, doing the things monks traditionally do, and finding that my life had meaning. To me the Benedictine way of life was co-natural to my being. I was young, but I knew that many people at such an early age made life-determining decisions. Although I hesitated at first, I decided to risk it all in one throw of the dice and said my yes. I have never regretted that toss.

*   *   *

Returning to Rome, I discovered that Father Augustin had been appointed rector. He continued to be understanding when, on Sundays, I went to visit my sister Betty and the Bianchi family. I had settled in at Sant'Anselmo now and felt right at home. Many of my friends had returned and the new students added still more variety with their cultural backgrounds. I was more secure in my Latin and Italian and enjoyed the year immensely. I lived in a new monastic-cell on the top floor with my favorite view of Monte Testaccio, the Piramide, and beyond. A quiet rumble from Via Marmorata way below filled the air when the window was open and the odor of espresso coffee from the street was constant.

That year (1949-1950) I took special interest in patrology, especially in the Greek Fathers, relished again Father Cyprian's lectures, and still found time for piano and theory lessons as well as practicing on the Bechstein. It was my best year in Rome. I was now acclimatized to the cold and survived in better fashion. Although I was enjoying immensely the lectures at Sant'Anselmo, I realized that we were not reading much on the side or in preparation for class. The system was still that of attending the public lectures, memorizing the *notulae,* or summaries of the lectures, each professor handed out, and cramming for exams. No time was allowed for reading and debating other points of view. Years later I began to evaluate this Roman system in a less favorable light, especially in contrast to what I would later find at Juilliard and Columbia.

In those days it was easy to obtain tickets for a short papal audience, a *baciamano,* at which you had a chance to greet the pope, say who you were, and then kiss his ring. I did this several times in those three years when I had to accompany groups of tourists from the States. Pope Pius XII was austere and had deeply recessed eyes behind thick glasses, giving the sense that he was looking right through you. He had a certain princely demeanor, unruffled, almost as if he were in another world.

My second immersion summer (1950) was spent in Munich, where I stayed at the Ottienkolleg near the English Gardens. The prior of this student monastic house, Father Wendelin, was glad to have an American visitor. Only a dozen student monks were there during the summer, which gave me a chance to speak German all the time or just listen to the Bavarian dialect. Almost all the men were older and had served in the German army. I heard bitter debates during meals and recreation about the role each had played in those years. Since many had a defensive attitude, I was reluctant to ask too many questions of them, especially about the treatment of the Jews. I cannot say I heard any clear anti-Semitic expressions, but was occasionally surprised to hear vigorous criticism of the German bishops and their lack of courage in standing up to Hitler.

Rome (1948-1951)

Munich had been destroyed by the war and was in the course of being rebuilt. Occasionally I went to operas, which were staged in the Prinz-regenttheater since the opera house had not been restored and where a marvelous performance of *Tristan und Isolde* was my first exposure to Wagner. The conductor was Wilhelm Furtwängler and featured Martha Mödl. I continued my piano studies with Franz Dorfmüller and under his guidance tackled Beethoven's *Sonata, op. 31, no. 2,* often called "The Tempest," several preludes and fugues from Bach's *Well-Tempered Clavier,* and some Chopin *Études.* He was a strong disciplinarian; this rigor was good for me.

Several events during that summer have stayed with me. One Sunday in July, I attended Mass at the university church, St. Michael's, because the noted writer and scholar Father Romano Guardini was to preach, and, knowing his writings, I was eager to hear him. The Gospel text of the day had the difficult passage: "Make friends with the mammon of iniquity." He admitted that his interpretation might not be exegetically correct, but he understood Jesus to say that one had to embrace the whole of the human condition, the existence of sin, and the underside of one's own nature to arrive at any degree of personal holiness or to create a just society. He knew that there were Communist cells in the university and that the students were tempted either to cynicism or to the formation of ideological schemes for creating a perfect world. Taking into account the human condition meant accepting that imperfection; evil would always be a part of the person and society and no person or society would ever be perfect. Forgiveness and reconciliation, thus, had to have a place in one's personal growth in holiness and in one's relationships and life in society. It was a sober word of wisdom for those of us just twenty-three years old. Though I do not remember many sermons I have heard, Guardini's made a lasting impression on me. After hearing those words of wisdom, I accepted my own self more willingly and without hesitation. I seemed to come to terms with who I was and began to relax.

The second event was my ordination to the diaconate. (I had been ordained a subdeacon the previous spring at Sacro Speco, a cave overlooking the monastery of Subiaco.) It was usual to be ordained deacon without much fuss in those days. The bishop of Augsburg performed the ceremony in one of the parish churches, as the cathedral was not yet restored. The ceremony went well and afterward we were treated to a German feast. The bishop rose at the end and saluted us all with a jolly *prosit* as he waved his enormous mug of beer. The celebration ended with some rousing German songs.

Among those ordained deacon that day was a classmate from Rome,

Lothar Kloss of the abbey of St. Ottilien. He had had a brilliant military record, but had lost a leg and been fitted with a wooden one. According to church law at that time he was permitted to be ordained but could not celebrate Mass in public because he could not genuflect and this might give scandal to the people. He was a wonderful character, feisty, opinionated, brilliant, and sharp as a whip. He spoke excellent English and we got along fine. He loved the opera more than I did and was a good companion. He was a frank, questioning free-spirit, who knew how to bend the rules when needed. Lothar with all his wounds was not out of place at the opera; it was hard to find a man there who was physically whole.

At the end of the summer I made my way back to Rome for my third year of theology, my last year of studies at Sant'Anselmo.

*   *   *

1950 was not to be an easy year for us students at Sant'Anselmo; it was a Holy Year, the first since the war. Although not many pilgrims were expected, we students would be required to sing for various papal Masses and ceremonies. Thus, I was present in the Square of Saint Peter's when Pope Pius XII declared the dogma of the Assumption on November 1, the feast of All Saints. Because there were fewer pilgrims in those days, the atmosphere was more casual than today.

I knew that all these experiences had to come to an end. The date for ordination to priesthood was set for June 24, 1951, the feast of John the Baptist, and again at Sacro Speco, the mountain cave behind the abbey of Subiaco in which St. Benedict had spent two years of solitude. The abbot of that monastery, Simone Salvi, was the bishop who would do the ordaining. At 7:00 in the morning in that simple, damp cave he ordained to the priesthood a motley group of seven — one Brazilian, two Hungarians, one German (Lothar), one Flemish, one Tyrolean, and me. Betty had come out from Rome at that early hour, together with some of the monks from Sant'Anselmo, including my confreres Demetrius and Alphonse. I have always loved that cave at Sacro Speco and was pleased that I could be ordained there in the utmost simplicity.

I had made a long retreat in preparation for ordination and, although I knew I was very young (I had just turned twenty-four in April of that year), I felt as ready as anyone could be. What consoled me was the conviction that God could and does work through people, their gifts, their talents, and even their weaknesses, and I saw myself as called to the priestly role.

Rome (1948-1951)

After the ordination, we all returned to Rome, where Betty had arranged an elegant dinner at the Hotel Massimo d'Azeglio for a dozen of our friends. The next morning, with Father Alphonse at my side, I celebrated Mass at Sant'Anselmo, and the following day on a side altar, that of Pope Pius X, at St. Peter's. In the meantime I had packed my bags and shipped them to the *Queen Elizabeth* for the trip home.

I had grown to feel at home in Rome, still charmed by its beauty. Even more, Archabbot Alfred's wishes for me had been fulfilled: studying at Sant'Anselmo with such a diverse group of monks, being able to live, even briefly, in other centers of monastic life in Europe, and receiving a solid theological foundation had been a challenging experience. I had only been away three years, but I had changed, I had grown up. My studies at Sant'Anselmo prepared me for the theological trends that emerged with Vatican Council II ten to fifteen years later. Italy had begun to soften me in my more rigid and judgmental stances and prepared me for what I would find in the next years in New York at Juilliard and Columbia.

CHAPTER 4

Experiencing a Second Novitiate

New York–Milan (1952-1957)

M y formal priestly formation and education was now finished, but my continuing musical education lay ahead. In between, from August 1951 to June 1952, I returned to my monastery, St. Vincent, where I easily reintegrated myself into the life of the community. In addition, the abbot asked me to live in the college to assist the priest in charge of the minor seminarians — some ninety of them. Working with these fine, idealistic, young men was a privilege and a rewarding experience, and the long winter passed quickly. Although the college students kept a different schedule than the monks, the abbot expected me to be up at 5:00 for Matins and Lauds and play the organ for the Mass and Vespers. I took long siestas in the Roman style and managed to survive this arduous daily schedule.

Once a week I again made the trek into Pittsburgh for piano lessons. Selmar Janson had retired and I studied with Ferguson Webster, brother of Beveridge Webster, one of the best-known piano teachers at Juilliard. From Webster I discovered a special affinity for the music of Brahms, especially the last pieces, a love that has grown over the years.

It was no surprise when around Easter time 1952, the abbot called me in and said I should think of enrolling in some conservatory to study music. When he asked which one I thought was the best, I said Juilliard. He grinned and asked if I thought I could get in, and, when I said yes, he urged me to try. Father Ralph consulted a Catholic member of the Juilliard faculty, Robert Hufstader, to find out who among the piano faculty would be teaching summer school. The name Alton Jones surfaced and I wrote to ask if I could study with him that summer in preparation for taking the entrance exams at the beginning of September. I also wrote to the New York chancery office to find a parish rectory where I could live. They assigned me St. Philip Neri at 3021 Grand Course in the Bronx. All was in order and in late June off I went to New York for the next phase of my education.

St. Philip Neri was a very large and busy parish. Some of the priests assigned there were sick or on leave and, for the first time in my priestly life, I found myself doing an enormous amount of pastoral work. The only time I saw the pastor, Monsignor William R. Kelly, was on Sunday mornings. The many hours in the confessional were fulfilling, but several times I had to tell the pastor that I had class and could not do more in spite of his insistence. I was on duty almost every Sunday, presiding at many baptisms and weddings. As fulfilling as this was, it did not prepare me for the entrance exams to Juilliard! With Professor Alton Jones I brushed up some pieces I had previously learned, e.g., several Bach Preludes and Fugues from the *Well-Tempered Clavier,* the Beethoven *Sonata, op. 110,* the Chopin *Ballade in A Flat,* and a set of Debussy pieces. At the entrance exams I presented these and was accepted.

Monsignor informed me that if I wanted to stay on at St. Philip Neri through the winter I would have to be on duty three days a week and carry a full program at the parish just like any other associate. I felt he was really telling me that he did not want me there, as he knew that the terms were impossible for me to fulfill and continue my studies. When I telephoned Archabbot Denis about this demand, he responded with an absolute no and advised me to find another place to stay. I hated to leave this parish since I liked the people and found the music exceptionally good. The choir was called the Welch Chorale after its conductor, and was far above average.

When I wrote to the New York chancery seeking a new parish, the chancellor responded at once that Monsignor James O'Reilly at St. Malachy's parish off Broadway on 49th Street was looking for a student priest to live in the rectory. I ended up there. God's ways are strange; it was a perfect fit for me. I spent four incredibly rich years of my life at St. Malachy's — four of the happiest years, too. My stay there was my "second novitiate": the first introduced me to Benedictine life, this second one just to life. I came to learn about the best and worst of the human condition as it played itself out in the heart of a great metropolis like New York City.

In 2002 I made a short trip to New York and began my visit by spending some time just sitting in St. Malachy's church and reflecting on the old days. As I sat there in the beautifully renovated space, I recalled especially the pastor, Monsignor James O'Reilly, and the first associate pastor, Monsignor Pat Gallagher. The latter was about as old as the pastor, full of wisdom and Irish charm, but one of the most compassionate priests I ever came in contact with. They must both have been in their fifties then; in the house I was the baby priest at the age of twenty-five with much to learn.

The five-story rectory was sandwiched between the church and Sam Goody's record store. I lived in the front suite on the fifth floor. There were actually two churches, an upper and a lower: the upper was Gothic and severe in style; the warmer basement church was known for its shrine to St. Genesius, the patron of actors, and was thus officially designated the Catholic Actors' Chapel. Both churches had adequate pipe organs.

Weekends were busy. The first Mass, primarily for tourists and a few actors, started at ten minutes after midnight on Sunday mornings. Three priests were always involved: Monsignor stood at the door to keep out any intoxicated people who wandered in off the street; one priest heard confessions and then helped distribute Communion; one celebrated the Mass and preached for five minutes. The upper church was always packed at this hour. The second Mass was celebrated at 4:00 in the morning in the lower church; confessions started at 3:30 and Mass began at 4:00 sharp. Printers, the chorus girls from Rockefeller Center, and some actors preferred this Mass. The sermon was two minutes. The Sunday morning Masses began at 7:00 with one at each hour till noon, two extras being sandwiched in at 11:15 and 12:15 in the lower church. Monsignor always celebrated the first of the morning Masses so he could greet all the people coming and going at the later ones.

The number of actors who attended Sunday Mass was impressive, more than one might have imagined. Some were well known, living for a limited time in New York because of their appearance in a specific play (like Don Ameche), while others, when they were not on the road, made New York their home (like Fred Allen). Then one could count on the large number of lesser known actors struggling to make their way in the theater. The largest group was composed of the chorus girls, the dancers, the singers, and all those who worked behind the scenes in New York's theaters. There was a small but significant group of older women whose days were past, having been dancers in the Follies or at Rockefeller Center; they now lived on meager pensions in one-room apartments farther west toward 9th Avenue. I used to take Communion to some of them on First Fridays if the other priests were busy. Finally, there were a number of poor and struggling local families who lived farther west on the edge of Hell's Kitchen, as the neighborhood was known.

The morning I arrived from Latrobe, I was shown by the sexton to my fifth-floor room and then taken to the lower church, where I celebrated Mass at a side altar. After breakfast on the second floor, I was ushered into Monsignor O'Reilly's library on the third floor. He was very short, a typical Barry Fitzgerald type. He greeted me, had me sit down, and laid down the clear rules of the house.

His first words, uttered slowly, softly, and authoritatively, were: "In this parish everything is done my way. Do you understand that? The only time you are your own boss is in the confessional, and God help you if you make a mistake there!" These last words were punctuated with his hand raised high in the air. His second rule was that no one was permitted to ask for an actor's autograph before or after Mass. "They are here to pray, not to be disturbed by tourists." The third rule was that I was absolutely forbidden to ask them for any money, regardless of how good the cause might be, and never to ask them for theater tickets. I was expected to celebrate Mass each week day at 7:30 and then hear confessions at the beginning of the 8:00 o'clock Mass. I was to celebrate two Masses each Sunday, rotating in the schedule with the other two priests in the house and with the priests who came and filled in from one of the high schools. I was expected to hear confessions each Saturday afternoon from 4:00 to 6:00 and from 7:30 till I finished, my confessional being the first one on the right when you entered the lower church (always the busiest one). Finally, I was to be on duty every third Sunday (this meant I was on call for anyone who might ring the doorbell or for any emergency sick call).

He surprised me by saying that I would receive room, board, laundry, a stipend of ninety dollars a month, and Mass intentions totaling a hundred and fifty dollars a month. Almost every month he found some excuse to give me more money for some extra task he had asked me to do. Because of this generosity I was able to take care of almost all my needs and seldom had to write to the abbey for money, not even for tuition.

Monsignor also gave me this sage advice: if someone called in from a hotel wanting to see a priest, I should never enter the hotel room without having the manager or the security person with me. That proved to be a wise bit of advice, since I received more than one sick call from an inebriated person who was lonely and not really sick.

Each Sunday, Monsignor would go to the back of the church in time to hear my sermon. His rule was that the priest should turn and face the people (in those days the priest celebrated Mass facing the altar), read the Gospel in English, put the book down on the altar, and preach freely without notes. The church could hold a thousand people (this is what Monsignor said, but on seeing the space more recently I doubt that it ever held that many), and was usually full for the later Masses on Sunday. He did not permit any amplification. If he could not hear me from the back of the church, he would cup his ear as a sign to speak louder. After Mass and after he had greeted the people, he would come up to the dining room on the second floor while I was having breakfast and critique the sermon, adding whatever comments about the sermon people had made on the way out. After my first few sermons, he sat opposite me one Sunday at the breakfast table and solemnly said: "Young man, you say 'I think' too many times. No one gives a damn what you think. Just tell them what the Gospel says." Then he repeated his first rule of preaching: "And don't tell any jokes. These are professional storytellers. They know every joke you know, have heard them all many times, and can tell them a million times better than you can. Just give them five minutes of some solid spiritual thoughts." After several months he ceased coming and the other priests told me I had passed his course.

Over the years I began to understand Monsignor O'Reilly better and to appreciate who he really was. I would be putting it mildly to say he had no use for Cardinal Spellman or for Cardinal (then Bishop) McIntyre for reasons that he never articulated. Under that hardened surface was a genuine, dedicated, and extremely well educated priest. In his younger years he had been a bright light, having finished a PhD at Fordham University and been appointed head of the Catholic Near East Association. I knew he was a gifted financier and had made many trips at the request of the Oriental Congregation in Rome to obscure places around the globe where the local Church was in financial difficulties. I was impressed that already in those days he had hired a professional company to take care of the financial books of the parish, which he had audited yearly. He gave the surplus, usually over a hundred thousand dollars, not to the cardinal, but to poorer parishes for their schools.

Slowly I saw how wounded he was, a phenomenon that I would meet over and over again in church circles, a truly talented and gifted person who, with the change of superiors, felt he was an outsider in the church structure and began to go to seed. Monsignor had too much integrity and discipline to become addicted to alcohol, as many in those days were, but he suffered from deep depressions. At times he would just sit at table, nibble at his food, and say nothing. I soon learned the "hot buttons" that would get him started talking and involved in the conversation. Often I would bring up ideas new to me that had come up in class or in conversation at school and he would do the research on the matter for me. For example, we worked for weeks on the Church's stance on usury and how and why it had through the centuries changed. He sat glued to the TV during the McCarthy hearings, fascinated and repulsed at the same time, and always willing to talk about them. Bringing up the places he had traveled to would also elicit some comments and a discussion.

$$* \quad * \quad *$$

Several incidents during those years, all with similar outlines, remain in my mind. I present one, as far as I was privy to what had happened, because it epitomizes an attitude among the clergy that certainly had an effect on me and helped form my way of thinking.

One Sunday when I was on duty at the rectory the doorbell rang in my room. It was some time after midnight. I looked out the window to see who it was. If it was a policeman, as in this case, I would wave at him, put on my suit and collar, pick up my small case with the oils for anointing and the ritual (book of prayers for the sick), and rush down the stairs finishing the last buttons on the way. As usual, the cop was waiting for me in his car with the motor running.

On this occasion, as we drove to a nearby seedy hotel, he told me what I would find. A man was dead. The cop said he was a priest: they had found his car keys, examined the car's contents, and found in the glove compartment a breviary with the priest's name and address. In the same room I would find another man whom they were questioning. He was a medical doctor who said he did not know his partner was a priest. I would also see on the dresser signs of drug paraphernalia. It was the doctor who had called the police. After anointing the body conditionally (we did that in those days if the body was still warm), I called Monsignor O'Reilly, since the case seemed to be too important for me to handle.

Monsignor came at once. After I explained the situation, he sent me home and said he would take over. The next day he told me that the priest was from a nearby diocese but out of state. He had called first an Irish friend high in the police force and then an Irish undertaker, also a close friend; the body was moved to the priest's rectory. The newspapers the following day mentioned that Father X had died in his own bed of a heart attack during the night.

True, the reputation of a priest in trouble was safeguarded to save the good name of the Church. Clergy and laity both united to keep such affairs out of the press. But nothing appeared about the doctor in the papers either. It seemed to me that professional people in general were treated in a different way by the legal system. The anti-Catholic rhetoric during the bitter presidential campaign of 1928 when Al Smith, governor of New York, opposed Herbert Hoover had left the Irish community sensitive to any sign of anti-Catholic prejudice. That attitude was certainly alive when I was a student in New York in the 1950s and was looked upon as residual Nativism that would not go away.

Nothing about this incident was to be put into writing for fear that anti-Catholic forces would obtain the notes and use them against the Church. The generation of bishops before me kept few records for that reason. The attitude among bishops and church officials was that the less written down the better.

Yet at Juilliard and later at Columbia University, I never felt any kind of anti-Catholicism. Although no one ever said that I was accepted at Juilliard because I was a Catholic priest (the first in its history to be accepted on the graduate level), no one ever said I should not be accepted because I was Catholic or a priest. During the four years I studied in New York, I lived in two distinct worlds, the ecclesiastical one of St. Malachy's and the secular one of Juilliard and Columbia; I came to feel at home and very much respected in both worlds. If I spend some time now talking about the years at Juilliard and Columbia, it is because that half of my world was very important to me and formative in its own way. I learned to work with and respect people of all faiths and religious backgrounds — and none — and came to see many of them as deeply committed people with strongly articulated values that were evident in their lives and work. From those years I also gained respect for contemporary music and art and never saw it as "unChristian" just because it used modern techniques and means of expression.

During my first year at Juilliard, I took all the required courses, musical and nonmusical, so that during the second year I could work on my final recital. Alton Jones, my piano teacher, was not among the most famous professors at Juilliard but he was always available since he did not concertize much. He helped me fulfill my desire as a future teacher of piano to cover stacks of repertoire, not only the usual Mozart, Haydn, and Beethoven sonatas, but some of the larger works by Liszt and Chopin, with sufficient Schubert, Schumann, and Mendelssohn. The best music course I had was with Joseph Bloch on Mozart's piano concertos. Each student had to learn the solo piano part of a concerto and also supply the orchestral part, playing from the orchestral score of a different concerto where the solo was played by another student. The soloist was also expected to write his or her own cadenza. We worked through the concertos chronologically as a way of studying Mozart's style and how it changed over the years. It couldn't have been a more demanding and engaging class. At Juilliard I acquired my lasting interest in contemporary music, which continued during my years at Columbia. There I took a course in contemporary composition with Henry Cowell, a magnificent teacher whose system of teaching I later imitated. This interest in contemporary music has never abated.

Juilliard was a challenge for me, but I prospered. I felt so much older than the rest of the students (I was twenty-five), and could stand apart from the stiff competition that characterized the school. I certainly was well prepared in theory, harmony, and counterpoint, and was introduced for the first time to the Schenker method of analysis so much in vogue in those days. At the end of the first year, however, fearing that just piano study would not be sufficient to keep me busy, I decided that I would begin work on a PhD in musicology at Columbia University. Robert Tangeman, professor of music history at Juilliard, was the first to encourage me to go on for a PhD in music history. He felt my linguistic background and Benedictine preparation made me a superb candidate for majoring in medieval music. It was on his advice that I talked with Paul Lang at Columbia, a move I never regretted.

During those first years in New York, I was able to do some pastoral work as well. About once a month the Catholic students would gather at Professor Robert Hufstader's apartment on Park Avenue or in a classroom on campus for a moment of mutual support and encouragement. Without my asking for it or being officially named, for two years I became the Catholic chaplain at Juilliard. I never knew how many Catholics were among the students, but on Ash Wednesday there were more with ashes marking their foreheads than I would ever have guessed. Often, especially over lunch, students would seek me out to talk about religion or their problems regardless of their religious affiliation. I seemed to get along especially well with the Jewish students, tossing around my little bit of Hebrew.

The final exam at the end of the second year consisted in presenting a full recital program from which the dean could select what he wanted the student to play. The hardest part was that the total audience in that large auditorium was composed of only eight teachers. For example, I saw Roselyn Tureck, the famous Bach specialist, in the back as I began Bach's *Italian Concerto.* (We all were listening to the muted sounds coming through the closed doors in the foyer when the student before me presented the same piece on his recital program. His memory failed him in the second movement and he had to stop.) The rest of my program included Beethoven's *Sonata, op. 109,* the Chopin *Barcarolle,* and the Liszt *Ballade in B Minor.*

Afterwards some of those who were listening in the foyer told me they were surprised at how much feeling I put into the Romantic repertoire. For some reason, they thought a priest should specialize only in Bach and the Baroque. I often reflected on that comment and asked myself why they would have felt that way. I knew that I needed the Romantic repertoire as a way of expressing feelings I could not easily express in words.

I received my Juilliard degree at Commencement, May 1954.

*   *   *

At Columbia I was under the tutelage of Professor Erich Hertzmann, a true giant of a human being, though he was physically small and handicapped. Crippled and deformed from birth, he had to walk with two canes suspended from his arms. He had fled Germany at the last moment during the Nazi purge of the Jews, first to Switzerland, then to England, and finally to New York. He treated me as a son, very much like Archabbot Alfred, and determined the courses I should take. There were the usual ones in music history and, of course, the graduate seminars taught by himself and Paul Lang. He had me audit the course on primitive musical instruments taught by Curt Sachs, a course I thoroughly enjoyed.

He was especially insistent that my knowledge of medieval culture expand beyond musical interests. I took courses in medieval art and architecture, Chaucer, and medieval High German, and the Renaissance philosophy course of Paul Kristeller. And then there were courses with Professor William Jackson, a specialist in medieval German and Latin; I thrived in his course on medieval Latin paleography. For that class I sent to Brussels for a microfilm copy of a late ninth-century musical treatise, *De institutione harmonica,* by a monk named Hucbald. My analysis of that work became my first published article on medieval music (*The Musical*

Quarterly, 1956). I was flattered then to be asked by the editors of *Die Musik in Geschichte und Gegenwart,* a new multi-volume German encyclopedia of music, to write the article on that ninth-century theorist and composer.

Paul Henry Lang had a vast knowledge of music and culture for all periods of history, but could be an exasperating teacher. He would begin a new theme, force us to read all the literature on the subject in whatever language, make us peruse reams of music looking to prove or disprove the point in question, only to drop the whole search in mid-stream to take on a new topic. He felt at a certain point that the students could go deeper into the subject on their own if they chose. Some were frustrated with the loose ends that resulted, but I think I knew what he was about and accepted the challenge.

Hertzmann was more systematic, taught the medieval and Renaissance courses, but had a special love for Beethoven. The system of interpreting medieval Byzantine notation had just been solved a few years before, so he decided we should learn something about medieval Byzantine chant. Professor Oliver Strunk from Princeton University, a close friend of Lang and Hertzmann, was a renowned expert in this area and helped us to get started and kept us on track. From that first encounter I developed a close friendship with Strunk, who assisted me enormously in later years with my own thesis on Ambrosian chant.

During those four years in New York, I lived — happily — in these two different worlds, at home in both cultures. In fact, those years were among the happiest and most fulfilling of my life as a person, monk, and priest. I say as monk because they reinforced my desire to return full time to the monastery. At no time was I tempted to seek an academic career, even though feelers were extended to me, nor did I ever consider becoming a diocesan priest, as much as I found the pastoral work absorbing. I formed many lasting friendships, and came to know and esteem many wonderful professional women. For me, my life in New York was a healthy spiritual and human existence, one of growth and insights, of tolerance and acceptance, and of learning the best of what the Church had to offer at the time, mixed with the best of secular education. Most of all, the groups of people I associated with at the parish and at the school gave me a sense of well-being and fulfillment. I felt loved and esteemed, and although I was preparing for a future back at my monastery and in its school, I knew that I had also contributed to the lives of many at the parish and the university. My pastoral ministry as a priest — hearing confessions, preaching, and celebrating the sacraments — came naturally and I felt a great freedom in my work. Again in my life the musical aesthetic experience and the religious seemed to complement one another. God seemed everywhere.

But it had to end one day. In the spring of 1956 I took the doctoral comprehensives, which lasted three days. On the first day I was placed in an empty office with only a telephone on the desk. That test consisted of translating and analyzing four legal-size, single-spaced texts in four different languages — Latin, German, French, and Italian. I was asked to translate them, date the text as closely as possible, describe what it was talking about, then give a probable author. I recognized all but the Latin piece — much to the delight of the professors. On the second day I found on the desk some photos of medieval and Renaissance music. I was asked to transcribe them into modern notation, translate the texts, and describe and date the music. On the final day there were essays to write and items to be identified. The professors avoided almost all reference to chant and medieval music, as I recall, and the questions dealt mostly with later periods of music. Although the tests were tough, they were reasonable and certainly comprehensive. But there was real satisfaction in having them behind me.

Toward the end of 1955, after lengthy discussions with Professors Hertzmann and Strunk, I settled on a subject for my doctoral dissertation: "The Office Antiphons of the Ambrosian Chant." To begin this systematic study, I had to start by obtaining microfilm copies of the earliest available manuscripts. Since Milan, Italy, was the center of the tradition, most of the manuscripts were to be found there and in the cities and towns of northern Italy. I applied to Columbia University for a scholarship to spend a year in Milan to locate, study, photograph, classify, and index this whole body of chant as a foundation for my study. Columbia awarded me a $3,000 scholarship, a large sum for a student in 1956, and I made plans to spend the next year in Milan. After passing the comprehensives, I now could begin to concentrate on the thesis. I would be leaving by boat in mid-July and was eager to move ahead.

*   *   *

But I had one task to complete before taking off. Through a classmate of mine, Joel Newman, I had been introduced to Noah Greenberg, the founder and director of the New York Pro Musica Antiqua group. At that time Noah was looking for someone to write program notes for a concert he entitled "The Virgin in Medieval and Renaissance Music." He found my notes to his liking and asked me to collaborate on other projects. Some time later he showed me a few pieces (processional antiphons, or *conductus*) from a medieval play called the *Ludus Danielis*, or *The Play of Daniel*, from the early thirteenth century. These pieces had been performed in English at Oxford and Noah wanted to sing them in the original Latin. He asked me to "put them back into Latin." I had to obtain a film of the original manuscript (British Museum: Egerton 2615) written about 1230 in Beauvais, France.

When I saw the whole work, I was fascinated, transcribing at once the pieces Noah had asked for, but moving ahead to study the whole play. What was most striking was the metric structure of each piece. I felt at once that this diversity should not be lost in a transcription in which each note had the same value. I knew from my study of medieval theorists that the rhythmic modes used in that period for troubadour and trouvère music could also be applied to Latin pieces that were metric. Having done so much transcribing of the French repertoire for a seminar with Professor Hertzmann, I set out to apply the same principle to these Latin texts. I was also convinced by scholarly opinions that medieval music also observed among its rhythmic modes binary and not just ternary meters and used the former for the processions, or *conductus*. I reread a manuscript called *Anonymous IV* from about 1270 that explained the theories of the rhythmic modes and applied them to the play.

After experimenting a bit and transcribing accordingly, I did the whole project and turned over the final result to Noah. He, in turn, checked it out with Strunk at Princeton who thought it was as close as anyone could come to the medieval rhythms. Noah then decided he wanted to perform the whole work, not in a concert version, but as a real play.

I put the final touches on the transcription and sent if off to him before leaving by boat for Italy that summer. We were to correspond through the winter as he worked through the details of instrumentation, costumes, and the like. The date set for the first performances at the Cloisters in New York was January 2, 1958. I would be back home by then and could attend the final rehearsals and first performances. I felt pleased by the transcription and was eager to hear music that had not been performed, at least not in this way, for over six hundred years.

The Play of Daniel was to become a great favorite, performed frequently by Noah and the Pro Musica. After the performing edition was published by Oxford University Press in 1959, the play could be seen and heard all over the world, especially on college campuses. Through the Pro Musica, I met the others involved in the project, Lincoln Kirstein and W. H. Auden. Auden had composed a text to be read between the scenes of the play. Its purpose was to enhance the audience's comprehension of the plot, a device not needed in the medieval period. I had suggested the reading of the pertinent biblical passages from the King James Version, but did not find the Auden text as out of place as some.

No one could have foreseen the success of the *Daniel Play.* The Pro Musica recorded it (Decca records) and continued to perform it in New York at the Christmas season and then all over the United States and Europe. I always appreciated what Paul Hume, music critic of *The Washington Post,* wrote about my transcription — "a fantastically demanding piece of scholarship, musicianship, and wizardry" (Dec. 20, 1964).

Through this collaboration I had come to know Noah well, and, of course, was shocked when his wife Toni called me at St. Vincent on Sunday, January 9, 1966, to tell me that he had died of a heart attack just three months before his forty-seventh birthday. He had seemed indefatigable and indestructible. He was not a perfectionist at all costs, but one who sought authenticity, refinement, and grace.

The Play of Daniel brought me my first recognition in musical circles and for that I am grateful to Noah. He also helped me see that medieval music was truly art and not just an esoteric hobby. Thus, with the tunes of the *Ludus Danielis* in my head and a Xerox copy of the manuscript and my transcription in my suitcase, I set off for Milan in July of 1956, thanks to the generosity of Columbia University and the scholarship they granted me.

*　　　*　　　*

My residency during my year in Milan was Casa Bertoni on the outskirts of the city near the Lambrate station. It was a parish run by the Stigmatine Fathers with a boardinghouse where some seventy university students — all Italian — lived. Three priests and a brother, all from northern Italy and Tyrol, ran the house and served the parish. It was ideal for my needs. Mass was celebrated there each day in the Ambrosian rite, different in many details from the Roman rite, especially in the texts used and the placement of features like the washing of the hands and the kiss of peace. Using this rite pleased me since I could then learn it as a form of living prayer and not just as the subject of my dissertation. Most of my work was done in the libraries of Milan, especially the Ambrosiana. Frequently when I had to go outside Milan to work in a small parish library that may have possessed a valuable medieval chant manuscript, I would take a professional photographer with me to get a microfilm copy of the pertinent material.

The president of the Istituto di Musica Sacra Ambrosiana, Monsignor Ernesto Moneta-Caglio, a distinguished, somewhat combative, scholar permitted me access to all the literature and periodicals I needed for my work and oriented me to the intricacies and historical facets of the Milanese rite. He sometimes drove me to parishes up along the lakes north of Milan where precious manuscripts could be found — like Bedero di Val Travaglia — and where the pastor might be reluctant to let me work with his medieval treasure. He in turn introduced me to all the Milanese scholars working on the rite.

Monsignor Moneta-Caglio also arranged a meeting for me with the then archbishop of Milan, Monsignor Giovanni Montini, my first encounter with the future Pope Paul VI, who immediately expressed his curiosity about an American Benedictine so deeply interested in medieval Milanese music. We spoke at great length about monasticism — a subject with which he was very conversant. He spoke of his struggles as a young man in deciding between becoming a diocesan priest or entering the Benedictine monastery at Chiari, just a few miles from his home. (At that time, Chiari was a community of French Benedictine monks in exile from Marseilles.) He decided, instead, for the diocesan priesthood but retained his attraction toward the monastic life. Over the years I came to understand how important this monastic side of his spirituality was.

I broke the rhythm of my work once during the year in Milan to make a trip to England to record a program on Ambrosian chant for the BBC Third Programme. It also provided me the opportunity to give a lecture at Oxford to the prestigious Plainsong and Medieval Music Society and to consult several musicologists. Most of the year, however, I remained focused on my work in Milan, which, to my delight, I found to be a well-organized city in which to do serious research. The students residing at Casa Bertoni were a lively group and gave me my first real introduction to the heated debates over Italian politics.

At the end of the year I returned to St. Vincent with a suitcase full of microfilm, reams of notes, and my portable microfilm reader, satisfied that I had done the necessary spadework on the thesis before me. I also came away with a different picture of Italy than the highly clerical one I wrestled with during my early years in Rome. The Church of Milan had its own proud tradition.

So ended my nine years of study — a kaleidoscope of spiritual, theological, musical, and simple human experiences. These studies gave me proficiency, not only in classical languages, but in modern European ones as well. They were my introduction to other cultures. Theologically, spiritually, and pastorally, I had been exposed to some of the best the Church had to offer in the early 1950s. I had obtained an excellent musical education at some of the finest schools in the United States. Without trying too hard, I believe I had integrated all of these experiences into a synthesis that made me who I was.

Returning to my monastery in Pennsylvania now filled my thoughts. I was thirty years old and looked forward eagerly to being again with my monastic community and to teaching. At the time, I believed my traveling days were over and I would settle down for the rest of my life at St. Vincent.

CHAPTER 5

Transitioning from Old Church to New

St. Vincent (1957-1963)

After nearly a decade of study, I returned to St. Vincent in 1957. I was happy to go back to the source of my spiritual life and to reenter fully the monastic rhythms with early rising for matins, lauds, and Mass — all in Latin and Gregorian chant. Once again, I was at my familiar post, the organ, for most of these services. Father Ildephonse still directed the choir; he and I worked well together. On great feasts the liturgies in the monastic Basilica with its barrel ceiling and echoing resonance that enhanced the sound of choir and organ were uplifting, even thrilling. I found our community prayer in both its ordinary and extraordinary forms deeply satisfying.

At the end of Vespers on the first Sunday of each month, I gave an organ recital transmitted on a local radio station. These concerts forced me to hone my organ technique and gave me a chance to keep Bach's major organ works alive in my fingertips while adding some of the big pieces of the Romantic period along with a few modern compositions. Once when I played Messiaen's *Dieu parmi nous* with its booming and discordant opening chords, some members of the community thought I had fainted at the keyboard and several came rushing over to help me!

Gradually the monks became accustomed to my more modern tastes — but never totally accepting of it. One day at Mass I played a newly composed piece based on a twelve-tone row. I called it *Emergence,* since the row started as a single note, was presented simultaneously at different speeds in four voices, until all twelve tones were sounding together. The whole piece was then played in retrograde, until it returned again to the single note. I kept each bar of the piece, however, in the same rhythm (a technique often called idiorhymic) so that it held together and had a sustained drive. The dissonance certainly woke up any dozing monks. At breakfast one of the older ones stopped and asked, "Rembert, what was that piece you played at the Offertory?" "Before you make any comments about it," I responded, "I should warn you that it is an original composition." "You mean," he said, "that it came out of *your* head?" "Yes," I said. "My, you must have felt better," he chirped as he left the refectory.

Keeping a regular schedule, teaching and playing the organ while continuing my research on Milanese chant was not easy. To these I would add quick trips to New York or Princeton University to give lectures on my progress or to be a reader for a dissertation on medieval music. I agreed to be the music editor for the *New Catholic Encyclopedia,* a task that forced me to read in all areas of church music and to perfect my skills of synthesizing large quantities of material. I was not musically starved!

Pastoral work, including outside the monastery, was part of our mission. All the ordained monks occasionally helped in nearby parishes, especially during Lent when we preached and spent long hours in the confessional. Questions raised there about contraception naturally led us priests to discuss among ourselves how to handle the matter. Most of us were reluctant to recommend the rhythm method as a solution since we had seen too many instances when it did not work and the Church was blamed for an unwanted child. The rhythm method also seemed dishonest since the intention of preventing conception was the same as if artificial means were being used. We advised penitents to look carefully at the Church's teaching and then decide in their own consciences what they felt was proper. We had been instructed in our pastoral training that the individual conscience was to be respected and to trust lay people to make the right decisions. Slowly we were learning not to make people's decisions for them. I do not remember any bishop coming down hard on us for taking this position. The whole question seemed very fluid in those days.

*   *   *

In the 1950s and 1960s, St. Vincent was by all standards a large and thriving monastery. There were about 250 monks who belonged to the community; of these about 190 were ordained priests. More than half resided at the monastery while others were in studies or worked in parishes and other pastoral settings. There were also resident at the monastery twenty-three professed monks studying for the priesthood and some novices. The thirty-eight brothers had a separate novitiate, recreation area, and daily schedule.

Life among us was generally peaceful and caring. Most of the monks came from large middle-class families and were accustomed to the give-and-take of living under one roof with many people. The monastery created a safe environment, protecting all of us in the observance of our vows; a simple but compelling religious motivation pervaded the atmosphere and kept monks from falling too far from the norm. And then, we had the example of those monks particularly happy in their choice of life and inspiring to live with. Of course as American men there was something of a spirit of rugged individualism among us; nonetheless we gave a good deal of unspoken support and understanding to one another.

How did such a large monastery function? First of all, it was much more democratic than most people might imagine (this was certainly one of its great appeals to me when thinking about becoming a monk; it allayed my anxieties about authoritarian superiors). A council of "seniors" composed of five monks in addition to the abbot — the prior, the subprior, procurator, and two monks elected by the community — acted as an executive committee. The vote of that council was necessary for many decisions in the ordinary management of the monastery. It also acted as a sounding-board for the abbot about any tensions within the community.

Then second, there was the monastic chapter, composed of all the monks in solemn vows. Their vote was required for all important matters as outlined by particular monastic law, such as the admission of novices and monks for temporary vows and for large expenditures of money. To incur an expenditure or indebtedness beyond a prescribed amount, the abbot had to call all the monks together, including those working outside the monastery; sometimes he also had to seek the approval of the president and council of the larger American Cassinese Congregation to which the community belonged. Although each monastery in the Benedictine legal tradition was considered independent, monasteries having the same monastic origins or following similar monastic traditions had joined into congregations (historically as a protection against interfering bishops). St. Vincent was one of eighteen monasteries belonging to this congregation. These processes had been worked out through the centuries and resulted in a situation where the abbot, to take on any major new commitments, had to convince the vast majority of the community of the rightness of the course he wanted to pursue. Clearly the whole system had many checks and balances.

This system came into play not long after I returned from my studies. In 1960 and for the next two years the community elected me a member of the council of seniors, though I was not very "senior." Being a member of the council gave me an inside view into Archabbot Denis's way of thinking and a singular vantage point in assessing the tensions that began to surface between the archabbot and the resident monks. Times were changing and the community was caught up in contested views about how best to move into the future.

The monastic community of priests and brothers was something of a two-class system. The brothers did much of the manual labor, from running the farm and the gristmill to the printing presses and the dynamos. The brothers did not attend the choir in Latin but recited their own specified prayers in English. They were good men, bright men, well trained in their crafts and skills, and the backbone of the financial stability of the community. Despite their critical contribution to the well-being of the monastery, they were not members of the monastic chapter and thus had no vote, not even in the election of a new abbot. The system was a carry-over from medieval structures; in the twentieth century it seemed anachronistic to many of us. Questioning the inequality of this old system was one source of the disagreements between the abbot and the community. And it was only one of the new ideas creeping into the monastery. These currents were to play a role in the events that led eventually to a visible break between Archabbot Denis and the majority of the resident community.

According to histories of our community, St. Vincent, through the first century of its existence, elected abbots alternating between "inside" men and "outside" men, i.e., between the resident community (thus interested in the schools) and those in the parishes (thus interested in the apostolates). Archabbot Denis came from the "outside" group. Even though he had been the director of a vocational high school for black students in Virginia, he had never worked at the monastery itself since his ordination and was never totally at home with the resident community, feeling, e.g., that he had not been its choice.

The young monks of Saint Vincent, like all young monks of that period in the United States, had been strongly influenced by new monastic thinking, such as the writings of Thomas Merton. Many newcomers came knocking at the monastery's door looking for a more rigorous contemplative monastic life. Archabbot Denis considered any talk of a more contemplative monasticism and less involvement in outside ministry as an invitation to laziness. Furthermore, he was always eager to take on more outside commitments as well as to admit more students to the school. This stretched the limits of the energy and abilities of the community members, especially the priests. Nor would he ever recognize that the community was overstretched with work.

In the post–World War II years, we began to receive for the first time candidates who presented a "category" problem; they simply wanted to be monks, i.e., they did not want to be ordained priests nor did they want to do manual labor with the brothers. They wanted to become academic specialists in preparation for teaching in the college or seminary. They had no problem learning Latin and of participating in the choir. Thus, these candidates, wanting to be neither priests nor brothers, were an anomaly for the community. Archabbot Denis did not understand these trends and distrusted the motives behind them.

But there were funds to build. The community had accumulated a sizeable amount of money during the war years by training military personnel and the monks who taught in the college and seminary were eager to use those sums to begin an expansion of the educational facilities. Shortly after being elected abbot in 1949, Archabbot Denis easily persuaded a willing community to build a new seminary to house the large number of candidates who arrived after the Second World War. This new edifice, finished in 1952, had none of the strength and rugged look of the monastic buildings constructed in the mid-nineteenth century by the European founding brothers; its plain and bland façade didn't fit in. Archabbot Denis prided himself on his ability to plan and supervise the construction of new buildings and had no use for architects. This issue of design and construction became another contributing factor to the rift between the archabbot and some of the monks, a disagreement that grew with each successive building project. Yet, throughout the country, there appeared a fervor among monasteries to build aesthetically challenging buildings in keeping with the monastic tradition of fostering beauty and not just functionality. The new church at St. John's Abbey in Collegeville, a historical rival of St. Vincent, was the chief example. That abbey's massive and imposing new church designed by Marcel Breuer and dedicated in 1961 was reproduced in many architectural and liturgical journals for its contribution to contemporary religious expression. Archabbot Denis, with all of his good intentions, dismissed this all as frills.

The G.I. Bill permitted many Catholic young men returning from military service to go to college, putting pressure on Catholic colleges and universities to grow rapidly. Archabbot Denis's response was an expanded building program for the college that began with the construction of a new gym and auditorium, a project completed in 1954. With the completion of the seminary, gym, and auditorium, Archabbot Denis proposed a third project, a new library to house in one building all the holdings of seminary, college, and monastery. It was finished in 1959. Again the design and location of the building created tensions in the monastic community.

To these tensions, add a shift in the minds of the monks about the nature of a liberal arts college, especially one sponsored by a Benedictine monastery with its unique ethos and history. This shift was shared by many Catholic colleges of the period. Archabbot Alfred had foreseen this by sending a large number of monks for graduate degrees. I was among them. To his credit, Archabbot Denis after his election continued to do the same. Many monks returned with advanced degrees in English and American literature, political science, biology, art, music, theology, economics, and so on. In addition, some novices had entered with already developed skills: Roman Verosko was a proficient artist, Rene Gracida a prize-winning architect. Excellence became the watch word in Catholic education.

The continual increase in the size of the student body became a growing concern among the monks. Benedictine educators across the United States were apprehensive that the growth of their schools would overshadow their identity as monastic communities and their own need for expansion. Archabbot Denis had little interest in questions of monastic identity, so his solution was simple: take in more students if they wanted to come. At St. Vincent all of these issues erupted over and over again in the monastic chapters, especially whenever the archabbot asked the monks to take on more outside work whether it was an additional parish or new construction for the school.

After one of the meetings of the chapter or the council of seniors that had become somewhat bitter, the archabbot would often ask me to see him the next morning. He wanted an explanation: What were the tensions all about? Why were the younger monks resisting his requests? He was a sincere man and a good man as well as a conscientious abbot, but he had had no experience with higher education and its competitive demands and was not much interested in newer monastic trends. Gradually, it became clear to me that he saw the problem as one of disobedience on the part of the younger monks, who he believed were resisting his prerogatives as abbot.

After the completion of the new library, Archabbot Denis was eager to move ahead and proposed building new dormitories for the college students. They were certainly needed. This time the resident monastic chapter stood firm, making it clear they would vote down any new buildings until an architect was hired and a master plan for the schools and monastery had been accepted by the community. The archabbot reluctantly gave in and a committee was appointed to select an architect for this task. With the help of that outside architect, Victor Christ-Janer, a master plan was drawn up for the entire complex, monastery and schools. It delineated areas for monastic privacy and development as well as for college and seminary expansion. The plan retained the abbey church, dining facilities, and library as a buffer zone where school and monastery could meet. In March 1961, the community voted to accept the master plan, and Mr. Christ-Janer was commissioner to design new college dormitories. The monastic chapter voted overwhelmingly to build them.

For the first time in some years, a sense of unanimity was palpable in the community. When the bids for the new dormitories came in, however, they ran over-budget, costing more than Archabbot Denis wished to spend. He delayed a decision till the last minute and finally said that he was rejecting all bids and the plans themselves. Subsequently he announced on September 25, 1962, that he had fired Mr. Christ-Janer. Right after, he departed for the first session of Vatican Council II. The resentment and disillusionment in the community reached a boiling point in his absence. Early the next year, he told the community that he had hired a new construction company, one he felt he could work with. He himself had designed the new dormitories and sited them contrary to the master plan. He insisted that this was his prerogative as abbot; that the community had a right only to allocate the money and not to determine how it would be spent. Some of us begged him privately not to do this as it would cause a rupture between him and the resident monks, but he was absolutely convinced of his position.

*   *   *

At the height of this turmoil, an event occurred that brought the community together in an unexpected way. On January 28, 1963, a disastrous fire struck the monastery and attached school buildings. The temperature that morning was a few degrees below zero. Shortly after 8:00 in the morning, after coming up from breakfast to my room, I paused in the hallway to say something to a passing monk and saw fire and smoke coming from the roof of the biology lab. That lab was attached to a chapel built in 1836; together the two formed the inner building that cut the courtyard into equal parts.

There are days in one's life that can never be relived. This was one. No fire trucks could enter the courtyards because the entrances were too small. The fire spread first in one direction and then, as the wind changed, in the other. The reality of the fire did not sink in until it was over and the ruins were all too visible. There was not much left of the double courtyard and of most of the monastery. The old chapel, the college biology facilities, and the entire high school were destroyed. The walls left standing were covered with ice. Eventually the choir chapel where we recited the Daily Office had to be gutted, but the old library below was salvageable and later became our refectory. The Basilica was not touched by fire, although all the sacred vessels and vestments had been removed along with the Blessed Sacrament. The loss of property and the buildings was estimated to be over two million dollars (in 1960 dollars).

The heroes of the day were certainly the brothers. We all took orders from them. They knew the buildings well, were in the best physical shape, and had been trained for crises such as this. During the fire, we all worked side by side, taking valuable items from the monastery and carrying the sick to the lower level in case they had to be evacuated. I did not try to reach my own monastic cell; my room was on the second floor and the fire was raging on the floor above it. Though I did rapidly make a mental list of my belongings to consider if there was anything of value that should be saved, I decided nothing was worth the risk involved since my work on Ambrosian chant was stored in my library carrel and was safe.

When, at the end of the afternoon, I was able to get back to my cell, I saw at once that dirty black water had soaked all my books, all my notes from my studies in Rome, and all my clothing. Everything had to be tossed out — a forced lesson in detachment. A few feet from the door to my room lay the three bells, cracked from the fall they suffered when the bell-tower went up in flames. That was the most striking symbol to me of the old now gone. During all my years in the monastery the ringing of those bells was an integral part of each day. No monk died in the fire, but everyone's belongings were destroyed either by fire or by water. Some lost valuable items that were irreplaceable; several men working on doctoral dissertations lost them in the fire and had to try to piece them together.

For years the monks in recreation would tell stories about the details of what happened that day. In particular, we remembered the many acts of charity: how the Salvation Army fed the monks; how some Protestant church supplied cots; how every available seminarian and college student pitched in; how the bishop of Greensburg, William Connare, cancelled every appointment, drove over to the monastery at once, and spent the whole day in the company of Archabbot Denis, who was visibly shaken by the force and extent of the conflagration — he seemed in a daze.

By mid-afternoon the fire was subdued and we could begin to assess the damage. At about 4:00 o'clock we all gathered in the recreation room to exchange stories. I do not know where the beer came from, but, through that old Bavarian tradition we had inherited from the founders, we seemed to be able to relate in a new way to one another that late winter afternoon. Then we went to the Basilica to pray Vespers together. We all knew things would never be the same in the community, but life would go on.

After the fire I took one of the "Protestant" cots, moved over to my music studio in one of the school buildings, put the cot under the grand piano, and made that room my living space. For the next several years I had to make many trips a day out doors to get to the Basilica for the Divine Office and Mass. In the wintertime that trip could be burdensome, but I never had a reason to complain.

Archabbot Denis, in spite of the tensions in the community and the disastrous fire, decided to move ahead with the new college dormitories. He called all the monks, including those from the outside apostolates where he knew his support was strong, to come to a special chapter meeting on February 19, less than a month after the fire. He insisted once again that the young resident monks were being disobedient to his wishes, and asked, as if it were a matter of obedience, for a vote approving the new dorms. Though the proposition passed, 68-63, the vote re-awakened all the old bitterness in the resident community at a moment when the monks had been coming together again. I am sure that most felt as I did: There were enormous issues facing the community after the fire and no one had the heart to make the dormitories a test case. We were too tired to argue and it seemed trivial in the light of the immense challenges the monastery faced. But this vote proved to be the breaking point.

As it happened, this February chapter took place in the middle of our triennial visitation. Every three years each house of the American Cassinese Congregation underwent a visitation by two abbots from other monasteries elected for that task. This visitation had begun on February 16. Each monk was expected to talk with the visitors and express his views about the life of the community. The visiting abbots' reports from 1954,

1957, and 1960 convey a growing concern about the tensions between abbot and community. In addition to the public report given to the whole community, they made clear in personal reports to Archabbot Denis that his authoritarian mind-set and ways were alienating the monks and causing serious unrest in the community. They begged him to take their advice seriously, to start giving spiritual conferences to the monks, to act as a spiritual father to the community, to proceed more democratically in his building projects, and to begin to heal some of the divisions. It is difficult to understand why the archabbot ignored this advice or minimized its seriousness.

In their 1963 visitation, the two abbots listened to every monk in the community and came to the conclusion that Archabbot Denis had lost the confidence of the monks and that he was not able to bring the community together to build a new monastery and the needed science facilities for the college. They told him that they were petitioning Rome to allow the community to elect a coadjutor archabbot with full jurisdiction to run the monastery. This was the equivalent of asking for his resignation. The archabbot was psychologically unable to resign or to even use the word; understanding this difficulty, the visiting abbots wisely proposed a coadjutor with full jurisdiction, an old Roman way of saving face. Rome supported the decision of the abbot-visitators. They also stipulated that Archabbot Denis, then sixty-seven years old, could stay on as president of the American Cassinese Congregation until his term expired in 1965; thus he would continue attending Vatican Council II. He called together the council of seniors toward the end of April to set the date for the election of the coadjutor, which would begin on June 25. In the meantime, he began construction of the college dormitories according to his own plans.

I have gone into detail about this tension in the community and the visitations that took place to show that the monastic tradition of visitations, one going back to the Middle Ages, was still remarkably effective in our own day. In this case, the process resolved an intolerable situation of authoritarian leadership. Furthermore, I learned a great deal from this experience. I watched a good man, one with deep sincerity and conviction, lose control of a community because he could not open himself up to new ideas, listen to the vision and aspirations of others, or articulate his own vision in a convincing fashion. Compromise was not a word in his vocabulary. I learned firsthand that exercising leadership was not the same as having power, and that leadership cannot be given to one; it must be earned.

St. Vincent (1957-1963)

*   *   *

On Monday evening, June 24, all the fully professed clerical monks gathered in the former monastic library, still intact after the fire, for the opening prayers and formalities connected with an abbatial election. The week before the election, I had gone to The Catholic University in Washington, D.C., where I was to teach several summer courses in medieval music history, chant, and music paleography. I arrived back just in time for the opening of the sessions.

The protocols for the election of an abbot and all the specific prayers for such an occasion are clearly laid down in the ceremonial of the American Cassinese Congregation and had deep roots in medieval monastic practice. Abbot Bede Luibel, one of our abbot visitors, presided. The monks sat in their order of profession, the juniors in the back of the room, the oldsters up front. The session opened with the monks singing *Veni Creator Spiritus,* a medieval hymn asking for the Holy Spirit's light and guidance. Then chapters two and sixty-four of the Rule of Saint Benedict were read, the one describing the qualities of an abbot and the other how the community should discern who had those qualities. This document from the fifth/sixth century seemed very real and pertinent to me so many centuries later.

Then preliminaries — tellers and secretaries appointed, the excuses of the absent read and accepted, their proxies and the monk they so delegated verified — had to be taken care of. There were about a dozen such proxies. The presiding abbot then asked each monk in attendance to write down the names of two candidates he wished to be considered by the community for the role of abbot. This procedure functioned as a straw ballot. These names were tabulated and then read aloud to the community starting with the one who had received the most recommendations. No voting took place that evening; the monks were expected to reflect on the names and pray for wisdom in making their choice the next day.

My name was near the top. After the preliminary rituals ended, I went straight to my piano studio and played a bit of Mozart. I spent a restless night.

The actual process of discernment began the next morning, June 25, after a Mass of the Holy Spirit. The monk-candidates to be "scrutinized" (that was the traditional term used) had to leave the room. The scrutiny began from the back of the room, with the youngsters having the first chance to say something about the candidate so that they would not be intimidated by what an oldster might say. Since abbots were then elected for life, it was assumed that the youngsters would have to live under the new abbot longer than the oldsters. The opinion of the junior monks about the worthiness of a particular person to be elected thus carried singular weight.

When my name was called, I left the room. Sitting in the hallway for a long time, I realized the community must be taking my candidacy seriously. When called back in, I sat down next to the monk who had entered the monastery with me and had sat next to me at table and in choir for many years. "Get ready, Rem," he said, "You're it." A few more names were scrutinized, but it was clear that very few wanted to discuss these candidates. Then the presiding abbot announced that the voting would begin.

As all of this was happening, the scene seemed unreal to me. The rules required that the person elected abbot had to have two-thirds of the votes on the first three ballots but after that a majority would suffice. The presider announced that 197 electors were physically present or through their proxies. On the first ballot, I received 91 votes, double the number of the second candidate. At once it dawned on me that the situation was serious and that I would probably be elected on a subsequent ballot. On the second ballot, the number grew to 100 for me and then to 110 on the third ballot. The fourth and final ballot came on June 26 and indicated 116 votes for me, not two-thirds, but a substantial majority. I knew the vote, however, indicated some hesitancy on some portion of the community. In my gut I understood the road ahead would not be easy because there would be a substantial, vocal minority. I would have to listen to them and gain their confidence.

Abbot Bede asked if I would accept and, a bit in shock, I said yes. As was to happen again in the future, I did not have much time to make the decision about accepting or refusing. In those days the Sacred Congregation for Religious had to confirm the election of an archabbot, and that confirmation followed by cable on June 27, officially making me the seventh archabbot in the history of St. Vincent.

At first I thought I was the candidate of the "insiders" rather than the "outsiders," but that did not prove to be a good analysis. On reflection I surmised I was the candidate of the younger monks seeking change, but not of many of the oldsters who, after the fire, were very worried about the finances of the monastery and thought it would be wise to have a more experienced administrator in charge. In any case, since I was thirty-six at the time and was elected for life, I marveled at the community's trust, especially after the fire and in such changing times.

St. Vincent (1957-1963)

Those years were optimistic ones for the Church and for the nation. The first year of Vatican Council II had passed and the excitement about its proceedings had not abated. In the United States, John Kennedy was president, giving Catholics the feeling of finally being fully accepted. There were problems facing the Church, but there was also a high idealism, a willingness to take risks, and a feeling that all would be well.

In this atmosphere it was easy to say yes to the challenges of assuming a leadership position. The discernment process and the subsequent election by my fellow monks gave me a sense of well-being, an inner peace, knowing that I would have solid support in the tasks that faced us as a community. The community was not irreparably divided and we could move forward. I said my yes because it seemed to me the right thing to do. From a faith perspective I felt the Holy Spirit had been guiding the community in its discernment process and that I could be at peace with the results.

*   *   *

My years as abbot at St. Vincent (1963-1967) overlapped with the Second Vatican Council, which began in 1962. Most Catholics had no idea what the council would bring, but many looked forward to something new and exciting for the Church. The period from John XXIII's election as pope in 1958 to the council's closing in 1965 formed an extraordinary moment. Many histories of Vatican II have been written and many more will appear. An important part of that history is how the council was received; it changed how many saw the future of the Church, igniting and fanning positive hopes and aspirations. It was in this context of hope and optimism that I took up my responsibilities as abbot. The council had a marked effect on me as a member of the Church and how I saw my place as leader of a monastic community.

I was not present at the council nor did I experience the debates firsthand. I avidly read, as did most priests and laity, accounts by those who were present as well as reports in secular and Catholic periodicals. Sometimes I was more influenced by a speech or a comment from a member of the council than by final documents, though it was years before I could read all the texts and fully absorb them. The very person of Pope John XXIII, his attitude toward the Church as all-inclusive, his positive assessment of the world, his love of the human person, his quest for peace, his inward tranquility, and his sense of humor — all added to the excitement. Although many of the stories told about him may not have been true, they helped make him a beloved legend. I remembered having washed his car at Solesmes in the summer of 1949. That was no legend!

Pope John XXIII's talk at the opening of the council had some pompous and traditional rhetoric that seemed old-fashioned, but it opened vistas for me. First of all, its tone was positive and optimistic, bordering at times on the triumphant. The pope announced that this was not a council to correct errors in the Church, rather it had a unique purpose: to bring the Church's teaching up-to-date (his famous word was *aggiornamento*). He hoped that the Church could look with confidence and without fear to the future, that it would become a leaven to the world. Although he emphasized continuity with the sacred patrimony, especially from the Gospels and the patristic period, he wanted the Church to be open to the modern world and its unique challenges. One sentence in particular struck me as a new and positive approach: "The substance of the ancient doctrine of the deposit of the faith is one thing, and the way in which it is presented is another." This willingness to look at how the teachings of the Church are presented to a modern mentality was heartening. There was none of the ranting against theologians not uncommon before the council and dominant again in our own time.

His talk was not the usual Jeremiad about the evils of the modern world and the need for the Church to close in on itself in order to avoid contamination. For the first time in my priesthood I could hope that the council would move the Church out of the paralyzing stance of seeing itself under siege — an attitude that went back at least to Pope Pius IX — into a more open and confident position. John XXIII also took a new approach toward what later came to be called dissent. He stated that the Church now "prefers to make use of the medicine of mercy rather than severity" and should meet the needs of the present day by demonstrating the validity of its teaching rather than by condemnation. I could hardly believe his words when I first read them. There was also a genuinely new focus on pacifism (recall that this was the height of the Cold War and the world had lived through the Cuban Missile Crisis in the fall of 1962); the pope observed that "Experience has taught men that violence inflicted on others, the might of arms, and political domination, are of no help at all in finding a happy solution to grave problems which afflict them." He also showed his desire for unity among all Christians by quoting Jesus' prayer at the Last Supper: "I pray not only for them, but also for those who will believe in me through their word, so that they may all be one, as you, Father, are in me and I in you, that they also may be in us, that the world may believe that you sent me" (John 17:20-21). He hoped for a dialogue for "unity in esteem and respect" with the other great religions of the world. He saw the council as but a beginning and stated that "it is now only dawn," more is yet to come.

If the council had ended there, I would have been satisfied. That opening talk set out clearly what had to be said. Instead of the cautious and tentative gesture, the pope opted for the dramatic and challenging. He certainly had shown the direction the council should take. Can anyone fault those of us who expected the council to usher in a new era for the Church as it looked at its heritage, tried to renew and up-date itself, and then contribute to a better world?

Gradually, as the council evolved, I found myself entering into its dynamic and subtly changing my approach to the faith and to its expression. I have spent long hours mulling over this shift in my thinking, trying to track its development and searching for the right words to describe it as clearly as possible. Though this is but one person's experience and others may have had different reactions, I am convinced that there are many aspects of my journey with which others my age will resonate.

Somewhere in those years I changed my image of God from that of enforcing policeman to one of a loving and caring parent. God the Father had not meant much to me, had not been a part of my spirituality. Now it dominated. Before Vatican II, I had a strong relationship with Jesus Christ but a very limited notion of the role of the Holy Spirit in building God's Kingdom. I did not question then the assumption that the Catholic Church had a monopoly on that Spirit. Sometime during the council, I realized that I had a narrow and restricting understanding of the Spirit's actions. How presumptuous it was to think that any earthly body could control God's actions — God's Spirit working in church and world. Discernment became a new word in my vocabulary. God's Spirit, the Spirit of Jesus Christ promised at Pentecost, blows where it will and is always out ahead of us building the Kingdom. We are but instruments of that Spirit. This was a freeing realization. With that, I was willing, even eager, to listen more closely to the Spirit breathing, acting, among my Christian friends, to discern the actions of that Spirit in those of other religions whom I especially admired as God-fearing people. As the council documents on the Church, on ecumenism, on dialogue with other religions, and on the actions of the Spirit in the world were issued, I felt confirmed in this liberating approach.

My attitude toward authority in the Church changed too. My fear of authoritarian superiors, which had been quiescent for some years, was re-awakened under Archabbot Denis. I felt a return of old fears going back to boyhood. The documents and discussion at Vatican II were reassuring in this matter. The model that God spoke only to the superiors and the superiors to the inferiors was gone forever. Like so many, clergy and laity alike, I resonated with the phrase "People of God" to describe the Church. Instead of a pyramid, the image was of a circle of all believers, among whom everyone had a rightful place, including popes, bishops, priests, and deacons. Ordained ministers were to be seen as servants empowered to develop the gifts of the others and help them reach the holiness to which their baptism called them. The servant model came to the fore.

All were called to holiness, not just the religious or the hierarchy. All had gifts of the Spirit, not just the hierarchy. This was not the same as saying the Church was egalitarian, but that the different gifts of the Spirit for building up the body of Christ had to be recognized and supported. If one accepted the importance of the Spirit's gifts in each through baptism and confirmation, then those gifts had to be discerned for building up the Body of Christ. Perhaps I saw in this new insight the possibility of recapturing the awareness of the Holy Spirit's action evident in the life of the early Church and the patristic period. The model of hierarchy was no longer a separated pyramid above the Church, but of service in a dynamic circle in which all equally belonged. One of my sorrows four decades later was to see the concept of "People of God" minimized or reduced in importance with a deliberate return to an emphasis on the prerogatives of the clerical state.

The document on religious liberty was a palpable victory for the Americans and a confirmation of the American experiment in separation of church and state. Rome had reacted with deeply negative appraisals of the Enlightenment after the French Revolution, and so the American experiment had always been looked on with critical, even fearful, eyes. The principle of religious freedom was reaffirmed — no one could be coerced in matters of faith. This affirmation of the council, although it was pleasing to me, did not really change my attitude; it just meant that I became less defensive in the eyes of my European friends.

Being Benedictine, I also became involved in the liturgical renewal of Vatican II and the implementation of its document, *Sacrosanctum concilium.* A genuine renewal of the liturgy was possible with a return to its earliest forms and pristine simplicity, thereby eliminating the accretions that had come through the ages and were no longer meaningful. Perhaps it was naïve to hope that liturgy would become the source of spirituality for the faithful and that popular piety would flow from it rather then being a substitute. Since liturgy by definition is a communal act, I was smart enough to know that the success of this renewal would depend on how strongly it could counteract the rugged individualism that characterizes our Western culture and had penetrated the Catholic population. At the beginning, because of my role as abbot, I was more concerned about how this liturgical renewal would affect monastic communities and only later focused on the pastoral implications for all God's people.

My interior antenna, glued to new thinking at the council, picked up the subtle change of attitude on the Church's relation to the world. I rejoiced at the suggestion that a specific document should address this critical issue. This "turn to the world" affected many monks and other religious, especially women religious. From its origins and throughout its history, monasticism implied *fuga mundi* — flight from the world. "World" in this context, as in the Gospel of St. John, meant the kingdom of evil. Monastic vows were a means of permitting interaction in a regulated way with the world, while not making this world the ultimate goal of monastic existence. Still, the tendency to divide everything into two categories, church and world, one good and one evil, and to place everyone and everything on one side or the other of this dichotomy was too easy a temptation for monks and Christians in general.

In looking through some articles from the mid-1960s that I had pored over and saved, there was one by Thomas Merton ("The Council and Religious Life," *New Blackfriars,* October 1965). When I first read it, I found it in almost every way to be on the mark. Merton recognized the challenge that monastic life would face if this dichotomy were to break down. After tracing the fifteen-hundred-year history of what he called the Augustinian dichotomy and its imminent collapse, Merton noted that the false temptation of American monks would be to assimilate themselves to the active religious orders rather than reconstruct medieval context in which monasticism had thrived. The monastic life could not survive this choice. His solution was to emphasize both/and, i.e., a separation from the world and a dialogue with the world. "However, one may look at it, one can neither admit a 'turning to the world' that would entirely destroy monastic solitude, nor a flight from the world that would leave the monk totally estranged from his contemporaries." Vatican II spoke of a single history in which the Kingdom of God grows up with the world, sharing its joys and sorrows, contributing its own perspective but not living apart from it.

Another attitude that changed in the period of the council was the approach to human sexuality. Formation in human sexuality received by Catholics of my generation was colored by the rigorist Jansenist approach brought to the United States through contact with the Church in Ireland and then blended with repressive moral attitudes inherited from the Puritans. Thus, in our formation as Catholics, human sexuality was presented in a negative fashion, as a danger to be avoided rather than as one of God's precious gifts. This negative attitude resulted in a demeaning attitude toward women — the woman as temptress — and the acceptance of an intrinsic relationship between original sin and human sexuality. Although we monks at St. Vincent did not receive a heavy dose of some of these traditional views, they were always lurking in the background, that sex was *per se* evil or at least "dirty." The bishops at the council put a strong emphasis now on family life, stressing it as a vocation, a true calling. We heard much about love in those days, chaste love, i.e., between husband and wife. All people, the married included, were called to holiness, not just the religious and priests. In the history of the Church few married people were ranked among the saints; now there was a scramble to find more.

But something more subtle seemed to be happening to the Catholic population. In the hierarchy of sins, those against the sixth commandment no longer appeared at the top of the most egregious list. Sexuality was seen, not as an evil, but as a good. I noticed this in the way people confessed, especially the younger crowd — whenever they came to confession. Perhaps, in fact, this may be one of the factors that played a role in the ever-decreasing number of those going to frequent confession. I personally did not find that people had lost a sense of sin, but rather that they had re-ordered their sense of sin by a different ranking of sins' gravity.

As I look back on that period, I now realize that the Church did not evolve a theology of religious vows that reflected this change of attitude toward sexuality. It is one thing psychologically to give up something that has been regarded as bad, but quite another to give up something now seen as a good. The continuing search for a valid theology of celibacy that corresponded to this new and more positive approach has not ended. Most of us fell back on the understanding that having chosen Jesus Christ as our model (as if lay people had not!) and that having remained celibate in his total self-giving to the Father, his example was sufficient reason for our celibate commitment.

New words and new understandings emerged because of the emphasis on baptism and the gifts of the Spirit to all. We began to talk about shared responsibility for the Church, the collegial nature of the hierarchy, the involvement of all with the working and functioning of the Church at the local level. These ideas came directly from the conviction that everyone had something to contribute to the life of the Church and to the Church in the world. From my Benedictine tradition I resonated with these ideas and saw them as a concrete way in which the Church as the People of God could be realized.

Finally, through Vatican Council II, I discovered the Scriptures. The biblical movement finally caught up with me. In the novitiate I had learned about *Lectio divina,* the way of making the biblical texts into one's prayer, but it remained somewhat extraneous to my life. Liturgy and the Divine Office in the vernacular helped me to rediscover the importance of the sacred writings. Ecumenical dialogue forced me to a deeper acquaintance with the implications of modern biblical scholarship. In any case, I consider this discovery one of the graces those decades provided. Such a discovery, however, also aroused in me new questions. I could not help but observe the contrast on the one hand between the proclamation of the Good News by Jesus and how it was lived out in the first Christian communities, and on the other hand, the heavy and highly structured Catholicism of our own time. Reconciling the reality of the Church today with the inspiration and practices to be found in its biblical and patristic roots remains an unfulfilled quest.

What I have written here about these ongoing changes of attitudes preoccupied my thoughts and actions for subsequent decades. I emerged from the experiences of Vatican II relaxed and positive. I had come to see God as a loving, merciful, forgiving God. Although I wrestled with how that God relates to human freedom, I became enthusiastic about the role of the Holy Spirit active in church and world. I accepted without reservation what the council said about how the Church could and should relate to the modern world. Without being very much aware of it, I probably had become more positive also about human sexuality and its beauty and about human nature in general. I relished the way the council fostered a new way of relating to other churches and faith traditions. I rejoiced in the renewal of the liturgy in an attempt to make it truly a communal prayer in which all could equally participate.

Some doubts, however, remained. In spite of the aim of the council to update the Church itself, I still wondered if such a renewal could ever really come about. My secretary in the monastery was Father Matthew Benko, a first-rate and wise canon lawyer. One day during recreation, after

I had spoken at length about the increased possibilities of participation by the world's bishops in decision-making and the involvement of clergy and laity on all levels of church life, he wryly commented: "Wait till all the bishops go home and the curia takes over again. I can assure you it will be business as usual. Mark my words: the curia will never give up its power." Perhaps those words were more prophetic than I wanted to believe at the time.

One thing is now clear to me: without the vision of the council and its documents the following decades would have been much more difficult for an abbot or anyone in a leadership position, regardless of the differences of opinion about the interpretation and implementation of the council. Optimistically I looked forward to serving as the abbot at St. Vincent with the high hopes raised by Vatican II.

CHAPTER 6

Testing Challenges of Leadership

St. Vincent (1963-1967)

*W*hen I returned to St. Vincent in 2002, I sat in my room and reminisced for a very long time about my four years as abbot. The guest suite I was occupying had been the rooms where Archabbot Denis, my predecessor, lived in retirement and the same rooms where my successor, Archabbot Egbert, resided after his term as abbot had expired. These rooms provided an appropriate space for reflecting on those years, 1963 to 1967.

In trying to capture the spirit of that period, I realized that it was like rafting in the rapids, with a continual stream of crises to be faced and serious decisions to be taken without delay. Some decisions were inevitable because of the fire — like building a new monastery. Some came from the adaptation necessary after Vatican Council II — like the introduction of English into the Divine Office and the integration of the brothers. Some were issues left in abeyance from my predecessor's time — like making new foundations. It had been many decades since the monastery had spun off a new foundation and the requests for monks from many foreign countries at that moment were many. The Benedictine tradition fostered the concept of sending off a group of monks to make a new foundation whenever the monastery grew large enough to support one and there was a need somewhere else. St. Vincent had traditionally made many foundations in its history and the monks were eager to take up that tradition again. In addition, there were demands on my time and energy stemming from the many requests I was receiving for talks or participation in various church projects. I had to limit myself to those coming from the Benedic-

tine Order and the U.S. Bishops Conference. It seemed that all of these issues had to be tackled simultaneously, and I felt pulled in many directions
at once. I knew though that it was important to guide the many and varied
projects that St. Vincent had to undertake and that we had to budget carefully since there were financial implications for the community, especially
after our disastrous fire.

Even before the abbatial blessing on August 29, 1963, I plunged into
the tasks that could not be delayed. Our taking over a monastic foundation in Brazil was pending and so I made a trip there to size up the situation and report back to the chapter at St. Vincent. We decided to make the
foundation. In October of the following year I sent four monks there and
accompanied them for the inauguration of the new priory. The second initiative came from Archbishop Yu Pin of Taipei, Taiwan, who wanted St.
Vincent to become a part of Fu-Jen University in that city. The university
had been founded in 1924 in Beijing by St. Vincent but later handed over to
the Society of the Divine Word. The community willingly accepted this
challenge in July of 1963. Again, in 1962, Archabbot Denis, at the invitation
of the bishop of Altoona/Johnstown, sent two monks to Penn State University as Catholic chaplains there. It had always been my hope that we could
establish a priory with a stable community of monks in the heart of a university. St. Vincent voted to take on this work permanently.

Finally, in 1966, the officers of the American Cassinese Congregation,
after a visitation to the priory of Sacred Heart in Savannah, Georgia, made
a decision to close it because sufficient monks were lacking. The property
and the high school were to be turned over to the bishop of the diocese. St.
Vincent, right after the Civil War, had played a leading role in its founding
on Skid-away Island as a school for blacks. Later it was given over to
Belmont Abbey in North Carolina and moved to Savannah. The island was
sold to the military. Because of St. Vincent's original interest and involvement in this foundation, I raised the possibility of the community taking it
over. Again the chapter was almost unanimous in agreeing to this endeavor.

To find sufficient personnel for all these projects, I proposed to the
chapter that we relinquish some of the parishes we administered. There
was less enthusiasm for that idea, but it was also accepted. The monks,
young and old, had the willingness at that time to risk a bit. It also served
to distract us from our internal problems and to focus on the needs of the
larger Church.

St. Vincent (1963-1967)

*   *   *

And then St. Vincent needed a new monastery building. Some in the community wanted me to rehire Mr. Christ-Janer, the architect whose blueprints for dormitories Archabbot Denis had rejected. This did not seem prudent since it would open so many old wounds. I appointed a committee of eight monks to begin interviewing architects. After they had examined about a hundred architects' portfolios, I asked them to list their three top choices. Seven of the eight listed Tasso Katselas of Pittsburgh and the eighth had him in third place. I asked Tasso to come up to the abbey to present his philosophy of architecture and to answer the monks' questions. He immediately won over the group who then voted to hire him, and I felt it would be easy for me to work with him Thus began an important relationship between Tasso and the monastery that lasted many decades.

Tasso was Greek Orthodox and possessed an innate understanding and appreciation of monasticism. His design for the new monastery was a building rising out of the hillside and going up seven stories. He convinced me and the community, now fearful of the medieval quadrangle concept with its courtyards, not to succumb to the temptations of creating a series of small units, like bungalows, that could be lost among the large and imposing college facilities. He also felt that a single building would avoid the dispersion of the monks and foster unity. A single building would hold its own on the campus and unify the community.

But we all feared that a large building might look institutional, like a hospital, with long, impersonal, and colorless hallways. He avoided this by breaking the corridors into clusters of rooms that seemed organically connected. The building materials, mostly brick and concrete, expressed strength and permanence. The building contained, in total, rooms for 180 monks. The novices were on the seventh floor with a view of the city of Latrobe in the distance and the surrounding undulating countryside while the recreation rooms were on the first floor. The architect placed the abbot's quarters on the fourth floor with a small, elegant private chapel cantilevered over the garden into the oak trees. As the plans developed we gave up the idea of a separate infirmary to be attached to the new monastery and instead redesigned the second floor, with its easy access to the monastic gardens, to house the elderly and the sick. In that way they remained integral to the life of the community. When the plans were presented to the community in 1965 for a final vote, there was surprising unanimity.

The cornerstone was laid on December 8, 1965, and the building completed and dedicated in July of 1967. I felt we had done as good a job as any community could have done in constructing a monastery in the twentieth century. It was true to the Benedictine tradition that the space in which monks lived was important in their quest for God. At the same time, the building fulfilled the aim of unifying the community and not letting it become dispersed. The monastery along with the new science complex exhibited an excellence in architecture that was to continue with all the later construction at St. Vincent.

A new monastery building was not the only challenge to be faced. Perhaps it was the easiest. The documents of the council posed real challenges to us monks. Among the council documents, *Perfectae caritatis* was specifically addressed to religious. It laid down three provocative criteria for renewal, namely, a re-examination of the biblical roots for the monastic way of life, a return to the charism of the founder, and an updating of these ideals to the demands of modern times. In the case of monks, this meant a return to the principles of monasticism as rediscovered in its origins and codified in the Rule of St. Benedict. It came at a propitious time in the history of monasticism because of the renewed interest in biblical exegesis and in the patristic sources for the monastic tradition. I tried in the conferences I gave the community to convey a sense of what that tradition was all about. Often I felt I was rowing against the stream because of the rugged individualism that was so much a part of our American version of monasticism and because of the excessively active nature of our work.

The documents of Vatican Council II also challenged us monks in two specific areas: the integration of all our members, brothers and priests, into one community and the reform of the liturgy. Liturgical prayer was central to Benedictine life and occasionally some of the monks expressed the fear that we would become a museum for those wanting to see something of the pre-Vatican Church and its life. As I reflect on that reaction, I recall how taken we were with the argument that we did not want to be caretakers of a past age simply because we happened to be monks. Merton, too, saw this danger in spite of all his warnings about giving in to the Zeitgeist.

Perfectae caritatis mentioned in paragraph fifteen that where there were lay brothers they should be associated more closely with the life and work of the total community. Perhaps not realizing that there were cases like ours where the brothers did not even have chapter rights, the document mentions only communities of nuns, especially enclosed nuns where there were two classes of nuns. The two-class system was to cease. We were eager and ready to face this challenge to unite the community, as it seemed to resonate, not just with the document's ideal of one single family, but with our own American ethos. Much of that integration would depend, of course, on permission from Rome to pray the Divine Office in English, a struggle that lasted till 1966.

In the monastery the integration was gradual. Those brothers desiring to make solemn profession were admitted to chapter, and, of course, obtained a vote in the election of the abbot. I asked the community for the possibility of dealing with each brother personally in this regard and they gave me *carte blanche* to do so. In that way each one could be at ease and not feel forced. Over the years the difficulties disappeared.

The fight for the vernacular was a more difficult matter. Conferences of bishops from around the world, especially the United States, Canada, and Western Europe, pushed immediately for their mother-tongue at Mass. Rome was under strong pressure from the bishops to grant these requests and seemed astonished that this movement had happened so rapidly. In the United States permission was received for the general introduction of the vernacular at Mass. Monks, too, eagerly accepted these changes, but still were obliged to retain Latin for the Divine Office. The abbots and priors of the several congregations of Benedictines in the United States created a committee and elected me its chair with the mandate to study the wishes of the Benedictines concerning liturgy and the Divine Office in light of the documents of Vatican II and, in particular, its desire for the vernacular in the recitation of the Office. In addition to the concern for praying in the mother-tongue, there was a desire to respect what came to be called the *veritas orarum*. According to the Rule of Benedict, the monks were to come together to pray eight times a day — for matins, lauds, prime, terce, sext, none, vespers, and compline — as a sign of sanctifying the whole day with prayer. In addition we had a daily Mass. It was the customary tradition in monasteries to bunch these hours into just four or five gatherings. Few monasteries in the world had the luxury of praying all eight hours at the designated times; the work schedule just did not permit it. Thus, a redistribution of the Psalter and the reduction of the number of hours to correspond to the reality of how monks came together to pray each day was a part of the discussion of the *veritas orarum*.

Perhaps it was a blessing that we did not move immediately into English in the Divine Office. Although we continued to sing chant, it was work enough for the musicians in the community to compose for the Mass in this gradual move to the vernacular. Father Ralph, Father Ildephonse, and I composed abundant pieces, many of them resembling chant, many with real value, some rather trite. When the permission for the vernacular in the Divine Office finally came for the American Cassinese Congregation, November 28, 1966, we already had a good deal of experience in its use at Mass. With this, I could begin to see the changes taking place in the monastery because of the documents of Vatican II, an updating that could not be denied.

Other important matters also had to be attended to. Ecumenism and interfaith dialogue became a part of the post-conciliar Catholic Church in the States and I felt it was important that St. Vincent be a part of that movement. When I was asked by the U.S. Conference of Bishops if St. Vincent could hold the first dialogue between Jewish and Catholic scholars in the light of Vatican II's document on the relationship with non-Christian faiths *(Nostra aetate),* I readily agreed. Twelve Catholic and twelve Jewish scholars from all over the country came together at the monastery in January 1965. I was the twenty-fifth member and chaired the sessions. The monastery did everything possible to make our new Jewish friends feel at home, catering kosher food from Pittsburgh, forty miles away. The results of these sessions were published in the book *Torah and Gospel* edited by Philip Scharper. From the dialogue, close friendships emerged with many rabbis, many of whom I would meet again and again as the dialogues continued. In particular, I prized my friendship with Rabbi Marc Tannenbaum that began at that event.

It also seemed wise to me to have new monastic superiors who could help me unite the community after we had passed through such a difficult period. I asked the community for suggestions for a new prior and wholeheartedly accepted their choice, Father Marcian Kornides, a pastor of a large parish known for his balanced judgment and amiable spirit. In addition, I knew that all the issues surrounding the question of excellence in the schools had to be talked out if the problem that had divided the community was to be resolved. In the monastery and schools I began slowly to name new officials, known for their dedication to excellence in education. I appointed Father Demetrius Dumm rector of the major seminary and Father Maynard Brennan president of the college, both well qualified for those tasks and capable of helping the community move the schools onto a new level of excellence.

St. Vincent (1963-1967)

*   *   *

How well did I succeed during these four years as abbot? I have often asked myself that question and did so again as I sat in my old rooms in 2002. The building of the new monastery went well and I am proud of what was accomplished. The new foundations were right for the time and brought a new interest in the community for the larger Church. The adaptations after Vatican II were, by their very nature, the most divisive issues in the community and the results the hardest to judge. Still the integration of the brothers and the formation of one community came about successfully after the whole liturgy was finally permitted to said be in English. The adaptation of the Divine Office into English was not as difficult as I had assumed. In hindsight, I agree with those monks who hold the opinion that we could have retained more Gregorian chant than we did.

However, I do not think I had enough time in those four years to reflect with the community on more important issues, like how a monastery such as ours could possibly maintain its spiritual monastic roots under the heavy burden of work we had assumed. It was compounded by the large number of monks living outside the community, especially in parishes. I probably shed little light on the proper balance and, in fact, probably caused more tension among the monks than was helpful. Nor did I accomplish what I had hoped I could by asking other demanding questions. For example, what challenges should a monastic community pose to the affluent American culture that surrounds it? How would those challenges affect the kind of education the students would receive in our schools? What kind of witness should monks give to be effective examples of a Christian community in our day? These thoughts rushed through my mind in those days when I was abbot. They found some expression in the buildings built and in the appointments made, but were not sufficiently articulated to be effective. Perhaps with time that may have come about, but I doubt that I was mature enough at the time to provide the leadership necessary to ask such demanding questions.

We had many vocations then. It is true that I listened attentively to their aspirations and hopes. But I felt I listened best during the chapter meetings when the oldsters dominated. In fact, I know it sounds strange, but I liked meetings, especially of the council of seniors, but also of the chapter. All the changes were aired in those meetings and voted on by the members. As abbot, I found this system a sign of strength and not weakness in leadership. I kept the unwritten formula in my mind that if seventy-five percent of the community could not be convinced of a significant project, it was dangerous to follow through with it. Often, too, I looked to see if the *pars sanior,* as Benedict called them in his Rule, were in agreement. These were the leaders among the monks who had a good sense of the traditions of the community and of what monasticism was all about, but who were open to new ideas and not threatened by them.

In this process of decision making I felt encouraged by what was coming out of Vatican II: authority in the Church should function in a consultative way; I considered this a discovery on the part of the bishops of what monastic practice had long known.

As I look back over those four years as archabbot at St. Vincent (1963-1967), I confess that there were differences among the monks on serious issues and even at times resistance to any change, but no one ever attributed such differences to bad will. Sometimes the enthusiasm had to be dampened so that the community could move together, but there was a pride about ourselves and what we were doing that helped pull us through and maintain unity. The Church, too, was not as divided then as it is today. People had not yet frozen into unbending positions.

*   *   *

The monastery was not my only focus of attention in those years. The Church was changing and there were many forces drawing me to tasks for the larger Church. Pope Paul VI appointed a committee to oversee the implementation of liturgical reforms; it had the cumbersome title *Consilium ad exequendam Constitutionem de sacra liturgia,* Consilium for short. In May of 1964 I was appointed a consultor to the Consilium and made a member of Group *(Coetus)* 14 on liturgical music. (That group met three times in 1964 in Europe, and I decided I could not spare the time to make those trips. They agreed that, as the liturgy moved rapidly into the various modern languages, it became more and more the competency of the national conferences of bishops to deal with issues such as music in the vernacular and that a central Roman committee could only talk in generalities.) In 1968 when I was resident in Rome, I was appointed a member of the Consilium itself, the overall guiding committee.

In 1965 Cardinal Dearden, archbishop of Detroit and president of the U.S. Conference of Bishops, asked me to chair a subcommittee on liturgical music. We held a fruitful first meeting in Detroit in May of 1965. Archbishop Paul Hallinan of Atlanta, chair of the committee on the liturgy for the bishops, attended and briefed us on what the bishops were looking for.

The members of the subcommittee seemed to have no difficulty in describing what they in turn wanted, namely, music of good quality, but disagreed on how that related to the pastoral needs of the people. Some of us were naïve enough to hope that we could do as well as the Anglican Church had done under Queen Elizabeth I. She brought together the finest English composers of her day; we had hopes that we could bring about a renaissance of church music in English for Catholics.

The advice we gave composers was good — that it be music of good quality and well suited to expressing the texts. We emphasized the need to respect the different roles as pointed out in the conciliar documents, namely, music for celebrant, cantor, choir, and congregation. To ensure this quality I suggested we move, as had the Episcopalians and Lutherans, toward a national service book approved by the bishops and controlled by them. I proposed that at first it should be a loose-leaf binder so that music could be added and removed till we were sure that the best had surfaced. I felt it would take some time for this to happen and before a costly hymnal and service book could be published. Cardinal Dearden opposed this idea and felt the American way was to leave the matter to the open market and the publishers. I regret now that I had not been more insistent then, for the music that emerged lacked quality and became more and more banal. Being market driven began to mean, through the years, that quality was put aside for what would sell.

This division among church musicians, apparent at the time, has persisted. But it was more than a division among people: I felt the division within me, as did many church musicians. On the one hand, I wanted good music, well-composed and aesthetically pleasing, but I also understood the pastoral needs of the people; they needed music they could sing. In good Catholic fashion, I thought we could have a both/and position and not an either/or. For me this did not mean a search to preserve the old as much as a stimulus to create good new music. Experience has shown that both sides lost. I am afraid that most of the music composed for the liturgy over the last decades, unlike the music composed in previous centuries going back as far as the Gregorian chant, will be consigned to oblivion.

Right after the council, many monks began asking what the documents of the council might mean to their lives. As early as January 1964, one of the elders and most revered abbots of the Benedictine confederation, Emmanuel Heufelder of Niederaltaich in Bavaria, sent a letter to all the abbots of the world urging us Benedictines to ask serious questions about how the council was affecting us, especially with regard to liturgy. Since many Benedictine monks had been involved in the liturgical movement and had provided some of the scholarship that led up to the reforms of Vatican II, this was a reasonable idea. But the abbot primate at that time, Abbot Benno Gut, was reluctant to permit such a discussion. Still, some two hundred abbots from around the world were scheduled to meet in Rome in 1965, the last such meeting having been held in 1959. Under pressure, Abbot Gut permitted a group of European abbots and priors to meet to discuss what the congress of 1965 should take up. This group was under the chairmanship of Abbot Gabriel Brasó of Montserrat in Spain who had taken the initiative. The first suggestion of this committee was that the meeting planned for 1965 should be postponed till 1966 since there was not sufficient time to prepare and that a second session should be planned for 1967, one year later. Abbot Gut eventually accepted the idea. The committee then called for an in-depth planning session at Montserrat for December 4-7, 1964, and invited Prior Damasus Winzen of Mount Saviour monastery near Elmira, New York, and me to attend it to represent the fifty-some monasteries in the States. I flew with Damasus to Barcelona.

This preparatory committee first made a list of the issues to be discussed, most of them dealing with liturgy. Under the heading "liturgy," the most contentious point was the use of the vernacular as a means of uniting all the members of a community into one choir; and then the list went on: how to maintain the *veritas orarum;* suggestions for possible redistributions of the 150 psalms over the week; and other liturgical problems. It was reassuring that not only the Americans were posing these questions. It was good that Prior Damasus was present because he was originally a monk of Maria Laach in Germany; he had come to the United States in the late 1930s to found a monastery that would have no school and thus be more contemplative in nature. His was a strong voice among the Europeans, convincing them that these were needs for all monks and not just the active American houses.

Next, the committee focused at great length on the way the abbot primate should function. There seemed to be a need for more communication if the primate was to represent the whole order in Rome and not just one or the other position. The primate's relationship to the college of Sant'Anselmo was also on the agenda. The feeling was that he should be freed up to tend to issues regarding the whole order. It was a profitable meeting and the minutes circulated in the monasteries throughout the world, receiving overwhelmingly favorable responses.

St. Vincent (1963-1967)

Montserrat was an ideal place to hold this meeting. It was renowned for its musical and liturgical tradition but openness to new things as well. At the end of the sessions I was celebrant for pontifical Vespers on the eve of the feast of the Immaculate Conception, i.e., on December 7, wearing, as is the Spanish custom, an ample blue cope trimmed in gold. The only miter that fit me was one that had belonged to Dom Gregory Suñol, a famous Montserrat monk who lived in the early part of the twentieth century and was recognized as a competent musicologist, especially in the field of Ambrosian chant. This miter, also trimmed in gold, was ornamented with symbols of harps and images of St. Cecilia. Father Damasus afterward told me I looked like the Infant of Prague!

In September of 1966 I left for Rome for my first Congress of Abbots. Taking the *Michelangelo* gave me ample time to prepare for the meeting, since I had to give one of the first talks focusing on the use of the vernacular and the unification of the community.

*   *   *

Upon arrival in Rome at Sant'Anselmo, we abbots found on our desks a document signed by Pope Paul VI with the title *Sacrificium laudis* (The Sacrifice of Praise), dated August 15, 1966, and addressed to those who pray the Office in common in Latin, monks being the primary example. It very bluntly declared that these groups had to retain Latin in the Office and sing the traditional Gregorian chant. *Sacrificium laudis* was a formidable document, placing everything on the level of obedience to the pope. It stated: "The Church has introduced the vernacular into the liturgy for pastoral advantage, that is, in favor of those who do not know Latin. The same Church gives you the mandate to safeguard the traditional dignity, beauty, and gravity of the choral office in both its language and its chant." Abbot Gut opened the meeting by saying the pope had spoken and we would thus deal only with other issues, like the needs of the Sant'Anselmo, discipline among the students, and the like. The whole planned agenda for the meeting worked out in Montserrat would have to be scuttled.

Abbot Christopher Butler of Downside in England, president of the English congregation, saved the day. Having been a distinguished member of the council and having written many works on it, he was listened to when he spoke. His word carried special weight. He defended our prepared agenda and boldly argued that we had to see the pope as the *abbas abbatum* (the abbot of abbots). If one of us had a group of monks in our

121

community, he said, who were disturbed by one of our decisions and felt it was not for the good of the community, we would hope that those same monks would come to us and open their hearts. So, too, the pope, he said, would expect us to tell him our difficulties with his decisions. We should at this congress respectfully discuss our issues and present them to the pope with the same filial trust that monks would show in telling their abbot about the difficulties they faced. When the vote was taken, only a few sided with the primate to scuttle the prepared agenda. Most felt we should move ahead and present our problems to the pope after we had discussed the issues thoroughly and had voted on them.

At that first session of the 1966 congress, I gave one of the first speeches whose theme was the need for the vernacular in the American houses that had both brothers and choir monks. Speeches followed from abbots all over the world in a similar vein. Because of my linguistic background I found myself acting as an intermediary between European and American abbots about the issues that had arisen. Many of these abbots I knew from my years of study in Rome. We ended this session with the decision to return in a year and then to present our views to Pope Paul VI.

When we met again in September 1967 much had changed. The presidents of the congregations, a kind of executive board for the confederation, had met in Rome in January of that year and had gone directly to the pope to point out the difficulties that we were having with Abbot Gut. Pope Paul VI, in his typical gentle style, said he would take care of the situation. He did so by naming Gut a cardinal that year and offering him a post in the curia. We thus opened the second session of the congress without a primate. Abbot Brasó, since he had chaired the preparatory committee, was elected to chair the 1967 meeting.

Before leaving for Rome I heard rumors that my name was circulating as a candidate to succeed Gut as primate, and I went to ask the advice of Father Quentin, my former novice master. After much deliberation and hesitation, he said he thought that if elected I should accept, even though we were in the middle of many projects at St. Vincent. With his advice in mind, I left for Rome. The 1967 Congress of Abbots was one of free discussion; I soon noticed politicking among the American abbots to have me elected primate. I had turned forty that year, the required age by church law to be the superior of a religious order.

At the election for a new primate, the abbot of Montecassino presided, according to the law of the confederation. There was no straw ballot, no scrutinium, so the first ballot acted as a sounding board. The vote was split four ways: Abbot Brasó received one-fourth of the votes, Abbot Augustin Mayer one-fourth, I received one-fourth, and one-fourth was dispersed among many members, some being Americans. On the second ballot I had picked up most of the votes from Brasó and many of the dispersed votes. Between this voting and the next ballot, I met with Abbot Emmanuel Heufelder in the hallway to seek his advice. He begged me to accept saying: "Es ist, Rembert, vom Heiligen Geist. Du musst ja sagen" (It is of the Holy Spirit, Rembert. You must say yes). And so it happened. On the third ballot I had reached the two-thirds required and was elected.

Saying yes this time did not come so easily. I had been abbot of St. Vincent for only four years; there was so much more to do. St. Vincent was my home and my community and, as in politics, I felt that all church life is local; the real life of the Church is in the local communities and not in Rome. In addition, at that point, my monastery was thriving. There were many novices of exceptional quality. A new monastery building conducive to a more reflective life had been built. The college was moving into the ranks of the best among liberal arts colleges and was thriving. Most of all, St. Vincent was a living faith-community with many gifted, generous, and remarkable monks, people I would truly miss. The abbot primate had no stable community of his own. Sant'Anselmo was first of all a school and secondarily a temporary monastic community of professors and students from monasteries all over the world. But from both American and European abbots, voices were pressing me to accept the challenge. Caught up a bit in the euphoria of the election, I said I would accept the task and try to be the kind of abbot primate the abbots were seeking.

On September 29, 1967, I became the fifth abbot primate of the Benedictine Order and abbot of Sant'Anselmo. It was now my task to meet with Pope Paul VI and tell him of our difficulties with his letter *Sacrificium laudis*. When I finally waited in the antechamber for the appointed audience to relay to him the abbots' views, I truly hoped he would be the "abbot of abbots." At that moment, I could not foresee how many more times I would be sitting in that same room waiting to see him about one thing or another.

PART II

Ye goon to Caunterbury — God yow speede,
The blisful martir quite yow youre meede!
And wel I woot, as ye goon by the weye,
Ye shapen yow to talen and to pleye;
For trewely, confort ne myrthe is noon
To ride by the weye doumb as a stoon;
And therfore wol I make yow disport,
As I seyde erst, and doon yow som confort.
And if yow liketh alle by oon assent
For to stonden at my juggement,
And for to werken as I shal yow seye,
To-morwe, whan ye riden by the weye,
Now, by my fader soule that is deed,
But ye be myrie, I wol yeve yow myn heed!
Hoold up youre hondes, withouten moore speche.

Chaucer: Prologue, *The Canterbury Tales*

(You're off to Canterbury — Godspeed, and the blessed martyr reward you!
And you mean to entertain yourselves by telling stories on the way, I'll be
bound; for there's certainly no sense or fun in riding along as dumb as
stones; and so, as I said before, I'll devise a game that'll give you some
amusement. If it pleases you all to accept my decision unanimously and to
do as I'll tell you when you ride off tomorrow, then I swear by my father's
soul you can have my head if you don't enjoy yourselves! Not another word
— hands up, everyone!)

CHAPTER 7

Adjusting to the Eternal City

Rome (1967-1973)

The 1967 Benedictine congress closed with the solemn singing of the *Te Deum*. The abbots of the confederation, some 200 in all, vacated their rooms and left the Eternal City for their home abbeys. In departing, each greeted me warmly, not expecting to see me again until the 1970 congress. Gradually, the house fell silent. Only the ten elderly but sturdy German brothers who took care of the physical needs of the plant and I were left behind. It was then that I began to realize the enormity of the task ahead and the uncertainty of it.

Abbot Basil Hume of Ampleforth in England was among those who encouraged me most. Before leaving Rome, he came to my room to thank me for accepting this sacrifice. In parting he added: "Look upon the task as one of giving to the whole order some of the vitality and spirit you have given to your own community. We want you to visit us and give us some of that spirit too." He urged me to make Ampleforth my "home away from home," and to come as often as I could. We did see much of each other in the ensuing years and I visited Ampleforth frequently. Basil had a strong influence on the confederation in those post-conciliar years; the abbots had elected him to committees preparing for the congresses of 1970, 1973, and 1977.

In the middle of my hesitation about accepting the election, I recalled the encouraging words of Father Annibale Bugnini, secretary of the Commission for the Implementation of the Liturgy. Between the first and second ballots on the morning of the election, I went to his office in the Vatican to present a petition from the American Benedictines about the structure of the Divine Office. He pleaded with me to accept the role of primate if elected. He pointed out that though the primate might not have the same juridical authority among the Benedictines that superiors of other orders have over their members, he insisted that at this juncture in history the primate had much personal authority in Rome, more than most other superiors or even bishops. Paul VI openly favored the monastic orders, Bugnini told me, describing him as a pope with a monk's soul and sensitivities, a "crypto-monk." I later learned how true this was.

Bugnini confided that the members of the curia were expecting either Abbot Gabriel Brasó or Abbot Augustin Mayer to be elected primate. Both were well known in Rome. Brasó, former abbot of Montserrat in Spain, was president of the Subiaco Congregation, a sprawling, diversified grouping of monasteries with provinces in many separate nations, its headquarters being hidden away in the old Jewish quarter of Rome. Brasó had chaired the just-completed congress of 1967 and the abbots had become a bit wary of his authoritarian approach. Mayer had lived and worked in Rome since the 1930s, first as a professor of theology at Sant'Anselmo and then as its rector. His home monastery of Metten in Bavaria later elected him abbot. Perhaps the abbots hesitated to elect either one as primate because they felt the two had become "Roman."

Cardinal Antoniutti, as prefect of the Congregation for Religious, was the person with whom I would have to deal in my new job. I did not know much about him but had heard good things about his work as papal nuncio in Canada. He had also been nuncio to Spain in the 1950s during the Franco period right before being named a cardinal by Pope John XXIII in 1963. It was rumored in Rome that, in the contentious conclave which elected Paul VI after several days of balloting, Antoniutti had been a serious opposition candidate, the one most favored by the cardinals of the curia and their conservative supporters. As I look back on my relationship to these three me — Antoniutti, Brasó, and Mayer — I wish I could say I felt confident that all of them would aid me in the tasks ahead. Instead, the unsettling premonition I felt in those first weeks, namely, that they would not be my friends but my adversaries was to prove true.

I began my new job with mixed feelings. On one hand, I felt challenged by the new confidence placed in me, but also frightened; secret fears and anxieties came to me at night as I tried to fall asleep. What if I were to fail or did not have the high energy that the job required? What if I found I disliked the work? I was also convinced that the true vitality of the Benedictine Order — and of the whole Church for that matter — could be found on the local level, in the individual abbeys, and not in Rome. This ambivalence forced me to ask myself some questions. Was I psychologically and mentally strong enough for the inevitable tensions? Would this kid from the little town of Patton, nestled in the Appalachian hills of Pennsylvania, find himself over his head in waters where he never would learn to swim with ease?

After I was settled in at Sant'Anselmo, I asked for an audience with Pope Paul VI and was immediately given one. How many times I made the trip to the papal apartments over the next decade! Entering by the Bronze Door on the right of St. Peter's where Bernini's colonnade begins, I passed between the two Swiss Guards as they executed a call-to-attention and saluted me with their halberds. I checked in with the officer on duty. Nothing was ever said. After one or two visits the guards would recognize me and some pleasant banter was in order. One guard made summer trips to Johnstown, Pennsylvania, near my hometown of Patton, so we had much to talk about. I knew they checked to see whether the pope expected me and phoned ahead to the receptionists at the elevators and the papal apartments.

Slowly I would climb the broad and impressive Stairs of Pius IX. One had to take the steps slowly because they were graded so a prelate did not really have to pull up his cassock to keep from tripping. At the top, I would pause to catch my breath and then exit into the Courtyard of San Damaso, crossing slowly over the cobblestones, and then taking one of the elevators to the papal apartments on the top floor. Again, after one or two occasions, the elevator operators recognized me, and we exchanged a few pleasantries in Italian. I rarely took the *Scala nobile* up to the papal apartments. It was expected that one would use the elevator.

One of the pope's secretaries would be waiting for me in the reception area. Before long I came to know most of them; each usually wanted to chat a bit, considering me an insider — gossip was a major currency in the Vatican! I preferred to have some quiet time to go over my notes and to review all the points I wanted to make. For the items I hoped the pope would act on, I would type up a page for each and leave the sheets with him as a reminder. (I learned from personnel in the curia that he would often write his responses on those sheets in his very fine, miniscule handwriting and send them on to the appropriate departments.) We always spoke in Italian, his Northern, chiseled accent easy to understand, even when he indulged himself in his customary, long periodic sentences with many qualifying clauses and with the verbs in the required subjunctives.

Paul VI always received me in his library. I loved that room. It was spacious and had been redone in light browns, yellows and gray. There were no traces of the usual dull red damask. Without being obtrusive, I often tried to glimpse the high paneled ceiling and frieze below it, all softly illuminated by recessed lights. There were windows on one side of the room overlooking St. Peter's Square covered with sheer curtains permitting light to penetrate but through which no one could see in. The brown valences also contained hidden lights that seemed to extend the windows to the ceiling. The whole room, including the bookcases and the books all bound in light brown leather, had a soft and tranquilizing glow. In the center of the room there was usually a large working table with chairs around it, removed at times for large receptions. As one entered the room from the waiting area, it was easy to overlook the pope's large and sturdy antique wooden desk to the right, one that looked well used. Paul VI always stood when I came in, permitted me to kiss his ring, but gave me no time to genuflect, and had me sit on a chair placed to the side of the desk and not opposite him.

Usually he had prepared some Benedictine trivia with which to open the conversation and put me at ease. On this first visit he had a copy of the Rule of Benedict that had belonged to Cardinal Ildefonso Schuster, his predecessor as archbishop of Milan, the margins of which were filled with Schuster's hand-written annotations. Schuster, a well-known and prolific scholar in historical and liturgical matters, had been abbot of the Benedictine community of St. Paul-Outside-the-Walls in Rome and then appointed archbishop of Milan in 1929, being its archbishop through the Second World War till 1954. Confirming the stories that he favored the monastic orders, Pope Paul would sometimes talk of the visits he made in his youth by bicycle to the old Franciscan monastery at Chiari, then housing exiled French monks from the Savoia; other times he talked of spending summers as a cardinal at Engelberg in Switzerland. He always addressed me with the formal title "la Sua Paternità" (Your Paternity), which, although proper by the old protocol, seemed a bit overdone.

At this first audience, the pope said he had been surprised by the negative reaction of the abbots to his document *Sacrificium laudis* in which he had stated we should keep the Divine Office in Latin. He felt he had been wrongly informed, hoping that by publishing this document before we met he could save us much time and discussion. He said quite directly that he

Patton, Pennsylvania, the author's birthplace

The author's mother, Mary (Kane) Weakland, c. 1921

The author's father, Basil Weakland, c. 1921

The Palmer House Hotel in Patton, c. 1924

Above: The author at five months of age
Right: The Weakland family during the Depression, c. 1935; top row, left to right: Barbara, Mother, Betty; bottom row: Marian, Lee, the author (the author's brother Bill is missing)

St. Vincent Archabbey, Latrobe, Pennsylvania, before the fire of January 28, 1963 *(Courtesy of The Benedictine Monks of St. Vincent Archabbey, Latrobe, Pennsylvania)*

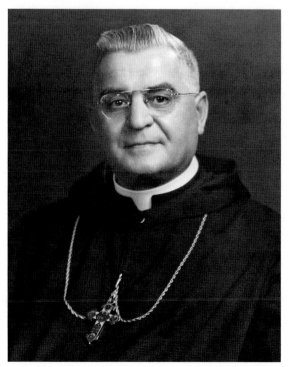

Archabbot Alfred Koch, abbot of St. Vincent from 1930 to 1949 *(Courtesy of The Benedictine Monks of St. Vincent Archabbey, Latrobe, Pennsylvania)*

Father Quentin Schaut, the author's novicemaster *(Courtesy of The Benedictine Monks of St. Vincent Archabbey, Latrobe, Pennsylvania)*

Father Ildephonse Wortman, choirmaster at St. Vincent in the 1960s and 1970s *(Courtesy of The Benedictine Monks of St. Vincent Archabbey, Latrobe, Pennsylvania)*

Father Cipriano Vagaggini, professor of theology at Sant'Anselmo, Rome *(Courtesy of the Archdiocese of Milwaukee Archives)*

Father Augustin Mayer, professor of theology at Sant'Anselmo, appointed an archbishop (1972) and then a cardinal (1985)

The garden at Sant'Anselmo, with the monastery in the background

With Archabbot Denis Strittmatter (left) after the author's election as coadjutor-archabbot, June 26, 1963

First meeting as Abbot Primate with Pope Paul VI, Rome, September 1967

Being presented to Patriarch Athanagoras of Istanbul by Father Pierre Duprey of the Secretariat for Christian Unity, Rome, Saint-Paul-outside-the-Walls, October 26, 1967

Thomas Merton in Bangkok, Thailand, December 1968, shortly before his death there *(Courtesy of the Archdiocese of Milwaukee Archives)*

Welcoming the patriarch of the Buddhists, Bangkok, December 1968 *(Courtesy of the Archdiocese of Milwaukee Archives)*

Playing a recital at the Juilliard School of Music, 1954

The Weakland family, 1975; left to right: the author, Betty, Barbara, Mother, Lee, Marion, and Bill

was impressed by the arguments for the vernacular — uniting the community and making sure that the new and younger generation could pray in a comprehensible way — and had told the various curial offices to grant all the permissions the abbots requested. He made it clear that he would not inflict his personal tastes or wishes on a religious order, especially if its superiors felt it would harm their communities in any way. He ended by expressing the hope that we Benedictines, regardless of the language used, would retain our pristine tradition of praying the Divine Office in a way that edified the listeners, quoting St. Benedict's Rule for Monks.

This was one of many audiences I would have, and I always looked forward to them. Pope Paul VI did indeed have a monastic soul and sensitivity.

My first official encounter with Cardinal Antoniutti in the Congregation of Religious took place on the morning of October 5, less than a week after my election. It conveyed a very different tone. His office was on the right in the last building at the end of the Via della Conciliazione, the street leading to St. Peter's from the Castel Sant'Angelo. He received me in his private office rather than one of the several reception rooms. He certainly had a list of topics to go over with me. He prefaced his remarks with the frank assertion that he had not been in favor of my election and had expected that Abbot Brasó would be the abbots' choice.

First, he talked at length about the university St. Vincent had founded in Peiking, China, in 1927. He had been in the Vatican embassy there from 1927 till 1933 and made it clear that he was not happy with how St. Vincent, and especially Archabbot Alfred Koch, had handled the school's financial affairs, which resulted in civil lawsuits in the United States and forced St. Vincent to give over the university to the Divine Word Missionaries.

His second topic was women religious. He was emphatic that men and women religious, even when they followed the same rule, should not have meetings together, especially renewal meetings. (In Africa, Asia, and South America it was customary for Benedictine men and women to meet together, and I here confess that I permitted that custom to continue into the future, knowing it would bring disapproval but convinced it was helpful to both groups.) Then, for some reason, he took time to speak in anger about the Benedictine sisters in the United States and their negative attitudes toward authority. It was easy to see that I was being lectured. To keep my blood pressure down, I just sat there and looked out the window at St. Peter's Square, a beautiful view from the cardinal's office. I watched the flock of people who came and went and wondered where they were from and what they might be praying for, hoping they would include an abbot primate then being badgered just beyond the window.

His third topic was the monastery in Cuernavaca, Mexico, which his Office had closed some months before. He pointed out that it would be my task, as outlined in a memo he had sent to my predecessor, to reclaim all the property for the Benedictine Order and to place each monk in a new monastery. I explained to him that the Benedictine Order did not own any property outside of Sant'Anselmo and that I would not establish a precedent. When a monastery was suppressed, it was our tradition to leave the property in the ownership of the local church. He bristled at that and said that under no condition should the bishop of Cuernavaca, Bishop Mendez-Arceo, whom he called an *ipocrita,* get his hands on the property. I also had to explain that it was the Benedictine tradition that each monastery had the right to vote in admitting anyone to its community and that I did not have the power to put men in other monasteries. Though I would help each member find a new home, I could never ask a community to take in someone they did not want. He responded by saying he would give me the power to transfer a monk's stability. I responded that I did not want such a power, which was contrary to our centuries' old tradition. The discussion ended on a sour note.

Little did I know that we would continue to discuss the monastery of Cuernavaca for the next year. Fortunately the abbots had elected a *Consilium pro re urgentiori* (a committee of three elected abbots that I could call on for emergency situations that arose between congresses). This committee, which included the abbots of Solesmes and Monte Cassino, totally agreed with me and Cardinal Antoniutti finally desisted. The Vatican secretariat of state took our side on the property question, since church property in Mexico at that time was held in the name of lay individuals and not by the Catholic Church. As often happened, I won the battle on the question, but many more skirmishes with the cardinal were in store.

I left his office with much on my mind, joined the crowds entering St. Peter's, and made my way down to the high altar to say a prayer at the tomb of Peter. That evening I wrote in my notes: "The Congregation of Religious wants a primate who will carry out their orders and take the blame if things go wrong. Such a procedure will be out of the question; if their decisions go against my judgment, I am afraid they will have to execute them themselves." It was clear that some of the members of the curia found our Benedictine spirit of independence a real challenge to their concept of authority and its exercise in the Church. Within a week of taking on the role of primate, I had a feel for what was to come.

Sant'Anselmo was to open on October 15. As I waited for the professors to return and for the students, new and old, to arrive, I decided to spend some quiet time reflecting on what the abbots wanted of me and planning what the next six years — the term for which I was elected — would look like. I wrote down some of my objectives. I combed through all the resolutions from the abbots' 1966 and 1967 meetings to get a better idea of what they expected. I made a list of their expectations. I tried to imagine the changes they wanted in how the abbot primate should function.

My predecessors had not traveled much, restricting their visits to Europe for ceremonial occasions, making perhaps one trip in their tenures to the United States and only to attend a special event. Their interests were primarily in Sant'Anselmo and in representing the confederation in Rome. The position was more honorary than effective. Many of the changes proposed by the abbots at the congresses of 1966 and 1967 were based on the assumption that the role of the primate should change. They felt that, in order to represent the needs of the monks, the primate should have a first-hand acquaintance with life in the monasteries around the world. They wanted the primate to travel frequently and be a link between Rome and the monasteries.

This was a major development in thinking. When Pope Leo XIII proposed a Benedictine confederation at the end of the nineteenth century, the abbots of the world had been negative to the idea and the creation of the post of abbot primate. They all feared centralization — which was ultimately the pope's aim. Now, however, they wanted more communication among the monasteries, more thought given to inculturation, and an abbot primate who would bring them together but avoid any kind of centralization.

Some also feared the monasteries becoming museums of the past. Among them was Abbot Christopher Butler, president of the English Congregation, who had been an active participant at Vatican Council II. In January 1965, knowing I was on the preparatory commission to prepare the congress of 1966, he wrote me the following (the underlining is his): "Personally I would hold strongly that people are underestimating the significance of the Vatican Council II. I hold that this is a moment in history for us to press for the twofold aim of local authority and diversification, and real adaptation to the cultural milieu. I dread the idea of Benedictines becoming a backwater or antiquarian survival — a sort of coelacanthus of the Church." That sentence summed up for me the fears of the abbots who had elected me primate, and I took these seriously.

Respect for pluralism had to be the first principle I should keep in mind. Pluralism would permit monasteries to adjust to modern times according to their traditions and needs. It would permit more inculturation as monasticism was brought to new parts of the world. It would also avoid a kind of uniformity that stifles. The second Benedictine value I knew I had to protect was subsidiarity. The independence of each house had to be safeguarded and any attempts toward centralization avoided.

These principles were especially important for the way monks prayed the Divine Office. The abbots would no longer accept a uniform breviary for the whole order. I knew that from their discussions, but I also knew that members of Roman curia, especially those who had pushed for the issuing of *Sacrificium laudis,* would try to impose one. As time moved on, I was to find that fulfilling this desire of the abbots in liturgy would not be an easy task.

The abbots asked for a change in the authority structure of both the monastery and the school at Sant'Anselmo. The prior of the monastery and the rector of the school were to truly run these institutions so that the abbot primate could travel more. The changes involved more participation of professors and students in the life of the monastery and in the running of the university. This kind of participation they felt was a part of what Vatican Council II wanted in all aspects of church life. That is how they interpreted the council and how it should be implemented. To help the primate accomplish all of this, the abbots elected for the house and school what they called a *curatorium,* three abbots who had previously been professors at Sant'Anselmo, to advise the primate and support him in these changes. This was helpful to me in facing the curia since these abbots were very supportive.

The abbots wanted a monastic chapter consisting of all the professors and a representative number of students elected by their peers. From three names given to me by the chapter, I was to name a prior to whom I would delegate whatever jurisdiction I could legally concede. That prior would then have full authority, calling the chapter to vote on all matters of more serious importance. The abbots also asked that there be an academic senate composed of the faculty and a number of elected students for the school, the Pontifical Academy of Sant'Anselmo. Again, the primate would choose the rector from three names, and the rector would truly run the school.

The abbots also voted that the primate should assist the Benedictine nuns and sisters to take their proper role in the Church. Benedictine particular law for over a century had specified that monasteries of Benedictine nuns *(moniales)* and congregations of Benedictine sisters *(sorores)* could be "affiliated" to the confederation. (In what follows, I will always keep the canonical distinction between nuns and sisters. Nuns live in a community with a clear enclosure that they leave only under specific conditions. Sisters are usually involved in active ministries outside of their monastic community.) It became clear to me as the years passed that Benedictine sisters needed little help in defending their wishes and desires. The enclosed nuns were in a more difficult situation. Some belonged to federations of their own; some were affiliated with individual congregations of monks; some were directly under the local bishop.

Frankly, I knew nothing about enclosed nuns till I was elected primate. Assisting them in this time of renewal, much to my surprise, would become one of my most consuming and, in many ways, most fulfilling tasks, a task that gave me an awareness of the spiritual contribution of these nuns to the order and to the whole Church. Those experiences were also later to affect my life as a bishop and my attitudes to the need to facilitate ways women could use their gifts in the Church. As I looked at this program of the abbots, I had no idea how important it would become and how much opposition it would generate from Cardinal Antoniutti and many members of the curia.

The abbots were also concerned about stimulating ecumenical interest among monks throughout the world and created a commission to assist the primate in this regard. I found it a wise and good suggestion in those post-conciliar years.

There were lesser items on the abbots' list of tasks — revising the proper law for the confederation, overseeing changes in monastic law for the Revised Code of Canon Law (finally issued in 1983), arranging another meeting of the abbots in three years, and overseeing all the commissions established to set the agenda. Given the tenor of the times, the abbots also set up numerous committees to assist the primate in all these duties and then elected members to those committees.

*   *   *

Waiting for the monastery to fill up and the school to get started, I also outlined for myself a program for traveling and visiting the various coun-

135

tries where our monasteries were numerous. From the primate's office I took the catalogue of the order. There I found about 320 monasteries of monks belonging to the Benedictine confederation, 350 houses of enclosed nuns, and approximately 30 congregations of Benedictine sisters. Some I knew from my days of study in Rome and summers spent in Europe. Some I knew from being abbot of St. Vincent and the foundations we had made. But most were just exotic names all over the world.

I was particularly eager to visit the monasteries in Eastern Europe, those lying "behind the Iron Curtain," as we said in those days. They were struggling for survival and had had little contact with the West. It was embarrassing that I recognized the name of only one of those monasteries, Pannonhalma; several members of that community had been classmates of mine at San'Anselmo. The monasteries of the Slav Congregation had been totally suppressed and some of these monks had regrouped in exile. In Poland we had two houses of monks, but over a dozen monasteries of enclosed nuns and several congregations of sisters. Only one small monastery of monks existed in Yugoslavia, but eight convents of enclosed nuns were nestled in some of the beautiful islands that dotted the old Dalmatian coast.

The names of the monasteries in Africa enticed me, but I knew nothing of them. To understand them, I knew I had to visit. Many monasteries there — like those in Senegal, Togo, Dahomey (later Benin), Upper Volta (later Burkina Faso), the Ivory Coast, and Congo Brazzaville — had been founded after the Second World War from monasteries in France. Other African missions and monasteries were older, having been a part of the former Belgium colonies in the Congo and Rwanda. Missionary monasteries from Germany had made large foundations in South Africa (where Flemish monks were also very active), Tanzania, and Kenya. There were fledgling monasteries in other areas of Africa as well, e.g., in Madagascar and the Cameroons.

The monasteries in Asia, too, were relatively new and struggling with concepts of inculturation and adaptation. We had a few new monasteries in India, a place seen as especially fertile for monasticism, but where Benedictines were struggling. Monasteries in Vietnam were living under very strained conditions. Monks and sisters from North Korea had fled to the South and were growing rapidly. Taiwan and Japan were also the centers of new monastic endeavors.

Finally, we had many new monasteries of men and women in Central and South America. It was of interest to me that the Spanish conquistadores had not invited the Benedictine houses of Spain to make foundations in the New World since they were not interested in contemplative communities but only in evangelizers. Thus, our monasteries in the Spanish-speaking areas were relatively recent and not a part of the early colonial thrust, which proved an advantage. The Portuguese, on the other hand, accepted the Benedictines from the beginning so that magnificent Benedictine baroque churches and monasteries established at the end of the sixteenth century could be found in the major cities along the coast of Brazil.

I knew I would have ample opportunity to visit the houses of Europe and North America since they were closer and such visits were less strenuous. I would not neglect them in their search for *aggiornamento*, but find ways of making quicker and shorter trips.

Visiting all of these monasteries would be an enormous undertaking, but I decided to start as soon as I had made the adjustments at San'Anselmo desired by the abbots.

I also had to pull together a staff. The abbots had created a new post called the secretary of the confederation. I asked Father Paul Gordon of the abbey of Beuron to assume that role. He was the most gifted linguist I had ever met, being adept in German, French, Spanish, Portuguese, and more than sufficient in English and Italian. I asked one of the American houses for a priest secretary and asked the same of the Italians. In this way all the correspondence in all languages could be covered.

I had decided then to send periodically to all of the communities circular letters to maintain good communication. This was not always an easy task; it meant editing each communication in several languages, and the postage bill was not insignificant. But it was worth the effort. In most monasteries these letters were read at table. Whenever I visited a community for the first time, it was not uncommon for some monk or nun to ask how one or the other monastery they had read about in the circular letters was doing, monasteries, they admitted, they had never heard of before.

As I sat gazing out the window, with pen in hand and notebook on my lap, I felt uneasy. Traveling and visiting monasteries of men and women could not be an aim in itself. I had to bring them a message that would be hopeful and realistic, a list of the significant Benedictine values and how they were important for church and world today. Because I was convinced that Benedictine monasticism had perennial values important for all times and places, especially after the council, I had to set out to encourage monasteries to see their role in the contemporary world and Church as one of making a positive contribution. I was convinced of the worth of monastic values and had no fears about their being inculturated differently in different parts of the world.

Among these values one could mention, first, that of belonging to a stable living community where common prayer focused on Christ and inspired by the liturgical year was central to the lives of the members. The Benedictine way of life kept a balance between the value of personal spiritual growth and the role of a living faith-community. Balance between prayer and work was also an evident part of the Benedictine heritage and one that answered a contemporary need.

These thoughts would become clearer to me as I visited the monasteries of men and women, listened to their questions, and tried to respond as well as I could. With time I became more and more convinced that Benedictine spirituality had a message not only for the monks, nuns, and sisters I would be visiting, but also for the contemporary lay person. Persuading communities to reflect on how they could share these values with the local Church and the world became a part of my task.

Realistically, I knew I had not given enough thought to the on-going training and learning I needed to penetrate more deeply into the life and culture of the many communities I would be visiting. I wrote down, nevertheless, some personal goals. I determined to keep abreast of all that was happening, especially theologically, in the Church at that time. It was a tremendous privilege to be able to travel all over the globe during the period of renewal after Vatican II and see how it was affecting the Church everywhere. It was also a privilege to live at Sant'Anselmo with its very competent scholars and avid international student body. Residing there was an excellent source of continual intellectual growth; almost weekly, famous scholars visited Rome for meetings of the various post-conciliar commissions, and would be invited to Sant'Anselmo for dinner. After meals there would be coffee in the parlor. One could not help but be aware of what was taking place in church thinking.

Although it was helpful to think out what was before me in the next six years and what I would need for intellectual growth, I did not give a thought to the toll these years could take on me spiritually. I did not ask myself what kind of spiritual tools I would need for survival. I did not grasp how powerful the tensions would be living in Rome, both within the community at Sant'Anselmo and with the Congregation for Religious. More seriously, I did not have any idea of the strain so much travel would entail, or how the loneliness I felt at the beginning of this new mission would increase a hundredfold. To be constantly on the move and not able to form more stable relationships had not come to mind. In retrospect, I wish I had had a mentor with similar experiences and to whom I could unburden myself as the years passed.

One by one the professors returned to reclaim their living quarters, and the old and new students trickled in. Classes began on October 15. On October 19, I called together the first chapter of professors and students at Sant'Anselmo and gave them the task of presenting three names to me from which I would select a prior for the community. I explained the wishes of the abbots that the prior would have more authority than in the past and would truly run the house. The next day I did the same in the school, telling the academic senate to present to me three names from which I would select a rector for the school.

I had not anticipated how politicized the process would become. National affiliations came into play among the members of the linguistic groups. In addition, members divided on the question of whether the prior and/or the rector should be chosen from among them or come from the outside. Academics were not used to the give-and-take required in any institution. Although the abbots had insisted that students be on both councils — school and monastery — many of the professors were viscerally opposed to this idea.

From the three names the members of the chapter of the monastic community submitted, I picked to be prior an outsider, Father Ambrose Watelet of Maredsous in Belgium. My choice for rector of the school fell on Father Basil Studer of Engelberg in Switzerland, one of the professors and thus an insider.

When I began to travel frequently and be away much of the time, and as the prior took over more and more responsibility, I could not help but see myself less and less as an abbot and more and more as a figurehead. As logical and inevitable as this new arrangement seemed, I do not feel I was totally prepared psychologically for such a change. Perhaps, too, because of the divisions and bickering in the community, I never had the same feeling of joy I had experienced in my own monastery after returning from a long absence. It was different now, and I knew in my brain that I had to accept this change.

*   *   *

Back in Rome after a few hectic weeks in the States to pack and say farewell to my community, I settled into my new quarters at Sant'Anselmo. The apartment was on the floor above the main classrooms and accessible by a convenient elevator. My bedroom was on the courtyard side so that at night all I could hear was the splashing of the small fountain in the goldfish pond. Now I also would have my own bath and shower, plus a small kitchenette. Off the elevator entrance was an ample reception room and then a large commodious office. Unlike so many apartments in Rome, it had been furnished with a figured parquet floor that gave the room warmth and color. My five-foot grand piano fit neatly into one corner of that room on the opposite side from my desk. The best feature of all was the large, high French doors that opened on to a sturdy balcony with a spectacular view that only Rome could provide. Below my windows the monastic gardens and walkways stretched out at the top of the embankment to the right and to the left, all meticulously cared for by the German brothers. Far below one could see and hear the traffic of Via Marmorata with the bustle of its shops and rumble of its trams. Directly opposite the balcony — I almost felt I could reach out and touch it — was Monte Testaccio, an artificial hill created by the broken potsherds *(testae)* discarded by vessels plying their wares on the Tiber that flows at its feet. When the city celebrated a feast with fireworks, Testaccio was their launching pad and I had the prize seat. To the right one could see the Piramide and the entrance to the English cemetery, where Shelley and other famous English poets were buried. In the far distance one was tempted to think that, on a clear day, it was possible to see past Ostiense to the sea.

Adjacent to my office and on the same side of the building could be found another large room that acted as an office for my secretaries. Beyond it were the archives. The arrangement was well thought-out and well organized — a tribute to my German and Swiss predecessors. I never complained of my rooms during my days as abbot primate. In the summer my bedroom was air-conditioned. A few years later, when my mother saw my quarters for the first time, she admired their beauty and remarked: "That's the last time I will send *you* a care package!"

My role was minimal in running the school. When it came to a decision I had to be involved in, such as acquiring new Benedictine professors, I did my best to beg the abbot of the monk in question and put as much pressure on him as I thought prudent. Tensions remained in the school, but they were mostly inevitable conflicts among strong personalities. One of the main areas of bickering centered on the way in which the Liturgy Institute and the Faculty of Theology were related. With time, we were able to work out a solution in which the Institute was autonomous in the granting of its own degrees. I was proud of how the school, both the theology and the liturgy departments, maintained their enrollment, especially of diocesan clergy from all over the world, and thus contributed to the life of the Church. This large number of non-boarding diocesan clergy in the classes was the major difference between the school that I had attended in the late 1940s and the one I returned to in the late 1960s as primate.

Life in the monastery seemed to generate more turmoil. In typical Benedictine fashion, the most acrimonious disputes almost always centered on liturgy and the daily recitation of the Divine Office. During my many absences in 1968, Father Ambrose, the new prior, wrote me painful letters about the debates in the chapter. He worked with some of the professors of the Liturgy Institute to determine what would be the best form of the Divine Office for Sant'Anselmo, a unique community of professors and students with a daily rhythm that involved many hours of classes and study.

The committee suggested the following arrangement. The morning hour would be a single more extensive one with material from both vigils and lauds and prayed in six language groups: Latin, Spanish, English, French, German, and Italian. The Mass would follow in those same groups. At noon there would be a single, extensive midday hour in Latin in the chapter room. Vespers and compline would be sung as before in the traditional Gregorian chant in the church. On Sundays, the Mass would be sung in Latin in the church.

As one can see, this was a compromise to permit some Gregorian chant, but also to allow the monks to pray in their native tongue. I gave my permission for this change. As a matter of good communication, I informed Archbishop Bugnini and Cardinal Antoniutti of these changes and sent them a copy of how we were arranging the Psalter in the morning and at midday. The division followed the guidelines Bugnini had worked out with me for experimentation on the Office for the whole Benedictine confederation.

As I should have foreseen, Cardinal Antoniutti summoned me to his office and demanded that we cease and go back to the former pre-conciliar usage at Sant'Anselmo with the entire Office, including vigils, all in Latin and with some of the hours bunched together and others recited privately. I was prepared for this scenario and showed him the pertinent passages in the particular law of the Benedictine confederation that gave the abbot primate the power to make these changes. As usual he was angry and retorted that I had not heard the end of the affair.

Some months later I met, by chance, Archbishop Antonio Mauro, the second in command in the Congregation for Religious, a kind but ineffective person. When I asked about the question of the Office at Sant'Anselmo, he replied that it was all in the hands of the secretary of state. I was a bit surprised that something so picayune would have to be dealt with at such a high level. Nothing happened for months and I surmised that Cardinal Antoniutti had simply dropped the matter.

Shortly after the beginning of the new school term in October 1968, I had an unannounced visit from Abbot Norbert Calmels of the Premonstratensians, often called Norbertines. He said Cardinal Villot, secretary of state, had asked him to visit Sant'Anselmo and speak with all the professors about certain criticisms of what was happening in the school and house. Nothing was listed specifically. Since the issue involved several different Vatican congregations, namely, Religious, Liturgy, and Education, the secretary of state had become involved. I refused to let Calmels approach the professors since there was no specific list of complaints; it was not clear who was making them, and how serious they might be. I said I would speak first with Cardinal Villot. On November 6, I met with Villot and we had a good airing of the problem. He was exceptionally kind and gracious. I will never know why the secretary of state himself handled this issue, since matters involving the curia were usually within the competency of Archbishop Benelli, the undersecretary of state. Perhaps the pope had personally asked Villot to intervene.

Someone from the faculty had reached the pope with complaints, the nature of which was not very clear to the cardinal, but he knew that the new disposition of the Divine Office played a major role among them. The suggestion of a canonical visitation by the Congregation for Religious came from Cardinal Antoniutti. To avoid such a visitation, Cardinal Villot, knowing a bit of the situation, took the matter in hand himself. He suggested that Abbot Norbert Calmels, a man we both admired and respected, should just visit the school and talk with each professor. Then the matter could be laid to rest. I protested that if even such an unobtrusive visit on the part of Calmels took place, it would be known all over Rome the next day, much to the detriment of the good name of the school and its future. The Vatican resembled a small town where everything was known to everyone and where rumors flowed freely. It was impossible to keep anything secret, especially in the schools where many people were involved. Even the hint of an apostolic visitation meant that something serious was afoot, e.g., that heresy was being taught. The enrollment would decline.

What concerned me most was that the Divine Office, the first issue discussed and voted on by the new house chapter and then approved by me, was the matter for this visit. It also involved the expertise of the department of liturgy of the school. If the proposal voted on positively by the chapter of monks was nullified, then it would give the impression that any member who was on the minority side of an issue could run to the Congregation for Religious to have the chapter vote changed. The whole process could thus be blunted. If the issue was one about the orthodoxy of what an individual professor was teaching in the school, then it should be taken up, not by the Congregation for Religious, but the Holy Office in the proper way and according to the rules of that office. Since I had a good rapport with Cardinal Seper, prefect of the Holy Office at that time, I felt certain he would have informed me if there were a problem with some teacher. Cardinal Villot knew these were delicate issues; how they were handled would be important in trying to get new professors to teach in Rome. Finally, he saw the problem and asked me to look for another solution.

After a little give and take, I countered with this proposal. Before each Congress of Abbots, a canonical visitation conducted by three outside Benedictine abbots was to take place and the results sent to each abbot of the confederation prior to the next congress. Such a visitation was scheduled two months later, in preparation for the congress of 1970. I would tell the visitators of these complaints, ask them to see if there was anything serious going on we did not know about, and then send the cardinal the results of their interviews. Villot thought this a splendid idea and told me to tell the three abbots when they came to find out which professor or professors were making the complaints to the curia and what the exact nature of these complaints might be. I went home satisfied that it would all work out.

Villot, taking seriously my fear that some negative rumors may have leaked out about a possible visitation of the monastery and school, came to lunch at Sant'Anselmo the next week. After lunch with the community, he gave a speech in the refectory in which he told the community in glowing terms how pleased he was with the school and monastery, and praised the professors for the contribution they were making to the Church and to the order. It was more than I had expected.

He was still worried that some complaints may have reached the desk of Pope Paul VI and said I should sit down with the pope to find out if there were any questions the pope wished answered. I made the trip to the Bronze Door, up the Stairs of Pius IX to the Courtyard of San Damaso, and took the elevator to the top floor. The pope received me in my favorite room, the library. This time I was a bit nervous, but there was no need to be. The pope understood the new arrangement of the Divine Office and agreed that he did not like the previous one where the young monks were expected to pray vigils privately. It just did not seem to be in the Benedictine tradition to him. He brought up no concerns about what was being taught by any of the professors. I recall, too, in that meeting that we had a lengthy discussion about whether monks should see movies (perhaps this was among the complaints). We agreed that it was the same question as whether monks should read novels; he dismissed it as trivial. I felt embarrassed that the pope himself should have to deal with such picayune nonsense, even though it was a good chance to talk with him about lighter matters.

The three abbots elected by the last congress came in February, did the visitation of the house, and informed me which professor was very disgruntled and "poisoning the well." They surfaced only one name. I wrote the abbot of his monastery, who immediately called him home. I sent a copy of the visitation report to Cardinal Villot and Cardinal Antoniutti; Villot was very pleased; I never heard again about the matter from Antoniutti. In fact, as a positive result of this intervention I became a close friend of Cardinal Villot. He would invite me on occasion to lunch if he had as a visitor a bishop from a diocese in which a Benedictine monastery was located or when he thought the discussion would be of importance to me.

*   *   *

In the ensuing years I tried not to abuse this friendship with Cardinal Villot by jumping over the curial offices and taking my problems directly to him, but I recall there was one exception. The point in question was vital since it involved the help needed by the women following the Rule of Benedict and my desire to implement fully the programs involving them that the abbots had outlined in the congresses of 1966 and 1967.

After re-reading the acts of these congresses, I was convinced the abbots were urging the women to see this period after Vatican Council II as an important challenge. The abbots expressed a hope — perhaps at that moment more like a dream — that these women would become more organized among themselves and thus be more effective in articulating and fostering their own vision about monastic life and its future. It was a vision in which they hoped the nuns and sisters would form federations and then a confederation similar to that of the men. This confederation of sisters and nuns would then work together with the confederation of monks so that the insights of one could be shared with the other.

This dream arose from an examination of the chaotic situation in which so many houses, especially of Benedictine enclosed nuns, found themselves. Some few were affiliated directly with the confederation of monks, but the meaning of that affiliation was not clear. Most of the monasteries of enclosed nuns, by church law, were directly under the jurisdiction of the local bishop, even if they were affiliated or aggregated to a congregation of monks. The abbots seemed to sense that this situation was not healthy for most monasteries and that a closer union among all the women following the Rule of St. Benedict could bring much benefit.

As I began to visit the monasteries of men and women in Europe, especially in Italy, I realized how important the vision of the council was for Benedictine women. I soon came to learn that those monasteries which were already affiliated to a congregation of monks had less trouble keeping their Benedictine values and way of life alive. These women, in turn, helped the monks think through any changes with attention to music, art, and the monastic environment that men so often neglect.

My pressing concern, however, was for the isolated monasteries of enclosed nuns who could easily fall prey to the private devotions of any chaplain assigned to them by the bishop or any retreat master to the detriment of the Divine Office. One of the reasons for this ambiguity may have been that the nuns were reciting or singing all the hours of the Divine Office in Latin, at times spending over three hours a day, and yet knowing little if anything of what they were praying. I brought this up once to an abbess. She curtly responded to me that it was not necessary that the nuns understand what they were praying since God would understand! Such a mechanistic concept saddened me.

Perhaps part of my uneasiness came from the way some of the abbesses treated the nuns in the community. By law, the abbot primate had the right to enter the enclosure of the Benedictine nuns. It was not rare for me to be visiting an abbess in her study when a nun would enter, kneel before the abbess, and ask for some trivial thing like paper and an envelope to write a letter. Some abbesses were overly maternalistic so that I got tired of hearing them use the phrase "le mie figliole" (my little daughters) over and over again. If I saw excessive maternalism among the abbesses, I saw the counterpart of excessive infantilism among the nuns.

I had only visited a dozen monasteries of enclosed nuns in Italy when I was called to a meeting in the Congregation for Religious on November 25, 1967. The theme to be discussed was described as "a discussion of the expression of separation from the world in the enclosure of nuns." When I arrived at the Congregation for Religious and was ushered into a large meeting room, I saw sitting around the highly polished wooden table about thirty men, all superiors of orders that had a rule followed also by nuns.

Cardinal Antoniutti did not attend but his place was taken by the second in command, Archbishop Mauro. As the head of the oldest order represented, I was placed at his right. The archbishop opened by saying the specific issue the Congregation for Religious wished to decide was whether in the parlors of enclosed nuns there should be a single or double grill, the latter, apparently, being recommended but not yet mandated. I had not had much experience in sitting in monastic parlors of enclosed nuns, but how well I remembered from my first visits the grills, those thick iron bars that separated me from the nuns. Most convents had single grills, but occasionally they had crisscrossed or double bars, in which case one could see almost nothing of the person with whom one was talking. For the most part I found these parlors dark, dreary, and uninviting. I never knew if I was the one who was expected to be doing the penance or if it was those on the other side of the grills. In some of the chapels of the nuns I had visited, the grills were so thick and formidable that it would have been impossible for the nuns ever to see the altar or the presiding priest.

After the archbishop had presented the case and the leanings of the Congregation toward enforcing a double grill, he asked me to give my opinion. That evening I wrote up what I felt at that moment, and how I expressed it to the group. I wrote: "I found it all very, very sad indeed. It seemed curious to me that in this day and age thirty men would be sitting around and discussing the fate of thousands of women as if they were mute cattle in stalls. I stated that what really mattered was how to help the nuns receive a better theological, spiritual, and cultural formation. The rest, I stated, would take care of itself."

The poor archbishop was dumbfounded. He went around the table asking the other superiors if they agreed with the views of the new young American abbot primate, and, much to my surprise, the support was unanimous. The archbishop, a bit befuddled, thanked us for coming, closed his handsome leather folder, and walked out. One of the superiors general of German origin with the reputation of being among the most rigorous and traditional came over to me and thanked me for finally saying what they all felt. He laughed when he added: "We need your American frankness around here."

Through the next year or so I visited some monasteries in Germany, France, and especially Italy. I met some impressive nuns and superiors. Once I pretended amusement when a nun told me that the elderly abbess of her community had the reader at table select from the daily newspaper only the stories of murders, rapes, and burglaries to be read during the meals. In this way she felt the nuns would be happy that they were in the monastery and not in the world.

With all of these concerns about the women religious weighing on me, I phoned the convent of Sant'Antonio, a house of Camaldolese Benedictine nuns, and asked to speak to Mother Ildegarde Gnassi. My calendar shows it was January 17, 1969. The convent was only a few blocks away from Sant'Anselmo where the Aventine hill rises up from the Circus Maximus. It was a noisy corner, but, once inside, it seemed quieter, the thick medieval walls keeping out most of the roar of the automobiles as they raced up the Via Lavernale.

I will always remember that meeting. Mother invited me into an inside parlor where she had coffee and biscotti prepared. We spent a good hour-and-a-half talking. In the ten years as primate I returned often to that parlor to talk with Mother Ildegarde. Like all nuns, she seemed ageless, but she must have been in her fifties then. She made up for the little formal education she had had the opportunity to acquire with life experiences and just plain wisdom.

This time I poured out my heart to her about what I was seeing and how shocked and sad I was. I knew there were 120 houses of enclosed Benedictine nuns in Italy alone and that there would probably not be vocations to fill all of them, but it seemed to me we should help where needed to raise the spiritual and human level of their lives. Then I proposed a plan. I knew I would have to find a different solution for each nation, but right now I hoped I could do something for the Italian houses.

Sant'Antonio had a large guesthouse with about forty rooms. The nuns rented it out to American colleges for programs of studies abroad. It was simple and clean. I asked Mother if there were times when it was not used, as I knew they relied on these foreign students to keep the community solvent. She said there were down-periods when the retreat house was vacant for several weeks in a row. My plan was to bring forty nuns to Rome during these down periods for courses in Sacred Scripture, the Rule of St. Benedict, liturgical spirituality, basic psychology, and so on. She was as excited as I was about the possibility and gave me the dates that year when the retreat house would be available. What pleased me most was that there seemed to be no need to explain to Mother Ildegarde what benefits such courses could have. Perhaps with her years of experience and knowledge of other houses, she knew better than I did the depth of the need.

By the time the meeting was over we each had our tasks. She was to contact a nun she knew, Suor Anselma, from Citerna in Tuscany, who had degrees in education and could help organize the classes professionally. My next step was to ask professors at Sant'Anselmo if they would be willing to add to their already heavy schedules these new courses. Of course, I had no money to pay them. They all agreed and were as excited as I was. Knowing, too, that some communities that might wish to send nuns could not afford it, and not wanting to put any financial burden on Sant'Antonio, already very generous, I wrote a begging letter to Mr. Harry John of the DeRance Foundation located in Milwaukee asking for a few thousand dollars for the project. I received a rapid, positive response, and we were ready to begin. We sent a notice to all the abbesses giving a list of the courses, an outline of their contents, and the names of the illustrious professors from Sant'Anselmo who would be teaching them. We waited for the responses to flow in.

Right after that I went on one of my long trips to visit monasteries. My secretaries kept writing me ominous letters that several bishops in whose dioceses the monasteries of our nuns were located had called Cardinal Antoniutti about whether they could make an exception to the rules of enclosure so these nuns could travel to Rome and attend such courses. His response was negative and stated emphatically that no one should attend. I returned home to find that word had spread among the abbesses that the Holy See did not approve of the courses, and, thus, no nuns were registered. I also found a note that I was to go to Antoniutti's office the day after my arrival back.

The meeting was brief. I did not even enter his office, but stayed in the somber antechamber. He said his decision had been made and I would be wasting my time even to try to persuade him otherwise. He added that the nuns did not need any more formation, intellectual or spiritual, than that which they were now receiving. In fact, he stated, such study could be dangerous to their vocation. As far as he was concerned, the matter was ended.

I left his office deciding that it was useless to argue with him. I walked dejectedly over the cobblestones to Saint Peter's, climbed the softly graded steps directly in front of the façade, and went in through the main entrance to my favorite praying spot in Rome, the confessional over the tomb of Peter. I knew I had to reach Pope Paul VI and that he just might understand.

I shortened my prayer, exited the Basilica, and found a public phone behind the Bernini colonnade. It was good I had a *gettone* (the token used in Italy for pay phones) in my pocket. I called the Vatican switchboard and asked to talk to the monsignor who was Cardinal Villot's secretary. The sister at the switchboard put me right through to the cardinal, to whom I explained my dilemma as rapidly as I could. Villot said he would be seeing Pope Paul in late afternoon and would call me at home that evening. The call came through about eight. The cardinal said the pope would fit me in next day at the end of his morning appointments, i.e., about one o'clock. He bolstered my spirits by adding: "I can tell you he truly understands and is on your side." I, in turn, called Mother Ildegarde and told her to keep the sisters praying intensely and that I would call her after the audience the next day.

That night I spent an hour putting all my arguments in order, hoping that I could convince Pope Paul that such courses would be of help to renew the Benedictine monasteries of women in Italy. I believe I argued with myself in my dreams.

I arrived early the next day. It was only about twelve-thirty. I was completely out of breath since I took the steps of the Stairs of Pius IX too fast and did not pause before crossing the courtyard. The monsignor who was the receptionist that day smiled when he saw me and said teasingly: "This is getting to be a habit, but we are always glad to see you here rather than some of the others," and he raised his eyebrows and looked up at the ceiling.

I did not have to say much to the pope that day about what I was trying to do. He understood perfectly. He said, as archbishop of Milan, he had to deal with the same issues among cloistered nuns. He had asked the monks of Montserrat in Spain to find chaplains for the Benedictine nuns there and to help them with conferences and the like. He promised to call Cardinal Antoniutti and express his wishes that the courses be held. More than that, he promised to receive the nuns attending them in a private audience and give an address to be published in the *Osservatore Romano* (the Vatican newspaper) on why such updating was important.

He followed through, and the courses were a great success.

Before long the abbesses themselves asked for a few weeks of courses geared specifically to their needs. This was easily worked out, and we included some lectures on psychology as well. As the years passed, I was pleased to see some of the brightest nuns with good academic backgrounds becoming the teachers of the courses so we no longer had to rely exclusively on professors from Sant'Anselmo. Often newly elected abbesses were taken from those who had attended the courses. In addition, some regions of Italy organized courses in their own monasteries so that all the members of the community could attend and benefit from them. Such courses continue to this day.

*   *   *

From the meetings of the Union of Superiors General (USG), I learned I was not the only one having difficulties with Cardinal Antoniutti. At several gatherings in 1968, the subject had arisen in earnest, and so the superiors general had decided to ask the Holy Father for a meeting to air their difficulties. Despite Archbishop Benelli's opposition to such a meeting, the Holy Father agreed to it. Father Arrupe announced these positive results to us at our first gathering in January of 1969, and so the meeting took place.

It turned out to be a relaxed and profitable event. Ten of us, the members of the council of the USG, were invited to the pope's library for the discussion. At the beginning the Holy Father said there would be no tape-recorders and no notes taken. He simply wanted us to speak to him frankly about why we asked for the meeting and, without fear, about the difficulties we were having. It wasn't long before the truth came out: the problem was our relationship with Cardinal Antoniutti.

Pope Paul said he knew of that difficulty and begged us to have patience. As superiors, he added, we could sympathize with the dilemma he found himself in. Often a superior does not want, at a particular moment, to remove a person and must tolerate the situation for a time. A change, he said, might just make matters worse and be imprudent in the long run. He said that was the position he felt he was in. I admired his honesty and that he treated us as mature people able to understand and did not cover up the difficulty. If the rumors that Antoniutti was the runner-up for the papacy and favored by the curia and some of the conservative cardinals, then the pope was saying he did not want to offend Antoniutti and lose the support of the more conservative group.

We dropped that subject then and spoke about other aspects of our work. The pope asked intelligent questions, did not presuppose he had all the answers, and the time passed rapidly. Out of this meeting came then the idea of regular meetings between the officials of the Congregation of Religious and sixteen superiors general, eight men and eight women, to clarify issues that could be the source of unwanted tension. That practice lasted for many decades.

There are few occasions when one can claim to have had the experience of watching a pope chair a meeting involving free discussion. From this occasion and from similar ones about liturgical matters, I came to see that Pope Paul VI was a most adept and practiced leader of discussion. I do not know why it surprised me that he always seemed perfectly at ease in such situations and showed a particular skill in drawing out what people thought, without their being afraid of saying something stupid or out of place. Perhaps that facility was gained when he was chaplain to university student organizations.

Of course, our problems with Cardinal Antoniutti did not end there, but at least we knew the pope was aware of the difficulties and, as in my case, was doing his best to make it all work out. In the long run, I am not sure, however, that the solution he chose, i.e., simply reversing the decisions of a lower authority, was a wise one since it just made that lower authority angry and vindictive, sensing his position was being disregarded. It also pointed to a deeper problem, namely, how Pope Paul felt he should deal with those who perhaps had opposed, or at least not totally accepted, the documents of the council. To leave them in office in the curia in that vital implementation period could send a mixed signal that in the end would not be healthy for the Church. It also left many of us superiors caught in the middle between two post-conciliar dynamics. The religious for whom we were responsible often picked the one they wanted among those forces and cited authorities to show that their interpretation was the legitimate one, thus creating divisions and disagreements.

By the time I arrived, the USG was well organized and very active. Pope Paul VI had approved of its establishment in May of 1967 with the hope that it would foster better relationships between the superiors of the major religious orders of men and the Congregation for Religious. Apparently this was not working out. A similar group for women superiors had been established a few years before, but, since most superiors of women religious did not have their headquarters in Rome, they were a less effective group. When we elected officers each year, Father Pedro Arrupe of the

Jesuits was always elected president and, from my arrival in Rome and for the next ten years, I was always elected vice-president.

We met at least yearly for one longer meeting of several days out at Grottaferrata or Villa Cavalletti, and most of us planned our travels to make sure we would be home at that time. During the year, those who happened to be in Rome gathered monthly, usually at the Jesuit residence, for less formal talk and for sharing experiences. The very first meeting I attended was at the Jesuit generalate. In fact, it was the afternoon of October 5, 1967, the very day I had met for the first time with Cardinal Antoniutti in his office! What a contrast! I knew I had found among the superiors general a group in which I would experience strong support and that would keep me sane. Thus, on one and the same day, I found myself torn between two different visions of post–Vatican II Catholicism, both reflected in the Roman scene during Pope Paul VI's pontificate. It was an experience that would repeat itself over and over during the next ten years.

My notes from that very first meeting show how impressed I was by the superiors general and, in particular, by its president, Father Arrupe. The atmosphere was informal, and everyone said what was in his heart and on his mind. There was no need to reach a consensus on anything. There was no rivalry, no one-up-man-ship. Arrupe, to my surprise, was very short but with strong, prominent features. He resembled perfectly what I imagined St. Ignatius would have looked like. He laughed easily and made all of us feel at home. For the next ten years I would find myself working closely with him. I count that relationship as one of my great blessings during my years as primate. As I came to know him better and better, I realized that he was the most saintly person I had ever encountered — free of all bias, truly compassionate, deeply prayerful, trusting of others, and intellectually very sharp. Perhaps his experiences in Japan during the war, his presence at Hiroshima with the dropping of the atomic bomb in August 1945, and his many years as a superior contributed to making him such a holy and yet totally human personality. If, from all the people I have known in my life in the Church, I had to select only one for sainthood, it would be Pedro Arrupe.

The topic at that very first meeting, as at many later meetings, seemed to get around to authority in the Church and how it should be exercised. That evening I wrote in my notebook: "Arrupe's observations that since the present crisis in the church involved authority and faith, it was unwise to force negative condemnations since they were pointless and did not help win confidence in the positive leadership of authority." I recall that he added: "When authority is the problem, authority is the least capable of solving it."

The meetings of the USG became one of my ways of continuing my intellectual formation. The themes we chose for discussion included the expected ones, those that most post-conciliar meetings among religious dealt with. There was, first, discussion about the nature of the new vocations entering religious life, how they differed from previous generations in preparation, in age, and in life experience. We also discussed and examined the motives of those seeking dispensations and leaving religious life.

We also broadened our outlook by selecting topics I had not heard discussed in the States. These more extensive themes occupied our thoughts at the longer meetings out in the Alban hills. We took up, under the guidance of expert theologians, themes such as secularization (very important at that time in Europe), inculturation, and justice and peace concerns. All three of these lengthy discussions were important to me and assisted my work when I began to travel and visit our houses all over the globe.

What a fine group of men had been elected generals of their orders in those post-conciliar days! I am afraid to mention them lest I miss some, but those that come at once to mind are: DeQuenongle, Koser, Cuskelley, Barrosse, Tutas, Calmels, Charles Henry, Thomas More, Lecuyer, Lalande, Systermans, van Asten, Musinsky. The only dissenting voice among us at that time was Archbishop Lefèbvre, superior general of the Holy Ghost Fathers. He came occasionally to the meetings, seldom entered into the discussion, but at the end before we moved on to another topic would interject a discordant negative commentary on what we had just seemed to agree on.

The difficulty we all felt was that we were on the road so much that it was difficult to get to know one another as we would have liked.

*   *   *

As a member of the USG, I was elected to attend the synods of bishops in 1969 and 1971, both of them memorable gatherings.

The synod of 1969 was declared by the pope to be an extraordinary one with the participation of about half the usual number of bishops, i.e., the heads of the major offices in Rome, the presidents of the national conferences of bishops, and only three elected members from the USG; I was privileged to be one of them. Because of its smaller size, this synod was not held in the new auditorium prepared as a part of the Papal Audience Hall designed by Nervi, but in the more intimate "Room of the Broken Skulls." This old storage area for damaged ancient sculptures had been converted into a meeting area without losing any of its charm and original intent. Its bar, called Bar Jona like the one found in St. Peter's during the council, became a gathering place for refreshments — an espresso or what have you — as well as news and gossip. As usual, much of the business and exchanges that really mattered took place here.

At the beginning, the theme of the synod, namely, the nature and authority of bishops' conferences, did not excite me. It became, however, the occasion for me to think through more seriously my concept of collegiality in the Church and to watch the growing efforts of the curia to reassert itself and regain any power it may have lost at Vatican II. The refrain of the participating curial officials, reiterated over and over again, was that nothing should come between the pope and each individual bishop. It seemed curious to me that these officials saw the conferences, not as a sign of subsidiarity or collegiality among bishops and between bishops and pope, but as an impediment to the relationship between pope and the individual bishop.

The strongest voice for the curia's point of view at the 1969 synod turned out to be Cardinal John Wright, former bishop of Pittsburgh, now prefect of the Congregation for the Clergy. He asserted, with his usual eloquence, that the bishops at the council had voted for the erection of the conferences of bishops only as an administrative, consultative group, and had no intention that such groupings would have jurisdiction or come between the individual bishop and the pope. The council documents do not seem to support this unequivocal position, since already in the very first document on the liturgy, much is relegated to the national conferences, and the same can be said of later documents. Cardinal Wright spoke emphatically against any powers being "delegated" to the conference of bishops, arousing fears in the members of the synod that such delegation would simply produce multiple temptations toward Gallicanism and the creating of national churches.

I realized, then, that the subject was of more interest to me than I had at first imagined. It touched the heart of the question of primacy and collegiality, a topic that had plagued the Church since the First Vatican Council and that was not clearly resolved in practice by the documents of Vatican II. Was the theology of Vatican II confirming that the bishops by reason of their ordination assumed real responsibility for the government of the Universal Church *cum et sub Petro* (with and under Peter) to find no concrete, visible, realizable structural component except every few centuries in an ecumenical council?

Other members of the curia and Cardinal Jean Danielou, an appointee of the pope, emphasized the problems of weak faith among the people that the Church must now confront. They proposed strong, more decisive papal pronouncements about what people should believe to allay the doubts of the faithful. Further, bishops should agree not to disagree so that there would be unanimity of thought and thus the faithful not be perturbed in their faith. I am sure these comments were in response to the negative reactions around the world to Pope Paul's encyclical on birth control, *Humanae vitae*. The solution proposed by the curia was to create an even stronger central authority and then to impose unanimity among the bishops around that authority. This idea among officials of the curia was not to die with this synod.

When I had a chance to enter the debate, I took a totally opposite point of view, namely, that the crisis of faith would grow worse if different points of view among the bishops or in the Church at large were hidden or masked in the name of loyalty and charity. I spoke in favor of openness and honesty without false or merely exterior manifestations of agreement and the need for a space where these disagreements could be expressed without fear of intimidation. I affirmed that the greatest scandal would come from hiding or glossing over differences rather than confronting them. What we needed, I asserted, were new structures within the Church where these differences of opinion could be expressed and worked out in a spirit of charity and honesty.

Second, I publicly disagreed with Cardinal Wright and his fear that conferences of bishops would end up falling into the evil of exaggerated nationalism. I felt we had to accept cultural differences to be a healthy Church. Yes, we had to avoid exaggerated nationalism, but at the same time we had to avoid imperialism and the absolutism of conformity. I ended then by saying that therefore the bishops' conferences should be strengthened.

At the break, I went out to Bar Jona to get a coke. There I found Cardinal Wright ahead of me. I greeted him and asked: "I hope, John, you were not upset that I took a position different from your own." He was livid with rage. Not answering me directly or even looking at me, he called over to Cardinal Vagnozzi at the other end of the bar sipping an espresso, and asked him if he did not agree that I was the stupidest ass he had ever seen. (The rest of what he said is not fit for print.) I took my coke and went over to a window at the other end of the room and let him stew. Cardinal John Dearden of Detroit, president of the conference of American bishops, had overheard the exchange and came over to me and, in a low voice, whispered: "Don't take him seriously, Rembert. You were right and he was wrong. He'll get over it." He did, but it took many years.

These positions the curia voiced surfaced over and over again and finally became very much a part of the thinking during the pontificate that was to follow Pope Paul VI's.

The synod of 1971 was a regular (ordinary) one with over two hundred members and, thus, ten members elected from the USG, of which I was one. It was called to discuss two themes: the ministerial priesthood and justice in the modern world, this latter a theme dear to Paul VI.

Since one-third of the priests in the world at that time were members of religious orders, we superiors took this theme of the pastoral ministry of priests very seriously. We formed commissions of experts to prepare ourselves, held many meetings to discuss our approaches, and used questionnaires to sound out all the superiors general. Fifty-four of us spent several days together at Grottaferrata (May 26-29, 1971) to discuss the issues involved. Our presentations at the synod relied on all this collected material.

Naturally, the question that was on the minds of the members was the position the synod would take on mandatory celibacy for diocesan clergy. After consulting all its members, the USG relayed to the assembly the position these members supported. They affirmed that celibacy was truly a value for the church and should be preserved in the Western church, but saw religious life as the means for preserving this value not the diocesan clergy. Many superiors had voiced the opinion that the nature of religious life and vocations to that form of life would be clearer if celibacy among diocesan priests was not obligatory. The synod, they added, should feel free to discuss without fear two problems that were urgent at that time: Is it opportune to continue the practice of ordaining only those who have the charism of celibacy or should ordination eventually be conferred also on married men? Second, should those who had left the active ministry to marry be reinstated? On the question of the admission to active ministry of those many priests who had left the priesthood to marry, seventy percent of the superiors general said no, thirty percent said they should be treated as all other laity, emphasizing that the issue should be decided by the needs of the communities to be served and their willingness to accept a married priest.

It would be naïve to think that this position of the religious on celibacy did not raise a strong reaction on the part of many bishops attending the synod. Cardinal Seper, then prefect of the Holy Office succeeding Cardinal Ottaviani, publicly proposed on the floor that the religious superiors and bishops of the Eastern Churches should not be permitted to vote on these issues but only Latin rite diocesan bishops. Pope Paul said no; he wished to hear also the voices of the religious superiors and the wisdom of the Eastern bishops who had had the experience in their tradition of a married clergy.

Although much else about the priesthood was discussed at this synod, I cite these issues of celibacy because they were the ones in which the religious seemed the most involved. In the final document, the bishops and religious present were asked to vote for one of two alternatives: (1) Without denying always the right of the Supreme Pontiff, the priestly ordination of married men is not permitted, even in particular cases; or (2) It belongs solely to the Supreme Pontiff, in particular cases, by reason of pastoral needs and the good of the universal church to allow the priestly ordination of married men, who are of mature age and proven life *(viri probati)*. In the linguistic group to which I belonged, there was much consternation when we were told that the ballots had to be signed by each member so the Holy Father (and the curia?) would know how each member voted. Some bishops, especially from third world countries, asked for an anonymous vote, so that the members could feel reassured that there would be no repercussions for how they had voted. This was rejected and each ballot had to be signed. The first proposition received 107 affirmative votes, the second 87. There were a few abstentions and a few null votes. I was surprised, though, that the vote was as close as it was.

If I learned anything from the way this topic was treated, it was that issues that are not confronted clearly, openly, and thoroughly do not go away. They just continue to surface and disturb the whole group for years.

But it was the second theme on the agenda that touched me most: Justice in the Modern World. The document produced by the members of this synod shows the first real influence of bishops from the third world on church life and thinking. It was a privilege to have been a part of those discussions and feel the strength of commitment of those third world bishops to social justice.

Until then I had a general background in the papal documents on Catholic social teaching, but this synod created within me a deeply emotional involvement in these global concerns. Some of it came from the discussion among the bishops, but much of it came from one person, Barbara Ward (often called Lady Jackson from her husband's family name and because of the honors she received from the British Crown). She sat behind me each day in the synod hall, we religious having the last seats after the bishops and the lay observers occupying the seats behind us. She was the first lay person to address the bishops at a synod. I confess that her speech brought about a conversion experience in me. She was a well-known and distinguished English economist who had written many books on the subject of the disparity of wealth among the nations. She was also a reporter for the English periodical *The Economist.* Most of all, she was a gifted and moving speaker. It was a treat to hear an economist with fire in her belly who was not afraid to draw moral conclusions from the inequalities in the world and the consumption of goods and energy.

Her analysis of the striking differences between the rich and powerful nations of the world, on one hand, and the poorest and defenseless, on the other, struck me forcibly. After the talk, I went out and bought many of her books and devoured them. In general conversation with her in the mornings before the sessions or during the breaks, she impressed me as very humble and unassuming, but one could see true passion behind her words.

I understood that, if the Catholic Church was now truly to be identified with all cultures and national diversity, the economic questions and life styles of its members were also going to be important. Perhaps this sudden discovery on my part was more an intellectual conversion, but it was real and continued to smolder within me for decades. Social justice became an issue I would continue to make my own and in which I would begin to form new attitudes and judgments. For this I am grateful to Barbara Ward. Though I never met her again after the synod, she stands in a special place in my intellectual and social development.

*   *   *

But 1971 was to end on a different note. That September Pope Paul VI named Abbot Augustin Mayer, one of the opposing candidates when I was elected abbot primate, secretary of the Congregation for Religious, second in command to Cardinal Antoniutti, and raised him to the rank of archbishop. In the future I would have to deal with Mayer for most Benedictine matters. One abbot of the confederation wrote me a letter soon after Mayer's appointment stating clearly the general feeling at Sant'Anselmo and among most members of the Benedictine confederation: "I was dismayed and unhappy at the news that Gus Mayer was appointed to the Congregation for Religious. It appears that dear old Antoniutti is trying to box-in a certain progressive abbot primate."

Many abbots felt that the appointment did not augur well for the future of the abbots' recommendations discussed at the congresses of 1966 and 1967, many of which were already well under way. I was curious, moreover, why from all the potential candidates in the world capable of assuming this position Pope Paul VI had chosen Mayer. Only time would give a clear answer to that question.

I took this appointment in stride because I felt that Pope Paul had been supportive of what the abbots of the confederation wanted and would continue to be so. If at that moment it seemed like a strange selection to me, with time I came to realize it was typical of Pope Paul VI. It was another example of how he tried to balance the currents of thought in the Church after Vatican Council II. He must have known at that time that Cardinal Antoniutti would soon reach the age of mandatory retirement and that it would be good to have some continuity. He must have seen Mayer as that point of continuity. Later, when he appointed a successor to Antoniutti, it would be clearer what was at play.

CHAPTER 8

Traveling the World Over

(1967-1973)

During my first six years as abbot primate, I made 362 visits to monasteries of Benedictine men and women outside of Rome; by the end of my term as primate in 1977, the number added up to 598 visits. I have reconstructed those visits from the circular letters I wrote to the monasteries, the scant and hardly legible notes I scribbled on my trips, and the letters to officials back at Sant'Anselmo. Finally I browsed through the letters and picture postcards, more like travelogues, that I wrote my mother from various places along the way.

In compiling the list of monasteries I visited, I see I did not follow my intention of focusing on third-world monasteries and those behind the Iron Curtain. Some monasteries I visited several times; others only once. I was on the road over six months each year. Except for the canonical visitations in the eight monasteries directly under me, which, by church law, I had to perform every five years, the visits to the other monasteries were friendly and unstructured; I was free to be more innovative. I sought to reinforce the role of the local abbot and never to undermine it. Perhaps, more than anything else, I wanted the communities to seek their place in the local and larger church and not become inward-looking. Balancing the needs of the monastic community with participation in the life of the local church and society has always been a challenge to monasteries. Bishops too easily see monks as a work force at their disposal, while monks often feel a need to guard their community life and stability.

In the years after the council, the local churches in particular were full of excitement. My task, as I saw it, was not to destroy or weaken this enthusiasm, but to use it to examine monasticism's spiritual roots more deeply and to articulate how they could be lived out in the contemporary world. The excesses I sometimes saw stemmed more from immaturity than from ill will. The instability arising from changes in society and church also brought hope. Yes, it was a period of experimentation, and one was not, as in later years, afraid to use that word. It was a period of searching in which I worried that church authorities would squelch this enthusiasm too soon, out of fear that these experiments could lead to imprudence. Zeal once stifled is not easily rekindled.

I came to see that one of my roles was to be a *provocateur*. If a monastery was not making any changes at all or, out of fear, not even willing to discuss the need for *aggiornamento* after Vatican II, my task was to encourage the monks to ask serious questions about their role in society and church in the light of the council's theology. On the other hand, if a monastery was moving too rapidly, making changes without serious reflection, I had to encourage the monks to a more realistic assessment of the modifications they were proposing and to ask how these would enhance monastic values and assure future stability.

Another insight of these visits, which quickly became evident, was how lonely many abbots and abbesses could be and how eagerly they sought a willing ear to listen to their problems of leadership in a world where all authority was being questioned. I spent long hours trying to support those who felt isolated. Often my task was to be a leader to the leaders and to give them courage. At the same time I came to appreciate the fine leadership qualities of many men and women superiors in the order.

Another aspect of twentieth-century monasticism that became apparent was the strength of its missionary spirit. I don't know why this surprised me since my own monastery at Latrobe was born of that spirit, and was still very much alive when I was elected abbot. There were other congregations with a similar thrust.

What was life like on the road? In every monastery of men or women I would preside at the community Mass and preach, give a lengthy conference or two, open the floor to a dialogue about any point the members raised, and answer questions about what was happening in other monastic communities around the world. I never felt that being an American was an impediment or the source of any prejudice. I put my whole self into the visit by entering fully into the life of the community. I wanted to know and understand each community as well as I could in the short time available, convey as much information as would be helpful to the members, communicate a positive feeling about their role as followers of Benedict in the contemporary world, encourage and challenge them.

Because these visits made up such a large portion of my efforts as primate and were so important to my understanding and growth, I want to recount some of what I saw and experienced. I have assembled a list of the monasteries I visited (with apologies to the readers, but perhaps to the benefit of historians). In some cases, I have added a comment or observation that will give a sense of monastic life in those heady years following Vatican II.

*   *   *

1968

March 21: Athens, Greece, to talk with a small group of women wanting to be Benedictines seeking a monastery of nuns in Europe to help them get off the ground and give them a deeper appreciation of how the Rule of St. Benedict could be lived out in our contemporary world.

March 23: Jerusalem, Israel — the end of the Six-Day War made possible a trip to the Orthodox monastery of St. Catherine at the foot of Mount Sinai with Dr. Ilse, Secretary of Religious Affairs for the State of Israel, and Abbot Leo Rudloff of Dormition Abbey in Jerusalem.

Somewhat to my surprise, this pilgrimage to St. Catherine turned out to be a deeply moving religious experience, one firmly embedded in my memory. Such experiences of an overwhelming awareness of God's presence are rare in life and usually can be numbered on one hand. Arriving at Mount Sinai and seeing the monastery of St. Catherine's nestled in its bosom gave me an overwhelming experience of the transcendent. I remember saying: "God could truly speak here!" Perhaps the historical and biblical roots I associated with that mountain — Moses speaking with God — combined now with a specific monastic component, became a symbol of my vocation, i.e., of being inserted into salvation history and God's embracing care. The simple architecture of St. Catherine's, the faith-filled ancient mosaics in its church, the magnificent manuscripts in its library, the monks' warm and outgoing hospitality toward us — all of these stay vividly with me.

June: visitations to two monasteries in United States, Weston Priory in Vermont and Mount Saviour, Elmira, New York — visit to Benedictine sisters in Tulsa, Oklahoma — speech in Shawnee, Oklahoma, at meeting of Benedictine abbots of my own Congregation.

July: meeting of French abbesses at Méry sur Oise in France, a thoughtful dynamic group — visit to the old monastery of Ligugé for discussion of Benedictines and ecumenism — visits to Camaldoli and Santa Giustina, Padova, Italy.

August: whole month spent visiting all 21 Benedictine monasteries of men and women in Austria with their large baroque facilities — added Säben and Muri-Gries in Tyrol district of Northern Italy at end of trip.

How often I heard it said: "Österreich ist klösterreich" ("Austria: Land of monasteries")! The Austrian monasteries are among the most beautiful in the world, but unfortunately one can easily forget about the lives of the people who reside in them. Most live very modestly, occupying only a small section of these gigantic baroque buildings. I found the communities relatively small, perhaps about twenty members, delightfully relaxed, bright, and adaptable. Although they seemed at that time perplexed about their future and how they should adjust to a younger generation, they were hopeful. I felt very comfortable celebrating Mass bedecked in baroque splendor, with shimmering, gold-trimmed vestments, to the singing of Haydn, Mozart, and especially Schubert Masses.

October 28 to December 17: long trip to monasteries in Asia; second visit to Dormition Abbey in Jerusalem, Israel; then flew off to India to visit monks at Asirvanam and nuns at Shanti Nilayam near Bangalore.

At Asirvanam I consecrated the first Benedictine church in India. I also encountered the first signs of external cultural adaptation, e.g., bare feet in church during ceremonies, no meat in monastery, simplicity of life, native furnishings, clasped hands and bowing as signs of respect and gestures of reverence during the liturgy reflecting those of society. This trip forced me to think differently about inculturation. I realized that it was happening all around me, in the United States as well as in Asia. Although the Rule of St. Benedict is the same everywhere and the Church's liturgical rubrics do not vary from place to place, each region brings its own way of

doing things and of interpreting the Rule and these rites so that, uncon-
sciously, inculturation is taking place. It cannot be avoided.

November 8: flew on to Vietnam, where war was raging, for a visit to mon-
astery of Thien-An, situated outside of Hué in the demilitarized zone be-
tween North and South — monastery building set on fire during Tet offen-
sive — four monks buried alive and prior killed in bombing raid shortly
afterwards — went also to visit Benedictine sisters from Sainte Bathilde in
Thu-Doc, but American military insisted I return before dusk — saw fields
of high grain along the road being strafed for hidden Viet Cong — brave
sisters, indeed!

The text of the Introit of the Mass at Thien-An that day proclaimed its
own message: "The Lord says: 'I think thoughts of peace, and not of afflic-
tion. You shall call upon me, and I will hear you; and I will bring back your
captivity from all places.'" The Gospel was also appropriate — raising the
magistrate's daughter and restoring her to life (Matthew 9). I remember
that my sermon on that occasion was one of encouragement: God had not
forgotten or abandoned them.

A sumptuous meal followed in the old chapter room under an open
sky shaded only by the charred and splintered beams. The monks brought
in a giant fish baked in banana leaves, the enticing aroma catching my attention immediately, and, on a separate platter, presented me with the
eyes, the part they considered the most delicious. Remembering my childhood Lenten practice of not eating candy till Lent ended at noon on Holy
Saturday, I said to myself: "Holy Saturday noon. Jelly-beans!" Then I swallowed the eyes whole with a slug of whiskey that the monks had gotten
from the U.S. army. The meal did nothing to make my diarrhea any better.
(It was one of the first instances of a problem I faced during almost every
trip; I often said that I held the Guinness record of having had diarrhea in
thirty-seven different countries!)

This visit to Vietnam in the middle of the war helped me realize that
the abbot primate was not just an office, but a symbol of unity.

November 12: On to the Philippines for visit to monastery of San Beda in Ma-
nila, having been there when I was abbot of St. Vincent — then to Japan:
Benedictines still just beginning there at St. Anselm Priory and parish in
downtown Tokyo — then Korea from November 18 to 27 for visit to large mon-
astery of monks at Waegwan and sisters at Taegu and Pusan — stopped in

Taiwan to spend some time again at the priory founded by my monastery that I had visited in 1966.

If the abbot primate were allowed to have a special love, I would admit that I loved the Korean culture and the monastic communities there. They were very musical and creative. Vocations were plentiful and the monks and sisters had no difficulty in providing for the economic stability of their communities. Although I could not speak the language, many spoke some German, the monasteries having been founded by German-speaking monks of the Ottilien Congregation and sisters of Tutzing. Some also spoke English. It did not seem to matter; we communicated with facial expressions and gestures. It was clear that the future of these monasteries was secure.

December: flew on to Thailand for meeting from December 9 to 15 at Samutprakarn, 20 miles outside of Bangkok — about 65 to 70 monks and nuns present. Aim: bring together superiors of monastic houses in the Far East and superiors of founding monasteries in Europe and America to hear experts discuss similarities and differences between eastern and western monasticism, because the superiors from Asia felt need for more freedom in determining what forms of inculturation their monasteries could assume. Much excitement that Thomas Merton of Gethsemani Abbey in Kentucky was permitted to come to conference and speak because of his knowledge of both western and eastern spiritual traditions — Archbishop Jean Jadot, apostolic nuncio, most enthusiastic.

The meeting was held in a tropical Asian park with sculpted gardens, small ponds full of iridescent fish, variegated colored flowers, running streams spanned by graceful wooden footbridges — all surrounded by lush green foliage. Archbishop Jadot had made these arrangements for us and had also seen to it that the patriarch of the Buddhists, Somdet Para Ariawong Sankarat, would come to greet us at the first session. The patriarch gave permission for our members to visit and stay over at any of their monasteries, an auspicious and rare happening for the year 1968. He had also been told that Americans shake hands, while I had been told not to touch the patriarch but just fold my hand and bow as I approached him. Both of us came from opposite sides of the platform, he with outstretched hand, I with folded hands and bowing. All laughed. It was the best possible way to break the ice.

Merton's talk was to be the high point of the conference and we all eagerly awaited it. My own relationship to Merton was typical of many my age. I had already joined the Benedictines and had finished my theological studies when I read *The Seven Storey Mountain,* published in 1948. Merton had a negative attitude toward us "black Benedictines" (he considered us inferior monks, hyper-activists not to be taken seriously). I did not agree with him; nevertheless, I continued to read his writings, but with mixed reactions. His more serious mystical works did not seem to evolve out of lived experiences, but seemed formulated from academic reading. Other works, like those involving social justice, I found to be on the mark. I was impressed and stimulated by his writings and reflections on the meaning for monks of Vatican II. I cannot say much about Merton as a person since I did not know him well. He was always polite with me, but I could sense a bit of aloofness around superiors, not surprising given his troubled relationship with Abbot James Fox, his former superior at Gethsemani. At times his self-assurance bordered on arrogance.

Merton spoke on Tuesday, December 10: "Marxism and Monastic Perspectives." The talk did not fit into the aims of the meeting and there was general disappointment in the group, a view I shared. Had Dom Jean LeClercq of Clervaux Abbey, our contact with Merton, sufficiently explained the purpose of the meeting? (When the letters between the two were later published, it was clear that Merton had selected the topic and Le Clercq had agreed.) Some had the impression that the talk was not well prepared; it roamed broadly over many issues. Nonetheless, some comments were pertinent and would permit the members to probe further in the discussion that evening.

At about 3:00 that afternoon, a monk came running to tell me Merton had been found dead in his room. I ran to his bungalow to find the body on the floor, face up, arms extended, hands free but slightly gnarled. A floor-fan had fallen on his body leaving strips of burn marks on his arm where the fan lay. Sister Edeltrud Weist, a medical doctor and prioress of our monastery in Taegu, Korea, said he was internally electrically burned, an accident which had stopped his heart. His body was still warm and I anointed him.

The Thai police and coroners were called. The coroner's certificate stated "death was caused as a result of fainting — due to acute cardiac failure and electric shock due to accidental falling against the electric fan to the floor."

Shortly after one in the morning the next day the undertaker took his body away. The conference's participants had kept vigil at the body with prayer services till then. I went into the city to the Vatican embassy to call the abbot of Gethsemani who, at first, asked for an autopsy, but the embalmers were reluctant to do so without written permission from the abbot, who finally agreed that the body should be embalmed and returned to Louisville.

The next day I presided at a funeral Mass and preached on Merton's insatiable search for God — a search that had preoccupied him for his whole life and that now was fulfilled. All agreed to continue the conference as planned; the mood was calm but serious.

The publicity surrounding Merton's death brought an awareness of the need for East-West dialogue in the Church to a new level. We had learned the importance of a dialogue based, not primarily on doctrine, but on spirituality, every future meeting referred back to this one as the true beginning of the dialogue.

Merton's death was premature. He had not been given time to integrate fully his studies in Buddhism with his Catholic beliefs: they seemed to stand beside each other in parallel columns and had not converged into a living, breathing whole. There were other areas of Benedictine spirituality he had not totally assimilated, e.g., his writings lacked a good foundation in biblical theology based on the best historical, critical, and literary exegesis. I also searched in vain for the deeper liturgical spirituality expected of a monastic writer. In other words, there was something incomplete about the whole Merton endeavor that left me puzzled. Merton's contribution, I recognize, was enormous, in spite of these lacunae that have always troubled me. God has His ways.

*   *   *

1969

In January of 1969 I received at Sant'Anselmo a visit from Father Ulrich Monsberger, prior of the Benedictine monastery of Pannonhalma in Hungary. Life for Benedictines in the countries behind the iron curtain was very difficult, especially in Hungary. In 1944 the monks belonging to the Hungarian Congregation numbered about 270 living in ten monasteries, all maintaining prestigious high schools. Under Communist rule, all religious orders of men and women in Hungary were officially suppressed with the exception of two Benedictine houses, Pannohalma and Györ, which were allowed to continue on, not as monasteries, but as schools. By 1968 the number of monks had diminished to about seventy. From Rome's point of view Pannohalma remained an *abbatia nullius,* i.e., a monastery with a small territory where the abbot acted with the rights of a bishop. For this reason, the abbot of Pannonhalma was a member of the Hungarian bishops' conference. As a part of a 1968 compromises agreed upon between the Vatican Secretariat of State and the Hungarian government, Archabbot Norbert Legányi was forced to resign, being a *persona non grata* to the government.

The prior, Father Monsberger, told me that he had asked Jozsef Pantner, president of the Bureau of Religious Affairs in Budapest, if I could visit in preparation for the election of a new archabbot. The prior informed me in a stage whisper that Pantner mentioned to him they had done their research on me. Pantner had asked him who I was and the prior gave the information that I was "an American in his late forties." Then Pantner, speaking slowly for emphasis, said to the prior: "We know, Father Prior, that he is exactly forty-one years old and will be forty-two on April 2." Though the prior was obviously frightened and uneasy, I readily agreed to the trip.

To gauge the situation, I went to visit Archbishop Agostino Casaroli who had negotiated with the Hungarian government. Casaroli was pleased that I was going, but observed that Pantner would assume I was carrying a name in my pocket representing the Holy See's candidate for abbot. But, Rome had no candidate, he told me, and I could act freely in recommending whoever seemed right for the community — if the government would accept the choice.

Casaroli also gave me the names of several of the monks who were under government control and who would be reporting everything I said and did to Pantner or the secret police. Pantner reported directly to Moscow and the archbishop gave me the name of the Russian official who was Moscow's local control on Pantner. At first this information unnerved me, but I made up my mind not to let the secrecy and the fears that it engendered trouble me.

Since I would be meeting also with all the bishops in Budapest, Casaroli named those favored by the government and those not. He also said that I would need to find out who was the bishops' candidate for abbot as he did not know. Casaroli doubted that I would have access to the school or meet any of the students since, being a young American, I did not fit the image the government projected of the Catholic Church, namely, a relic of the past.

A week or so later I applied for a visa at the Hungarian consulate in Rome. I was taken out of a long waiting-line, ushered with much formality directly and personally into the Hungarian Consul's office, treated with unusual deference, and granted the visa at once.

March 21: after Mass, I drove with two secretaries across Italy to Ancona — put car on ferry — early morning passed through lovely islands dotting old Dalmatian coast — arrived at Zadar in Yugoslavia — stayed overnight with bishop there — next night stayed in Zagreb at archbishop's residence — crossed border by car into Hungary — drove up along Lake Balatan with its light green water — finally, in the distance, Pannonhalma came into view.

No abbot primate had visited Pannonhalma since 1938, and I noticed tears in the eyes of some of the older men as I arrived. For many decades they must have felt abandoned. Once again, I saw the symbolic importance of the abbot primate.

I was lodged in the apartment of resigned Archabbot Norbert; the prior whispered in my ear that the rooms were under the immediate control of the "Office of Fine Arts" so that no piece of furniture could be moved. Some pieces were very handsome antiques, but curiously nailed to the floor. I assumed the rooms were bugged because no one felt free to talk to me there, and the prior also informed me that the phone was tapped. I was surprised that the preferred language was German, the second language of the prior and of Father V., headmaster of the school, who Casaroli said was the government's connection within the monastery.

For admission into the community, the government had imposed a *numerus clausus,* i.e., only a certain number of new "professors" could be admitted each year. This placed an enormous burden on the junior monks since each one had to finish his professional teaching degree before a new member could be admitted. The training period consisted of novitiate, five years of theology, and at least four years at the university. I encouraged them to do the professional degree before finishing their studies for ordination, as some more modern religious orders do. To complicate matters, some of the monks were stationed in parishes and thus the government did not consider them members of the faculty of the school, depriving them of the right to vote for their abbot.

Next morning after breakfast the subprior, Father M., waited for me and whispered in French (constantly looking about him) that Father V. was the government contact person and would be relating everything I said to

169

the community to the civil authorities. Furthermore, every monk would be called in and interrogated separately by the secret police about what I said and did. He was full of fear. That day I met all day with officials of the monastery that included a triumvirate of monks elected by the community to assist the prior in running the monastery in this interim period. Father V., the government connection, had been elected by a very small margin to this group. At first I was surprised, but then realized that the others would know from his reactions what the government's position was on all issues. In the discussions the others kept noting his responses. During the next few days some monks who were afraid to talk privately with me, slipped me short notes, asking me to read them and flush them down the toilet.

Many older monks lived under an ever-present and debilitating fear that seemed to have warped their minds. Searching for ways of living in peace, they had created worlds of their own into which they had receded. No wonder they could not have a communal recreation as all monasteries do. The tactic used by the government was not one of coercion but of slowly draining the vitality out of the men and creating in its place a slow-working paralysis. The younger men noticed this phenomenon. The degree of cooperation with the government had become a source of division between them and the oldsters. The younger generation was afraid that I would hear only the ideas of the older, more fearful generation.

My immediate reaction was one of sadness. Once, this had been among the most prestigious monastic communities in the world with one of the highest levels of academic training and learning. In spite of the diminished numbers of monks and the deleterious effects of the political situation, the power of that tradition was still visible. Those who had remained in the country under these harsh conditions were doing their best to keep alive a monastic tradition under insurmountable hardships. Although I was troubled for a time, I decided I could not judge them severely but simply had to help them find the best solution for a community living under almost impossible circumstances. We had to come up with the best compromise possible.

Pannonhalma served also as a place of "house arrest" for older and infirm members of other religious orders suppressed in Hungary. About 120 men, mostly Jesuits and Franciscans, lay in beds in large dormitories. I went from bed to bed promising I would inform Father Arrupe, the superior general of the Jesuits, or Father Koser, the minister general of the Franciscans, or whomever that they were still living and wanted to be remembered.

The women who did the cooking were former Benedictine sisters whose houses had been suppressed but who tried to remain together as lay people. We gathered in a secluded area off the kitchen in the cutlery. No words were needed; we cried and hugged one another and prayed in Latin some prayers we all knew. How many would survive to see better days? Their fidelity and strength of commitment, at great personal risk, impressed me. I am sure there were many other people in Hungary who were performing similar acts of heroism, hoping and praying that somehow their ideals would be preserved and passed on to another generation.

I kept asking Father V. if I could see the school, and as Archbishop Casaroli had predicted, he always found excuses that made it impossible. Finally he agreed I could visit on a specific afternoon at a specific time. When I arrived, all the students were away at a soccer match! I was taken from one empty schoolroom to another. I was surprised, however, that one student was permitted to come over to the monastery whenever he wanted. He spoke English fluently, saying he learned it visiting his girlfriend in East Berlin! He kept lamenting that he would not be able to get into the specialization in college that he wanted because his dad was a nobody in the Party.

In the evening I had a chance to spend some time with the whole community. I had to do most of the talking; the few questions were extremely well formulated and intelligent. However, the community knew very little about the renewal of religious life after Vatican II, having had other more pressing matters on their minds. I noted in my diary that they were not closed-minded, just not informed.

On Thursday the prior and Father V. took me to Budapest to visit Pantner's office in the government headquarters, then to the gathering of the Hungarian bishops, followed by an evening with the junior monks studying at the university. Not wanting to look pompous or princely, I insisted on dressing as an American priest, i.e., in suit and Roman collar and not in full habit. Both Father V. and the prior were very displeased.

Joszef Pantner in the Bureau of Religious Affairs was not an academic type; he had come up through the party ranks. Through the German-speaking interpreter, he lectured me on Vatican II and its new approach to the world, a cleverly constructed talk peppered with quotes from the council documents but always taken out of context. The meeting ended with coffee and excellent Hungarian Tokay. Through it° all the prior remained nervous and patently obsequious. I had noticed a thin, wiry man sitting at a small desk in the corner of the room, facing the wall and feigning to read a newspaper through the meeting, all the while chain-smoking. I took advantage of the moment when wine was brought out to go over to greet him. As we shook hands, he gave his name: it was that of the Russian control on Joszef Pantner that Archbishop Casaroli had mentioned.

Lunch with the Hungarian bishops was enjoyable; their greeting was warm and sincere. They made it clear to me, without much reserve, who was their candidate for abbot of Pannonhalma and insisted I have a chance to meet this monk while in Budapest. That opportunity came a bit later in the day when I was given a tour of the city. I found him humble, shy, perhaps a bit frightened, but well informed theologically. The encounter that evening with the ten young monks studying theology at the seminary was a good one. What a bright and impressive group! It seemed to me that if most of them stayed, the future of the monastery would be in good hands. They were more idealistic than the oldsters and more aware of the effects of too much compromise with the government.

We left Pannonhalma for Rome the next day. A slight covering of snow on the ground made walking difficult, but all the monks gathered in the courtyard to say farewell. The young student who said he had learned English in East Berlin appeared too. He asked if he could drive my Fiat around the courtyard and I said yes. As he was doing so, the prior whispered in my ear: "Treat that lad well. His father is high up in the Communist Party." It was a perfect note on which to end the trip: one never knew whom to believe.

I promised the monks that if everything worked out to the satisfaction of all sides, I would return for the blessing of the new abbot they would elect.

March 29: Drove to Vienna, Austria — visited with Cardinal König, the eyes and ears of the Vatican for Eastern Europe — returned by car to Rome — met at length with Archbishop Casaroli to relate all that I had heard and seen and what were my perceptions of the situation, pointing out the contentious canonical points before moving toward the election of a new abbot.

After returning to Rome this time, I went out to Sacro Speco, the cave monastery where Benedict had spent two years of his life and where I had been ordained a priest. I wanted to spend a week in reflection and prayer about my trip to Hungary; I needed time to digest all that had happened. If anything, those experiences heightened my fears of despotic rulers, within the Church as well as outside of it. I saw firsthand how fear destroys people and communities so that normal relationships became impossible. To live without trusting those around you is a condemnation to living alone.

Let me end the story of Pannonhalma by saying that I returned there in March of 1973 for the blessing of the new abbot, Father András Szennay, who was agreeable to the community, the bishops, and the government. I made another trip to Hungary in September of 1975 for a longer stay to do an unofficial canonical visitation to assist the abbot in his duties. A new minister of religious affairs had been appointed, a classmate of the abbot's from college days, and some of the tight restrictions had been loosened. (In 1989, to my great joy, the new government restored the Hungarian Congregation to its former independence and officially recognized the monasteries and schools.)

May: spent month of May visiting houses of England, first of three trips to visit all the houses of England, Scotland, and Ireland — during this trip, visited eleven monasteries of men and seven of women — surprised that such a small country with so few Catholics could have so many Benedictine houses.

The English monasteries, with their long tradition of excellent schools, but also with their medieval and deeply mystical heritage, fascinated me. The English houses had taken ecumenism seriously, especially with the Church of England. I vividly recall going with Abbot Basil Hume to Selbey Cathedral for Vespers during my trip. It was Sunday, May 25. Selbey Cathedral had at one time been a monastic church. We went first to the Catholic parish where a week-long vigil had been taking place and processed with the parishioners through the streets to the Anglican Cathedral where they also had been celebrating a week-long vigil. Basil preached at that service.

Basil and I also talked much in those days about interfaith dialogue, and he encouraged me to work for more contacts with Eastern monasticism. He felt that contemplation was a universal phenomenon and agreed that it could be a new form of spiritual ecumenism.

There were many convents of enclosed Benedictine nuns as I now discovered to my surprise. Many of them had not had vocations for some time. I learned during that trip not to judge too quickly the mystery surrounding vocations. Based on purely human standards, some Benedictine monasteries throughout the world merited vocations but had none. They contained observant, happy, fulfilled women or men, but no youngsters knew about them and none applied. Other houses were more narrow-

minded and judgmental with an observance that exhibited external conformity; nonetheless, they seemed to succeed at recruitment. That the
number of incoming novices was the scale for calibrating the health of a
community struck me as a new form of materialism. Some monasteries, to
keep the numbers up, were not discriminating enough and ended up with
many problem cases. Often I felt the question of vocations depended, at
least for us Benedictines, on the vitality of the local church and the conditions of the sociological strata from which recruitment came.

*June: Visitation at Trier and visits to Münsterschwarzach and Beuron in Ger-
many.*

*July: Visits to several houses of Italy — conference at Maredsous in Belgium
on authority in monastic life — visitation at Mount Saviour and Weston in
U.S.A.*

*November: Visits to Le Bec-Hellouin in France and Sainte Marie in Paris —
visit to Saint-Lambert-des-Bois in the diocese of Versailles — canonical visitation at Le Bouveret in Switzerland.*

*December: Second trip to England for visit to some houses and Synod of Presi-
dents at Douai.*

*   *   *

1970

*January: Visit to all the monasteries of Sicily: thirteen of women and one of
men — the first abbot primate to do so.*

*March: Visits to Rosano and Sorrento in Italy, conservative but large commu-
nities of enclosed nuns with a higher level of education and instruction.*

*April 9–May 15: began trip that would take me to Brazil, Uruguay, Argentina,
the west coast of U.S.A. and Canada — clocked a total of 58 hours in the air —
flew in 21 different airplanes, from 707s to Piper Cubs — in addition, traveled
thousands of miles by trains, ferries, and cars — first part of trip: visit to monasteries of Brazil — stopped, first, at monastery in Rio de Janeiro founded
from Portugal at end of 16th century with its splendidly gilded baroque*

church from 1595 — situated majestically on promontory overlooking naval yard and Rio harbor — April 13 began trip of over 1000 kilometers, driven by abbot in small Volkswagen, to visit monasteries of nuns at Petropolis, Belo Horizonte, and Juiz-de-Fora — flight to Recife in northeast to visit monastery of Olinda, nuns of Nossa Senhora do Monte and the thriving Tutzing sisters from Germany — flew to Bahia to visit monks and nuns there — preached at Sunday Mass to large congregation in gigantic baroque church — April 29 flew down the coast to São Paulo, a monastery in the heart of the city that dates back to the late 16th century — visited nuns founded in 1911 from Stanbrook, England, origin of most of the monasteries of nuns in Brazil — flew by small plane to Curitiba and back to visit new foundations of sisters and monks there — by car to Piritiba and then by car to Vinhedo, monastery founded by St. Vincent — by car to visit nuns at Uberaba and then monks at Riberão Preto more in the interior — May 13 off by plane to Montevideo in Uruguay to visit new foundation of nuns from Argentina.

When I was abbot, St. Vincent took over in 1964 the monastery of Vinhedo some fifty miles inland from São Paulo, then a community consisting of only four German monks. That visit whetted my fascination for Brazil and Brazilian culture. Now, I had my first opportunity to travel to parts I had never seen before, especially the northeast, and to study with more leisure and intensity Brazilian monasticism and the transitions it was making. My first impression was of the vitality, openness, and youthfulness of the Brazilian monks and nuns. The newer foundations were full of young, eager, friendly faces. The nuns in particular exuded happiness. Although they held themselves to a more rigorous enclosure than the Benedictine sisters and staffed no schools, they were busy counseling people in the parlors, translating into Portuguese books and articles for publishing firms, taking care of guests, especially sisters from active communities seeking a place for a quiet retreat, and looking after the needs of the many poor who knocked on their doors.

I noted with satisfaction the competent leadership among both the monks and the nuns. Among those Beuronese monks who came to Brazil in the 1930s was Father Martin Michler. Through his work in the universities of Rio de Janeiro, he was able to attract to the Benedictine way of life a large group of very competent professional men, doctors, lawyers, teachers, and the like. Many of these men became monks and some were later elected abbots; some were named bishops. They brought with them a sophisticated approach to Brazilian culture and Catholicism. I could see that the monasteries under them were moving from the older Beuronese traditions they had accepted to newer Brazilian ways of doing things.

To this transition was added the *aggiornamento* demanded by the documents of Vatican II. In Brazil this updating had led to a special concern for the poor and the marginalized in society and the identification of the Church with them, one of the important Gospel imperatives that gave birth to liberation theology. Although the monasteries were very concerned about the problems of poverty in their localities and were seeking concrete solutions, they were less inclined to give in to the tendency to see material or economic advancement as the equivalent of spiritual progress.

At that time, there were many enlightened bishops in Brazil who were close to the people and also to the monks. For example, when I visited the monastery of Olinda in the northeast, in nearby Recife I gave a public conference sponsored by the men and women religious there. How well I recall that night! A powerful thunderstorm accompanied by slashing rains left pools of water all over the muddied streets. The bishop then was the diminutive, gentle, beloved, and charismatic, Dom Helder Câmara. He came alone by public bus to the conference, arrived a bit late, soaked from head to foot, eager to be a part of the discussion and to bring some encouragement to the religious. From that encounter and the long conversation we had the next day, we became friends, sharing many of the same ideals for church and society.

In addition to these older establishments, there were many new foundations in Brazil, begun either by Brazilian monks looking for a simpler life and seeking to be more embedded in the communities of the poor or by monasteries from other parts of the world with similar intent. The picture of monastic life in that period was a kaleidoscope of experiments. It was also a period of tension as these cultural tendencies sought confirmation in the texts and documents of Vatican Council II and especially how the Church should relate to the modern world and share in both its anxieties and joys. In Brazil women and men religious worked together at finding solutions. Without trying to diminish this thrust of being one with the poor, I attempted to keep the monks together in community so they would not be absorbed by the desire to find immediate solutions to all ills that would tear their communities apart.

During the following decades and under a new pontificate, the Church took a very strong position against liberation theology, first through cautionary official documents from the Congregation for the Doctrine of the Faith and censures of prominent liberation theologians, then with the appointment of new bishops who had publicly taken stands against liberation theology. Perhaps Vatican leaders were frightened by forces and tendencies proposing radical solutions that included violence. Rome seemed to accept and work with dictatorships in Central and South America, while having such a grave fear of socialist or populist tendencies. Ultimately new bishops were appointed who suppressed the enthusiasm for identification with the poor and stifled the thrust of human development that had been so much a part of liberation theology. Their fear — in so far as I could understand it — was that the Church was becoming too "democratic," too "grass-roots" in emphasizing an option for the poor, economic development, and lay leadership while neglecting the spiritual nature of the human person. These new ideas were seen as a threat to the Church's hierarchical nature. It has always saddened me that this effort to suppress liberation theology led to the de-vitalization of the Church, a lessening of its identification with the poor, and a withering of the zeal that had characterized the Brazilian Church in the years after the council.

May 15 to May 27: visit to five monasteries in Argentina — first, Buenos Aires — visited monastery of men in heart of city — celebrated Mass on feast of Pentecost with nuns of Santa Escolastica — what a powerhouse of extraordinary women! — by car to Los Toldos, foundation in 1948 from Einsiedeln in Switzerland — back to Buenos Aires and then train to Rosario and small Piper Cub to cross Parana river to visit monastery of Niño Dios, founded around 1900 — outstanding abbot and busy community — on by train to Tucuman to visit monastery of Siambón, and return to Buenos Aires by train.

In the Spanish-speaking countries of South America, unlike Brazil and the Portuguese colonies, the Benedictine monks did not arrive with the *conquistadores.* They have had the advantage of not carrying colonial baggage, such as large, imposing structures, and a history of clericalism. On the other hand, being recent, they find themselves adjusting to a culture that is itself in flux.

These new monasteries were no longer dependent on their founding European houses and yet were not fully inserted into the local culture. They seemed isolated and lacking in vision and direction. The clearest tension showed itself in their attitudes toward engagement in social and pastoral activity outside of the monastery. They had not yet found a balance between their prayer life and their outside commitments. What seemed to me to be their biggest asset was that the quality of leadership they had produced would lead them to solutions.

For the first time they talked to me about the possibility of forming, together with the monasteries of Chile, a new Benedictine Congregation. I pursued this idea with the European founding monasteries and the European congregations to which they belonged and eventually we were able to form the new Congregation of Cono-Sur, with its own structure and leadership.

May 27: Long flight from Buenos Aires to Los Angeles and on to Portland, Oregon, for dedication of impressive new library at Mount Angel Abbey designed by Alton Aavar — on to Olympia, Washington, to St. Martin's Abbey — by car and boat to Island of Victoria in Canada for visit to Benedictine sisters — by car and ferry to Vancouver and monastery of Westminster.

June 5-14: flight to Pittsburgh and visit to my own monastery of Saint Vincent — dedication of spectacular new monastery and church at St. Procopius Abbey in Lisle, Illinois — back to Rome, Italy.

July 19 to August 18: flew from Milan to Warsaw — spent almost a month in Poland — visited two houses of monks, Tyniec and Lubin, 16 monasteries of enclosed Benedictine nuns and three congregations of Benedictine sisters — traveled some 2,500 miles by car (a Polish Fiat) all over Poland to visit these houses — celebrated conventual Mass at Tyniec on feast of Assumption — took train on August 16 to Vienna, Austria — visit with Cardinal König — train to Venice, Italy, for short stay with monks on island of San Giorgio — return by train to Rome.

A trip to Poland meant a visit to Cardinal Stephan Wyszinski, which was always a great delight. He was truly a prince of the Church: the primate of Poland who acted with that conception of his role. He told me Pope Pius XII had given verbal permission for him to make necessary decisions for the Church in Poland without constantly referring matters to the curia. He believed that all the Polish bishops had to be of one mind so that no disagreement could be used by the government for its advantage. I am sure he felt that democratic processes at that time would be a weakness when unity was absolutely necessary.

On the other hand, he was always kind and open with me. Difficulties were not hidden. I came to see him as an astute analyst of the situation in which he found himself and perceived clearly the power and support he received from the Polish faithful. He knew how much pressure to put on the government and when to keep silent. I also visited the young cardinal of Krakow, Karol Wojtyła; our monastery of Tyniec was in his diocese. He was more difficult to read than the primate. He seemed always to speak in questions and kept his cards close to his vest. When the conversation was over, I had no idea where he stood on any issue. But I learned from the monks that he was much esteemed by the intellectual community.

August to November: visited several monasteries in Italy: Montevergine outside of Naples; Faenza (Camaldolese and Vallombrosian nuns); monks of Praglia and Padua: nuns on Via Belotti in Milan.

December 8-9: Einsiedeln in Switzerland for burial of Cardinal Gut.

In September of 1970 the abbots of the world returned to Sant'Anselmo for the Congress of Abbots. This meeting was very relaxed and there was little material to be voted on. It was also our first meeting with simultaneous translation. Formerly, when the discussion on the floor had to be in Latin, only a few abbots spoke. I found that, by moving to simultaneous translation into five languages, all could express themselves with more assurance and accuracy. Having spent so much time traveling, I now knew every abbot by name, a fact that facilitated chairing the meeting. The most important talk was given by Cardinal Jan Willebrands of the Secretariat for Christian Unity. The emphasis he and the whole congress gave to the specific role of monasticism in ecumenical endeavors was significant. The spirit was good.

*　　　*　　　*

1971

January 3 to 16: Second trip to England — Ealing Abbey in London — Stanbrook Abbey of nuns in Worchester — Ampleforth for lectures — nuns of Holme-Eden — Scotland: Fort Augustus on Loch Ness, Pluscarden way in the north, and the priory of Carlekemp — visit to Olivetan monks and sisters at Cockfosters in London.

April 16: Back to England for meeting of "Free Association of Benedictine Nuns of British Isles and Ireland" at Grayshoot — then to France for meeting of abbesses of France at monastery of Juarre — meeting in Paris of A.I.M. — a few spiritually refreshing days at Solesmes (monks) and Sainte Cecile (nuns) nearby — then on April 29 at Maria Laach in Germany for meetings of German-speaking abbesses.

May 30 to July 5: first trip to Western Africa — to Paris, France, for briefing — flight May 31 to Dakar, Senegal — met at airport by Father Omer Bauer, monk of monastery in Yaoudé who had spent over 20 years in Africa — monasteries visited were — Senegal: Keur-Moussa (monks founded in 1961) and Keur-Guillaye (nuns founded in 1966) — Burkina Faso, formerly Upper Volta: Koubri, men's monastery (founded 1962) and women's (founded 1962) — Ivory Coast: Bouaké, monastery of monks (founded 1960) and nuns (founded 1962) — Togo: Dzogbegan, men's monastery (founded 1961) and women's (founded 1963) — Benin, formerly Dahomey: convent of sisters at Toffo (founded 1965) and monastery of men (founded 1963) — Cameroon: priory of sisters at Bamete (founded in Otele in 1938, moved in 1961) and monastery of men at Yaoundé (founded in 1932 and moved to capital in 1964) — Congo-Brazzaville: monastery of monks at La Bouenza (founded 1958).

This was the first of three extensive trips I made to Africa where I fell in love with the continent and its monasteries. Almost all the foundations were recent and all made from different monasteries in France. It was like visiting with adolescents and wondering how they would grow up and what they would look like in ten or twenty years. One fact was evident at once: the founding monasteries had made significant sacrifices by sending some of their finest monks and nuns to these missions, especially as superiors.

Naturally my instincts were attuned to any inculturation that was taking place. Then it was called "Africanization." Of course, it was happening all around me but in ways I had not expected. The monks there were closer in spirit, thought, and traditions to the time when the Rule of Benedict was written. Many were recent converts to Catholicism, zealous, and not afraid of sacrifice. Their way of life was simple and not characterized by our Western consumerism. Life in community was taken for granted, a mirror of the extended families in which they grew up. Living in dormitories was no novelty; they would not have understood having a room of their own. They certainly were not afraid of manual labor but, because of the heat, did not overdo it. The role of abbot resembled their traditional concept of the chieftain of a tribe. In general, I found them open and less complex in their approach to monastic life.

Monastic poverty — everything being held in common — was no problem, but not being able to beget children and have a family was, of course, foreign to their cultures. It was not easy for them to speak about such matters with me, especially the nuns. Because of the subservient role women played in most of these societies, intellectual and spiritual formation seemed a new challenge to them. But I insisted that receiving a good intellectual and spiritual formation, for women as well as men, had to be a priority. Their previous schooling before entering the monasteries had been minimal. In some areas their grasp of Catholicism consisted in catechetical recitations with little understanding. Often the Catholic tradition was seen more as external rites than as interiorized, lived expressions of the faith.

At the *palavras,* or informal meetings, in the evening as we gathered around the fire or under the thatched roofed pagodas, they posed questions of a nature different from the ones I usually heard in European and American monasteries. They asked where they should be buried, at the monastery or with their families and clans. They asked what gifts they could give guests — a traditional obligation — without breaking their vows of poverty. I was sometimes surprised how frequently they asked about personal prayer, finding liturgy and communal prayer easier to understand. Religion had not become privatized for them as in the West. Another of their questions, especially if the French founders were not present, might be: Why do we have to learn so much about the history of France or the greatness of French philosophers if we are to become monks? Some also asked if it might be possible sometime to meet with other African monks like themselves and not just with the French founders. They felt a need for such solidarity and for exchanging experiences of monastic life in Africa.

All the monasteries were involved in inculturating local African traditions into their prayer life, especially the monastery of Keur-Moussa, where the monks had introduced native instruments, like the balaphone, tom-toms, and especially the stringed kora. In Koubri in Burkina Faso, I heard for the first time at Mass an old musician play the *arc musicale,* as they called it, a bow with a single string that vibrated on the lips of the player, forming visible calluses and creating an ethereal sound with very little volume and sustaining quality. The nuns were making their own adjustments. For example, if there were any grilles, they had become symbolic, perhaps, made of bamboo. In both the men's monasteries and those of women, hospitality was a given and reflected the African care for guests.

The aspect of their lives that seemed to be the most pressing, however, was the basic one of earning a living. Because of the severe climate, hard work did not always produce much. At the monastery of Koubri, a community situated in one of the poorest areas I saw in all Africa, during a *palavra* a monk asked if I thought their standard of living was too high compared to the lives of the villagers who lived near them. I answered that they should not give up the well they had dug for water or their agricultural insights but share them with the villagers, seeing that they too could have wells and not have to walk miles to get water at the common spring. They had difficulty in thinking beyond immediate needs and did little to save for the future. But in all of these circumstances, I felt as if I were living in the time of Benedict in the sixth century when the monasteries were centers of agriculture and learning as well.

There are specific moments and images from this trip I will never forget: tasting guava ice-cream for the first time; hearing the old codger play the *arc musicale;* the prodigious memories of the cantors and catechists in translating my homilies from French to the native language; the stories told around the fire by the elders at the *palavras;* the many gifts — especially eggs — from the villagers whenever I visited them; the patterns of scars on the faces of some of the monks, indicating the tribe they came from, especially the Mossi; the refectory at Koubri where the places at table were the tops of old school desks, the ink-hole enlarged for the water-glass, the pencil trough used for the silverware; the sweet root beer they made there; the fine, delicate architecture of Bouaké; the yogurt some of the monasteries made; the many dispensaries, each monastery having one, and the long lines of people waiting there for assistance; the beautifully constructed monastery at Dzogbegan in Togo on a plateau that seemed to have a perfect climate and where everything seemed to grow well; the flight from Abijan to Lomé when, right after take-off, an engine was on fire and we had to make an emergency landing; the elegantly dressed women Oblates at Lomé and their dancing and singing of entire psalms by heart; the train ride from Brazzaville to La Bouenza (five hours to go 150 miles); and on and on.

I ended this visit at La Bouenza by going to one of the villages for the first Mass of a newly ordained monk, the first in the history of this monastic community. At dusk of the evening before the ordination, people began to gather from all the surrounding villages. Some oldsters slept on the benches in the church, but most quietly prayed and danced around several fires that had been lit, sharing food and song. The Mass began the next morning when the bishop arrived. To the delight of the large crowd, I had the honor of presenting the candidate for ordination to the bishop in the local dialect called Benbe, having memorized what one of the monks wrote out for me. The liturgy was full of singing, with drums and rhythmic accompaniment, much swaying and occasional dances. Giving out Communion, I noticed how the rows of recipients kept time with the music, swaying and articulating the beat with their bodies as they sang. Most received Eucharist in the hand, often audibly slurping as they lapped up the host.

As I flew back from Congo Brazzaville the next day to Paris, my mind was full of contrasting images. I wondered what would become of these monasteries. It was clear that their cultures were changing rapidly. The image that stuck in my mind was one from Koubri in Burkina Faso: I watched a young man come out of the savanna, no clothes on, but with a transistor to his ear as he listened to the Beatles' latest recording. What would Africanization be like in the future? How many of these monasteries would find support to continue to grow and flourish and be independent from Europe? What would they begin to look like when the French founders died and the monasteries had only indigenous monks? I had a thousand questions, but I was at peace.

*   *   *

August-November: Visit to the two monasteries of Ireland; visit to my home abbey of St. Vincent followed by a retreat for the Sisters at Ferdinand, Indiana; visit to Montserrat in Spain for meeting of the presidents of all the Congregations to prepare for next Congress of Abbots — visited Father Arrupe at Manresa.

November 18 to December 22: Second trip to Africa — joined by Abbot Ghesquière for flight to Cotonou in Benin — took a DC3 to Parakou for meeting of superiors of monasteries of French-speaking West Africa, Benedictine and Cistercian, with one native monk from each house — warm reunion with these monks I came to love and respect — then flight to Nigeria to see Sister Mary Charles, a native Nigerian founder of a contemplative Benedictine convent — on to Kinshasa in Democratic Republic of the Congo (then called Zaire) — informative meetings with Cardinal Malula and Bishop Tshibangu — then flight to Lubumbashi in Katanga (Shaba) region in South East where the Benedictines have been active for over 60 years — visited monastery of

Sainte Marie de la Source at Kiswishi — visits to missions of Fugurume, Kansenya, and Kapolowe, all constructed on same lines: group of Benedictine monks to do the pastoral ministry, Benedictine sisters and lay people — especially married couples — from Belgium and Congo working side by side with the priests, especially skilled in catechetical, agricultural, and healthcare needs — visited convent at Likasi of Benedictine sisters, almost all native, engaged in educational endeavors — visited sisters at Emmaus who have home for widows — on November 11 flew on DC4 to Goma, still in the Congo, traveled along Lake Kivu and then on by car to Rwanda to monastery of sisters at Kigufi on Rwanda side of the lake — drive to our house at Gihindamuyaga outside of Butaré (founded 1958) through thickly populated regions, one small hill after another, all unpaved, gravel roads lined with lush, dense, green foliage — visited the nuns at Sovu, already an independent monastery of mixed Belgiums and natives — day at Kigale where a group of Benedictines and Taizé monks form a single community — flight to Entebbe-Kampala, Uganda, to visit nuns in Tororo founded in 1960 from Holland — flew back to Rome, Italy, on December 22.

The work done by the Belgium Benedictines in the province of Shaba in the Democratic Republic of the Congo, because of their persistent energy and missionary zeal during those sixty years, was visible everywhere. When they first arrived, they did not set out to establish monasteries but to create centers of missionary activity. Thus, the monasteries were relatively new and resembled those founded from France in West Africa. It was not clear to me what the future would be like for the missionary activity as they handed over this work to the native clergy being formed. The monasteries I felt sure would continue.

I was impressed by some of the older missionaries who were truly rugged individualists with remarkable courage. Sister Gregory, a strongly built and weather-beaten, middle-aged sister was a fine example. I did not know how much medical training she had, but she made regular trips into the hills on her motorbike laden with all kinds of medical supplies for minor operations and midwifery. She carried sweets for the kids, clothing of many sorts, and, of course, catechetical material. In talking with her, I found she was one of the best informed persons I had met in the missions, reading everything in sight, with an insatiable curiosity about the world and Benedictine affairs. Such colorful, old-time missionaries I noticed were disappearing.

One day the native monks in the community of Kiswishi asked if they could spend some time alone with me. They took me swimming in an abandoned tin mine a few miles away. In typical African fashion, at dusk they built a fire, cooked something to eat, and then began a *palavra*. Stories were told and finally the issue became clear to me. They realized that soon they would have to elect a native superior, but the one they wanted, an African from the local tribe, was not a priest. I had met him often and knew whom they meant, even though they did not name names. They had been told that Rome would not approve of such an election if the community also had priest members. I admitted that this was the rule, but that I would fight for an exception if such an election took place. Later, this wise brother was elected by the community and, after much debate with the officials of the Congregation for Religious, an exception was made and permission was granted for him to be the monastery's superior.

*   *   *

1972

February 6–March 12: visitation at Sankt Matthias, Trier, in Germany; visits to monasteries of Northwest Germany: monasteries of monks at Gerleve, Nütshau, Meschede, Siegburg, Kornelimünster, and Tholey — monasteries of nuns at Hamicolt, Osnabrück, Dinklage, Vinnenberg, Holzheim-Kreitz, Herstelle, Bonn-Endenich, Köln-Raderberg, and Steinfeld — visit to sisters at Marienfried.

Northwest Germany, Münsterland, Sauerland, and the Saar, had about 3,700 Benedictine men and women. I was amazed at the variety of monastic expressions, with older and vital solid traditions, many with remarkable recruitment. The monasteries of nuns were especially impressive. I suppose that the Benedictine Order does not have many monasteries with the quality that one finds, for example, at Herstelle, where famous Benedictine liturgists like Odo Casel had been chaplains for many years. On that tour I received more than I gave.

April 9 to June 2: my third trip to Africa, including South Africa, Madagascar, Tanzania, and Kenya — flew through the night from Rome to Johannesburg in South Africa — taken by car to Pietersburg where the abbot is a bishop and most of the priests of the diocese are from the Flemish monasteries of Belgium — moved on to monastery of Inkamana founded by monks of Ottilien Congre-

gation and Nongoma hospital staffed by Benedictine sisters of Tutzing — visited Benedictine sisters (all natives) at Twasana and the Sisters of Saint Alban — then on to monks at Eshowe in the Zulu area — bishop of Eshowe also Benedictine — met the chief of the Zulus, Gatsha Buthelezi — went on to Durban for a visit to Archbishop Hurley and then flew on to Madagascar.

There was a similarity between the work done by the French-speaking Belgium monks and nuns in the Congo and that done by the Belgium Flemish monks here in northern South Africa. In South Africa many knotty political problems had to be faced under apartheid. Some of the younger and less compromising German monks were thrown out of the country for their attitudes, and attempts to form integrated monasteries lagged. Their patience through those difficult times has born fruit.

This was my first visit to missions established by the Ottilien Benedictines. Since they had a long tradition of missionary work, they were adept at creating large, significant institutions. Everywhere I went I noticed how many sacrifices, in both material contributions and personnel, the founding monasteries made. For the first time, I saw how important the brothers, not just the priests, were to their missions; their skills were indispensable for the well-being of the large monasteries and for the maintenance of the parish structures. I could see that all these monks were going to leave to the native clergy in the parishes well constructed, functional buildings. Again, I saw the strength and energy of the Tutzing sisters who created well-organized medical and educational facilities wherever the monks went.

April 18: on to Madagascar — visit to monks at Mahitsy, high above sea level back in the hills, founded in 1955 — visited by small plane sisters in Manajary at other side of the island — hot tropical climate — visit to large monastery (40 natives) of Benedictine sisters at Ambrosistra — well inserted into life of local church.

The culture of Madagascar came as a surprise to me. It had traces of Africa but still seemed to possess Indonesian traits. What pleased me most were the musical instincts of the monks and faithful. Without realizing the complexities of what they were doing, they sang all the time in harmony, resembling a Russian choir. As a result, the Office and Mass were excellent. The monastery of women, founded in 1934 from Vanves, Paris, was already highly developed, with an exceptional superior, Mother Bénigne Moreau.

May 5 to 30: visit to monasteries and missionaries in Tanzania — from Dar-es-Salaam flew to Mtawara on southern coast of country to visit monastery of Ndanda and the Benedictine abbot/bishop of the region, Bishop Viktor Hälg, O.S.B. — trip by car (13 hours) to monastery of Peramiho — Abbot/Bishop Eberhard Spiess, O.S.B. in hospital at Litembo and visited him there — visited monastery of Hanga — Office in Kiswahili — visited native Benedictine sisters of Chipole (85 in final vows and 110 in temporary profession) — visited monastery of monks at Uwemba in diocese of Njombe and Tutzing sisters there — nuns at St. John's Corner — and back by car through Mikumi Park to Dar-es-Saalam.

For this part of the trip I had a fine and instructive companion in Father Siegfrid Hertlein. It was still the rainy season and the mud roads were like glass. Both Ndanda and Peramiho were large, like medieval cities, with many buildings and workshops. When I was there, the monks were struggling with the desire of the government to nationalize the schools and healthcare centers that formed a part of the whole complex. At Peramiho I celebrated Mass on the feast of Pentecost. The monks ran an impressive seminary that has produced many priests for the region.

For the first time I heard many discussions about the influence of Muslim religious practices and the tension between them and Catholics. It was a problem that would continue to vex the missionaries in Africa in some regions for years to come. It was not easy to talk about the interfaith attitude of the bishops at Vatican II since the monks and sisters felt in the minority and that it was not a level playing-field. Catholicism seemed still to be a Western and colonial importation that had not adapted to the native culture.

It was not easy for the old German missionaries to remain on in parishes they had established as assistants to native pastors, but many were doing so. These transition periods made it all the more urgent to establish native Benedictine houses to continue the work, and I was pleased to see that this was being done and that they were most successful. In the Catalog of the Confederation of 2000, e.g., Hanga, the native monastery, is listed as having 133 monks after having made several foundations!

May 30–June 2: flight from Dar-es-Salaam to Nairobi in Kenya — visit to three Swiss Benedictine monks beginning a new mission in the Kerio valley — lived for a few days in a tent, got to know the surrounding tribes, saw the monks trying to learn two new languages from Kiswahili — later monastery moved to more populous region near Nairobi.

Without much time for repose, on arrival back in Rome, I began to prepare for one of the longest trips I was to make as primate.

July 20 to September 8: trip to Brazil, Chile, Peru, Colombia, Venezuela, Trinidad, Martinique and United States: — meeting in Rio de Janeiro, Brazil, of all the superiors of the Brazilian and Spanish-speaking houses, full of tensions over the role of monks and social justice, between sisters and nuns, between native Benedictines and European and American superiors: a microcosm of the tensions in the Church there — longer stay at Vinhedo with monks of my own monastery — August 11 flew to Chile to visit Las Condes — to Peru for visit in Lima to monks at Ñaña — and then to Colombia from August 17 to 25 for visits to the recent foundations of Benedictine men and women in Bogota, Usme and El Rosal — a visit to the beautiful city of Medellín and the monks there — flight on August 25 to Venezuela for visit to monastery founded in 1923 by Ottilien Congregation in Caracas and school at Maracay — August 29 flight to Trinidad to visit monastery at Tunapuna — August 30 to Martinique, one of my favorite little monasteries in the Caribbean — September 3 to St. Vincent in U.S.A. before returning to Rome.

September 11 to 18: Synod of Presidents in Admont, Austria.

September 19: Trip to Israel for visitation at Dormition and visit to Tantur.

October 13 to 19: Meeting at Maredsous in Belgium and visit to sisters at Loppem and Maredret.

November: visits to several convents in Italy.

*　　　*　　　*

1973

January 8 to March 8: long trip to U.S.A. to visit a number of houses: Mount Saviour (visitation); Weston (visitation); St. Anselm, Manchester, N.H.; in California, Woodside in Portola Valley, Big Sur, Valyermo, Glenora (sisters), Oceanside, San Diego (sisters); Pecos and Christ of the Desert, in New Mexico; Dallas (sisters), Texas; St. Benedict and Covington (sisters), Louisiana; Jonesboro (sisters), Arkansas; New Subiaco and Fort Smith (sisters), Arkansas; Kansas City (sisters), Kansas; Atchison, Kansas to visit sisters and monks;

Conception Abbey and Clyde (sisters) in Missouri; Marmion Abbey and St. Procopius in Illinois — back to Rome, Italy.

March 19 to September 1: Visits in many countries of Europe: March 19: Hungary for the blessing of the new archabbot of Pannonhalma, Andrew Szennay — visited also Győr; Austria: Schottenstift in Vienna, Münsterschwarzach in Germany; Subiaco, Genoa, Vallimbrosa, and Livorno in Italy; Paris, Saint-Lambert-des-Bois, Limon, La Pierre-qui-Vire in France; Le Bouveret, Disentis, Curaglia, Altdorf, Seedorf and Sarnen in Switzerland.

The extensive trip at the beginning of the year to the United States meant I had to be away for a even a longer period of time. It was not as strenuous as many of the others since I was familiar with the culture, especially the food. I found the American Benedictine houses very much alive and not yet feeling the diminishing number of vocations that other religious orders were beginning to notice.

These many trips were exhausting but satisfying. They provided a living picture of what was happening in monasteries all over the world as they struggled to implement the Second Vatican Council's admonition to let biblical roots and the charism of their founders inspire them again as they made the adaptations needed to be effective in the contemporary world. Now I knew the abbot of almost every monastery by name and understood the local struggles he had to face. The abbots had asked me to do this traveling for that very purpose and their wisdom was bearing fruit. The visits also acted as a perfect preparation for the coming Congress of Abbots planned for September 1973 in Rome.

CHAPTER 9

Applying the Wisdom Learned

(1973-1976)

Although I thought I had done as primate what the abbots wished of me, some clouds began to appear on the horizon during the months before September 1973. The presidents of the Benedictine congregations had met with me the year before in Admont, Austria, to examine the agenda. At that meeting Abbot Kolomon, president of the Austrian Congregation, came to see me and inquired whether there was any truth to the rumor that, if re-elected, I would not accept to continue on as primate. He wanted me to know the Austrian abbots would be very disappointed if I would not accept. Then Abbot Brasó came to tell me that he thought, out of friendship, I should know that I would probably not be re-elected primate. The German-speaking abbots, he asserted, were upset with the way I managed Sant'Anselmo. In January 1973 when I was traveling in the States, Father Paul Gordan, secretary of the confederation, after a trip to Germany, wrote me that some German abbots were opposed to my re-election, and reported that "Sie werden abermals gegen B[rasó] eintreten müssen" (You will have to once again stand against Brasó).

Through the following months, I heard rumors from members of the curia that Abbot Brasó and Archbishop Mayer were saying openly in the Vatican that I would not be re-elected. This was confirmed by several incidents. An official working on the revision of the Code of Canon Law asked to see me about a matter touching on the confederation but then he later called to say he had better take up the matter with my successor since the discussion could be protracted into the following year. Then in April, on the feast of St. Anselm, patron of the school, the guest at the monastic dinner was Cardinal Gabriel-Marie Garonne, prefect of the Congregation for Education and Seminaries. After the meal I invited a group up to my room for coffee and asked him to join us. He had never seen the primate's quarters and marveled at the view. Then he nonchalantly said to me: "How you will miss this when September comes and you will not be living anymore in these quarters!" Finally I went to Monsignor Monduzzi of the Papal Household to make arrangements for the usual papal audience during the congress. Monduzzi said of course there would be an audience, but the Holy Father thought it would be best to hold it after the election of my successor so that the new man could be presented to him.

Already sensing that Brasó's "friendly" information may have had some truth in it, I decided when in the States in March to talk to Archabbot Egbert Donovan, my successor as abbot of St. Vincent, about the situation. I repeated the rumors that I might not be re-elected circulating in Rome. I added the confederation might want to move in a direction to which I was opposed; in conscience I could not then accept to be its leader. He understood. We discussed the possibilities: I was interested in the priory that we had established on the campus of Penn State University, it would be a place where I could do good work and be happy. I also expressed an interest in St. Vincent's foundation in Brazil. He listened and then said that if I were not re-elected or did not want to accept a re-election, he would certainly help me make a decision about my future and the work I would do. It would be a positive choice and I should have no worries. With that, I simply left it all in God's hands — and the abbot's — and moved ahead in the preparations for the congress with inner peace.

The theme selected for discussion among the abbots was "The Experience of God," and though there was some fear that it was too theoretical, in the end it appeared to be a specifically monastic theme that could be beneficial to all and not divisive. From my many travels I had come to see that the abbots had much to share with one other about what Vatican Council II meant to their local communities. They were not interested in themes that would just bring more agitation; a more deeply spiritual theme seemed just right. I was pleased to see how much the abbots were imbued with the theology of Vatican II concerning the action of the Holy Spirit in the community and in each member; certainly it was not a discussion that could have occurred before. Many spoke of the gift of prophecy as typical of the monastic vocation; several abbots nuanced this understanding by adding to prophecy the gift of wisdom, also a part of the monastic heritage. In fact, the Rule of Benedict is permeated with more quotes from the Wisdom literature of the Old Testament than from any other section.

On a more practical level, the abbots, to my satisfaction, voted to simplify the administration of San'Anselmo, the school and monastery, by reducing the number of councils and committees. Finally, with my positive encouragement, they voted to meet every four years in the future since every three years seemed too frequent. The urgency of the post-conciliar years had disappeared, and more time was required to prepare adequately for each congress. Since the abbots would be meeting only every four years, a new person would be elected primate for eight years with the possibility of being re-elected for any number of four-year terms.

When the time for the election of the primate came, the abbot of Montecassino, according to an old tradition, presided. On the first and only ballot I was re-elected for a term of four years by a vote of 180 to 30. Among the thirty there were sixteen votes for Abbot Brasó and fourteen for other candidates. A few days later, we were received by Pope Paul VI. He set aside his prepared talk at the beginning to say how pleased he was that the abbots had re-elected Abbot Rembert and by such a large margin. It was a sign, he felt, that the renewal we were engaged in had the confidence of the body and showed a clear unanimity of direction. Word spread rapidly through the curia that I had not only been re-elected, but that I enjoyed Pope Paul's public support. Mayer and Brasó had been wrong. I admit that I smiled on the inside.

My last four years as primate in Rome passed rapidly, and I seemed to be learning how to navigate the Vatican's complicated maze of offices and people. In addition to the visible support my re-election gave me among Benedictines, the public commendation by Pope Paul made life in Rome easier. Word was on the street that it was better to give Weakland what he wanted or he would go to Pope Paul and get it anyway. I tried not to abuse that privilege.

Many changes of personnel at Sant'Anselmo lightened the burden for me. In 1974 Father Ambrose Watelet, prior of the house, asked to be relieved of his duties to return to the community of Maredsous in Belgium where he was much needed. I coaxed Abbot Basil Hume of Ampleforth to release one of his monks, Dom Dominic Milroy, to be prior. Although Dominic had not studied in Rome, he was a gifted linguist with a winning personality and was well suited to run an international college. He did so in the thoughtful, laid-back style that the English possess in abundance.

In March of 1974 Father Cyprian Vagaggini, one of my former professors whom I had invited back to Sant'Anselmo to teach, was elected the
school's rector. The Congregation for Education and Seminaries asked
each Pontifical University in Rome to offer a distinct specialization and
not to compete with one another. In addition to the Monastic Institute
that served primarily the confederation, it was immediately obvious to the
Academic Senate of Sant'Anselmo that the Liturgy Institute would be emphasized as the most logical specialization. Under Cyprian's guidance and
persuasion, the senate also chose to add a specialization in Sacramentol-
ogy, the history and theology of the sacraments, to complement liturgy.
These specializations were determined in March of 1975 and gave the
school a clear direction and a unique contribution into the next century.

Since I did not have to worry much about the monastery and college of
Sant'Anselmo, I continued in earnest my travels. My only additional trip to
Asia was scheduled for immediately after the abbots' congress of 1973. This
second meeting took place in Bangalore, India, and assumed a different
format from the previous one in Bangkok five years before. It was much
more a dialogue between Eastern and Western monasticism with a good
representation of members of Eastern religions, including Buddhists, Hin-
dus, Jains, and Sufis.

It was at that meeting that I realized how many of the Eastern traditions had a resemblance to historical Western practices of mysticism and
contemplation and how important and fruitful such contacts could be. I
knew that some day we would have to probe more deeply our differences,
but it was still too early. My deepest hesitation at that time centered on a
lack of clarity on the aim or ultimate goal of Eastern practices. Were they a
way of evading the stresses and tensions necessary for human social relationships? Would they make this world a better place in which to live? I
guess I was too Christian and Benedictine in my spirituality with such a
strong emphasis on scripture, liturgy, and social outreach to give myself
over totally to most of these Eastern traditions.

During these next four years I returned twice to Hungary and made a
second trip to Poland. Visiting monasteries in France, Italy, Germany, England, and the United States took up a great deal of time as I came to know
many of the communities of men and women I had not been able to visit
earlier. I also made my first trip to the French-speaking sector of Canada,
namely to the monks of Saint-Benoit-du-Lac and the nuns at Mont-
Laurier and Sainte-Marie des Deux-Montagnes. I completed my tour of the

houses of Italy by including the monasteries hidden away in the interior of Sardinia, and even spent some time with a very isolated monastery of nuns in Corsica.

To complete the visits to the communities of Central America and the Caribbean, I made a long trip to Mexico, Belice, Guatemala, Puerto Rico, the Bahamas, and St. Lucia, returning for a lengthy visit in Trinidad. I spent more time in Yugoslavia, especially with the eight convents of nuns on the many islands dotting the Adriatic coast. More systematically than in previous trips, I spent time in all the houses of Benedictines in Belgium, both the Flemish- and the French-speaking ones, fourteen of women and seven of men.

Only in the summer of 1977 did I travel to Holland and come to know our monasteries there. There were four communities of men and seven of nuns in Holland. The general ferment in the Church had affected them, although we had never been as numerous there as in other parts of Europe. Before the council, all four monasteries of had been a part of the Solesmes Congregation. In 1969 three of them, Oosterhout, Egmond, and Slangenburg, formed a congregation of their own, the Congregation of the Netherlands. The monastery of Vaals, which had attracted many of the more traditional elements from the other three monasteries, decided to remain in the Solesmes Congregation. In this way there was relative peace in the monasteries, but I was not sure that all of them could survive the decline of vocations that had begun in that country.

During the first six years as primate I had made many trips to Montserrat in Spain but I had not made a systematic tour of the Spanish monasteries; now I made two trips. The first took me to the Catalan region and Majorca, the second to the rest of Spain where the Benedictines are represented by six monasteries of men and fifteen of women, including some very impressive communities.

Invitations to give conferences and talks to monasteries around the world multiplied. I wanted especially to accept those that came from meetings of Benedictine nuns. One of my dreams came true in September of 1976 when all the abbesses of Italy came to Sant'Anselmo for a week of meetings. They faced the rigors of living at Sant'Anselmo with good will and playfulness, although the buildings had been constructed for student-living, with bathrooms at the end of the halls and no elevators to the various floors. The showers were centralized in a separate building. The planning committee of nuns asked me to buy ninety-five bidets, one for each room, and I did!

Pope Paul VI greeted the nuns with graciousness when I presented them in a special audience. His talk reinforced all that I had been trying to do for them. One does not solve all the problems of *aggiornamento* in a week-long meeting, but giant steps were made toward helping them come to know one another, recognize leadership qualities among themselves, and face the future optimistically.

*   *   *

How did all this traveling and the pressures of working in Rome affect me personally? During the lengthy travels, but especially after them, an increasing depression set in. Because I was more fatigued than usual, I assumed this was natural. Perhaps I should have seen it for what it was, a profound loneliness. Among my papers from that time I found a poem I had written, an attempt, even if somewhat awkward, to describe my feeling. I called it *Aequalis Omnibus Caritas: On a Banner of Silver Flames* from the motto on my coat of arms.

Lord, I cannot hear you:
My eardrums are taut — not slack, or loose,
    but they remain unresponsive.
My heart beats out its call, but no answer returns.
All has been sounded: nothing rings true.

My body vibrates in its tenseness,
    but sympathetic love responds no more.
I listened for your answer,
    but heard only my own echo.

You told me, God, through your Son,
That I would find you in those others,
But all I found was me,
    loud, blaring, oppressive me.
How can they respond to my call?
Can they fill this void?

You have placed me in an echo chamber.
There is no escape,
You created in me a need for response

195

and failed to nurture that need.
You created others like me:
   each with his own tune and timbre.
You told me to blend, to harmonize,
Not to smother or blur their tones.
It is too difficult a task, Lord.

Or are my musical images all wrong?
Let me put it this way:

On one hand, you created me on fire;
On the other, commanded me to consume not.
Since you will not take that fire from me,
Teach me to live enflamed;
To touch, not extinguish, the spark of that other,
Not to scorch or mar its source.

Lord, you are in that other's spark:
Lord, you are in those flames.

Loneliness was not something a monk spoke about except in the old terminology of the desert fathers, like being afflicted by "the noonday devil."
Monks, except perhaps hermits, did not talk about being lonely, as that
would reflect badly on the community and the quality of the monastic environment. I reconciled myself to the self-evident fact that everyone was,
at the deepest point of one's being, lonely, including married couples; one
had to tolerate that reality and "offer it up." Spiritual directors reiterated
that point to me.

But why, without denying that reality, had loneliness become such a
problem? I was already over forty and wanted to pass it off as a middle-age
crisis. Had I become a superior when I was too young, before having settled into a more mature personality? I knew that I had to be the servant of
all and not worry about myself. That would have seemed narcissistic, too
self-serving. I was willing to give my all to the tasks asked of me, only now
did I see that there was a toll to be paid. Had I adequately calculated the
cost?

I do not know if my secretaries noticed those moods. From my earliest
days as abbot I resolved that my relationship toward my priest-secretaries
would always remain strictly professional; I would never expect a secre-

tary to become a companion — and certainly not an intimate one. In Rome and in the States I noticed that some bishops expected their priest-secretaries to be a constant companion with no personal life of their own. These men needed their own circle of friends of their own age, their own vocations, their own avocations.

Since I saw myself as an intellectual, and was someone who lived in his head, I tended to downplay the importance of emotions. And as a religious superior, I thought I should not let emotions sway my decisions; it was important to keep cool and be somewhat detached. This seemed to me proper behavior, but perhaps it was not psychologically or even spiritually healthy. Furthermore, with my heavy traveling schedule, I did not have time to play the piano, which had always been a great emotional release for me.

My spiritual director spoke about having a stronger relationship with Jesus Christ, not just an intellectual one, but an existential one. There had been moments when such a relationship was very real to me — I have mentioned a few already — and I tried to keep these in mind, but I soon realized that a relationship with Jesus Christ, as intense as it might be on the spiritual level, could not fill the emptiness rising from the lack of the physical presence and reality of another human person. In fact, it may have contributed to my tendency to intellectualize everything. The spiritual did not adequately fill the empty hole I felt, and I was often left dry, as spiritual writers say, for days on end. I read what I could about spiritual dryness among the saints and their means of coping with it. But transposing their terminology into modern psychological terms did not provide any easy answers.

And so the void remained. Traveling so much from community to community and visiting many different cultures with the barriers they raised to personal communication and lasting friendships demanded their own human price. I came to realize I had to learn to deal with it in a positive way. But could I? I wrote to one of the St. Vincent monks that I was coming to realize that celibacy made sense only if it incorporated into one's consciousness the most important act of all — dying. Then, human relationships ceased to be of meaning. One had crossed the barrier into a new life alone with Christ. No wonder the Eucharist was called the viaticum, the companion on the journey.

As I reflect back on that period of my life from the advantage point of almost forty years, I sense that I was going through personally what many other religious were sensing in that same period. It was not a change in moral theology, but rather an awareness of human sexuality that had been deeply suppressed in our training. After much pondering I cannot fully understand why that sexual awareness began to permeate the lives of so many religious and clergy in the church. Perhaps we saw many of our confreres leave the religious life or active ministry as priests and found ourselves faced with the realization that we too had to have stronger convictions about why we were staying. Previously we had not permitted ourselves to even think of the option of leaving, but the number of the good men and women we saw choosing to return to the lay life forced us to reflect. I wish now we had done more profound studies on why this exodus was taking place.

My training for a celibate life-commitment was, as I have already described, typical of the 1940s and 1950s. It focused on avoiding forbidden sexual acts and developing the necessary discipline. How those acts functioned within the whole psyche of the person was never broached. As in all religious orders, particular friendships were forbidden among Benedictines. This negative mandate, perhaps unintentionally, gave the impression that all friendships were dangerous and would lead to sin. No superior, spiritual director, or confessor ever talked about the phenomenon of falling in love, certainly not the inherent beauty of such feelings and their mysterious nature and origin. It would have been unthinkable for me to raise such issues to someone in authority, especially if they involved a same-sex relationship. For the first time in my adult life, at the age of forty-five, I was becoming acutely aware that I, too, was a sexual being. My consciousness of my own sexual orientation was gradually emerging. First of all, it had never occurred to me that I could be attractive to others; I had never seen myself as a sexually attractive being. And then, I would not have known how to deal with sexual attraction, especially if it was a same-sex attraction. Some spoke of "the third way," of seeking deep intimacy with another but remaining in religious life or in the priesthood. I found this unconvincing: it was an injustice to the other person, unrealistic, and a compromise of the deepest meanings of one's vow of celibacy. Taking the risk of being vulnerable in friendship would have been a new experience for me. It also became more evident to me that the celibate commitment was not one of avoiding evil, but of giving up what was enriching and good.

In studying the history of the Benedictine Order, writings on friendship, like those of St. Aelred of Rievaulx in the Middle Ages, were mentioned, but with little comment. The beauty of human relationships was never mentioned, only the dangers. Observing monks and nuns around the world as well as in the Sant'Anselmo community, I saw that many of them seemed to have resolved this dilemma and were living full and positive celibate lives. In contrast, I observed many monks and nuns who seemed like dried up old prunes; their celibacy may have been perfectly intact but their lives seemed a caricature of what God intended for human and spiritual development. Instinctively and without much in-depth analysis, I knew I did not want to grow old that way.

My travels brought me into contact with many sensitive and remarkable women, and I prized my friendship with them. Their presence was enlivening for me; for the first time I realized how unbalanced my life and circle of friends had become since graduate school, rich with so many different men and women. All of this made me more aware of the lack of the feminine dimension on the Roman scene and especially in the offices of the curia. My travels brought me into contact with women who had a depth of human and spiritual understanding that I had never encountered before.

I realized that I should have dealt with all these questions when I was a teenager, but to have done so, especially to have tried to work out same-sex relationships, would have been totally unheard of when I went through formation for religious life, indeed, unheard of in the culture at that time. Only now in my mid-forties could I come to terms with my basic orientation, admit it to myself, and then rethink what this meant to me. I never doubted my vocation or the significance of the vows I took; but now I had to see them in a new light, namely, not as the avoidance of sin and evil, but as a new way of living the gospel of love that Jesus Christ preached. I wanted to be a person who lived by love not fear.

I do not regret these late struggles with how to make the observance of celibacy a positive moment of spiritual and human growth. In a mysterious way, the effort made me a better superior: the complexity of the human person and the beauty of the human condition became clear to me in a new way. I ceased to be judgmental; I stopped categorizing people as good or evil. I saw the good in those struggling to find a balance in their lives but who did not always succeed. Good and evil, it was now clear, could be found in everyone. If not, then why the need for redemption and grace?

In all of this thinking and reflecting and struggling, there were categories that never came to my mind or my attention because I did not have to deal with them personally. No one spoke of people who have a sexual attraction to children and adolescents, or of the relationships between sex and power or sex and violence. These were not on the radar screen of church or society at that time. Even today, psychological studies have not found adequate explanations. Like many aspects of the human person, they remained obscure and unnamed and were never mentioned.

Perhaps the spiritual crisis I found myself in was more widespread among religious, even Benedictines, than I had imagined. In 1975, I was not surprised that the committee *De re monastica,* set up to prepare the Congress of Abbots of 1977 and chaired by Abbot Basil Hume of Ampleforth, proposed that the theme for that congress be "sexuality and spirituality." The presidents debated this suggestion and agreed unanimously, provided, they said, it would be presented in a positive fashion. They, too, were seeking ways of integrating sexuality and spirituality and of discovering the implications of seeing sexuality as a positive aspect of the human person. I looked forward to the papers that committee would prepare, and then the discussion among the abbots in 1977.

*   *   *

At the Congress of Abbots in 1973 the abbots again pressed me to keep open the liturgical privileges the monasteries then enjoyed, each congregation having obtained from the Consilium, or later from the Congregation for Worship, what they felt helpful to their members. But I knew that members of the curia wanted to close that door and bring about a greater uniformity. Earlier I mentioned that in September of 1971 Pope Paul had appointed Abbot Augustin Mayer secretary in the Congregation of Religious, making him the second in command to Cardinal Antoniutti. The pope had a distinctive way of maintaining equilibrium among the various theological groups evident during and after the council. His strategy surprised me at first. In the same curial congregation, he would often appoint contrasting personalities to the positions of prefect and secretary. Or he would name as successor to a departing official a person with a differing point of view. In this way he kept representatives of the various currents in constant contact and dialogue — or, more often, in tension. But the appointment of Mayer was an exception: he was definitely of the same mindset as Cardinal Antoniutti, which seemed strange to me. Two years later, in 1973, Cardinal Antoniutti having reached the age of retirement, seventy-five, dutifully wrote his letter of resignation, expecting, it was rumored, that it would not be accepted. But it was.

Mayer took advantage of this interim before a successor was appointed to push his liturgical agenda. In February 1974, he took the initiative of calling a meeting in his office at which Archbishop Bugnini from the Congregation of Worship would be present to discuss his liturgical proposals for the Benedictine Order. I was surprised when Mayer attempted to interfere in the liturgical practices of the confederation, since, strictly speaking, these were not matters for his department since they were decrees to individual Benedictine congregations granted by the Congregation for Worship or the Consilium. The situation was delicate for me since Mayer had been one of my professors at Sant'Anselmo, then rector from 1948 to 1950, my last two years of studies. He was also the runner-up to be abbot primate when I was elected in 1967. It became apparent that we had different views on many things, especially on the degree of centralization that should exist in the Benedictine Order, he advocating more uniformity, I seeking more subsidiarity to meet local needs.

I agreed to the meeting but brought with me the members of the liturgical committee for the whole confederation, all elected by the abbots at the 1973 congress: Cassian Just, abbot of Monserrat in Spain; Théodore Ghesquière, president of the Belgium Congregation; Salvatore Marsili, abbot of Finalpia, formerly professor of liturgy at Sant'Anslemo and then president of the Liturgical Institute; and Father Henry Ashworth of Quarr Abbey, professor of patristics at Sant'Anselmo and secretary to the Commission. The members unanimously agreed that the way we were moving was the right one and defended a pluralistic solution for the recitation of the Office in the monasteries of the confederation. After that meeting Mayer realized he could not really impose a uniform Breviary on the Benedictines and ceased to pressure me to do so. On such important matters, I was able to prevail against Mayer's efforts.

To succeed Antoniutti, Pope Paul appointed Cardinal Arturo Tabera, of Pamplona, Spain — a very sensitive and shy man who found it difficult to make decisions — and who died prematurely in June of 1975. As his successor Pope Paul then appointed Archbishop Eduardo Pironio, an outgoing, friendly Argentine. Pironio had been archbishop of La Plata and had shown a high level of pastoral sensitivity and care, a trait that dramatically changed the climate in the Congregation for Religious. Pironio loved religious life and was very comfortable and relaxed working with men and women religious. Like Pope Paul VI, he possessed a truly Benedictine soul, having been very supportive of our monasteries in Argentina. Almost immediately we became close friends. It was evident to all of us that he did not get along well with Archbishop Mayer, who became his second in command and more representative of the school of Antoniutti. Thus, most of us avoided taking matters to Mayer and went directly to Pironio.

Later that same summer Cardinal James Knox was appointed prefect of the Congregation for Worship. Knox was an Australian who had been in the diplomatic corps and brought a more pragmatic attitude to the discussions than his predecessors. I took advantage of his appointment to sit down with him and Archbishop Bugnini to bring some conclusion to the question of how Benedictines would recite their Divine Office by seeking official approval of the congregation for the document the liturgical commission of the confederation had meticulously drawn up. Instead of a uniform Liturgy of the Hours, the committee proposed a set of guidelines, a framework within which the communities could work out their prayer life. On February 10, 1977, Knox approved two documents the liturgical commission of the confederation had drawn up; one was called a *Directorium* (usually cited by Europeans as the *loi-cadre,* or "approved framework"), the other a *Thesaurus,* or set of examples, that could be followed if a monastery so chose. They are still thirty years later the guiding norms for all Benedictine houses throughout the world.

These documents are an excellent example of how a global Church must work. That is why I fought, vigorously and relentlessly, to have them approved. It was clear to me that this argument over how the Divine Office would be recited among Benedictines was not just a debate about an internal Benedictine affair. Much more was at stake. Mayer represented the highly centralizing curial position that demanded that all monasteries, regardless of their work or cultural needs, recite daily the same breviary. The stance of the abbots of the confederation, one that I had to defend, was that some guiding and uniform principles should be established, especially those found in the Rule of Saint Benedict, but that there should be flexibility in their application to given circumstance around the globe.

At that time I felt our documents were a test-case for the aims of Vatican II, liturgical and ecclesial. More than anything else, it involved trust in the wisdom of local communities to make adjustments according to their specific regional needs, but within a framework that assured unity. In these documents pluralism is accepted, inculturation is made possible, and the tradition of sanctifying the day by recurring periods of community prayer is respected.

*   *   *

How much was Pope Paul personally involved in these liturgical issues? From what Father Bugnini shared with me, I knew that he was constantly keeping the pope informed, even about the wishes of the Benedictine Order. I also knew he was under pressure from those voices, especially in the curia, who were unhappy with the liturgical changes after Vatican Council II and were insisting on more discipline and uniformity. It would not be wrong to say that the changes in liturgy were the most divisive of all the issues Paul had to face. The persistent demands of the bishops' conferences from around the world required a serious and generous response; his appointment of Father Bugnini as secretary of the Consilium signaled his sincerity in trying to implement the vision of the council with care and rapidity. But strong voices to the contrary remained. I could see the mounting opposition through my personal involvement in the post-conciliar liturgical reforms.

In May 1964, when I was still abbot of St. Vincent, Pope Paul had appointed me a consultor to the Commission for Liturgical Reform (the Consilium) with an assignment to the committee on church music. After I took up permanent residence in Rome, in January 1968, he appointed me a voting member of the Commission's board. That year was a critical one for the liturgical renewal; the Consilium's committees were working on the final drafts of the *Missa normativa,* i.e., the changes in the rubrics for the celebration of the Mass of the Roman rite.

Because of his intense interest in our work, the pope wanted to experience the new Mass in various degrees of solemnity ranging from one with no music to one with almost everything sung. He asked that three Masses be arranged on three successive evenings in the Capella Matilde, on the floor below his private quarters. January 11, 12, and 13, 1968, were set aside. All the Masses, because they were to resemble Sunday worship, were to include three biblical readings, the recitation of the Creed, and a homily. Someone had told him that the revised Mass would be too short and would be finished in fifteen minutes or less. He wanted to see for himself. Since the idea was to replicate a parish Sunday Mass, he asked that a small congregation be present and for each evening invited about twenty-five people. I was among them. Out of the corner of my eye I noticed that the secretary of state, Cardinal Cicognani, and his next in command, Archbishop Benelli, had slipped quietly into the chapel. On the last night, the pope, in the chapel, thanked all of those who came, stressed that this was an "historic moment," and begged for feedback. Each evening after the Mass, Pope Paul invited a small group, five to seven of us, to discuss our reactions; I attended all three evenings.

We sat around a table in his library. On the first night there were two Italian bishops, Father Bugnini and Carlo Braga from the office of the Consilium, and myself. On the second and third evenings, the pope invited two more to join us, Archbishop Ferdinando Antonelli, secretary of the Congregation of Rites, and Bishop Luigi Rovigatti, representing the Italian bishops' conference. Our small numbers made it possible to have a truly effective discussion about what had transpired. I am sure Pope Paul received the reactions of Cardinal Cicognani and Archbishop Benelli privately.

This was yet another occasion when I had a chance to observe the pope at his best. He had selected one of the bishops to be present because he was the bishop of that area of Rome and because of his reputation for being a compassionate pastoral person, but not too well-informed in matters liturgical. He was up in years, understood very little of what was being discussed, and made comments that usually had no point. The pope would very kindly thank him and then turn what the bishop had said into a very valid question so that he would never feel put down. The whole conversation was a most frank and open exchange. The first evening the reflection with just five of us present lasted an hour-and-a-half. I suggested that with three lessons being read each Sunday, a pause was needed after each of the first two in order to absorb their meaning. Pope Paul remarked that it was just like a Benedictine to want more contemplation even during the liturgy, but agreed that the Mass on the second evening should have a pause after each reading. When we returned to his library that second evening, he agreed that the pauses were an improvement and should be kept.

After the second and third Masses, the discussion lasted about three-quarters of an hour. The pope turned out to be a good listener who made clear his feelings about the areas he thought were weak — the opening penitential rite, the offertory prayers, the words of consecration with the placement of "mysterium fidei" (mystery of faith), and so on. On the third evening, after a Mass sung by students of the Germanicum, as we were gathering in the library the pope asked me, with a twinkle in his eye, if I had heard the story about what two Italians, two Greeks, and two Germans do when they meet abroad. When I answered in the negative, he explained that the two Italians open a barbershop, the two Greeks open a restaurant, and the two Germans start singing in four-part harmony. My first and only papal *barzelleta* (humorous story)!

Over the next year, the Consilium meetings considered many notes from the pope as each modification we had agreed on was sent to him. His observations were written in his clear miniscule handwriting. These comments, it became clear to me, were always geared toward winning more support from curial officials. He wanted their agreement before promulgating the final version which would make the changes obligatory for the whole Church. For this reason he felt he had to pass judgment on every change. He would send back his comments on our work in minute detail, but would never force his changes on us, simply asking that we freely debate them and get back to him with the results of that debate. After going over the notes from our meetings, he did not hesitate at times to hold to his own position, even if it had not been supported by the majority of us.

The long process continued until April 28, 1969, when he announced the publication of the New Order of Mass, the *Novus Ordo*. Though he had signed the decree in January, he hesitated before promulgating it, fearing that some would not accept the New Order but continue to claim that only the Tridentine usage was valid. He often repeated that the New Order was a revision of the Tridentine and thus there would be but one Roman rite in the Catholic Church. In sum, Pope Paul feared to make any decision that could be an excuse for a new division within the Church, accepting as axiomatic that the unity of the Church was expressed in a unity of rite. Still the council had accepted that there could be cultural modifications according to pastoral need without destroying the unity of the rite.

Pope Paul must have remembered as well the debates during the council on the intimate relationship between the use of the words "rite" and "church." In treating of the Eastern Catholic Churches and their patriarchs, the bishops at the council had ceased speaking of the Roman Catholic Church as composed of many rites — a terminology I grew up with — but now recognized that the Catholic Church had in its body many distinct Churches (such as the Armenian, Coptic, Ethiopian, Chaldean, Maronite, Melkite, Ruthenian, Romanian, Bulgarian, Ukrainian, Syrian, Syro-Malabar, Syro-Malankara) in union with Rome, but each with its own rite over which that Church had authority and jurisdiction. The council explicitly stated that its practical liturgical norms did not apply to the rites of those churches in union with Rome. Several rites within one church would have seemed to all of us at that time as an anomaly — a dangerous one.

Having heard Pope Paul speak his mind with frankness and sincerity about the importance of these revisions of the Roman rite, I knew he considered them among the most important acts of his pontificate. In April of 1969 when he promulgated these liturgical changes, he was probably still reflecting on the negative response to *Humanae vitae* and knew that they might bring the same reaction. They did, but from totally different groups within the Church. Those who had expected more forward-looking changes after the council were disappointed with *Humanae vitae,* but happy with the liturgical changes. Those who were happy with *Humanae vitae* tended to be unhappy with the liturgical changes. The pope was again isolated.

In the years following the council, the Consilium had received many requests from the conferences of bishops, especially from the United States, France, Germany, Italy, the Low Countries, Africa, and Asia to introduce more vernacular. Now requests from these same countries for new liturgical permissions increased, like the use of more Eucharistic prayers and the addition of alternate freely composed orations. Most commentators tend to underestimate the major role the national conferences of bishops played in the implementation of the council's liturgical reform. After all, the bishops knew best what they had voted on.

In May of 1969 the Consilium was dissolved and merged with the Congregation for Divine Worship. Father Annibale Bugnini was appointed secretary of that congregation and, in February 1972, was made an archbishop. The work of liturgical reform continued at a remarkable pace with the publication of a new lectionary, rituals for all the sacraments, and a total reform of the Liturgy of the Hours. I marveled at the amount of work coming out of his office, the many committees and meetings organized, and the number and quality of scholars from around the world involved. Bugnini knew liturgy well, especially its history, and was a superb organizer. But he also became the focal point, I feel unjustly, for all opposition to the liturgical reforms of Vatican Council II.

∗   ∗   ∗

One of the blessings that came my way during these last four years as primate was my election by the superiors general to the 1974 Synod of Bishops on Evangelization. It was the last of the truly significant synods of bishops, even though it ended without any clear final document. In its ambiguity, it mirrored the state of the Church itself at that moment. Many of the leading cardinals and bishops from Vatican II, though now aging and somewhat less vigorous, were still alive and present. The curia had won its point: insisting the synod should be held every three years, rather than two years, and that the pope should select one theme for consultation and not a series of themes as in the previous synods. Nonetheless, 1974 had the spirit of the council and previous synods. The *relator,* the cardinal-theologian appointed by the pope who was expected to pull all the divergent opinions of the many groups together into a synthesis, was the young, impressive Cardinal Karol Wojtyła of Krakow.

Moreover, the participation on the part of bishops from Africa, Asia, and especially South America was outstanding. Those churches, especially in Latin America, possessed a rostrum of articulate, courageous bishops, all well aware of the poverty that plagued their faithful and of the ruthless dictators they had to confront. Their people had been evangelized, as one bishop put it, by the sufferings of the cross, and not by the hopes of the resurrection. Most of these remarkable bishops I had come to know through my travels. For the first time, we were also hearing from the thoughtful Asian bishops who were most concerned about inculturation and the relationship between Christianity and the other religions of their region.

Evangelization was a most popular theme in those days. What the word meant was the subject of much debate, but in general it included living the gospel more completely and bringing that gospel message to others. It was a theme dear to all of us religious superiors by the nature of our office because it touched on inculturation, i.e., the insertion of the gospel into many, divergent cultures. I was totally engaged in the arguments and debates during this synod; they vindicated the direction the Benedictine confederation was taking.

Differences of approach were real and evident from the very first talks by the appointed theologians. The first part of the meeting took a newer, experiential approach where most of the bishops felt at home in the discussions. They were summarized by the special secretary appointed for that task: Father Duraisamy Simon Amalorpavadass from India. From his presentation, I had the image of the Church as a gigantic quilt where each patch had its own lights and shades, its own joys and struggles, but all tightly sewn together by a common bond of faith. The second part was to deal with more systematic theological themes. Father Dominico Grasso, a theologian from the Gregorian University in Rome, presented a classical summary of ecclesiology with an image of church that was abstract and disembodied, ignoring almost totally the local atmosphere where the gospel would be preached.

Cardinal Wojtyła was unable to blend the two points of view — one experiential, the other theoretical — but leaned toward the latter. For that reason the propositions worked on so assiduously by the secretaries for a final document were, for the most part, rejected. Some of the bishops who had attended Vatican II felt they were reliving history and realized that the synod itself was a living experience of tensions between more traditionalist viewpoints and those rising in the third world, especially among the new native clergy. In the coming years, these tensions became even more pointed. At the synod, these different points of view never totally coalesced and we 200 bishops did not have sufficient time to write and issue a final document. All of this material with its differences was simply put into Pope Paul's hands to write up; he seemed to let this tension hang in the air at the end of the meeting. A year after the synod he published a synthesis of the meeting in a document called *Evangelii nuntiandi* (Evangelization in the Modern World), a statement that could never have been written without the input of the discussion that took place at the synod. In his typical approach, it was a both/and solution. That post-synodal exhortation became an indispensable guideline for me in the years ahead, a valuable tool for much of my future thinking as a bishop.

What were the issues that divided the synodal members and how did Paul formulate these? He accepted the need for personal conversion of each individual, but also recognized the need for more just societal structures. The gospel message was not outside a given culture, but transformed every culture, forming a *tertium quid,* something that had its roots in both, and that was thus both new and old. Paul saw liberation as not neglecting the economic, political, social, and cultural aspects of life, but as going beyond these to include an openness to the Divine, to the Absolute. Evangelization and ecumenism went hand in hand, since a divided church could not evangelize fully. In this way Paul brought together some of the issues that had divided the members.

Only two points in the document, at the time, did not ring totally true to me. First, Paul wrote of the gospel as if it were in itself free from cultural influences in its very formulation, as if it were an abstract a-cultural proclamation outside history and thus culture. Second, I felt a similar neo-Platonic approach when he talked of the relationship between the universal church and the local churches. He rejected the idea that the universal church is the sum or a federation of different local churches. Still he did not explain how and where this universal church incarnated in each local church exists. At times he appears to identify it with the Church of Rome and Peter, "a flock which a single shepherd pastures." I was not surprised when, for the next decade, this tension between universal and local remained a part of Catholic life. It was just another aspect of the relationship between collegiality and primacy that was not clearly spelled out in the documents of Vatican II.

During this synod on evangelization I realized how privileged I was in my role as abbot primate by having the opportunity to travel the world over for so many years. My participation in the synod now was inspired from concrete experiences and not from theories, however good they may have been. I had come to know many participating bishops, having met them in their own dioceses when visiting their countries. The contrast, however, between the atmosphere in this synod compared to those I attended in 1969 and 1971 was apparent. Then the bishops from the Council were still present in large numbers; the synods seemed like extensions of the council. Then the press was full of interviews with cardinals and bishops well-known for their views at that time — Suenens of Brussels, Marty of Paris, Döpfner of Munich, and the like. Now the press was more muted and less curious. Slowly one could see changing attitudes among the bishops, with newly appointed ones being less open. Pope Paul himself appeared less optimistic and more fearful of the direction Peter's bark was taking.

CHAPTER 10

Ministering in the Last Years of Pope Paul VI

Rome (1973-1977)

M y years as abbot primate of the Benedictines coincided almost exactly with the pontificate of Pope Paul VI, whose thinking had a marked influence on me as a person and as a religious superior. As I write, his presence keeps coming to mind. Before me on my desk, there are the chalice and paten he gave me in 1976 on the twenty-fifth anniversary of my ordination to the priesthood. They are not large, but heavy and modern in style; they bear Paul's coat of arms. He loved modern religious art and surrounded himself with it. I continue to celebrate Mass regularly with that chalice and each time make a special *memento* for him because of his many acts of kindness to me.

After his death, whenever I would return to Rome, I was surprised and saddened by the freedom with which many members of the curia openly criticized him and his pontificate. They blamed him for all that they thought went wrong in the implementation of Vatican II. This was harsh criticism despite the degree to which he extended himself so that there would be neither winners nor losers after the council; no doubt, this must have created a good deal of personal anguish for him.

Every time I would meet with Pope Paul VI he would ask me what trips I had made and what was happening in all the countries I had visited; he seemed especially interested in their liturgy. If I was about to leave on a trip, he would beg me to greet those communities and tell them of his concern for them. In Benin, the French monks told me that the catechist translated "the pope has great concern for you" into the native language with "the Great White Chief in Rome told me to tell you that he had carved out a niche in his heart and placed you there." Inculturation, I learned, also included making our Western abstractions into vivid images! No wonder there were so many uuuhs and aaahs and every one danced around the fire.

But I knew that not all the tensions I felt in Rome were due to the council and its implementation during the pontificate of Pope Paul VI. Many curial officials had a pervasive negative feeling — almost a disdain — toward the Church in the United States. They did not regard us very highly. Americans were considered intellectually inferior, without an appreciation for the arts; we were pragmatic and superficial, traditionless and without any reverence for historical treasures. This negative attitude toward American Catholics was deeply rooted in historical and philosophical differences. Though American Catholics had changed after World War II, it was unclear to Roman officials how the Church in the United States would evolve. Their mental picture of the pre-war American Church included its deep Irish roots, its rigorist adherence to church observance, and its almost childlike, docile nature and loyalty to Rome. That image was often articulated and reinforced in Rome by Cardinal Amleto Cicognani, papal delegate to the States from 1933 to 1958. He arrived during the Depression years, stayed through the war years, and continued into the immediate post-war period. The men he favored as bishops reflected his image: practical men who were known for their administrative skills, simple unquestioning faith, external piety, and absolute loyalty to Rome. The Church in America did not pride itself on its contribution to theology, that area having been stifled since the beginning of the nineteenth century because of the "modernist" purge under Pope Pius X. The U.S. Church, as Cicognani knew it, lacked theological sophistication.

Cicognani became secretary of state under Pope John XXIII in 1961 and still held that position when I came to Rome in 1967. In 1969 Pope Paul VI appointed Cardinal Jean-Marie Villot to succeed him. A few months after my arrival, Cicognani asked me to come and visit him as he wanted to talk about the Church in the United States. He invited me several times in the following years. Even after resigning his position as secretary of state, he continued to reside in the same set of large musty rooms, certainly from another century, with their imposing furniture, heavy dark curtains, and thick dark-colored rugs. But he was a simple person and the splendor of his surroundings did not seem to bother him. Each time the theme of our conversation was the same: what is happening to the Church in the United States? He knew that a change was taking place; he had probably seen it start in his time there, but could not imagine what was happening. The image he had projected on the States he knew was no longer holding up.

But what was taking its place? We talked about the G.I. bill providing education funds for returning soldiers and the rise of a Catholic laity; these developments were gradually changing the way Catholics participated in American political, academic, and economic structures. He asked about the Catholic universities and the gradual formation of a whole new cadre of Catholic lay and clerical scholars. He knew of the affluence of second- and third-generation Catholic immigrants and that this change in economic status brought changes in attitudes. He seemed to represent the feelings of other curial officials by mentioning that he did not know how to relate to this new phenomenon. In fact, I felt I discerned a slight fear of the power of the American Church and what might happen if it were to reach deeply into its local history and make an ecclesial declaration of independence.

But there was also a deeper level of concern. The Church in Europe carried many wounds from the political and social struggles that came with the Enlightenment, the French Revolution, and the unification of Italy. All these movements were inspired by the Enlightenment philosophy of freedom and democracy and forms of anticlericalism that accompanied them. These new ideas were followed by the efforts of newly formed nation-states to control the Church, whether it was Gallicanism, Josephinism, or Febronianism. Rome, with its prodigious memory, did not forget any of the sufferings of the nineteenth century. While all this was happening in Europe, the Church in the United States — founded on the very Enlightenment principles that the European Church feared — was thriving. Furthermore, the American bishops praised the new freedom Catholics had to live their faith and expand and grow.

Freedom and democracy were not positive terms in European Catholic clerical circles during the nineteenth and twentieth centuries, and this created hesitations about the American political experiment and its potential impact on the Church. In addition, I realized for the first time how important the Spanish-American War of 1898 had been to the Church in Europe. To us Americans it was a blip in the history books. To European prelates, on the other hand, that war was more than the defeat of Spain by the United States. It became a symbol of the defeat of a country with deep Catholic roots by an upstart nation built on principles whose ultimate purpose, they believed, was to destroy the Catholic Church. To someone like the powerful Cardinal Merry del Val, a highly influential prelate of English-Spanish origin, that war inspired fear. He was active in the administration of Pope Leo XIII during the period of the condemnation of "Americanism"; in 1903, he was appointed secretary of state by Pope Pius X and participated in the pope's efforts to purge the Catholic Church of any trace of "modernism."

Although I had understood in theory these ambivalent feelings of the Roman curia, I never felt their full force until I became abbot primate and had to deal at a deeper level with members of the curia. The Cicognani stereotype of U.S. Catholics was giving way to a new stereotype of U.S. Catholics: lawless experimentalists with no sense of tradition or continuity and without awareness of the lessons the Church had learned through suffering. The new and more lay-dominated Church rising in the United States had to be controlled and kept within clear boundaries. How often I would hear a Roman official say that whatever the Church in the States did the whole world would be doing within a few months. That attitude explained why Rome paid no attention if something happened in Canada, but would be quick to intervene if the same thing happened in the States. At the root of the unease was an undifferentiated fear of a Church with so much power and potential. It had to be carefully watched and controlled, especially at a time when a new Catholic population was coming to the fore with a diminished loyalty to Rome and an enlarged sense of its own capabilities.

I was convinced that Pope Paul did not share this ambivalence about the U.S. Church. He certainly never manifested any antipathy toward the country in his dealings with me. On the contrary, I felt he instinctively liked Americans. Because his formation and tastes in both theology and culture were rooted in French sources, most U.S. Catholics of my generation found his documents easy to read; we would have known where he was coming from. Like many in my generation, I had been educated in the French neo-Scholastics, having studied Jacques Maritain and Etienne Gilson. I read theologians like Henri DuLubac, Yves Congar, and Jean Daniélou. The writings of Paul Claudel and Charles Péguy, of Francois Mauriac and Georges Bernanos, were standard fare in Catholic colleges. I felt at home in Paul's ecclesial world and its thinking. Moreover, I thought this French influence was evident in his writing style. He wrote well, often expressing himself in long periodic sentences, carefully polished, but with balanced and, at times, even elegant phrases. Sometimes I would hear theologians and other scholars say that if you wanted Pope Paul to read something you wrote, try to have it published in a French periodical, like

Études, since he would be sure to read it. He admired the works of the theologian Jean Guitton, probably the person closest to him in his last years. It was evident why he had appointed Cardinal Villot his secretary of state. Villot epitomized the classical French prelate with his strong but relaxed bearing, suave handling of delicate affairs, charm when needed in social circumstances, and clarity of thought and speech.

During my final years in Rome, I could not help but notice how Pope Paul was failing physically and how much more depressed he seemed at times. From that period comes a stark remark, one often quoted in conservative periodicals. In a homily preached on June 29, 1972, he spoke of the post–Vatican II period as a day of clouds and storms and darkness, and attributed this state to the work of the devil. "The smoke of Satan," he menacingly declared, "has entered the temple of God." One can see why those who had opposed the council would frequently cite his phrase. Although it gives the impression that he had soured on the work of the council, he continued to implement it as he had before, but with less enthusiasm and more caveats.

Later in 1974, during one of my long trips to Central America, I promised a bishop who was in a very difficult political position that I would personally relay a sensitive message to the pope. On returning to Rome, I called Cardinal Villot and asked for a private audience. When I named the bishop from whom I was bringing a confidential message, the audience was immediately granted. At that time Pope Paul was in one of those negative or dark moods that characterized his later years. I had decided at the end of the audience to give him a brief pep talk and so had prepared a little speech designed to cheer up a depressed pope. After I had relayed the message to him exactly as the bishop had asked me and he had taken a note about it, I got up to leave.

As he ushered me to the door and I was ready to start my speech, he unexpectedly said that he knew I was in trouble again with some cardinal of the curia. I expressed my astonishment that he knew this. He laughed about it and commented that the pope knows everything. Then he added: "Do you want to know why you in are in trouble?"

"Of course," I replied, "I would love to know why the pope thinks I am always in trouble with some cardinal."

"You are very American, you know. You always say exactly what you think, and we are not used to that over here. But you have the complete confidence of a pope," he added, "Why worry about a little cardinal?"

As he opened the door and ushered me out, I was on a high and never did deliver my speech cheering up a depressed pope.

Pope Paul also became more and more isolated. It was sad to see the unfortunate misunderstandings that arose between him and Cardinal Giacomo Lercaro or between him and Cardinal Joseph Suenens. It seems Suenens had made remarks in many interviews that had offended Paul. Suenens had been very influential right after the council in suggesting new names and faces for the curia and the diplomatic corps, and Paul had accepted them. But Paul had drifted further and further away from his friends in the more progressive bloc of council bishops, all of whom had been delighted by his election as pope.

Why this alienation? As I analyzed the situation in which Paul found himself, I concluded that the dominant motivation behind much of what he did in that post-conciliar period could be found in his conviction that he had to reach out to the curial and other conservative cardinals. If rumors in Rome were correct, it was they who, after many inconclusive and painful ballots, finally gave him the two-thirds vote needed to be elected. His sensitivity to their opinions was evident in the liturgical reforms. After he had appointed Cardinal Gut head of the Consilium and then prefect of the new Congregation for Worship, he asked me in a casual conversation what the Benedictine monks thought about this appointment. I admitted it surprised most monks since Gut was up in years, had had difficulty handling even the slightest difference of opinions within the Benedictine confederation, and now would find himself at the vortex of the most persistent tensions in the Catholic Church. Pope Paul replied that he hoped this gesture would please the conservatives and help them accept the Consilium's decisions. In the same way, I noticed that whenever he would suggest a change to any document proposed by the Consilium, he would add that he hoped the proposed alteration would help the whole project gain more support from the curial group. The slight alterations he made on his own to the documents already approved by the bishops at Vatican II, like the one on ecumenism and the *Nota praevia* as an explanatory note to preface Chapter III of the Constitution on the Church, and the bold decision to take the question of contraception out of the hands of the council to write his own document — all these uncharacteristic acts were aimed at placating the conservative cardinals who feared he might betray the First Vatican Council (1870) and its definition of papal infallibility, key to the pope's role as they saw it. We see this fear clearly expressed in the published notes of their leader, Cardinal Giuseppe Siri of Genoa.

Paul's sensitivity to the conservatives, especially the curial cardinals, prevented him, after the council and during the period of its implementation, from appointing at once to head the various congregations men who had been leaders in the majority during the council debates.

Instead of giving in to one side or the other, Paul tried to keep peace by creating parallel bodies, called Councils or Secretariats, headed by more forward-looking cardinals. Thus, the Congregation for the Doctrine of the Faith did not take up the dialogue with the other Christian Churches, but Cardinal Bea's secretariat for Christian unity did. This contrast continued on in the dialogues with the Orthodox Churches. It was not the Congregation for Oriental Churches who pursued such a dialogue, but again Bea's secretariat. In liturgy the reforms were given over to Cardinal Lercaro and the new Consilium for Liturgical Reform, and not to Cardinal Arcadio Larraona, prefect of the Congregation for Worship. Paul created a new council for Justice and Peace, but those of us who represented the religious orders in that office noticed at once that it was always caught between its own bolder stance and the pragmatic decisions of the secretary of state. This two-track system during the implementation period perpetuated irreconcilable differences and gave an official platform for concepts that had been rejected by the council. In this Pope Paul failed to give the implementation of the council a clear direction. At the time, I was convinced his plan was to create, slowly but effectively, unity in the church, but that did not come about.

His second way of attempting to be fair consisted in the way he named people to the various curial offices. I already mentioned that often a prefect and a secretary would represent two almost opposing view points and that a prefect from one perspective would be followed by a prefect from the other. He knew of the continued opposition to the liturgical reforms in the curia itself and was constantly seeking ways of gaining more support from the opponents. From liturgical watch-dog groups around the world he was receiving an avalanche of letters describing the many liturgical abuses they were uncovering. Perhaps that is why he brought Cardinal Knox, an Australian pragmatic diplomat, into the role as prefect of the Congregation for Worship. Pope Paul's nervousness reached a peak in summer 1975, and without warning or without offering reasons he announced the merger of the Congregation of Worship with the Congregation for the Discipline of the Sacraments. As a result, Archbishop Bugnini was without a curial post. For six months, his friends noticed that he remained almost incommunicado, staying in his two small rooms where he lived at the house of the Vincentians, his religious order. Six months later, January 1976, he was appointed papal nuncio to Iran — an easy assignment everyone in the curia said, since "nothing ever happens there." He distinguished himself during the hostage crisis (1979-1981) and died prematurely in 1982.

The Bugnini case is another instance of the way in which Pope Paul caved under pressure from those opposed to his reforms. Perhaps it is the most striking example of how he ceased to support someone who had faithfully carried out his orders and how he then ostracized that person. The rumor circulating in those days in the curia was that Bugnini was a mason, a rumor he publicly vehemently denied. (Many lists of Vatican prelates who were "masons" appeared in the conservative Catholic Italian press from time to time.)

Pope Paul did other things that caused unrest among those who worked in the Vatican and thereby isolated himself. In 1967 he restructured the curia, including the newly formed councils, so that they all fell under the authority of the secretary of state. That office was divided into two subdivisions, one for internal affairs (matters touching the inner life of the Church and the curia) and one for external relationships with states (the Council for Public Affairs). In early 1967 Pope Paul had called Archbishop Giovanni Benelli from service in Senegal to Rome to work on the new structuring of the curia and appointed him to the office in charge of internal affairs. He then appointed Archbishop Agostino Casaroli head of the office for external affairs. This arrangement had just been put in place when I arrived in Rome in the fall of 1967. These two men, Benelli and Casaroli, are synonymous with the pontificate of Pope Paul VI. As Pope Paul grew older, we all noticed that he relied more and more on these two faithful collaborators.

Although Paul may have made his life easier by making the secretary of state a stronger position, the curial officials were very unhappy with the idea that they did not report directly to him. I recall hearing Cardinal Wright, appointed prefect of the Congregation for the Clergy in 1969, say that, before taking that position, he did not know that it would be so difficult to obtain an audience with Pope Paul VI or that he would be reporting to Benelli. I believe he had hoped he would have regular access to the pope and be able to influence his decisions directly — not, I judge, an unreasonable hope for the head of a Roman congregation.

In addition, Pope Paul compounded the anxieties in the curia by naming, at regular intervals, many new cardinals, most of them non-Italians, and by raising their number so that the Italians and the curia cardinals no longer dominated. He wanted to recognize the fact that the Church was now global and needed representation from many nations and cultures. Over time, the curial cardinals would become a smaller bloc in future papal elections. He even went further and in November 1970 decreed that no cardinal over the age of eighty could vote in a papal election, thus eliminating over twenty-five cardinals at once. Shortly after that edict was published, I invited the French cardinal, Eugène Tisserant, to lunch at Sant'Anselmo. Tisserant was a brilliant, frank, uninhibited, and delightful person. Being eighty-six at the time, he publicly — contrary to all correct cardinalatial protocol — displayed his anger with the decree. At table that day he did not hesitate to let us know how upset he was. He emphatically declared that he wanted to outlive Pope Paul VI so that he could see the rule abolished by Paul's successor.

Pope Paul also appointed as diplomats men like Archbishop Jean Jadot who had not attended the diplomatic school in Rome or worked his way up the career ladder. This distressed some in the lower ranks of the diplomatic corps. The volume of these rancorous remarks reached their highest decibels when Jadot was appointed papal delegate to the United States, a prize position. It was not pleasant to go over to a curial office for some business touching the Benedictine confederation and listen to the constant laments of those who feared that their advancement would be affected by these changes.

Pope Paul even sounded out the possibility of a new way of electing a pope. Rumors abounded. First one heard that he wanted the pope elected by the presidents of the conferences of bishops from around the world, most of whom were not cardinals. Then it was rumored that, instead, he would decree that the election would be done by the cardinals and the elected council of the synod of bishops that included non-cardinal bishops from around the world. Pope Paul, by putting out these feelers, must have had some hesitation about the ability of such a large number of cardinals to elect his successor. Perhaps he saw, if only intuitively, that they would not know each other well and would be forced to fall back on a well-known curial cardinal as their candidate. Perhaps he also saw that a body not appointed by the pope but elected by the bishops themselves would have the possibility of producing a result more acceptable to twentieth-century lay and clerical Catholics.

These tentative suggestions floated around Rome for months; then in November 1975, he published a document on the election of a pope to take effect January 1, 1976. The electors were to be 120 cardinals, but only cardinals under the age of eighty. Although Paul was reducing the power of the curial cardinals, he was not creating truly effective instruments of administration involving all the bishops that had been foreseen in the formation of the episcopal synods. He conceded to the wishes of the curia by permitting the synods to become less and less important.

What caused Pope Paul VI to turn toward a stronger centralization during this implementation period after Vatican II and to minimize any emphasis on shared responsibility on all levels of church governance? At that time, it seemed to me that the answer could be found in his reactions to events in the Netherlands and then in the German-speaking nations. Between 1966 and 1970 the Catholic Church in the Netherlands organized a National Pastoral Council composed of bishops, priests, and laity. Local synods in Germany and Austria followed. Every imaginable topic was discussed and voted on. It was as if the flood-gates had been opened by Vatican II, and every discontented person or group could present for a vote what they wanted changed, from disciplinary to doctrinal questions. Or, at least, so it appeared to the curial officials. Enormous energy went into preparing and debating these issues with no regard, they said, to the desires or thoughts of the rest of the Church. These meetings inflamed the fear that the curia already had of national churches being formed.

The council and its thrust hit Holland in the midst of its own sociological changes after World War II: a large number of Catholics, as in the United States, had moved up political, academic, and social ladders and had a new sense of their power and influence. Their views were dominant in the Dutch pastoral council and alarmed Rome because they seemed to project a model of church that was a local, congregational, and democratic alternative to a traditional, hierarchical model. The curia saw these Dutch synods as splitting the Church and setting one faction against another. Pope Paul became alarmed and in 1970 appointed very conservative new bishops in Holland. The reaction was more bitterness and division among the bishops, priests, and faithful. Holland saw an even larger number of priests leave the active ministry than in other countries. This phenomenon among the diocesan clergy and among the religious orders also shocked and frightened the pope. It was sad to see such a vibrant Church as the Dutch disintegrate.

One thing became certain: the council had brought an enormous flow of energy to the Church especially among these newly educated, socially mobile Catholics, not only in Holland, but in the rest of Europe and in the

United States. Paul felt helpless against the onslaught and responded by appointing more rigorous authority figures, but to no avail. The final result was a much smaller Church, in Holland first and then in the rest of Europe, depleted of its former vitality and energy. He was unable to channel that energy in positive ways. The Church for the most part gradually became dormant. In many circles, including the curia, the council and weak bishops were blamed for this outcome. Pope Paul's solution did not solve the problem; the Church in Europe was not a stronger Church, but a depleted one. Though he understood the situation, he felt helpless in responding.

At the same time, he suffered immensely from the defection of Archbishop Marcel Lefèbvre, former archbishop of Senegal and apostolic delegate for French-speaking Africa, later bishop of Tulle in France, and finally superior general of the Holy Ghost Fathers. Lefèbvre resigned this latter position and formed his own seminary in Switzerland. After many attempts at reconciliation, Pope Paul had to suspend him in 1976, but it was to no avail. If Pope Paul was disturbed by those who seemed to be carrying the changes of Vatican II too far, he was equally disturbed, if not more so, by Lefèbvre and his followers, who refused to accept the council and separated themselves from the Church. Paul had tried so hard to maintain unity in the Church and avoid a schism and he felt defeated.

If Pope Paul felt rejected by the faithful of the world after the reactions to *Humanae vitae* in 1968, he must have suffered that same feeling of rejection by his own staff in Rome. All of this must have deeply wounded him; there were hints that he wanted to resign at the age of eighty. Although he wrote no more encyclicals after 1968, he continued to generate important documents, especially on social issues. He fostered warmer relations with other churches, especially the Orthodox. The importance of liturgical reforms in the Roman rite remained a priority. But there was one over-riding fear that determined his shifting attitudes — to avoid schism in the Church. Trying to placate all sides gave the appearance of indecision or insecurity. His fear, coupled with an innate wish not to offend or hurt anyone, often forced him to shift course mid-stream and support the conservatives; in the process, he alienated his most loyal supporters and collaborators.

*　　　*　　　*

In one area Pope Paul's ardor did not seem to diminish — ecumenism. This fervor on his part was helpful to us Benedictines and to me personally. If my personal interest in liturgy had its roots in my Benedictine vocation, so did my interest in ecumenism. At each Congress of Abbots I made sure this latter topic was discussed. In 1970 Cardinal Jan Willebrands, successor to Cardinal Bea as prefect of the Council for Christian Unity, spoke to all the abbots to inspire more ecumenical endeavors and to encourage the Benedictines to become more deeply engaged. In 1973 Monsignor Charles Moeller, secretary of the Congregation for the Doctrine of the Faith, did likewise. Because the Benedictine Order antedated the split between Catholic and Orthodox in 1054, it seemed to have a natural affinity with the Orthodox Churches. Monasticism was a common bond between these two ancient branches of Christianity.

Pope Paul VI knew of this interest. In early November 1975, his secretary, Monsignor Macchi, called and asked that I drop in to see the pope. The ecumenical patriarch of Constantinople, Dimitrios I, wanted to observe the tenth anniversary of the lifting of the anathemas of 1054, an event that had taken place between the two churches on December 7, 1965. This was to be commemorated on December 14, 1975, by Patriarch Dimitrios in his Cathedral of St. George in the Phanar in Istanbul, with a similar celebration presided over by Pope Paul VI taking place simultaneously in the Sistine Chapel in Rome. At the ceremony in Istanbul, Dimitrios wished to announce the creation of a pan-Orthodox theological commission in order to start an ongoing dialogue with the Catholic Church.

As I waited in the pope's antechamber, the secretary remarked: "I hope you have a valid passport." I knew I was going to be traveling somewhere. Pope Paul was in a light-hearted mood and simply asked if I would accompany Cardinal Corrado Ursi of Naples to represent him at the ceremonies in the Phanar. In Istanbul we would meet the third official representative, Bishop Pierre Dubois, the vicar apostolic in Turkey. Cardinal Ursi, Pope Paul told me, had given the Greek Orthodox faithful a parish church in Naples and thus was well esteemed by the Orthodox and a logical choice for the trip. I had been picked, he added laughing, because in 1054 the papal legate, Cardinal Humbert of Silva Candida, fulminated the excommunications against the patriarch Michael Cerularius on the altar of Hagia Sophia; Humbert was a monk of the Benedictine monastery of Moyenmoutier. It was time, Paul said, that the leader of the Benedictines return to Istanbul and make amends.

Patriarch Dimitrios appointed as my guide the young Metropolitan Bartholomew, secretary of the Holy Synod, now Dimitrios's successor as the ecumenical patriarch of Constantinople. In addition to the long liturgies on Sunday, the exquisite dinner that followed at the Phanar, the exchange of gifts, and the laying of a rose on the tomb of Patriarch Athanagorous, we had a chance to visit all the other Orthodox and Catholic heads of Churches in Istanbul. Our visit to Hagia Sophia was memorable. Since Metropolitan Bartholomew would not enter because it functioned as a mosque, I wandered around and absorbed it all at my leisure, sensing the weight of history that Hagia Sophia embodies. I said a prayer for Cardinal Humbert, for Pope Paul, and for Patriarch Athanagorous.

While we were at supper that same evening, someone from the Orthodox delegation in Rome phoned to recount the events that morning at the papal Mass in the Sistine Chapel. Monsignor Virgilio Noe, papal master of ceremonies, told me that Pope Paul, after Communion at that Mass, whispered to him: "Do not try to stop me now from what I want to do." He went over to the small throne where Metropolitan Meliton, the leader of the patriarch's delegation, was sitting, fell on his knees before him, and kissed his feet, calling to mind the words of St. Paul: "How beautiful are the feet of those who preach the good news" (Rom. 10:5).

One of my Orthodox companions at the table that evening recalled a story about a metropolitan from Constantinople who visited Pope Pius IX in the middle of the nineteenth century. According to the Orthodox version, the metropolitan knelt to kiss the feet of the pope, and Pius IX, through inadvertence or because of embarrassment at the gesture, kicked him in the face. If Pope Paul knew this story — and he may well have — his gesture was exactly the right one to rectify any hard feelings. It may also have been why I saw so many Orthodox around the table with visible tears in their eyes as the telephone conversation was repeated.

Each time I celebrate Mass with the chalice and paten Pope Paul gave me, I recall this event of reconciliation and this gesture toward unity. I learned that healing memories is essential to ecumenism and can be done by gestures in a more memorable way than by words.

The next day we made a trip to Izmir (Nicea) where we recited the Nicean Creed together at the ruins of the basilica where in 325 the Council of Nicea had condemned Arianism (yes, we Romans recited it in Latin with the *filioque*, the Orthodox without it).

*   *   *

Pope Paul was very gracious to my family. In the spring of 1970 my brother and his wife visited Rome. I asked for a *bacia-mano* (a short visit just to kiss his hand) to present them. At that time I mentioned to Pope Paul that my mother would be coming to Rome in the fall. "You must bring her over so I can meet her too," came the response. To my surprise, at the end of the summer Cardinal Villot called to ask when my mother would arrive so he could arrange the audience. The pope received us in a small and intimate reception room with just a couch and a few comfortable chairs all upholstered in the light brown and gold characteristic of his tastes. My oldest sister, Betty, was traveling with Mother so Pope Paul received the three of us together. He sat on the couch with my mother, took her hands in his own soft ones, and spoke to her in halting Italianized English. "Mrs. Weakland, your son good boy; does good things for Benedictine Order," and so on. At the end, he gave Mom a rosary he had just blessed. It became her prize object for years.

As we left this little reception room and were walking down the gallery toward the elevator, I said slyly to her, "Don't forget, Mom, he is infallible." "Yes, I know," she replied. "That was the first faith crisis of my life."

Again in 1976 on the twenty-fifth anniversary of my ordination to the priesthood, many of my family were able to come to Rome. On June 16, Pope Paul received us and had a gift for me — that modern chalice and paten that was his and that was embossed with his coat of arms. I used it for the first time the next day at Sant'Anselmo for the big Mass of celebration. Cardinal Wright preached on that occasion (all difficulties between us seemingly resolved) and Cardinal Eduardo Pironio and Archbishop Bernardin Gantin, an old friend from Benin in Africa and now in Rome, concelebrated. We made a trip to Subiaco where I had been ordained twenty-five years before for another Mass and then two days later to Monte Cassino for Mass. On special occasions I still use this Pauline chalice and paten and cannot do so without reflecting on his kindness to me and especially to my family.

On the evening of February 17, 1976, Cardinal Villot called to let me know that Pope Paul VI had decided to name Basil Hume archbishop of Westminster in London. At that time Basil was chair of the committee *De re monastica* for the next Congress of Abbots scheduled for September 1977, and I knew I would be losing a close collaborator. Hume asked me to come to London for the event on March 25, to stay at his residence next to the cathedral, and then to preside that afternoon at Vespers in Westminster Abbey. Over the course of years, I had met many of his relatives and was delighted to do so. The ceremonies were done with the usual English seriousness and grandeur, slowly and without haste. Basil seemed actually to be very relaxed. He told me that Pope Paul had told him the best preparation for being a bishop was to have been an abbot and not to worry about his capabilities.

When the ceremonies in Westminster Cathedral, the Catholic Cathedral, were all over and everyone a bit refreshed, we went mid-afternoon to Westminster Abbey for Vespers.

The Abbey of Ampleforth, where Basil was a monk and abbot, considers itself the continuation of the Benedictine community of Westminster Abbey, dissolved by Elizabeth in 1559. The whole community of Ampleforth, some 120 in number, descended on Westminster Abbey that afternoon, and for the first time since the mid-sixteenth century, the monks sang Vespers in that historic church. It was the feast of the Annunciation, March 25. It was my privilege to preside. Basil preached. Later those working on dialogue between the Anglican Church and the Catholic Church often quoted his sermon. Basil used the image of the two sisters, Mary and Elizabeth, buried side by side waiting for the ultimate resurrection, as a sign of reunion. Pope Paul picked up this image when calling the Anglicans a sister church.

*   *   *

In September of the next year, 1977, the abbots again came to Rome for the four-year congress. By that time the confederation consisted of twenty-one congregations, and 227 independent monasteries of men. We had determined to discuss three themes: celibacy and sexuality, social justice, and inculturation. I was completing ten years as primate and some of the presidents privately came and begged me to continue for at least four more years. I had agreed I would accept if elected again but would want three months off before beginning another term — one month for rest, one for study, and one for a thirty-day retreat. They all thought this was reasonable.

But Pope Paul VI had other ideas. We began the congress on Wednesday, September 4, 1977, as planned. Friday evening I received an urgent phone call from Cardinal Sebastiano Baggio, prefect of the Congregation for Bishops, telling me to be in his office the next morning at 9:00. I responded that this would be difficult since I was presiding at a meeting of all the abbots of the world. He cut me short by saying that what he wanted to talk to me about would affect the abbots' meeting and took precedence.

When I mentioned to the prior that I had to absent myself the next morning, he simply smiled and said he thought it would be a bishopric.

And so it was. Cardinal Baggio, in the name of Pope Paul VI, asked me to accept the position of archbishop of Milwaukee in Wisconsin. I, in turn, asked him if the pope himself was really doing the asking or if this was just a *pro forma* procedure. He assured me Pope Paul VI himself was making the request. When I asked how much time I had to decide, he replied: "Five minutes." The plan, he informed me, was to talk with me that Saturday morning to get my assent, telegraph Archbishop William Cousins in Milwaukee on Sunday, prepare the press kit on Monday, and make the public announcement on Tuesday at 12:00 noon. My successor as abbot primate would be elected on Thursday and the papal audience would take place on Friday. He then added that theoretically I had till noon on Tuesday to withdraw, but it was not easy to stop the process at that point. Cardinal Baggio explained that I had the usual privilege of consulting one or another counselor of my choosing.

I took a deep breath. Only one thought came to mind: Although theoretically I could have said no, how could I refuse the personal wish of the pope and still be at peace with myself? I said my yes, knowing that over the week-end I could think and pray about it, consult some wise people, and, if I thought it was a wrong decision, call the cardinal on Monday morning.

I returned to Sant'Anselmo with mixed feelings. Saturday afternoon I was able to visit my spiritual director and talk over my hesitations. I had never wanted to be a bishop, otherwise I would never have become a Benedictine monk. I knew very little about bishops or what kind of life they led. Never having been in a chancery office, I did not understand the structure of a diocese and its officials. My director responded that not aspiring to be a bishop was probably the best criterion for becoming one. He also remarked on the advantage of being back in the States, a culture I knew well and where I felt at home. He knew the Roman atmosphere with all its gossip and small-mindedness did not always agree with me. We tossed the positives and negatives back and forth; I began to see that there was some logic in taking on this new challenge at the age of fifty.

My most serious reservations centered on my intellectual integrity. As primate of the Benedictines I enjoyed a certain intellectual freedom — a freedom that I prized. I was intellectually curious, and it was part of my nature to withhold assent till I found adequate reasoning to support an argument. I questioned the logic of a decree and hesitated in closing a debate if I felt all the evidence was not on the table. At times, the decisions of the curia seemed to lack strong theological underpinnings; in some cases it was difficult for me to defend them. These misgivings about more serious theological decisions could make the task of being a bishop difficult. Until now, as head of a religious order, I did not have to take public stands on issues like the non-ordination of women or contraception. Having been trained in theology in the style of the old manuals, I knew the degrees of certitude attached to various teachings of the Church and used them as guides, knowing that they were not cast in stone; there were difference between those doctrines *de fide definita* (defined as a part of the faith) and those that were *pia opinio* (pious opinions) and all the grades in between. We also talked that afternoon of my reservations about the natural law theories of some moralists, a subject I had wrestled with for many years.

On the positive side, I agreed that I would enjoy preaching more and presiding at sacramental liturgies like confirmations. Pastoral ministry appealed to me; I had an avid interest in social justice and work with the poor. I liked to write and could communicate in that way with many more people. Above all, I liked people and had no problem working with men and women alike. In addition, I was engaged by ecumenism and interfaith dialogues, deeply appreciating what that could contribute to the life of the Church.

My director wisely advised me to talk to a theologian we both knew and who was then in Rome. This would allow me to work out some of the negative issues — issues the director did not see as major obstacles. He used the oft-repeated phrase: "when one is asked to be a bishop, he is not asked to leave his brains at the doors." He emphatically believed that a bishop should feel free to be a part of the discussion on all theological issues and express his views in all honesty. If a bishop is not free to think and speak, who in the Church is able to? He asked me to think more about the positive aspects of collegiality as envisioned at Vatican II and how important that was for the future.

The theologian met with me on Sunday afternoon while all the abbots went by bus to Subiaco. We talked at length about the kind of faith a bishop, in general, should have; we spoke specifically about my doubts. It was the theologian's opinion that I should have no qualms whatsoever about consenting to be a bishop; in fact, he rejoiced in the thought.

I spent more time than usual in the chapel those few days asking for light and guidance, trying at the same time to analyze my hesitations, wondering about how I would adjust to a new kind of life, and asking for wisdom in this decision. The confidence Pope Paul had shown in me was my strongest support: he trusted me and thought I was suited to the task. Few being named bishop could say they had that same personal confidence. At the time I gave no thought to the possibility that I may have been another "Bugnini" and that Pope Paul would have been happier if I were not remaining in Rome. It was only later that I would hear that rumor.

At 11:45 on the morning of Tuesday, September 20, I called out of the assembly of abbots the abbot of my own monastery in Latrobe, Archabbot Egbert Donovan, to tell him the news before I spoke to the others. At 12:00 I took the microphone and said that, as of that moment, I ceased to be abbot primate and had become the archbishop of Milwaukee. The translators in the booths for the various languages heard the message correctly but had trouble with the name of the city. That is how the story went around that the abbots were all saying: "Where? Where?" And the people in Milwaukee were saying: "Who? Who?"

On Thursday, Viktor Dammertz, abbot of Sankt Ottillien in Germany and president of the congregation with that same name, was elected my successor. It was a good choice. I highly esteemed Viktor, having known him years before as a student. Being president of a missionary congregation meant he came to the job with a good knowledge of the Benedictine world that I had lacked. He was an excellent canonist and chaired that committee of the confederation. It was an important role in Rome at that time since the canonists were hard at work revising the Code of Canon Law and we were all concerned about the way in which monastic life would be treated. He was youthful, vigorous, and fluent in Italian, English, and French.

I stayed in Rome for a few weeks to pack my bags and say my farewells. Father Arrupe had a gathering in my honor at the Jesuit house so I could see all the superiors general at one time. Cardinal Baggio had asked me to return to his office to take the oath of fidelity required of a bishop. When it was over, he said he thought it would be a fine gesture if I went in the same building to the office of Cardinal Pericle Felici, the one in charge of the interpretation of the Code of Canon Law and the revision in progress, for the oath against modernism. I do not know how many times I had already taken it in my life as it was customary to do so before major orders, becoming a pastor, or assuming major office. Felici seemed delighted and was in his usual outgoing, exuberant mood. We had met many times at synods and were both members of the Consilium. The ceremony was delayed since in that vast canonical library no one could find a bible! I had to place my hand on a breviary. The Latin of the old oath against modernism was very complicated. When I finished reading it, Felici smiled and remarked: "I believe you really understood what you were reading. That is more than I can say for most bishops." Then he presented me with a gift — a collection of homilies he had preached in Latin on the occasion of bestowing the pallium on archbishops.

For my retreat I went up to Assisi for a week, staying with the Franciscan Third Order Regulars. With me I took two books: the *Regula pastoralis* of Pope St. Gregory the Great and a recently published work, *Farsi uomo: Confessioni di un vescovo (Becoming a Human Person: Confessions of a Bishop)* by Luigi Bettazzi, the bishop of Ivrea. Bettazzi had been auxiliary bishop under Lercaro in Bologna and was president of Italy's Pax Christi.

These books had been gifts to me from the Comunitá di Sant'Egidio, a group of lay Catholics seeking a deeper commitment to the gospel and to the needs of the poorest of the poor. I had come to know them ten years before when Professor Andrea Riccardi, a well-known historian in Italy, first gathered a group of men and women in their late teens, all seeking an alternative to other more political Catholic groupings. Occasionally I would go down to Trastevere in the evening to attend and preach at their vesper service at the convent and church Cardinal Poletti had given them. They, in turn, introduced me to another aspect of the Church of Rome, not the sterile clericalism of the curia, but the enlarged pastoral vision of the needy and outreach to them.

*   *   *

During that retreat in Assisi, I had time to reflect deeply on the role of bishop. Many questions were going through my mind. When I said my "yes" to Pope Paul VI, what was I really expecting? How should I prepare myself? What was my life as a bishop going to be like? I knew that the original meaning of the word bishop was "overseer" — an idea that pleased me since it did not deny the gifts of others but implied discerning how those gifts could be used. The documents of Vatican II wanted to return to an emphasis on bishops as pastors or shepherds, following in the footsteps of Pope John XXIII, who used the image of the good shepherd as his model.

I also asked myself: What kind of church would I find back in the States? Except for occasional visits when I was mostly occupied with Benedictine concerns, I had been away for ten years. During that time I had not played an active role in the changing American Church and to the challenges those times brought. I had left in 1967 at the beginning of the student unrest in the colleges and universities and returned in 1977, right after the bicentennial celebrations of 1976. During those ten years the Church had greatly changed and so had the country: from Europe I had watched the American pullout and end of the Vietnam War, the Nixon period and his resignation, economic downturns, and a general feeling of unease. In the Church large numbers of priests had resigned from active ministry and married and the numbers of men and women religious began to diminish. A new generation of Catholics had grown up, one with a very different experience of the Church than their own parents. Some had stopped practicing their faith, having obtained little religious education in their families, their schools, and their parishes. And I knew that the Church had many dissident members who had not fully accepted the thrust of Vatican Council II and were resisting any changes. Many disconcerting stories had reached me in Rome but at that point I had no personal experience.

I also asked: Where does one find a role model for a contemporary Vatican II bishop? Historically I knew there were two perennial sources that would influence my thinking in this regard: the profile of the bishops of the patristic period and the role of the abbot in the Rule of Benedict. I had always held in high esteem the way the bishops in the patristic period conceived of their ministry, e.g., in the West, St. Ambrose and St. Augustine, and in the East, the Cappadocians, like St. Basil and St. Gregory of Nyssa. Those fourth-century bishops willingly accepted their role as teachers; in their writing and preaching, bringing together the best of the Catholic tradition of their day, grounding it in biblical soil with theological acumen and philosophical wisdom — all to form a pertinent Christian spirituality for the faithful. They were scriptural exegetes using the knowledge available to them. They were theologians and philosophers, seeing no irreconcilable differences among the truths propounded by either group. And yet they were astute politicians, like Ambrose, and compassionate, socially concerned leaders, like Basil. It was the "golden age" because of the synthesis they were able to create for the faithful of their day. Moreover, they saw themselves and neighboring bishops as the best qualified to face the problems of their region, not looking over their shoulders to any higher authority to solve problems for them; Augustine did not look to Rome or Basil to Constantinople. They were assiduous in attending the councils of their region. How I wished that quality of episcopal leadership could be regained in the Church!

In addition, I knew that my experiences as an abbot would influence how I viewed being a bishop. Benedict's words in his Rule for Monks on

how the abbot should regard his role, I was convinced, embodied his concept of how all authority should function in the Church.

How should one update these models in the last quarter of the twentieth century after Vatican II? I combed the council documents for insights,
outlining and meditating on paragraphs eighteen to twenty-seven of *Lumen gentium* that dealt with the theology of bishops within church structure and on *Christus Dominus* that was dedicated in its entirety to the
bishop's role. The bishops at Vatican II stated unequivocally that, among
the bishop's many tasks, preaching the gospel should be given pride of
place. They also pointed out that a bishop had to be an authentic teacher. I
took these tasks to be my primary responsibility.

The council documents were clear that a bishop was not to be seen as
the pope's vicar, but possessed his powers by reason of his ordination. That
certainly was the fourth-century bishops' concept. Through that same ordination the bishop became a member of the college of bishops and, thus,
had a responsibility *cum et sub Petro* (with and under Peter) for the whole
Church's well-being. These documents also pointed out that a bishop is a
member of the presbyterate of his diocese, sharing with the priests the
pastoral care of the faithful. Finally, they talked in a new way about the laity's role, not only of their rights and duties, but also of their participation
in the whole Church's mission. It seemed to me those texts created a
framework of relationships to be worked out in practice, a vision that was
still in its infancy after Vatican II.

*   *   *

I went to visit Pope Paul before leaving Rome. What would his last message to me be? By that time I had heard in the corridors of the curia the rumors that Weakland was another Bugnini, that the pope wanted Weakland out of Rome, that it was a case of *promoveatur ut amoveatur* (let him
be promoted to get him out of the way). I doubted there was any truth in
these rumors since Hume called me to wish me blessings and told me that
he knew for some time I was being considered for a bishopric and he had
encouraged it. Some older American bishops had been in Rome for something, I do not remember what, but had asked me about returning back to
the States as a bishop and that some had put my name on the list. I knew
as well that Archbishop Jean Jadot, papal delegate to the States, had been
submitting my name — or so an American bishop told me.

The pope was very talkative that day, delaying some ambassador who was waiting in the antechamber. He repeated what he had already told Cardinal Hume, namely, that the best preparation for being a bishop was to have been an abbot, and that, above everything else, the priests and people were looking for a spiritual message. He said that he knew I would like the Midwest and Milwaukee in particular; that he had distant relatives in Kenosha (whom I never did meet); that my name had been on the bishops' list for several years; that he liked what I was doing for the Benedictine Order and thus always said no to an episcopal appointment; and that I was fifty, a good age to begin a new challenge. He had agreed this time to my appointment provided the announcement coincided with the Congress of Abbots so that they would not have to reassemble to elect a successor.

As I knelt beside that antique desk for his final blessing, I felt a sense of deep gratitude for all he had done for me. He had suffered a great deal as pope and it had taken its toll. After I kissed his ring, he accompanied me to the exit, shuffling along beside me. I did not look back as I opened that doubly padded door, perhaps realizing this might be the last time I would see him. Not wanting to dwell on that possibility, I left rapidly.

In mid-October I flew to New York and on to Pittsburgh and was met by some of my confreres. A few days later, Archbishop William Cousins, retiring archbishop of Milwaukee, Bishop Leo Brust, auxiliary bishop, and Father Bob Sampon, chancellor, flew from Milwaukee to Pittsburgh early one morning to become better acquainted with me and to firm up plans for my ordination and installation. The ceremonies had been set for November 8. Archbishop Jean Jadot, apostolic delegate in Washington, was to ordain me. After that meeting and lunch in downtown Pittsburgh, we went to my mother's house, situated conveniently on the way to the airport. Archbishop Cousins and Bishop Brust easily won over my mother's heart. As they left in the late afternoon, she said: "With people like that out there in Milwaukee looking after you, I know I will never have to worry."

PART III

By proces, as ye knowen everichoon,
Men may so longe graven in a stoon
Til som figure therinne emprented be.

Chaucer: The Franklin's Tale,
The Canterbury Tales

(As you all know, if you carve away at a stone for long enough, in the course of time some image will be impressed on it.)

CHAPTER 11

Learning to Be an Archbishop

Milwaukee (1977-1983)

I was ordained bishop at Mass on November 8, 1977. Although that I could have happened in Rome, perhaps even by Pope Paul VI, I decided to be ordained in Milwaukee among its priests and people. I had an intense sense of finality during the ceremony. I recalled Basil Hume's words two years before when he became the archbishop of Westminster: "There is no turning back or changing course. It is truly for life." I was then fifty years old; the future of my life was determined. That realization gave me clarity and direction. Yet it was also frightening: What if I were to discover that this was not my calling? Moreover, I would be living without a monastic community's support, without daily companionship from those who shared the same ideals, and without the richness of a daily and balanced prayer routine that had structured my life till then. Even in all of my travels as abbot primate, I returned to the monastic spirit of Sant'Anselmo.

My first year was spent settling in and becoming acquainted with the staff and parishes of the archdiocese, but especially getting a firm grip on the finances. The archdiocese for several years had been running on a deficit budget, selling property to make up the difference, and was only slowly beginning to make ends meet. One of my boasting points was that for the twenty-five years I was bishop we never operated on a deficit budget. Most of all, I had to find a place to live that would bring me closer to my people. From my predecessor I inherited a house out in the suburbs that was comfortable but far removed. The cathedral rectory where I established the archbishop's residence the next spring was more convenient and accessible, even though it was not completely monastic!

* * *

The *ad limina* visits of the American bishops to Rome were to take place in 1978. The country was divided by regions, and Milwaukee belonged to region seven, which included the bishops of Wisconsin, Indiana, and Illinois; our visit was scheduled for October. Of course, I was eager to see Pope Paul and share my observations on what I found on returning to the States. God determined otherwise: Paul died on August 6. I was shocked and grieved at losing a strong supporter and a father figure. Having lost my own father when I was five, I found father figures in the Church — my pastors, my novice master, my cleric master, and, of course, my abbot.

On August 26, Cardinal Albino Luciani of Venice, taking the name John Paul I, was elected Paul's successor. I knew the new pope fairly well and looked forward to a visit with him. Over the years, I had given conferences to the clergy in Venice and once preached a retreat that Cardinal Lucianai attended. In the summer of 1977 we were both in Split (the then-Yugoslavia) speaking at the 1,000th anniversary celebration of the Benedictine Marian Shrine at Solin. Afterward, we spent several hours together waiting for cars that were to pick us up and talked at length about church matters. He was, above all, a good listener.

Significant events — especially the deaths of loved ones — piled up in those weeks. After the pope's death in August, my mother died in early September. It was not totally unexpected. In early June, she had come to Milwaukee for a visit. I looked for events she might enjoy; since she loved flowers, we began with a tour of the Boerner Botanical Gardens and Whitnall Park, and then visited the Mitchell Park Domes. By evening she seemed exhausted by the amount of walking. But the next day she was again full of vigor. She had been a schoolteacher so one of her strongest wishes was to visit a central city school. I picked St. Agnes, which afterwards she declared the highlight of her trip. One of the students, probably a fifth or sixth grader, named Troy Washington (if memory, after all these years, serves me correctly) became her guide and never left her side. Within a few days after her return to Pittsburgh, he sent a photo of himself. I noticed, after her death, that she had pinned to the corkboard beside her bed, pictures of her fourteen grandchildren, and there in the center was Troy's face. All together, we had a busy week and she struggled valiantly to keep up the pace.

In early August I went for a week's vacation to Mount Lebanon outside of Pittsburgh where she was living with my two older sisters. She and I watched on TV the announcement of Pope Paul VI's death, understandably her favorite pope. As she looked on, she kept fumbling the blest rosary beads he had given her. When I would glance at her frail features as she sat there slumped in her recliner, I felt her days were numbered. She was obviously failing physically, but her mind remained clear. A few weeks later, after my return to Milwaukee, she telephoned in the early afternoon of Sunday, September 3, to tell me she was slipping fast and I had to come — "but there's no great hurry," she added. She died a few hours later before I reached Pittsburgh.

After a funeral Mass in Mount Lebanon, another Mass in Patton, our hometown, and the burial in nearby Carrolltown, I returned to Milwaukee. There I faced a hectic schedule of appointments. I had been away most of August and was leaving on September 25 for the bishops' *ad limina* visit. Finally, packing my bag, I suddenly realized how tired I was physically and mentally, and perhaps even spiritually. I was feeling a bit unmoored.

This uneasiness was compounded on my way to Rome. I stopped in London to spend a few days with Cardinal Hume. Early on the morning of September 28, Hume knocked on the door of the guestroom to tell me that Pope John Paul I had died during the night. What was God doing to His Church? Though I knew that such questions were useless and shrouded in mystery — in God's hands — this did not relieve my bewilderment. Luciani's untimely death was a deep disappointment to me; I was losing someone with whom I could have talked freely and who would have understood the tensions local bishops had to face in those post-conciliar years. Hume, knowing I was still grieving my mother's death and that I was quite shaken by this added sorrow, suggested I rest another week in London. I changed my flight and flew to Rome for the funeral of John Paul I.

After concelebrating that funeral Mass, I lingered in Rome until the election of his successor. I was staying with a few other bishops who had made the trip to Rome at the North American College. When the announcement came that white smoke was seeping out of the chimney of the Sistine Chapel, I made my way down the hill to St. Peter's Square and joined the expectant crowd. I added my voice to their jubilant cheers when, from the central balcony, Cardinal Pericle Felici announced that Karol Wojtyła was the new pope. My first reactions were quite positive. John Paul II was a gifted man, a learned and scholarly bishop whom I had often met on trips to Krakow and during my years in Rome. Although I was encouraged by his election, some of the other superiors general — men and women with whom I had previously worked — showed less enthusiasm. They thought that the new pope did not understand religious life and liturgical renewal. Since all the *ad limina* visits were canceled, I did not have an opportunity to verify their views. I flew back to Milwaukee.

*   *   *

A few months later, I gave a talk to the members of the Milwaukee press club at their annual Christmas gathering. The party was lively and well attended with a very relaxed and informal spirit. It was off the record — or so I thought. I spoke of the new Polish pope in positive, almost glowing, terms, but used several unfortunate expressions; of course they were the only ones repeated in the press the next day. In contrasting Pope John Paul II's gregarious public persona with Pope Paul's soberness and stateliness, I described his way of working a crowd, such as kissing babies, as "like a ham actor." Unfortunate wording! I also contrasted his temperament with the perceived "waffling" of Pope Paul VI by saying the new pope was much more tenacious and used another unfortunate word, "stubborn."

Charles J. Sykes, a young reporter, quoted both those expressions next morning in the *Milwaukee Journal*. I also told the group that many Italians were disappointed that they had lost the papacy; it had been a year of tragedy, the brutal murder of Aldo Moro and the threats of the Red Brigade. The Italians' disappointment, of course, was not because the new pope was Polish, although some, in reading his article, interpreted my words in that sense. There was a storm of protest from the sensitive Polish community in Milwaukee that haunted me for decades.

Old wounds, that I was scarcely aware of, were reopened. The hurts and grievances of the Polish community went back for decades. Archbishop Sebastian Messmer (1903 to 1930) had treated them harshly. He was impetuous and rashly placed their Polish newspaper, parishioners, and pastors under ecclesiastical penalties. He established his own Polish newspaper, and the fighting between the two papers was bitter and at times scandalous. A truce seemed possible when Messmer in 1911 agreed to ask Rome to appoint a Polish auxiliary bishop for Milwaukee. The Polish priests and people were jubilant. But then he turned around and recommended that Bishop Joseph Koudelka, an unhappy Bohemian (!) auxiliary bishop in Cleveland, be transferred to Milwaukee. Rome, unwisely, agreed.

Understandably, the Poles in Milwaukee felt betrayed and never accepted the new auxiliary. After two years, Koudelka was transferred to Superior, Wisconsin. Not surprisingly after the article quoting me appeared, I received many irate phone calls; one caller even said: "We are getting even now with you for what Messmer did to our grandparents."

The furor finally abated when the leaders of Polish community sat down with me and we listened to a tape of the whole lengthy talk — actually laughing and enjoying it. The *Milwaukee Journal* laid the event to rest in an article putting the disputed passages in context. The *Journal* also expressed the editor's hope that the new archbishop would not let this one incident change the "openness, honesty and good humor reflected in his public speeches." The incident, however, did not die. Without reference to the tape or to the newspaper's exculpatory editorial, the story was rapidly repeated all over Rome and reached as far as Poland — as the Benedictines there soon informed me.

*   *   *

In June 1979, I was back in Rome to receive from the pope a *pallium*, a woolen stole worn by residential archbishops (metropolitans). No matter where I went or to whom I was speaking — cardinals or *minutanti* (the lowest officials) — I heard the same story: many negative rumors were circulating in the curia about what was happening in the Archdiocese of Milwaukee. The pope was displeased with me. To obtain some clarification I went to see Cardinal Sebastiano Baggio, prefect of the Congregation for Bishops. With remarkable bluntness he told me I had done two things that had raised eyebrows: I had held a dinner at the seminary for resigned priests and their wives and I had appointed a resigned priest to a chancery position. Several times, he repeated that there had been many objections from a number of cardinals in the United States and Rome to my being named Milwaukee's archbishop. (He verified rumors that I had heard.) He told me that these objections were based on an interview I had given the *National Catholic Reporter* some years before. I had said that I saw no convincing theological reasons against women's ordination, but added that there were many sociological and psychological barriers to be overcome. Cardinal Baggio told me that he had consulted those who knew me well; all of them agreed that Weakland in his heart of hearts probably favors the ordination of women, but that he would not act outside the episcopal body or without Rome's consent. This response satisfied any doubts or hesitation that Pope Paul VI may have been harboring. Because of this background Cardinal Baggio admonished me to "keep my nose clean" *(non creare fastidi)*. With similar frankness he told me how difficult it had become for him now to defend the decisions of local bishops, especially those in the United States. Complaints from disparate sources frequently arrived directly on the pope's desk, especially through the Polish community resident in Rome. They were acted upon before his office had a chance to clarify matters with the bishop in question. In my case, he told me that frequent complaints arrived from Monsignor Alphonse Popek, a Polish pastor in Milwaukee. These complaints were disseminated by Popek's contact persons in Rome.

How seriously should I react to these rumors? Wanting further advice, I consulted Cardinal Casaroli, who had been named secretary of state following the death of my friend Cardinal Villot. I also wanted to talk with him about the U.S. Church, how I found the situation on my return after an absence of ten years. He quickly dismissed the rumors concerning some of my administrative decisions, and asked to hear about the Church in the United States. He listened carefully, interposing here and there pertinent questions, and saying several times how difficult it was for him to obtain a clear picture of what was happening in the States. He urged me to talk to Monsignor Justin Rigali, the person in charge of the English-speaking desk in the secretariat of state, who, Casaroli pointed out, was the pope's chief interpreter of the American Church and who should hear my point of view.

I agreed and he arranged for me to go directly down the hall to a small, dark waiting-room where Monsignor Rigali received me. He did most of the talking, confident he was well informed about the situation in the States and in Milwaukee in particular. His advice for me was unequivocal and could be summed up briefly as follows: I should seek to follow clearly in all matters the Holy Father's mind as seen through the documents of the curia and conform myself to them for the sake of unity in the Church's teaching body or magisterium; I should demonstrate absolute loyalty to the Holy See and inculcate such loyalty in my people; I should become a paragon of doctrinal orthodoxy in my teaching and writings, relying principally on the teachings of the pope and the curia. In this way my diocese and the Church in the United States would be unified and strong. This refrain would be repeated to me by other curial officials many times in the years ahead. Whenever in subsequent visits I tried to bring up in conversation with members of the curia the question of collegiality between the pope and the bishops or among the bishops themselves, I was called "ideological."

After the *pallium* ceremony and before leaving Rome, I had a private audience with Pope John Paul. He received separately the nine archbishops to whom he had given a *pallium*. I had arrived, naively as it turned out, with a list of issues I wanted to discuss. First on my list was to draw out his views on the concept of collegiality with the bishops and how it might function. I soon realized that the audience was a *visita di cortesia* (a courtesy call), and my attempts to bring up substantial issues were fruitless. He said I should return to these issues at a later date. He also waved off the "Polish affair" I had stumbled into and did not want to discuss it.

Then, out of nowhere he asked me two questions. "How long have you been a bishop?" and then just grunted when I responded, "Less than two years." "And how long were you abbot primate of the Benedictines before that?" "Ten years," I responded. That provoked another grunt, but no comment. At that meeting he never looked me in the eye and never betrayed his feelings, a behavior I had noticed in Poland. That trait and the ambiguous grunting I then assumed he had acquired as a survival technique under the Communist regime. We had the usual photo opportunities and that ended the audience.

As I boarded the flight to Milwaukee and reflected on the trip, I realized that this visit had left me perplexed and a bit unnerved. I was not surprised to learn that my appointment to Milwaukee had not been well received by many in the curia. But I decided not to take their reactions too seriously, since I had a genuine distaste for the credence they gave to rumors and gossip. Of one thing I was sure: in the future, every opinion I uttered would be meticulously scrutinized by the curia, especially any statements on women's ordination or the possibility of the ordination of married men.

I felt a bit disillusioned on my return home, but made up my mind that I would do my best for the faithful and the priests of Milwaukee and not let myself be put in a dehumanizing straitjacket. I finally realized that the days of Pope Paul VI were over. I had moved from being an insider in his pontificate to an outsider in the new one. Though I had not fully analyzed the consequences, I could see that I would have to deal with this in the future. In my heart I knew that I would probably reject the advice of Monsignor Rigali, and at my own peril; ultimately it became evident that he was outlining how the reign of Pope John Paul II would function. He was correct.

*   *   *

Living in the cathedral rectory downtown, I was far from the chancery and archdiocesan offices that were still out on 94th Street. It would be useful to again begin to drive. During my last year as abbot in Latrobe, in 1967, I had learned to drive at the age of forty. I went to Rome the week after receiving my license; with so little experience, it did not seem prudent to drive in Italy and for the next ten years, I didn't. Now, living in calmer and law-abiding Milwaukee, I decided to take it up again. I went to a competent instructor in one of the high schools who was delighted to provide a refresher course. He was very encouraging and imparted a sense of self-confidence. I rather enjoyed zipping around town. I soon realized that I could be a bit distracted because I was always in a hurry. I came to see something was amiss when no one in the house would ever go with me when I drove. One Sunday morning, in a hurry to take a retired priest to the bus station, I ripped off a part of the bumper of the car next to mine in backing out of the rectory garage. I took a terrible teasing and my reputation as a driver, such as it was, was totally destroyed. From then on, though I kept a set of keys for an emergency, I ceased to drive.

I soon learned the city bus-routes and on a day off enjoyed riding the bus out to one of the malls, the zoo, or the museum. Milwaukee's excellent Art Museum I could reach by foot.

From my library/office I could watch people come and go in Cathedral Square. It was full of picnic benches, and there, during the noon hour, street people, munching on a sandwich given out at the rectory door, would mingle with young executives and tourists. I came to know the street people well — if not by name, certainly by face. One bitterly cold winter morning one of the street people we all knew was found frozen on a doorstep. A need for more shelter-space led us to open the old cathedral school building to the homeless when the shelters were full.

The running of the cathedral parish I left entirely in the hands of the pastor and associate. When, in 1979, the pastor Father Fliss was named co-adjutor bishop of Superior, Wisconsin, I selected Father Jim Brady to replace him. Jim's zeal for the poor and his pastoral sensitivities had impressed me. The rectory was almost always full: pastor, associate pastor, a saintly retired priest, a priest who headed an office in the chancery, my secretary Father George Rebatzki, and me. There were two guestrooms. The two sisters who cooked and cleaned lived in quarters on the ground floor off the kitchen. That was our community.

Each day we gathered in the living room and recited Morning Office together. On one occasion, Cardinal Hume, visiting from London and dressed in rather unkempt street clothes, joined us for prayer. He took a seat on the sofa next to Helen, a Croatian immigrant who cleaned the rectory and helped the sisters. Helen immediately tried to assist the cardinal by pointing out as we went along where the next prayer could be found and guiding him through the whole Office. He played along perfectly and feigned ignorance.

I was beginning to establish a regular rhythm to my life, but it became clearer and clearer to me that I had to learn how to be a diocesan priest rather than a monk and had to accept the changes this transformation required. Although my living situation was good, I had not yet made any friends and missed the ready companionship of my fellow Benedictines. About this time I met Paul Marcoux. I have described in the Prologue (Chapter 1) the sad and difficult outcome of this friendship, but I raise it here because this is the context in which I met him. I was lonely and probably more needy than I would have publicly admitted, and perhaps more vulnerable than I could admit even to myself. I needed company, someone with whom I could talk over this new experience that I was just beginning to understand and accept. Although I enjoyed my work, I was not yet sure of myself and needed greater affirmation than I was receiving. Those around me at the rectory and the chancery treated me with great respect — and distance as befitted my role. I was the bishop!

*   *   *

The archdiocesan offices were on the corner of West Bluemound Road and 95th Street near the Milwaukee Zoo (the priests referred to the diocesan offices as the zoo-annex!). Our building had been constructed as a grade school by the adjoining parish, but, for lack of funds, was never completed and the archdiocese bought it. My office retained something of its schoolroom look and atmosphere. Each time the cold winter wind swept up the hill, rattling the windows and chilling my bones, I thought of the poor third-graders who might have been using that room. Of course, the real Catholic life and tradition were to be found in the parishes and not in my office, and not through the occasional parish ceremonies I celebrated. On the other hand, I knew that the diocese had to supply vision and planning for the whole Church and provide expertise and direction in education, catechetics, pastoral training, etc. I was also this diocese's link to the larger Church, as well as to the civic and ecumenical community in the Milwaukee area, activities that made many demands on my time.

Even in these, I knew that the parishes had to be central to the Church's mission. Thus, creating vibrant parishes was the first aim; everything else had to be means to that end. Through twenty-five years, I never wavered in that conviction.

Ms. Delphine Meyer, a seasoned professional, was my secretary; she was part of the diocesan staff for over forty years, twenty-five of them as my secretary. She was supremely proficient and loyal; no one took dictation as fast as she; no one typed as accurately; no one uncovered a misplaced comma as readily. Her life was one of exceptional service. I soon learned that in Milwaukee there were many such dedicated professionals working quietly and efficiently for the Church.

My typical week as a bishop was like my life when I lived at St. Malachy in New York and studied at Juilliard and Columbia University. Saturdays and Sundays were always the busiest and most important days of the week. Saturday was full of meetings, especially with lay groups, and I still had to carve out time to finish my homily. Sunday's 8:00 broadcast Mass was a highlight of the week. I took preaching on the liturgical texts seriously and wanted my homilies to be based on scripture but pertinent to people today. On Saturday my "Herald of Hope" column for the *Catholic Herald* also had to be outlined and a rough first draft typed up in the computer for delivery on Monday morning. During the twenty-five years as bishop I wrote over a thousand such articles.

On Sundays I was up by 5:00 a.m. I would shower, shave, recite Morning Prayer, and have a light breakfast. Finished with these by 7:00, I would go over my homily twice in my mind — always from memory — to make sure I could recall how it should fall into place. And then, I tried to pray over it as well. I was always a bit nervous about preaching, especially on the radio.

Celebrating this Sunday Mass was always special and remained so even after fifty years of priesthood. In breaking open the scripture readings and presiding at the Eucharist, I imagine the assembly before me as part of a gigantic living icon depicting Jesus with his disciples of all ages gathered at the Last Supper. All those gathered in former times and we in our day are simply doing as he commanded, repeating that supper in memory of him.

When I preached, I formed the habit of taking the bible in hand, going out into the center of the sanctuary to be closer to my listeners and preaching freely from there. I hoped my sermons would challenge the listeners without alienating them, force them to think more deeply about issues without totally rejecting what I was saying. I feel one is not preaching Christ's word if the challenges at times do not sting people's consciences. In general, however, I felt that people trying to be Jesus' disciples in today's world needed to hear more about God's compassion, love, and forgiveness.

Each Sunday after Mass, I looked forward to waiting in the very large vestibule of the cathedral as everyone exited, staying far back from the door in cold and freezing weather, waiting just outside the door on sunny days. I was eager to greet the regulars as well as the shy newcomers, to stoop to receive a bear hug from an enthusiastic youngster or gently embrace a fragile oldster, trying to remember each by name as they rapidly fell upon me. I would then move on to hear an update about someone's health or to commiserate with another on the loss of a job, to give a word of encouragement or at least a promise of prayer, and on and on. I hope I don't sound presumptuous, but I often felt I understood just a little bit of what Jesus must have felt as he passed through the crowds, healing by his very touch, writing words of pardon in the sand to be swept away like their sins, and bringing to life those who had no reason to live. It was overwhelming, almost frightening.

In the afternoon I usually celebrated another Mass out in a parish. Those Masses were often confirmations or anniversary celebrations of the parish. These were always joyous affairs when I saw the parishes at their best. One of the most satisfying aspects of being a bishop came from confirming, especially when the minimum age was set at sixteen. Preaching to the teens was rewarding and I seemed to be able to reach them. I wish I had kept the thousands of letters those confirmands wrote me each year on why they sought confirmation. Some of those letters were truly insightful. They would bring me courage when I was tempted to think the next generation might not be strong in the faith.

One day, after a few years in Milwaukee, I was on a flight to Atlanta for a meeting of bishops. The man next to me was a middle-aged, neatly dressed African-American. Seeing my Roman collar, he asked if I was a preacher. I said yes. Then he asked where and when I preached. I said every Sunday morning at St. John's Cathedral in downtown Milwaukee. "Good," came back the reply, "I come to Milwaukee often and would like to drop in to hear you. At what time do you preach?" "Eight in the morning every Sunday," I replied. He hesitated a bit, thought, and then responded, "You preach at eight on Sunday mornings? Well, courage! Someday you may get better and they will give you a decent hour." I have tried over the years to do better, but never gave up the eight o'clock time slot.

Tuesday was my day off and I was rigorous in keeping it. I did not go to the office under any circumstance. After prayer time and breakfast, I went to my study overlooking cathedral-square with my yellow pad in hand. I read slowly and carefully the texts of the readings for the coming Sunday Mass, jotting down ideas that came to me spontaneously. Then, from the shelf I would take down a few biblical commentaries on the same texts and continue my jottings. I left the ideas marinate till Friday or Saturday before writing my outline.

In my first years in Milwaukee, Tuesdays I soon learned could be the days when I felt the loneliest. Most of the priests of the archdiocese had parents or brothers and sisters living around Milwaukee whom they would visit. They also had seminary classmates whom they had known since early school days and who had the same day off. The first months I found myself trying to figure out how to supply this need. Sometimes I walked up to Marquette University where I had a confessor and spiritual director among the Jesuits to talk about this loneliness, coming often to the conclusion that a bishop had little choice but to grin and bear it.

With time I came to enjoy being a bishop and the ministry it entailed. I loved the people and entered willingly into their lives with their hopes and disappointments, joys and anguishes. I threw myself into the work, using all my time and talents as best I could. Slowly, too, I was able to build a staff that challenged me and brought me to new levels of understanding. When I was in Milwaukee, Rome seemed thousands of miles away and I put out of my mind rumors that might be flying there. But the loneliness never seemed to abate. Being out in public so much, I felt as if I were on stage all the time.

*   *   *

In December 1979, I found myself again on the way to Rome to confront Pope John Paul II. The difficulty centered on the appointment of Father Richard Sklba as my auxiliary bishop; he was the seminary rector. Archbishop Jadot, the apostolic delegate, had made a thorough inquiry among priests and laity, both in the archdiocese and outside among seminary rectors, before placing Sklba's name first in the *terna* he sent to Rome. Rome had approved Sklba's nomination, but, one week before his ordination as bishop and long after his appointment had been made public and the invitations to all the U.S. bishops sent out, the pope cancelled the ordination.

Sklba had chaired a committee of American biblical scholars who issued a document stating that, from a strictly biblical point of view, the ordination of women could not be decided one way or the other. But a codicil was added that upset the pope: the committee further stated that a positive answer would be more in keeping with the biblical evidence. Sources in Milwaukee had faxed this information to one of the pope's secretaries who, in turn, had placed it on the pope's desk. Pope John Paul II made the decision to cancel the ordination.

I flew with Sklba to Rome for a painful few days during which I vented my displeasure to Cardinals Casaroli and Baggio. Both were helpful in acting as shuttles between the pope and us. Although I asked for a personal audience with the pope, Cardinal Casaroli responded that he did not think it was wise for me to see the pope one-on-one, since, as he said, "both of you are too angry to bring about any positive results." He also relayed that the Holy Father had stated that he would permit a theologian to have a position in this matter different from his own, but not a bishop. Casaroli added, "Even though we both know that this is not *de fide definita*," a phrase that means "defined as an article of faith." Several times Sklba was required to write up his position on the ordination of women, each draft of which was taken to the pope by Cardinal Casaroli. The pope kept rejecting these versions until late Saturday night when he finally gave in. Our plane left early Sunday morning, with the ordination scheduled for the following Wednesday.

The process was impersonal, demeaning, unjust, and, most of all, lacking in any human sensitivity or concern for the life and reputation of Father Sklba. Moreover, the event confirmed a growing tendency in Rome to give credence to a powerful network of unofficial complaints that were influencing papal decisions.

I am forever grateful that Richard Sklba became my auxiliary bishop. It is impossible for me to exaggerate the role he played in the archdiocese during the twenty-three years we worked together. Not only did he keep me from making many mistakes as an outsider, but with his thoughtful and positive approach to our ministry, he contributed to making my years as bishop a deeply rewarding experience. His knowledge of scripture and his personal sanctity were always evident. In this selection as auxiliary bishop, God was indeed good to me — and to the people of Milwaukee. The energy that went into clearing his name that week in Rome was more than worth the effort. It is true that he was not Polish but Slovak; that may have miffed some of the Polish pastors.

How long I reflected and prayed over the events of this brief but exceedingly disturbing visit to Rome! That trip galvanized me: I had to think out more precisely how I would offer my service as a bishop. I had dreamt of a functioning collegiality among the bishops "with and under the pope," one that would not reduce individual bishops to mere spokespersons for the curia but see them as true collaborators. As a bishop, the least I had expected was that my opinions and ideas would be listened to as coming from an equal. Now, I had to take more time to think how the Church after Vatican II should function.

*   *   *

What did I find when I came to Milwaukee? First, it had a solid Catholic tradition that went back to 1843. It inherited a disciplined Catholicism from its ethnic roots, especially Swiss, German, Irish, and Polish, possessing a typical Midwestern conservatism with a strong working-class base. It resembled the Catholicism I had grown up with in western Pennsylvania; I felt at home and liked the people very much. Second, Milwaukee was large with a Catholic population of about 700,000, worshipping in over 300 parishes and missions. There were 547 active diocesan priests, 73 retired, and over 50 permanent deacons. To those were added 518 priests belonging to religious orders. There were also 3,872 sisters with residence in the diocese and 216 brothers. Third, many religious orders had established their headquarters or at least a religious house here. Through their work in universities, colleges, hospitals, and various institutions they greatly enriched the Church of Milwaukee.

Most of the clergy were first-rate — well-trained, highly independent, open-minded, and zealous. I was helped in understanding them — and myself — in an unexpected way. Soon after my arrival, on one of those beautiful Wisconsin winter days when piles of clean fresh snow covered everything in sight and the city more or less closed down, including the schools, and when people did not show up for appointments. I found myself in my office with time on my hands. I started to clean out the closets and drawers to see what Archbishop Cousins left behind. In the back of one of the cabinets I found a dusty copy of two studies commissioned in 1972 by the bishops' conference. The first was written by Eugene Kennedy and Victor Heckler on the psychological profile of priests, the second by Father Andrew Greeley on the sociological profile. I blew off the dust and took them home to read.

The findings of the reports corresponded to my limited experience with diocesan clergy. In particular, I resonated with the statement that psychological and social immaturity was one of the most serious problems among diocesan priests; according to the authors this indicated a weakness in the formation process. It is difficult to define immaturity, but we often recognize it in others when we see it; and to be honest, I had to recognize that same immaturity in myself. In addition, I was becoming concerned that narcissism was equally a problem among the clergy; again, I could see this in myself. For us priests self-centeredness seems to have come with our mother's milk, and was later re-enforced by being treated as the favorite among our siblings because of our priestly vocation.

In one of the interviews I did during my first week in Milwaukee, a TV announcer asked me whether I was going to be a bishop for the priests or for the laity. I answered, "For both, of course." I knew the priests were important because they were the means by which the Church reached the laity, but I did not want to exclude the possibility of reaching the laity directly. From the beginning I knew that I had to learn about them and from them.

Milwaukee was ethnically diverse, always had been. But the African-American population that had migrated north during World War II was in a different situation than other groups. Migrants from the southern United States gravitated to the northern section of the city as the old German population moved to the suburbs. I found it incongruous that this relatively small black population worshipped in the staid, somewhat plain Nordic churches constructed for thousands of parishioners. Not many of these newcomers were Catholic, although there had been a small active Catholic black population in the city that went back to the nineteenth century. Unlike the Germans, the Polish held on to their ethnic parishes on the south side with the large and impressive churches that were the center of their tightly knit communities. Till then, they had been reluctant to abandon them in a move to the suburbs. At the same time new ethnic groups arrived, especially the Latinos, and several Asian groups, Koreans, Hmongs, and Laotians.

The archdiocese had a long history of involvement in social issues. This tradition gave rise to nationally known activists, such as Father Jim Groppi, a civil rights leader in the 1960s and 1970s. But there was a long list — priests, religious, and lay — who had been sensitive to social injustices and who had kept social action alive. On the practical level, many food pantries and soup kitchens provided direct help to the poor. This was a proud Milwaukee tradition that I resolved to continue. This movement was not an exclusive Catholic enterprise; all the city's religious groups were active. Milwaukee had a rich ecumenical and interfaith atmosphere, which I prized from the beginning. During the social upheavals of the late 1960s, Archbishop Cousins had joined with the leaders of other church groups and with the Jewish community to form "The Greater Milwaukee Committee for Religion and Urban Affairs," later named simply "The Interfaith Conference." The Catholic presence in these groups was essential and became a regular part of my experience: a lived reality, not a theoretical topic.

Milwaukee was not as theologically conservative as I had been led to believe. My predecessor, Archbishop Cousins, was kind and gentle, trusting of others, and thoroughly imbued with the spirit of Vatican II. He permitted leaders to emerge and to develop their talents. His permissiveness in the case of Father Groppi estranged him from the Polish parishes of the south side and wealthier Catholics in the suburbs. In addition, he had asked Rome to name Father Leo Brust his auxiliary bishop, much to the dismay of some of the Polish pastors who felt that this was not in keeping to the tradition of appointing a Polish auxiliary in Milwaukee — a throwback to the acrimony of the Messmer days.

When talking with other bishops, I liked to emphasize Milwaukee's ideal size: large enough to undertake serious projects, small enough to be governable and manageable.

*   *   *

As I wrestled with the multiple issues I faced as a bishop, I had to come to some conclusions, even if tentative, about the way a local church should function. In today's lingo, I needed an operative ecclesiology. Some had begun to use the word communion for the council's vision of church; while I agreed, it could not be a *communio* of superiors ruling over inferiors. If we really believed in the action of the Holy Spirit, received in baptism, working in and through all the members, it had to be a vision in which everyone shared and to which everyone contributed.

The vision that I absorbed from Vatican II's document on the Church, *Lumen gentium*, could be summed up in one phrase: *the Church is all the People of God on pilgrimage. Lumen gentium* began, not with the hierarchy, but with the well-known phrase "People of God" to include all the baptized. This thought was echoed in the document on bishops *(Christus Dominus):* "[The bishops] should ensure that the faithful are duly involved in church affairs; they should recognize their right and duty to play their part in building up the mystical body of Christ" (#16). The neat dichotomy between the Church's life *ad intra* (the clergy's domain) and the Church's mission *ad extra* (the laity's domain) could be exaggerated and unhelpful if taken in an exclusive sense.

This intuition is confirmed by paragraph twelve of *Lumen gentium,* but with one important addition. It says that the whole body of the faithful, because of its baptism and the reception of the Spirit, cannot be mistaken in belief. It speaks of the *sensus* or *consensus fidelium,* a supernatural sense of the faith found in the whole people, "when 'from the bishops to the last faithful,' it manifests a universal consensus in matters of faith and morals."

This difficult but important passage is based on Cardinal John Henry Newman's *On Consulting the Faithful in Matters of Doctrine* (1859). When Newman was asked why the faithful should be consulted, he answered: "... because the body of the faithful is one of the witnesses to the fact of the tradition of revealed doctrine, and because their *consensus* through Christendom is the voice of the Infallible Church." If one believes that everyone receives equally of the Spirit at baptism and the Spirit grants charisms to clergy and lay alike for the building up of the Body of Christ, then that presence of the Spirit in clergy, religious, and laity must be listened to and respected.

It occurred to me — and to many others — that, through the concepts of shared responsibility and discernment, the documents of Vatican II permitted an inculturation of Catholicism into contemporary culture, especially in the United States, that could be the source of a revitalized Church in our times. Americans believed deeply in the value of democratic processes; perhaps this is the most enduring aspect of our culture. But Catholics are being asked to live schizophrenically in two opposing cultures, a church culture where leaders determine what all must believe and do and a democratic culture where there are participatory structures that help shape decisions. The discussions on shared responsibility and the theology of the laity, especially if interpreted in the light of Cardinal Newman's insights, opened up new doors. If the hierarchy really understood the need to consult all the faithful in the way in which Newman expressed it, then it would take seriously the need to listen to that same Spirit among them.

I would never want to say that God's Spirit is limited to the majority vote of any group. Within the cacophony of voices we hear, it could well be the "small voice" that is truly guided by the Spirit (the *pars sanior*). The process of consultation becomes one of discerning with all the people in the midst of all the voices what Christ wants for his Church today. Thus, there is a need to listen and to discern together. That does not mean that taking a poll is the answer to every question; that is not discernment or even democracy, but populism. Nor would I want to say that every decision that is discerned together in the Church is necessarily the will of God; we cannot bind God's Spirit to our processes. Nor would I want to say that God foresees only one way of doing things and we have to uncover it. But participatory decision-making diminishes the margin of error, even on a purely natural level, and gives a sense of ownership of the Church and its decisions to all its members.

Here, then, are some convictions I arrived at during my first years as a bishop after meditating on Vatican Council II's documents about the Church and how it should function, keeping in mind the need for consultation described by Newman.

No single group — hierarchy, religious, or laity — has a monopoly on the Spirit's gifts. Moreover, that Spirit is one, although its gifts might be many and varied. Chaucer and his description of the rag-tag group on pilgrimage is more what the Church is all about than Dante's neatly defined layers of saints and sinners. This point seemed especially relevant to those of us living in a society that still has many traces in its social structures of a Calvinistic or Puritan determinism that has resulted in classifying people into good and bad, the latter as irreformable and irredeemable. The idea of pilgrimage means that perfection in this life is never achieved, only striven for, where the good and the bad grow up together till the final judgment that rests, not in human hands, but only in God's.

Everyone has a contribution to make in building up God's Kingdom, some within the Church, some in the Church's mission to others, some predominantly in society at large. In fact, not all gifts are for the Church's inner life; some — probably most — are for bringing gospel values to the world.

Within the Church, moreover, although the members of the hierarchy on the pilgrimage are in the driver's seat, as it were, the map is never precise: it must be re-created, re-discerned as the pilgrims move along and encounter new problems and challenges, experience new joys and sorrows. The hierarchy shares the creation of this map with the entire People of God, listening to them at every turn, discerning with them the direction that must be taken. That map is created from meditating on and interpreting the scriptures together, as has happened in Christian community through the centuries. From those struggles comes a lasting, cumulative tradition solidified through the experience of many trials and errors, but which results in clarity of doctrinal definitions and resolutions. Added to this heritage is the composite witness of all the saints through the centuries as well as in our own day, holy men and women, models of the living gospel. Finally, and not least of all, add the light that comes from the give-and-take, the prodding, critiquing, discovering, pushing, shoving, and, yes, truth-telling that comes from brushing up against the particular culture in which the Church found itself in the past and still must live and work.

If all the baptized are full members of the Church and have received gifts from the undivided Spirit, then that Spirit working in them must be consulted. The authority, called the *ecclesia docens* by Newman, must first of all listen, listen, and listen and then try to articulate and refine, through more listening, what it heard. My task as bishop was to articulate this vision of a functioning church community and to find ways of implementing it in this given part of the Kingdom called the Church of Milwaukee.

With such a concept of church, I knew that I had to put most of my effort into sustaining those participatory entities that Vatican II had named, beginning with synods and conferences of bishops on the international and national levels to the same kind of entities on the local level, priests' councils, diocesan pastoral councils, and parish councils. They had to be ways of listening to and discerning the Spirit working through all the members. Today's expansion of communication through modern technology was one of the great advantages we have to model such a church.

*   *   *

When I arrived in Milwaukee certain urgent decisions had to be made, one concerning the minor and major seminaries. In 1977 there were about 120 students in the high school (minor seminary) and about 50 students in the four-year college program. They used a relatively new complex that was much too large for those numbers. Though I had attended a minor seminary, I felt that to foster maturity in the candidates they should spend their teenage years at home and go to a school that provided more social contacts than an enclosed minor seminary. Thus I pushed for closing our minor seminary; the seminary board finally voted to do so. On the college level, it seemed impossible to me to run a first-rate four-year college program for fifty students, even with an excellent faculty. I floated the idea of creating a unified college seminary somewhere in the Midwest among the bishops of Chicago, St. Louis, Minneapolis, and Duluth, but without success. The seminary board voted to close the college and house the students in a separate building on the campus of Marquette University. I often had second thoughts about so much change in so short a time period. I know I was not sensitive enough to the fallout from such decisions.

The major seminary of any diocese acts as a weather vane: when problems arise in the Church, especially among the clergy, the seminary is the first culprit blamed for not providing sufficient or appropriate training. Milwaukee was fortunate in having a well-established seminary, St. Francis de Sales, founded in the middle of the nineteenth century. The priests of the archdiocese were deeply divided on how this pre–Vatican II seminary had weathered the changes after Vatican II. As a newcomer, I could see that the seminary had gone through a difficult period, but it was theologically very moderate and had maintained a solid academic reputation. Father Richard Sklba was rector when I arrived; when he became the auxiliary bishop I turned to Father Dan Pakenham. He was a priest of the archdiocese then working for the bishops' conference in Washington as director of the office for priestly life and ministry and a recognized expert in formation.

Lay people who wished to obtain degrees in pastoral theology were admitted to seminary classes and their number was steadily growing. I was impressed and encouraged that lay people were working for these degrees. The priesthood candidates were the only students in residence and had their separate formation program. This arrangement corresponded to that of the Roman colleges and universities. This system embodied a good practice: candidates for the priesthood and lay ministry could come to know one another. More importantly, we would know during their formation period whether a candidate for the priesthood was able to work with professional lay people — an important qualification for ordination. Over the years we were continually evaluating these programs and reassessing the kind of formation the Church needed. Moreover, entrance requirements had to be kept high because the temptation to accept unqualified people was always present, especially with the declining numbers of candidates.

*   *   *

In a document published (1965) on the role of the local bishop, the council urged that in addition to a priest senate, each bishop should create a diocesan pastoral council composed of clergy, religious, and laity "to investigate and consider matters relating to pastoral activity and to formulate practical conclusions concerning these" (*Decree on the Pastoral Office of Bishops,* #27). Archbishop Cousins established the senate of priests but hesitated over the archdiocesan pastoral council (APC). I accepted the challenge to make these new participatory groups work well because I saw in them not only the wishes of the bishops at Vatican II, but the way to prepare the Church to enter the twenty-first century. Listening and discerning were not qualities the American political system valued highly and all of us had to learn new skills. My Benedictine background helped me in this effort.

These entities were pivotal to the way I functioned as a bishop for twenty-five years. And in all honesty, I enjoyed them. In no other way could I have met, worked with, and come to appreciate so many leaders, clerical and lay. I profited immensely from their insights and fervor.

Of all the participatory entities, the priest senate was the one with which I first became acquainted and with which I felt very much at home. It was active and vital when I arrived in Milwaukee; Archbishop Cousins had supported them and never tried to rein them in.

The priests, working through the priest senate, had been dealing with significant pastoral and social issues; they were also preoccupied with many concerns about their own lives and mission as diocesan priests in the post–Vatican II period. Since this issue was relatively new to me, I listened carefully to the most respected leaders among the priests, those who possessed evident and clear pastoral insights. Priests were the important middle management without whom the Church simply could not function; everything that reached the people was funneled through them. They needed someone who would listen to them, trust their pastoral instincts, and confirm them in their ministry.

The archdiocese was divided into sixteen districts and one aspect of the priest senate that pleased me was that the priests met by district between their regular bimonthly sessions. In that way, each delegate could report, not only his own opinions on the issues at hand, but those of his fellow priests.

During my first years all of those concerns were in one way or another supporting the priests' desire for more self-reliance and accountability. Probably the most important was the naming of a vicar for clergy. In church law a bishop can appoint a priest his vicar for a specific area and delegate to him powers reserved to the bishop. The other topics were alternate residency, adequate salaries, clear assignment procedures, determined tenure in an assignment, periodic reviews of their life and work, and an agreed age for retirement; I approved all of them. This relieved much of the tension priests felt and gave them a sense that they were a part of the decisions that affected their lives. It awakened in them a sense of personal accountability as well.

At the *ad limina* visits in Rome I never received any negative reactions from the curia about these changes in the lives of the priests. One decision of the priest senate did bring strong negative reactions in Rome. The priest senate voted to sponsor a dinner for resigned priests and their wives at the seminary in June of 1979 after the students had gone home. I agreed and about 120 priests and their wives came, bringing the number of those attending to about 250 people. Instinctively I understood that this meal was to be a gesture toward healing — Pope Paul VI had taught me the importance of such gestures — and it was an effective one. Those who had been bitter or felt wrongly treated by Mother Church found in this meal a sign of reconciliation. But Rome was flooded with letters of protests from the Priest Forum (a small group of priests headed by Monsignor Popek) and members of Catholics United for the Faith (CUF).

*   *   *

The priest senate also recommended the creation of an archdiocesan pastoral council (APC). For Catholics, this was a new experiment. Each of the sixteen districts selected two members to this council; the priests elected several of their number for membership; men and women religious elected their representatives. Finally, I appointed a few lay members to make sure that all the ethnic groups in the archdiocese were represented and would be heard from. The wisdom of the committee that helped me set up this council could be seen in the clarity with which they refined its scope and its processes. It was to deal only with significant issues of a diocesan nature, related to the Church's total mission, and of pastoral concern. The recommendations, if they met these criteria, could come from anybody. By keeping these criteria in mind, the council was able to avoid entering into personality conflicts in individual parishes or complaints of a local nature.

The APC held its first meeting on December 9, 1979. Jeanne Bitkers of Sheboygan was elected its first president, served two terms, and gave it the professional character it needed. Through the years we were fortunate in having excellent leadership in that body, one that worked well with me and my staff. They had no preconceived agenda, were flexible, and were not ideological. Jeanne was especially effective. She was a teacher in the public school system in Sheboygan, very involved in her parish, comfortable working with priests, but sure of her own identity. She saw her role as supportive of the bishop and the pastors and of working for the betterment of the Church in this area of the world.

What kind of issues did that group deal with? The first was the transition from the older model of Catholic Youth Organization for youth ministry to one with less emphasis on sports and more on service to those in need and based on good scriptural and catechetical inspiration. Second came the pastoral care of prisoners in the state and federal prison systems and their families; it also took months to gather information and devise solutions that involved enlarging our corps of volunteers. One of the most sensitive issues involved the establishment of two residences for developmentally disabled adults; this included the difficult issue of clarifying more accurately what parish membership entailed. It was a good exercise in trying to combine a sense of full participation with compassion for those who could not fully participate in, or who were only peripherally joined to, the parish. The pastoral council came up with guidelines for confirmation, given the older age at which it happened; they tried to find a just formula for parish assessments (called the *cathedraticum*) to the central offices; they studied carefully the norms for the newly established parish councils; and so on.

Two items they worked on in the first years stand out now as having been important, but without their knowing it at the time. The first was an issue called "The Education/Training for Prevention of Child Abuse" that was introduced in 1983 and passed in early 1984. Their recommendations resulted in a joint project of the Catholic school personnel and Catholic charities for the training of special teachers to work with kids to detect any kind of child abuse. For this project the director of Catholic Charities, Tom Schneider, was able to obtain funding to train teachers who could be called in when necessary. Although this effort was at first directed primarily toward cases of physical abuse, we later used these professionals in all the schools where any priest or lay person had been accused of sexual abuse of minors.

The second issue from those same years called for a study of shared personnel and cooperation among parishes, especially adjacent ones. This was the beginning of an extensive project of collaboration among parishes that extended over many years and acted as a perfect preparation for the merging and closing of parishes that came about because of demographic shifts and the shortage of priests.

The school system at that time was excellent but with limited funds beginning to show signs of stress. As the number of sisters diminished, there was a growing core of lay teachers. The religious education programs, being predominantly staffed by volunteers with little training, were often criticized for lack of qualified teachers and real content. My staff worked hard to raise standards in both areas. However, I knew that funds would always be a problem, even though, at that moment, it had not reached a crisis stage.

With the advice of these bodies, I mandated parish councils in all the parishes. Discernment became the in-word for years among members of these groups. It was from the leadership that surfaced on this local level that the members of the APC were chosen.

*   *   *

One of the first proposals to come to both the priest council and to the archdiocesan pastoral council asked that the diocese engage in a program of spiritual renewal. I had noticed the importance of keeping a spiritual and biblical perspective in all the discussions at the parish and diocesan levels; how easily the councils could fall into attitudes that were more political or provincial than religious. We needed a program that would help the faithful reflect on the scriptures and the Catholic tradition and place their discernment in that light and in a context of prayer. In October 1979, the priest senate recommended the *Renew* program and later the APC concurred. In my *ad limina* report to Rome in 1983 I described the triple purpose of this program as follows: "1) a return to the primary teachings of our Faith as expressed in the New Testament, in our theological tradition, and in the sacramental life of the Church; 2) a renewal of the bond of Faith which should characterize the unity of each parish community; 3) a new commitment to the works of justice, peace, and charity." Our newly ordained auxiliary, Bishop Sklba, agreed to direct this spiritual renewal with a concern that the material used be biblically based and of the finest quality.

In August of 1981 all the preparations were in order and *Renew* began in 213 parishes. Each year for the next three years, during six weeks in spring and fall, all other programs in the diocese ceased (we observed that proviso rigorously) and the whole Catholic population devoted itself to the prepared prayers, studies, and reflections. The program was tied into the liturgical readings for the Sunday and so the Eucharist became the center for this renewal. The faithful were invited to come together each week in small groups in private homes for prayer and reflection on the Sunday readings. As many as 60,000 adult Catholics met weekly in these groups under trained leaders. After *Renew,* leaders with a more spiritual perspective came to be elected to parish councils. Many of these prayer groups continued to exist long after the official programs ceased.

*   *   *

One of the advantages of the APC was that women became more integrated into the decision-making processes of their parishes and of the archdiocese. It was good to see their number grow. With the strong support of the priest senate and the archdiocesan pastoral council, I formed in 1981 a task force on the role of women in the local church and society with Jeanne Bitkers as chair. They held hearings all over the diocese to probe this issue and came up with some helpful suggestions. In the meantime, as openings occurred in the staff of the archdiocesan offices, I began to appoint women to more and more leadership positions, recognizing the wealth of talent we already possessed in these women, lay and religious. As the years moved on, I can say that it was taken for granted that women would be found in all leadership positions in the archdiocese where ordination was not required by law. Outside consultants brought in to examine my staff and its functioning always gave me high marks for this support of women and the use of their distinct talents.

When the APC was organized, I noted that some ethnic groups, especially the new immigrants, were not represented. It was necessary for me to name members from those groups. This meant there were some whose gifts were not yet a part of the whole mix of the archdiocesan Church. For some time I reflected on how to raise up these voices. I knew it would take time — perhaps a generation.

One of the most important pastoral decisions to cope with the growing Hispanic population came about almost accidentally. When Bishop Ronald Connors, CSSR, of San Juan de la Maguana in the Dominican Republic invited our diocese to take over the poorest parish in his diocese, one on the southern coast west of Santo Domingo, I jumped at the chance. In that way we were always training priests in ministry to the Spanish-speaking. These priests returned to Milwaukee after five years to serve in our Latino community. I received much encouragement from Archbishop Cousins, who had sponsored a similar project some years before in Paraguay.

In the first five years I struggled with ministry to the African-Americans who lived for the most part in the Central City; the church and school complexes there had been built by German immigrants. After World War II, the German population began to move to the suburbs. Now a small, predominantly black, Catholic population was using these same buildings, swallowed up by their size and struggling to maintain them. There were many meetings to try to unravel that problem. Initially, we did not make much headway. I continued to follow Archbishop Cousins's decision not to subsidize any parish or Catholic school. We offered scholarships to families who wanted to send their children to a Catholic school, but did not pick up operating costs. We simply did not have nor could we raise that much money. This dilemma reached a critical point in subsequent years.

The Catholic black population was not growing. One of the most trying crosses of my ministry as a bishop was my inability to identify and implement the best form of ministry and evangelization to the African-American population. It grieves me even today to write this statement.

I had told Archbishop Jadot there was no ministry to the Native Americans in Milwaukee because we had no reservations in our diocese. I found out soon enough that, though there were no reservations, there were many Native Americans in Milwaukee. Shortly after arriving, I received a poignant letter from Sister Margaret Troy about their plight — so I hired her. Through her sensitive approach to Indian culture and her gentle ways that ministry began to blossom. First we established a place for them to congregate and worship with the establishment of Siggenauk Center in 1981 and then, some years later, I permitted them to erect their own parish called the Community of the Great Spirit. Every five years I could report to Rome on the growth of this ministry and its effectiveness.

The Asian community was slower in becoming more organized, but soon began to grow rapidly. Much of that growth, however, was yet in the future.

*   *   *

When a survey was done among the priests in early 1978, high on the list of their priorities were social justice concerns, no surprise given the history of the archdiocese. Although I had a good theoretical knowledge of Catholic social teaching and some personal experiences of the issues, I had never been engaged on the local level in the situations that Catholics there were facing. For example, I knew that the Church in most parts of the

United States had State Catholic conferences, but I knew nothing about what they did. Wisconsin was highly organized with an office in Madison, the capital. In the twenty-five years I was bishop we had only two directors for that office, Chuck Phillips and John Huebscher, both of whom had my complete confidence and trust. We bishops met three or four times a year to discuss what was coming before the state legislature, to decide which legislation we would take a stand on and why. The issues we became involved in touched the lives of Catholics and the Church, like educational changes, consistent life issues, hospitals and health care, cemeteries, and welfare policies. At the beginning the apparatus seemed heavy to me and more time-consuming than necessary; so, with the bishops' agreement, I streamlined the process.

In the Archdiocese of Milwaukee I found an active Catholic Social Services, led by Monsignor Joseph Springob. He was an invaluable source of wisdom to me and guided me through some difficult situations with the labor unions. He shared with me much about all the direct services we could provide to this diocesan community. Most of all, he taught me the need to work with other community groups; the Catholic Church would make a difference only by working with others and not by standing alone. Thus, I found myself taken up with the ecumenical and interfaith leaders on social issues. Where there were grassroots organizations among the parishes I encouraged the pastors to become members, obtained funds for them when possible, especially from the Campaign for Human Development, and gave as much support as I could.

Within the first three years of arriving in Milwaukee, I had in place a Commission on Human Concerns composed of Catholic leaders in the archdiocese to sort through our local issues. At that time, these ranged from ethical investment practices (e.g., no investing in companies producing abortifacients, none in companies with more than ten percent in armaments, etc.) to supporting family farms and agriculture. We studied thoroughly the draft of the bishops' letter on racism and took a special interest in integration, a vexing problem in Milwaukee for decades. The priest senate even asked me to hire a professional in this area to make sure we were doing everything we could as a diocese to conform to the law and support equal opportunity in employment.

But most of the efforts toward more social justice came by working with the ecumenical and interfaith community. I felt immediate rapport with the Jewish community, which like Catholics had been immigrants in the very first days of the city. We had grown up together, two minorities that shared many of the same social problems for over a hundred years. In fact, we celebrated with several common events in 1993 the 150th anniversary of our being in Milwaukee. Our leaders met frequently and discussed with freedom our feelings and concerns about the city and its social problems, often coming to an agreement in appropriate action.

On September 10, 1981 (as my notes show), I gave a talk to the members of the Muslim/Catholic dialogue and spoke on rising above our stereotypes and learning to know the best of each other's traditions. Archbishop Jadot, who by that time had left the United States to take over an office in Rome for the promotion of dialogue with the Muslims, told me that Milwaukee was one of the only dioceses in the world with such a dialogue and encouraged me to continue to support it because "it is going to be very important in the future."

Out of our mutual knowledge and the growth of trust, the religious leaders formed many dialogue groups to discuss topics of a more theological nature, which have continued to this day. Many friendships were formed and they enhanced the presence of all churches in the community for dealing with social problems, especially for bettering the conditions of immigrants and workers. These contacts affected positively my talks, writings, and sermons.

I seemed to flourish in the midst of all these discussions and projects. One aspect of these participatory entities I had not anticipated was the way in which I came into contact with people who were highly motivated, unselfish in giving of time and talent, compassionate, and God-fearing. The example of all these people who participated in these listening and discerning processes encouraged me.

During the first decade I was bishop I wish someone had told me I was trying to do too much. Wherever I went, even on short trips, I carried a bag full of books because of the Economic Pastoral and all my other pressing projects. A bishop had to be an expert in many different fields — from liturgy, scriptures, theology and education, on one hand, to cemeteries, poverty, sex education, health care, and finance, on the other. I was being pushed to the limit. To help ease this load of work, I restructured my staff by forming a cadre of middle management, a group I called episcopal delegates (I used this term instead of vicars so I could include women). They took up the more routine work for me and made the necessary decisions in my absence. I delegated well and the work was not neglected.

*   *   *

One of my priorities as a bishop was to participate fully in the work of the National Conference of Catholic Bishops (NCCB) headquartered in Washington, D.C. The full body of bishops, numbering around 280 at that time, met twice a year, each meeting lasting several days. To me this was an example of collegiality; thus participation for me was obligatory. When I joined the conference in 1977, I was impressed by the competency of its staff; all were acknowledged experts in their fields. In my twenty-five years as bishop I missed only one conference meeting, that held in the spring of 1996 when I was on sabbatical.

Whenever I was asked to do anything in the conference, I willingly accepted. For example, in November 1978 the bishops elected me, still a newcomer, to chair for a three-year term the bishops' liturgy committee. It was a busy committee: translations had to be approved and the proper liturgical books printed. But it was material I knew. Moreover, its staff, Fathers Thomas Krosnicki, SVD, and John Guerrieri, excelled in every way. The main concern I had to deal with in those three years was "inclusive language" in translations, a new phenomenon that could have been marked "tread lightly." Specifically, the neuralgic point was the words of consecration in the institutional narrative of the Eucharist that contained the phrase "for all men." After extensive debate, the body of bishops voted to drop the word "men" and Rome approved.

In the bishops' meeting of November 1980, because of many liturgical issues, I happened to be on the floor more than usual guiding the discussion. At that same meeting the bishops voted overwhelmingly for a statement condemning Marxism. After that vote Peter Rosazza, a young auxiliary bishop of Hartford, rose to make the suggestion that we write a letter on capitalism, since that is "what the bishops of the world would expect of American bishops." It was a fine idea and the vote to do so was positive. At that same meeting the bishops voted to write a letter on peace and the nuclear threat. It too passed overwhelmingly. Bishop Rosazza's proposal would drastically affect the next six years of my life. Little did I realize what I was getting into. (I give a full account of the Economic Pastoral, its process and outcome, in Chapter 12.)

*   *   *

Every five years I dutifully sent to Rome a lengthy report on the state of the Archdiocese of Milwaukee as requested by church law. Then, about six months later, I would make a trip there together with all the other bishops of the region. After the aborted visit of 1978, I made four such trips — in 1983, 1988, 1993, and 1998. Each time, we bishops would meet as a group with various curial officials in selected congregations. The bishop or archbishop of each diocese would also be granted a private audience of ten to fifteen minutes with the pope — a visit that became a mere formality since there was not sufficient time for any real dialogue. Some of us suggested we forgo these short visits so that the whole group could have time for a lengthy serious dialogue with the pope on the urgent issues the Catholic Church in the United States faced, but that suggestion was not looked upon favorably.

On every *ad limina* trip without exception, I noticed that I would be singled out (the other bishops were never aware of this) and told to meet privately with Cardinal Baggio in the Congregation for Bishops (or later with his successor Cardinal Bernardin Gantin in that same congregation) and then with Cardinal Joseph Ratzinger in the Congregation for the Doctrine of the Faith. Upon arrival at their offices, I would be presented with a list of complaints. These were actions or decisions of mine that seemed to irritate the pope and members of the curia. I always felt a need to stand tall and not be intimidated, making it clear by my demeanor and responses that I was engaging in a conversation as bishop to bishop and not as a "branch manager to the head office."

Cardinal Joseph Ratzinger, then prefect of the Congregation for the Doctrine of the Faith (the former Holy Office or Office of the Inquisition), later Pope Benedict XVI, always treated me professionally and respectfully. The first time we met in 1983 he had some of his staff present, but after that we always met alone. Although in private we sometimes spoke German together, when it came to these official meetings, he would slip into Italian where I was more comfortable and where he would not have a decided advantage. The complaints raised against me, it was evident, were provided by someone from Milwaukee who was monitoring my every word and action, mostly through the local diocesan and secular newspapers. Almost all the programs and lectures sponsored by the archdiocese, especially on sexuality, were being monitored. The cardinal never referred to scurrilous negative articles about me in ultraconservative Catholic papers published outside the archdiocese. Moreover, he made clear distinctions between matters that were of a dogmatic nature and those that were questions of pastoral judgment.

No real process was involved in these meetings; they just seemed like a friendly conversation, one that was not accusatory or threatening. Yet I knew better than to let the elegant atmosphere of that sitting room with its gilded baroque chairs covered in red damask seduce me into thinking these discussions were idle chatter.

In that first meeting in 1983 the cardinal brought up, as I had expected, complaints about the teaching of certain professors in the various colleges and universities in the Archdiocese of Milwaukee. He was always concerned about the question of women's ordination and mentioned that I should not raise false hopes that this might change even in a new pontificate. He was sensitive to the practice of inter-communion that, on some occasions, had been practiced by some priests of the archdiocese. As I expected from previous correspondence, he raised the question of the employment of resigned priests in the archdiocesan offices. I reiterated that I followed the policy set down by my predecessor Archbishop Cousins, namely, that, if the priest was officially laicized, I would not hesitate to hire him for a position that met the criteria set down in the document granting the dispensation. Finally, he brought up the complaints about the sex education courses. Since I had sent him all that material and he had responded that his experts found no fault with the contents, he did not dwell on that issue.

On every topic, I would distinguish facts from whatever gossip his informants may have picked up, clarify the record where the information was false or faulty, and then defend my actions if I thought the issues at hand involved a prudential judgment that was the prerogative of the local bishop. Finally I would concede if there were something I had not taken care of that I should have. I can honestly say I never feared these meetings. If they were meant to intimidate me, I certainly did not let them do so. Cardinal Ratzinger knew that no bishop could control all that happened in his diocese, having been himself the archbishop of Munich. When he would raise a point like girls serving at Mass, I could point out similar things happening in Rome, sometimes in the very shadow of St. Peter's Basilica.

It is true that I never was informed who had sent in the complaints or saw them ahead of time, but the large number of Xerox copies of articles from Milwaukee newspapers that he had before him made it clear that they came from someone in the archdiocese itself. As an aside, I can say that in all honesty I felt Cardinal Ratzinger's heart was not in this kind of policing, if that is the right word for what was going on. I always assumed then and still do that he was carrying out papal orders.

After meeting in 1983 with Cardinal Ratzinger I was asked to visit Cardinal Baggio in the Congregation for Bishops where the same subjects were covered. During that visit in September of 1983, I heard many stories circulating in the curia about the dinner for resigned priests, most of them untrue. In all honesty I had to admit I was upset with the negative attitudes I found in Rome toward those who had left active ministry, almost as if they were to be ostracized or treated as lepers. Although I never held the view that the best had left — as some were inclined to say — I did regret the inestimable loss to the Church of many very competent and faith-filled ministers.

For the private audience with the Holy Father, I had made a list of items I wanted to talk about. He seemed more relaxed in his manner of receiving bishops now, but commented very little on anything I said. The Economic Pastoral did not come up at all in the conversation. When I touched a delicate point like the role of women in the Church or his resistance to permitting resigned priests to return to the lay state, he just cast his eyes down, crossed his arms, and grunted. At that time Pope John Paul II had taken a more restrictive stance toward priests asking to leave active ministry, probably thinking he could put a stop to the hemorrhaging by denying dispensations. It wasn't working and only more deeply hurt those leaving.

At the end of that *ad limina* visit we bishops had the customary lunch with the pope. As we were finished eating, he asked if anyone wanted to bring up any specific issue not yet talked about. I swallowed a few times and then placed on the table the practice of not granting dispensations for resigned priests. I mentioned how, as a result, many excellent men and women were hurting. He went around the table asking the other bishops if they also knew of such men. Almost everyone replied in the affirmative. At the end, slouching in his chair, with elbows on the table and arms intertwined, he simply said: "But I'm hurting too," and ended the discussion.

*   *   *

When I wrote up the *ad limina* report covering the years 1978 to 1983, I felt rightly proud of the vitality of the Church in Milwaukee and all that was happening because of *Renew* and the ecumenical and civil involvement. But there were problems, vexations that did not go away, divisions that I was not able to heal and that perhaps were even exacerbated by my national involvement. Probably what surprised me most when I first returned from Rome in 1977 was how highly organized those groups opposing the implementation of Vatican Council II could be. One could always assume that negative and argumentative letters would appear regularly in local newspapers, Catholic and secular, opposing every decision of the bishops' conference and that I as a local bishop tried to implement. Almost every parish had a small vigilante group that was an irritant to pastors, parish councils, principals of the schools, and teachers of religious education alike. These groups had their own networks and channels of communication.

The pernicious enemy at that time was "secular humanism," a term taken from the Evangelical Protestants that meant a form of atheism. I recognized this term as redolent of fundamentalist thinking that came from the American religious right and was taking hold in the Catholic population, especially in the southern Bible belt. Beginning with my *ad limina* report of 1983, and in every subsequent five-year report, I tried — without visible success — to explain to curial officials a phenomenon I had uncovered here, namely, a new form of Catholic fundamentalism. These officials had no understanding of American biblical fundamentalism and thus of the kind of religious thinking — often very anti-Catholic — experienced not only in the Bible Belt, but in abundance on all our TV stations.

I pointed out in my report that some Catholics were becoming more and more "fundamentalist" in their approach to their faith. This did not always result in biblical fundamentalism, but more often in a tendency to treat all church teaching and papal pronouncements in a fundamentalist way. Some of these insistent groups wanted the pope to pronounce infallibly on everything in order to cast out all doubts and have unity in the Church. Struggling to raise their children in the Catholic tradition in a culture they found inimical to it, they expressed a deeply felt need for clarity in church teaching above all else, seeking unquestionable definitions of and solutions to all religious and moral matters. They were rightly concerned about many aspects of the contemporary American culture and saw the role of the Catholic Church, often in union with Evangelicals, to be a stronghold against all these culturally negative influences — at least as they defined them. Moreover, too many Catholics, I felt, were influenced by the mega-churches of the Evangelicals and really were looking to be entertained rather than challenged by God's Word and Christian discipleship.

During my years as archbishop I had a running battle with conservative groups that had risen up after Vatican II. Some of these groups were locally bred; others were national with a local chapter in Milwaukee. In their regard, Archbishop Jadot mentioned: Whenever you find a group of

laity who are obstructionists, look for the priest behind them. Two such instances in Milwaukee will suffice as examples.

In Kenosha Father Vincent Schneider began a local group, the
Thomas More Education Foundation, to monitor all the teaching in the
Catholic schools, especially the local high school. The members sought
out signs of doctrinal deviations as they understood them and would label
them heretical; this kept Kenosha divided and on edge for years. Another
group, national in character with an active Milwaukee chapter, was Catholics United for the Faith (CUF). In Milwaukee Monsignor Alphonse Popek
was its leader. Their concern focused first on the sex education courses
taught in the archdiocese and, in particular, one called *Valuing Your Sexuality.* The concept of that program was bringing together parents and
teens to assist parents in speaking about sexual morality with their children. The idea was a good one and very much appreciated throughout the
archdiocese by parents who admitted they were embarrassed to discuss
these matters because they lacked an appropriate vocabulary. They did
not want to use coarse street jargon, on one hand, nor medically correct
but abstruse terms, on the other. Members of CUF also objected to seminars for couples and married people that they considered too explicit. Not
being an expert on age-appropriate sex education and fearing that CUF really wanted courses on chastity, I finally sent all the material off to Cardinal Ratzinger's office. When he sent it back, I found the comments of his
Roman consultant theologically helpful, but realized that consultant was
not much more competent than I in judging age-appropriate specificity in
sex education. I did some tweaking on the material where needed and decided there was not much more I could do.

*   *   *

I cannot end this chapter without mentioning that in those first five
years I had to deal with my first cases of sexual abuse of minors by
priests. I have spent many hours in the last years reflecting on my knowledge of this phenomenon, my presuppositions about it, and my reactions
to it in those early years. At that time, no one used terms like sexual
predators or spoke about the phenomenon as we do now; no one was
aware of the extent of the problem, not as we are today. Nor had I yet
grasped the extent either. Never having been abused myself and never
having counseled anyone who had been and who had spiritual or psychological wounds, I was naïve in assuming that those abused would

gradually "grow out of those experiences." That is how most people described the effects back then.

I can say for certain that I had not had any occasion to think through seriously about my responsibility for the private or even public lives of the priests. No one had ever explained to me what *respondeat superior* meant; I had never heard that legal term. It was perfectly clear that the perpetrator was responsible for his own acts, but my role from a legal point of view was not clear. It would never have occurred to me that I could be in any way answerable for what diocesan priests did, much less for the acts of religious order priests.

The first case with which I had to deal involved Father Bill Effinger, a priest stationed in Lake Geneva. I didn't then and I still do not now comprehend how anyone can be sexually attracted to children or adolescents. Though it was an experience I knew nothing about or to which I could relate, I had to accept it as factual. I learned that there was often a relationship between alcoholism and acting on this sexual attraction. Perhaps the most important fact I learned was that there was no relationship between this acting-out and a priest's theological positions, liberal or conservative. Father Effinger fell into the category of conservative, as were many I was to deal with later. He did not support anything I was trying to do in the archdiocese and tended to be very critical. That may have made me feel a bit threatened by him or at least fooled and thus far too trustful in his statements that he would never act out again. After dealing with Father Effinger, I had to learn not to be fooled by the conservative stance; it could be a screen behind which to hide a serious problem, or perhaps it was an unconscious coping mechanism.

At the time no one spoke of criminal charges; I have long pondered why not. I could understand why parents would hesitate, not wanting to subject their children to the burden of being witnesses in a court trial. I could see why they just wanted the priest removed, feeling they could then deal with the damage, if any, to the child. Still, I ask myself why I did not even consider the possibility of reporting the matter to the police. It was simply not done. I do not remember in those years any kind of sex abuse of minors being reported in the newspapers as a crime, at least not if one was talking about such acts by professional people — doctors, lawyers, teachers, judges, and priests. Perhaps professional groups had their own systems in place where such offenders lost their license. But I knew nothing of that. The legal aspects of these cases, if any, I now suppose must have been handled behind closed doors.

In the Catholic Church a priest belonged to a diocese in a way that went far beyond being a member of a professional society or organization. He was "incardinated" into a particular diocese where he became a part of the presbyterate or body of priests and where he would remain and function for life. It was often described as being a member of a family. He was "wedded" to the Church that had, in turn, to take care of his every need. Thus, problems or difficulties were treated as they would have been in a family. These cases were not divulged to outsiders, just as families did not report untoward activities among their members. Moreover, bishops had the power to restrict the ministry of a priest, but not to dismiss him from the priesthood. Only Rome could do that, and, even then, I knew of no case in which this penalty was inflicted.

Furthermore, psychologists and therapists were not always helpful. They were not aware of the compulsive nature of such acting out, nor of the deep harm done to the young victims, who often carried unresolved problems that could surface years later. Psychologists seemed to agree with the general view, do not worry too much about the kids, "They did not understand what it was all about and will forget it." In addition, my years of being in Europe and my traveling around the world left me less sensitive toward post-puberty victims, since, in the majority of these countries, the legal age for marriage and also for consent was lower and sexual maturity and responsibility were presupposed at an earlier age than in the United States. I now regret this insensitivity and wish I had been more alert. In the States, I soon noticed that minors were often tried as adults but never regarding sexual activity. In retrospect, I see I was not sensitive enough to the situation of vulnerable youth in their mid-teens.

In dealing with those issues in the first few years of my being a bishop, I had to ask myself some questions about the role and strength of grace, of self-discipline, and of a strong religious motivation in controlling such attractions. I certainly did not think that grace of itself would cure an addiction, nor did I believe that, of itself, a deep religious motivation could keep such deep-seated addictive attraction under control. I did believe that a strong spiritual awakening could be a positive factor in trying to control an addiction — as in the case of alcoholism — if reinforced by other motives. The commonly accepted Catholic approach held to the belief that self-discipline under the impulse of grace could keep one from sinful acts and reinforce a sense of personal responsibility. Moreover, certain clear boundaries had to be in place if that control was to be effective. In the Catholic tradition we called that "avoiding the occasions of sin."

Above all else, I was simply unaware of the extent of this problem among the clergy.

In dealing with Father Effinger I did what I thought was best. After talking to the parents, who did not want to bring charges, I removed Father Effinger from the parish, telling him he would not be reassigned until this matter was cleared up. Later I sat down with him to talk about the situation and hear his side of the story. He admitted to drinking too heavily at times, a situation that reduced his self-control. I emphasized the need for a stronger commitment to his priestly vocation, a deeper spiritual and prayer life, and a clearer understanding of his vocation. Having been impressed by Alcoholics Anonymous, I also tried to stress the need to rely on God's help above everything else. I believed then as I do now that these recommendations are still valid. It was advice I repeated often enough to myself to be able to repeat it to others. I certainly did not understand the deep addictive nature of pedophilia, but I accepted the Church's teaching that no one was tempted beyond his or her strength; with God's graces, one could resist. But for that to be true, it was also evident that boundaries had to be set and rigorously maintained. I urged Effinger to avoid the "occasions" of sin, his drinking, in particular, but pointed to other more positive safeguards, like seeking mature friends in whom he could confide. I sent him to a psychologist for therapy and told him he would not be reassigned until the psychologist agreed that he was ready and that he understood these boundaries and kept them. Should I have done more? In hindsight, yes.

*   *   *

In addition to learning about the role of a bishop during those first five years, I also learned much about myself. I finally understood what an older bishop said to me one day: "Rembert, during this pontificate a bishop must, at a certain point, make a decision whether he will stand with his priests or with the curia." I came to see what he meant. If I had a weakness, it was that I seemed unable to keep from uttering my opinions even when they were not welcome in higher places. Perhaps I was speaking too much on too many issues.

From what I said and did in those first five years, the characteristics of my reputation were established. In the local papers I acquired the usual unspecific description of being "controversial." I was considered the most "liberal" bishop in the United States, and a bit unpredictable; sometimes I was called a maverick. The adjective liberal had lost its positive and original meaning and had become for many a pejorative term. I had to live with that term, although at the time I saw myself in church circles squarely in the center, a place where most of the bishops of the conference could be found. During the next decades, with the appointment of new bishops, that center shifted very much to the right. What surprised me and gave me thought was that liberal and conservative were always used with political overtones. Because one accepted something the Democratic Party stood for — say, a decent minimum wage — it was presupposed that one accepted the whole litany of liberal causes found in American society. The way in which party politics could alter the Church's presence in the society at large and the way it influenced how people thought and made judgments was new to me. I found this political influence in play when working on the Economic Pastoral Letter; I found it in Milwaukee when the churches there were involved in social projects.

Through all these experiences of my first five years in Milwaukee, I was learning by trial and error and coming to enjoy the role of bishop: I was using the best of my talents. If I missed anything from my time in Rome as head of the Benedictines, it was belonging to the Union of Superiors General. I needed people like Father Arrupe and the others with whom I could broach any sensitive subject and feel free to discuss the most controversial topic without fear of unwanted repercussions. The meetings of bishops did not exhibit the same close and trusting relationships. Any expression of disagreement with a Roman policy could easily be interpreted by some as being disloyal to the curia or the pope.

In 1983, I was only at the beginning of the pilgrimage and unsure of where it would lead me. I knew that we were now ready at home for an archdiocesan synod and that preparing the Economic Pastoral Letter for presentation to the bishops' conference would keep me very busy into the future.

CHAPTER 12

Drafting *"Economic Justice for All"*

(1981-1986)

I was surprised when, in January of 1981, Archbishop Roach, president of the Bishops Conference, asked me if I would chair the *ad hoc* committee on capitalism that the bishops had agreed to form at their 1980 meeting. Archbishop Bernardin had been asked to chair the committee on peace voted at the same meeting. Roach explained that his executive committee and staff had agreed on my name because they liked the way I had led the bishops through some of the more delicate liturgical issues we faced.

I said yes to Archbishop Roach. After some clarifications, he and I agreed on four other bishops: Peter Rosazza, auxiliary of Hartford; George Speltz, bishop of St. Cloud; William Weigand, bishop of Salt Lake City; Joseph Daley, bishop of Harrisburg, who, unfortunately, died soon after. Archbishop Thomas Donnellan of Atlanta took his place. Through the next five years we would come to know each other very well.

My background for this task was not strong. I grew up in the Depression and carried with me scars from the experience of living on welfare. My knowledge of Catholic social teaching was good, much of it acquired in Rome by representing the Religious on the board of the Office for Justice and Peace when Monsignor Joseph Gremillion, an American priest from Louisiana who had established a reputation for his knowledge of social justice issues, worked there. I could add my active participation in the synod of bishops on "Justice in the Modern World" in 1971 and the influence of the writings of Barbara Ward and her speech at that synod. But I had a passion for and identified with the poor, for those who were not making it in the U.S. society. Having traveled widely, I was sensitive to the exportation of U.S. culture, propelled — as third-world leaders asserted — by a bottom-line approach to all aspects of life from business to entertainment, and even religion.

The bishops' conference provided an excellent and competent staff coupled with outside consultants. Professor Donald Warwick of Harvard's Institute for International Development was to be the principal writer. A year later, Dr. Charles Wilbur of the Economics Department of the University of Notre Dame was added as a consultant. In retrospect I can say they were responsible for giving us bishops a brief updating in economic thought, a kind of Economics 101.

The first meeting of the committee was held at the O'Hare Hilton in Chicago, July 17, 1981. At that preliminary meeting we made some serious decisions. We knew, as a group, that the possibility of writing a pastoral critique of the economic theories underlying capitalism as such would be impossible. For our document to become one agreed to by all the bishops we knew it had to be of a pastoral nature. Thus we chose to limit ourselves to the American economic system, even knowing that it was beginning to move in a global direction. The decision to treat the U.S. economy and not capitalism from a theoretical point of view seemed inevitable to me at that time. Since we had not yet selected a title, we usually referred to it as the Economic Pastoral, just as we called the work of the Bernardin committee the Peace Pastoral. We knew, too, that we would be expected to have an excellent summary of how scripture treated these same issues and how Catholic social teaching, especially during the last century, struggled with them and over time developed a comprehensive approach.

The second decision, also a difficult one, was to determine the letter's degree of specificity. With less conviction and unanimity we made the decision to pick specific areas of the U.S. economy where we would apply the more abstract vision of Catholic social teaching. This question of specificity was not an easy one, and I confess to my own hesitations. On almost every issue, a detailed analysis of a particular subject would place the committee on the side of the Republican or Democratic Party and their party platforms. On the other hand, the tradition already established by the bishops in their previous statements leaned toward specificity. It was also felt that in some areas, like poverty and unemployment, some bishops had personal experiences for assessing the results of specific policies and they could contribute firsthand to the general discussion. We decided on specificity, or the application of principles to a limited number of specific areas,

With Cardinal Karol Wojtyła, Tyniec, Poland, 1975

With Mother on the twenty-fifth anniversary of the author's ordination to the priesthood, Sant'Anselmo, Rome, June 1976

Feeding the poor at the parish of St. Benedict the Moor, Milwaukee, Thanksgiving Day, 1977 *(Courtesy of* The Catholic Herald; *James Pearson, photographer)*

Visiting the Benedictine sisters at Mananzary, Madagascar, May 1972 *(Courtesy of the Archdiocese of Milwaukee Archives)*

Ordination as a bishop and installation in St. John's Cathedral by Archbishop Jean Jadot (left), being greeted by Archbishop William Cousins (center)

Palm Sunday in Cathedral Square, Milwaukee, 1980 *(Courtesy of* The Catholic Herald*)*

Being honored with other bishops by the magazine *U.S. Catholic* for support of women in ministry in the Church; left to right: Bishop William McManus, Bishop Michael McAuliffe, Bishop Charles Buswell, Archbishop Raymund Hunthausen, and the author

Receiving the Thirty-third Annual B'nai B'rith Human Rights Award; standing with the author, Philip Lerman; seated left to right: George Gay, Hugh Henderson, and Ardie Halyard *(Courtesy of* The Catholic Herald; *James Pearson, photographer)*

The signing of a covenant among Episcopalians, Lutherans, and Catholics, 1993; in the foreground, left to right: Bishop Peter Rogniss (Evangelical Lutheran Church of America), Bishop Roger White (Episcopal Bishop of Milwaukee), and the author *(Courtesy of* The Catholic Herald; *James Pearson, photographer)*

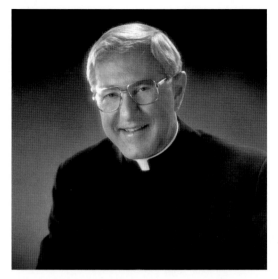

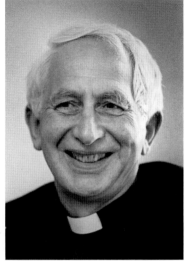

Bishop Richard Sklba, biblical scholar and former rector of St. Francis Seminary, ordained auxiliary bishop of the Archdiocese of Milwaukee, December 19, 1979 *(Courtesy of the Archdiocese of Milwaukee Archives)*

Cardinal Basil Hume, Abbot of Ampleforth, England (1963), Archbishop of Westminster (1976), named a cardinal by Pope John Paul II the same year, died June 17, 1999

Discussing the Economic Pastoral Letter with Rev. Brian Hehir of the staff of the Bishops' Conference, 1986; Bishop John Snyder of Saint Augustine, Florida, is in the background

With Archbishop Desmond Tutu, Milwaukee, May 18, 1995 *(Courtesy of* The Catholic Herald; *James Pearson, photographer)*

With Cardinal Joseph L. Bernardin, c. 1994

Above: Teaching a class in medieval music at one of Milwaukee's public middle schools of the arts *(Courtesy of* The Catholic Herald*)*

Left: Visiting prisoners at Waupun, Wisconsin, September 1, 1980 *(Courtesy of* The Catholic Herald; *Edgar G. Mueller, photographer)*

The author, 1999 *(Courtesy of* The Catholic Herald*)*

in the hope that Catholic universities and scholars would later continue this kind of reflection for many of the other areas we simply could not cover.

Naively, I thought we could finish the project in two years so that we could present the results to the bishops in the fall of 1983. It soon became clear that we should not hurry. Our committee began at the same time the committee chaired by Cardinal Bernardin started writing the Peace Pastoral. They began with a more defined theme and were ready to present the final results to the bishops in 1983. I assured the cardinal we would not be ready by that date and there should be no concern that the bishops would be overwhelmed by two hefty documents.

In looking back at the Economic Pastoral, I want to emphasize the importance of the process that we adopted. Since the Peace Pastoral was out of the gate ahead of us, we learned much from their procedures and just assumed that it was the right way to function in the post–Vatican II era. We began to hold hearings around the country. We also decided to present to the bishops a first draft, receive their feed-back, then present a second draft after more hearings, concentrating on the areas proposed by the bishops, and then present a third draft for amendments and a final vote.

I was glad our committee took more time since we five bishops had to become comfortable in the area of economic thought and to assess the divergent points of view among the leading economists. The planned hearing sessions became a form of continuing education for us bishops. In November of 1981 we began those hearings. They were to continue till the document was finished in 1986. One morning, for example, in August of 1982 we heard from and were able to ask questions of people as diverse in their views as Herbert Stein (chairman of Economic Advisors in the Nixon-Ford administrations), Charles Schultze (chairman of the same group under Carter), and Michael Harrington of the Institute for Democratic Socialism. As Don Warwick remarked when the morning session ended: "Any student in the Economics Department of Harvard would have been thrilled to have had this opportunity, would have paid a thousand dollars for it, and would have received two credits." Often those who appeared left a summary of their thoughts. All of this material became important to us bishops in forming our own opinions and ideas.

By the end of 1983, fifty-four economists, moral theologians, business people, labor-union officials, social services coordinators, and legislators had appeared in closed sessions to discuss what they thought should go into such a letter. We never asked the religious affiliation of the participants, although we did ask many to come because of their particular expertise in business, economics, or Catholic social teaching. Everyone we asked came willing to give us their insights and I could sense the excitement about the undertaking on the part of most of them, though some feared that our work would reflect negatively on the Reagan administration.

All accepted that the economic system, with its heavy accent on advertising and consumerism, did affect people's values and view of life, often negatively, and could contrast with the values articulated in the gospel. Most had not thought about these questions and entered eagerly into the discussion. Some of those we interviewed were concerned about the role of the worker and the labor unions, but also tended to criticize them for lack of foresight and flexibility. All agreed there were many people unable to participate in the economic system of the United States but gave different analyses and reasons for the existence of this sub-population. The role of government, from the beginning, was one that elicited the most striking differences of opinion, varying from total non-interference by the government to a government-sponsored and -financed welfare state. All of these differences of opinion were colored by the political party to which the person belonged or by the economic theory he or she endorsed. It was our task to absorb all this material and then ask what light the gospel and Catholic social teaching might bring to it.

But 1983 was also a turning point for the committee. The more conservative secular press reported on a symposium we had attended at the University of Notre Dame and said that our document would be critical of the Reagan administration's policies and would encourage socialism. That negative criticism, appearing before the letter was even written, became a burden to the committee that was never totally lifted. More than anything else, it shifted the emphasis in the public perception from the biblical and theoretical tradition of Catholic social teaching — the section we prided ourselves on and saw as the real substance of the document — to the application section.

But the bigger problem for me at that time was internal to the committee itself. Although there was a certain frustration that we were moving too slowly as a committee, I purposely did nothing to hasten the pace. It seemed evident to me that we bishops needed this time to become acquainted with the material and feel comfortable about what the bishops' conference would want to say on the subject. The bishops on the committee were not at ease with what our principal writer had written thus far;

the style was too technical to become a pastoral letter of bishops. We then asked different writers to draft sections of the letter and we moved ahead. The basis of the scriptural section was written by John R. Donahue, SJ, and highly prized by the committee and readily accepted. The section on Catholic social teaching was mostly the work of David Hollenbach, SJ. It also resonated with the drafting committee since it placed the human person at the center by judging any economic system by what it did for people and how it helped them participate more fully in the life of society.

By the fall of 1983, I was convinced we could have the first draft written for the November meeting of the bishops in Washington in 1984. But since that was also an election year, I agreed with the president of the conference and the executive committee that the draft would not be given to the bishops and the press till the election was over. In that way we hoped to make it clear that the document intended to look at issues over a broader period of time and not be limited to an analysis geared toward the election cycle.

During the first months of 1984, work on the Economic Pastoral gained momentum with intense rewriting so that the committee could present the first draft to the bishops in November. Having selected new writers for each section of the letter and having worked out a fairly good summary of what the final version was to contain, the drafting committee was able to move rapidly and steadily forward.

Once a month between January and October I took a week to fly somewhere in the country for a hearing and then a meeting of staff and committee.

As in the preceding years, the committee never received a refusal when it invited an expert to come and present his or her point of view. The most informative took place at the University of California in Berkeley in May 1984. The committee was able to consult an impressive list of thirty well-informed people with strong convictions on the subject, ranging from the 1972 Nobel Prize-winning economist Kenneth J. Arrow to the labor leader Cesar Chavez, and including stimulating thinkers like Robert N. Bellah and John T. Noonan. After those sessions my mind was spinning. More than anything else, what impressed me was the seriousness with which they took the work we were doing, their eagerness to contribute to it, and the encouragement they gave us.

In July of 1984 we planned two other significant hearings in New York, one with leaders of the Jewish community and one with Protestant scholars picked by the National Council of Churches. I wanted very much to be present for the New York hearings. The death of my oldest sister and performing her funeral kept me away. It was only meeting I missed in the five years of the project; I mention them because it shows the broad interest and support our work was receiving in ecumenical and interfaith circles.

Second only to the dialogue with the bishops and their written responses, for us members of the drafting committee the hearings were the most helpful part of the whole process. Although we obtained too much information for a pastoral letter, all of that information would be of help in the interviews and speeches we would be engaged in after the letter was published. There was never a point raised later in such discussions that our committee had not, at one point or another, been forced to consider, even if it did not find its way into the final document.

The drafting committee worked hard and finished the first draft of the letter on time for the bishops' meeting in November 1984. But the committee had two concerns. It did not want to make the letter public before the presidential election on November 6, lest it appear as a move on the part of the American Catholic bishops to influence that election. To prevent this, the committee recommended each bishop be sent a copy on November 7 and that the text be embargoed till November 11, the opening day of the bishops' meeting. The U.S. government had at least one thing to learn from us Catholic bishops: no leaks occurred!

The committee's second concern was to avoid any last-minute interference from Rome. I judged the only way that concern could be met was somehow to keep the Roman officials informed of the letter's contents and thus allay any fears or misgivings they might have. This gesture became even more important because of the spin that was being put on the work, especially by conservative Catholic and secular periodicals, namely, that the letter would advocate socialism. Experience had shown that people in authority feel more comfortable if they know ahead of time what is about to happen and are adequately prepared to respond when the event occurs.

I recalled that the drafting committee of the Peace Pastoral, chaired by Cardinal Bernardin, had to overcome one such road-block before ending work on their letter. In January of 1983, before the bishops voted on its final draft, the pope asked for a meeting in Rome of some U.S. bishops involved in the drafting process with other bishops from major European countries and bishops from the curia, especially from the secretariat of state. As I understood the situation, some tensions had arisen since not all of them were in agreement on the question of nuclear deterrence. I wanted to avoid any such last-minute problem with our letter.

For this reason, in late August 1984, I made a quick trip to Rome and spoke at length with Cardinal Casaroli in the office of the secretariat of state and answered the questions he thought the pope might bring up. Although I was willing to speak directly to the Holy Father about the letter, the cardinal informed me the pope thought it would be best if a meeting between us did not take place. The pope did not want to appear to be interfering in the process — an opinion expressed by some journalists after the meeting on the Peace Pastoral in the Vatican the year before. Instead of asking for a private audience, I attended the public Wednesday audience in the Nervi hall, sitting to the side with the other visiting bishops. The pope, at the end of the audience, came over to where we were all sitting, greeted each bishop individually, and simply said to me in Italian, with a knowing nod: "I know why you are here."

The point-person for the pope in all matters concerning Catholic social teaching at that time was Bishop Jan Schotte, vice-president of the office for Justice and Peace. Schotte was a pragmatic and efficient Belgian, well-informed and insightful on matters touching Catholic social teaching. While in Rome, I sat down with Schotte, explained what we were doing, and gave him an unofficial, personal copy of the draft as it existed at that time. I knew it was a risky thing to do and against the unwritten policies of the conference, but I emphasized that the text was not for public distribution and elaborated on the sensitive problem posed by the coming presidential election in the United States. I also assured him that any comments he wanted to make privately to me would be seriously reflected on. These comments, however, had to be "unofficial" and remain personal to me since the American bishops had not yet seen the draft. He agreed. He told me he would be coming through Milwaukee in less than a month and would bring along his comments. He did so and I found his comments perceptive and helpful. I put them, without authorship, into the list of all the other comments that had come in at the last minute without saying where they came from and was not surprised when almost all of them were accepted by the committee and incorporated into the final text. I can happily say, in addition, that there were no leaks of the document to the press from Schotte's office.

For this "Roman maneuver" of trying to put the Vatican officials at ease by leaving an advance-copy with Schotte, I received a rebuke from Monsignor Daniel Hoye, secretary of the National Conference of Catholic

Bishops, a fine administrator whom I highly esteemed. He wrote me in mid-October that my disclosure had been out of order. He reminded me it was the conference's policy not to share copies of conference statements or documents with Roman officials before the bishops had approved them. Yet, a shadow hung over this maneuver that haunted me. It was Bishop Schotte who wrote the published minutes of the Vatican meeting on the Peace Pastoral. That meeting was called by the pope himself with the presence of American, European, and curial bishops. Schotte began his minutes with an account of a presentation by Cardinal Ratzinger. The cardinal stated that the first question to be discussed should be whether a bishops' conference had any teaching authority whatsoever. In other words, it called into question the very right of a conference of bishops to write such a letter. This question — one that would remain unresolved at that time — cast a shadow over the whole Roman meeting and now over our document.

For me that question was of special interest because it brought back memories of the 1969 synod of bishops on the nature of bishops' synods and conferences and my disagreement with Cardinal Wright, which I mentioned in Chapter 6. In those first years after the council, hope still existed among some that the synods of bishops would become the primary advisory body to the pope and in that way give the bishops a vehicle to fulfill their responsibility of participating in the governance of the whole Church. That hope implied that the power of the curia would not come between pope and bishops and that there would be a gradual decentralization.

The practice of the bishops' conference in the United States after Vatican II had been set by Archbishop John Dearden of Detroit, its first elected president who served from 1966 to 1971. Dearden saw the wisdom of permitting the conference and its staff to work without interference from the curia. Twice each year, i.e., after the spring and the fall meetings of the bishops, he and the other conference officers made a trip to Rome to meet with the pope and the various offices in the curia to discuss the bishops' actions at their last meeting. It was an unwritten rule of the conference, then, that no document should be sent to Rome till it had been voted on by the U.S. bishops and could be explained by the conference's leaders. All subsequent presidents followed this practice. It was that practice I had "bent," and Monsignor Hoye protested.

However, it was clear from the question Cardinal Ratzinger raised at the 1983 Vatican meeting that Pope John Paul II wished to bring some clarity into these processes and was opting for more, not less, centralization.

After examining personally each line of the Revised Code of Canon Law with a group of selected canonists, Pope John Paul II saw to its publication in 1983. The code clearly stated that conferences of bishops had no legislative power that could bind the member bishops unless church law or Rome itself gave the conference such a mandate. All requests of this sort, to have any force, were to receive a two-thirds vote and be approved by Rome. Teaching documents, such as those on peace and the economy, by reason of the statues of the conference, had to receive a two-thirds vote to be an official document of the conference, but were not sent to Rome for approval.

*   *   *

The symposium on the economic letter held at Notre Dame in December 1983, as I said, aroused suspicion in the secular press that the bishops' document would condemn Reaganomics and, perhaps, even advocate socialism. That fear was reiterated by several committed lay Catholics who met and agreed not to wait to see what the bishops would write but decided instead to produce a counter-document of their own. This group called itself "The Lay Commission." The central figures in this group were William E. Simon and Michael Novak. Simon had been secretary of treasury under Nixon and Ford. Michael Novak was a prolific scholar at the American Enterprise Institute in Washington. Simon became the counter-letter's chair, Novak its chief drafter. Novak appeared three times before the economic pastoral's drafting committee, but seemed frustrated by the direction he surmised we would be taking.

In mid-July a few members, including Simon and Novak, flew into Milwaukee to meet personally with me to assure me that their document was to be seen as a contribution to our committee's work. I could not object to this initiative since it represented the kind of dialogue we bishops had hoped for. On the other hand, some members of the drafting committee of bishops and the staff were less enthusiastic about this commission and its endeavors, sensing this counter document would be an attempt to justify a neo-conservative political position and attempt to vindicate Reaganomics using Catholic terminology. Actually, their letter was much better than I had anticipated, even though somewhat limited in scope by seeking to endorse one form of American capitalism, the one corresponding to the neo-conservative point of view.

Some other lay scholars who had attended our hearings and some who were to do so in the future were upset that the group assumed the label "The Lay Catholic Commission." They pointed out that there were many lay Catholics who did not agree with the positions taken in the Simon-Novak document and thus found this title presumptuous. I began then to refer to the document by its title, *Toward the Future,* and to the group as the Simon-Novak committee. They decided to release their document on the evening of November 6, election day. Thus, the next morning, November 7, it was featured on the front page of the *New York Times.* A copy was sent express to every parish in the United States and to 700 other newspapers and formers of public opinion in the country. One of the weaknesses of the bishops' Economic Pastoral Letter was that it never treated the intrinsic relationship between wealth and power, especially political, in the American culture. The committee had to learn the hard way that this relationship was real!

The action of the Simon-Novak committee to preempt the bishops' letter contributed to the added publicity the latter received when it appeared a few days later. I presented the letter to a full room of reporters and TV cameras on Sunday afternoon, November 10, and then, on November 11, formally to the bishops. The *New York Times* the next day quoted large sections of the document, a great service to all. Over 93,000 copies of that first draft were sold within the first few months. Our committee could not have asked for more attention and discussion.

No list of my activities for that week can be found in the archives; I was too busy to keep a record. It was a whirlwind of events with many appearances on TV and radio, from the McNeil-Lehrer program to Ted Koppel. The results of the pre-publicity by the Simon-Novak committee meant that every TV station wanted someone from the bishops' committee or staff, especially me, in opposition to a member of the Simon-Novak committee. That week lingers in my memory; it was a very difficult few days. I felt often out of place on the talk-shows and doing interviews. We bishops were not prepared for such media exposure. Usually at the end of the day when I returned to the hotel, I was exhausted, both emotionally and physically.

I soon learned that I was useless in the yelling talk-shows, as I refused to engage in that kind of display. In addition, I tried to steer clear of political wrangling. Wherever I spoke, listeners were sharply divided along party lines, especially in dealing with questions like the role of government, treatment of the poor, inequality among nations or even within the U.S. society, the role of labor, and the role of religion in society. I felt more at ease doing radio or TV interviews rather than the usual TV panels. For example, I easily engaged in a discussion about poverty with Charles Kuralt on his Sunday morning program, "On the Road," and, as a result, received from a fish dealer in San Pedro, California, a whole refrigerated truckload of fish for the poor in Milwaukee.

This media frenzy dissipated after a few weeks. For the next two years, however, many colleges and university scheduled lectures and symposia on the bishops' Economic Pastoral Letter and wanted to pit one of the bishops or staff from the drafting committee against one of the Simon-Novak committee. Michael himself must have become as tired as I was of hearing the same questions and giving the same answers over and over again. We highly respected each other, both of us coming from Cambria County in Western Pennsylvania, with deep ethnic, immigrant roots.

The rest of the bishops' process took place between the presentation of that first draft and the bishops' vote on the third or final draft in November 1986.

At the bishops' meeting in June of 1985 at Collegeville in Minnesota, our committee and staff had the first opportunity to hear the bishops' reactions. I had separated out for discussion in small groups particular questions that were still of special concern to the committee, like the level of specificity, the role of government, the option for the poor, the linkage with the Peace Pastoral, and the implementation of the document. The drafting committee studied the results of these discussions with care. We wanted the bishops to be at ease with whatever conclusions the committee would recommend in those areas.

Most of the bishops rightly thought the document was too long and its tone too harsh. In particular, I recall the intervention of Bishop Michael Murphy of Erie, Pennsylvania, a precise thinker with a penetrating mind and a creative form of expression. He remarked on the floor that the letter sounded as if I had been listening too intently to Liszt's *Totentanz* (Dance of Death) and suggested that I needed to add to it more of Beethoven's *Ode to Joy* from the Ninth Symphony. (After returning to Milwaukee, I took out the scores of both of these pieces and wrote a pastiche that started with the *Totentanz* and ended with the *Ode to Joy*. Unfortunately, I never sent a tape of the final mixture to Bishop Mike and now cannot find it.)

One point was very evident at that meeting: the bishops had made the document their own. Any committee has to recognize the moment when a document passes from their hands into the hands of those whom they represent. After that meeting, I never worried about the letter's outcome because it was evident to me the bishops had taken possession of it as their document.

Responses from the bishops kept pouring in during 1985, some personal ones, some from their staffs, so that we were able to produce a second, much shortened, draft during the summer months and send it to the bishops for discussion at our fall meeting. In addition to the bishops' responses, over 10,000 pages of other suggestions came in during that period from individual Catholics and concerned citizens. That second draft was shorter, but seemed to please no one. Bishops asked that some sections be restored. We also were able to insert the section on agriculture that had been missing from the first draft. As a result of this process, the final draft presented in the fall of 1986 was more like the first draft in both content and length.

While we were working on the second and third drafts, we continued to hold hearing sessions, especially on how the U.S. economy touched the lives of people in other nations. This theme was the subject of two important hearings, one composed of economists from several developing countries around the world, the second with bishops from South and Central America. This latter was held at the request of the pope, since he felt these countries were very much influenced by the U.S. economy and should have a chance to point out how they viewed those effects.

In addition, we had another fascinating exchange with John Kenneth Galbraith on the morning of April 27, 1985. When the first draft of the letter was published, he read the excerpts in the *New York Times,* was impressed, and called me from Switzerland to express his encouragement and support. We set up a date when he could meet with the drafting committee. We had not scheduled any other person that day so that we would not be rushed. I can still recall his large frame filling the chair in the conference room and his ability to go on for some time on any issue in great detail without any notes. But what I remember most was his attitude toward us. I felt no trace of condescension. He treated us as colleagues and not as pupils. Most of all he emphasized our right to have our say in the public forum as religious leaders on these economic issues and encouraged us not to be intimidated and silenced. I cite this initiative on his part to show the seriousness with which some economists took the letter and its endeavors.

A list of all the official hearings held by the committee and those who appeared there is appended to each draft of the letter, but individual bishops attended other meetings, symposia, talks, and panel discussions that are not listed in these appendices. Some of these may have had an even greater influence than the official hearings. I cite as an example two meetings, one after the first draft of the letter and one after the second draft, I attended of Catholic CEOs of prestigious businesses where the discussion was challenging, thoughtful, and significant. They were organized by Edward L. Hennessy, Jr., of Allied Corporation (later Allied Signal). In inviting me, he emphasized the group did not want to be identified with the Simon-Novak committee and *Toward the Future*. The meetings were held at his corporation headquarters in Morristown, New Jersey. The comments of that group were helpful, especially in making the second draft of the letter more precise.

As often happens, sometimes some of the best discussion happens at the coffee break and over lunch — discussions that are not recorded anywhere in the archived boxes. Sitting, after the first meeting, in the bright glass-enclosed dining area with Hennessey and a few others who seemed more interested in the religious aspects of the document, I had the chance to hear in greater depth some of their preoccupations. I found it was necessary to calm a few who, like Hennessey, told me they came from blue-collar families, worked their way through a Catholic college, and then rose to the position they now held, only to feel they were being scolded by the bishops. I understood what they were saying because I saw my own life reflected in theirs, not in the field of business but in the Church. I reassured them that the letter was not a criticism of them personally, but an attempt to help them reflect on their new position of influence and the responsibilities that went with that position. I also sought to emphasize that there were broader issues to be discussed about the effects any economic system can have on the larger society, issues that go beyond a concern just for the bottom line. Such reflection seemed important because now they enjoyed powerful leverage in society.

In addition to profiting much from these two meetings because of the frank and detailed discussion, I have to add that the first one remains in my mind for another reason. I flew from Milwaukee to LaGuardia in New York that January afternoon, arriving right after dusk. A helicopter was waiting to take me to Hennessey's headquarters in Morristown, New Jersey. The two young pilots asked me if it was my first helicopter ride (I wonder how they knew!). They immediately put me at ease. During the flight they pointed out what we were passing over and what famous buildings could be seen in the distance. It had snowed the whole day and the ground, with its fresh white covering, glistened under the city lights. I had taken many boat trips and bus rides around Manhattan, but I had never seen the city from the air that way. For a first helicopter ride, it was truly spectacular!

After more feedback on the second draft, we prepared a third draft, longer again because every bishop saw something he wanted restored or another idea he thought should be included. That third draft of the letter, carrying the title *Economic Justice for All: Catholic Social Teaching and the U.S. Economy,* was sent out in June of 1986 and, after very few amendments, voted on by the bishops on November 13, 1986, receiving 225 affirmative votes and 9 negative. A standing ovation from the body of bishops for the drafting committee's work followed the announcement of the voting results.

*   *   *

At one of the press conferences, a reporter asked me to sum up in just a few paragraphs the contents of a document that ran over 50,000 words. When I said I was not sure I could do it in sound-bites and in just a few paragraphs, he reminded me of the Sermon on the Mount and said, "If Jesus could do it, you can at least try."

The bishops struggled with how to summarize the document and so added a pastoral message as a preface to it. In that summary they cited six themes that dominated in the bishops' thinking. (1) Every economic decision and institution must be judged in light of whether it protects or undermines the dignity of the human person. (2) Human dignity can be realized and protected only in community. (3) All people have a right to participate in the economic life of society. (4) All members of society have a special obligation to the poor and vulnerable. (5) Human rights are the minimum conditions for life in community. (6) Society as a whole, acting through public and private institutions, had the moral responsibility to enhance human dignity and protect human rights.

We wanted to put a human face on economic statistics and examine how people functioned in an economic system. How well we achieved that end will have to be decided by history.

The letter certainly had its deficiencies, even if it asked the right questions at the right time. Here are some of the many lacunae. Although we had discussed at length among ourselves the question of globalization, then in its infancy, we did not give it enough space, mostly because of the interest of the Midwest bishops in agriculture and local concerns. We did not treat the relationship between wealth and power in the American culture; that deficiency was pointed out to us later by many Protestant critics. Nor did we reflect sufficiently on the way in which a market economy and its concomitant thrust toward spending affects the whole of our culture, especially the young. We could have asked how advertising creates, especially among the young, ever-new and unnecessary "wants." We did not analyze how concepts of success in American life have been altered by the astronomic salaries of sports idols, entertainment stars, and corporate executives, and how people today have come to be evaluated by their salary and not by intrinsic virtues. In my many travels as abbot primate of the Benedictines, I had always smiled at the questions posed by friends in third world countries about life in the States. On their TVs they watched re-runs of *Dallas, Falcon Crest, Baywatch,* and other sit-coms and thought we Americans all lived like the protagonists in those melodramas. They just took it for granted that success for an American meant owning a big house, riding around in several flashy cars, and spending endless hours surfing on the beach.

Some of the issues hotly debated then will continue to be the object of division in the country, e.g., the role of government, not just in solving the problems of poverty or unemployment, but in taking an active part in subsidizing some industries and not others; our duties as a nation toward developing countries; states' rights versus federal policies; the potential for unrest with large gaps between the rich and the poor; and so on. One could name many more.

Finally, the manner of reasoning in which the document was written proved unfamiliar to many. The learning method of education in the United States is typically one of induction, i.e., from analyzing experiences the person arrives at the principles involved. This method, more frequently associated with science, has deeply penetrated the American culture. The deductive method used in religious discourse is less accessible to those imbued with American ways of thinking. Church documents begin with principles arrived at from Revelation or natural law and then apply them to personal or societal decisions. Everywhere I went in the States to speak about the Economic Pastoral I found these two methods in conflict. I often thought that if we bishops had had more time and more creativity, we could have written a letter that would have resembled the casuistic approach of the old Jesuit manuals of moral theology. Those manuals presented actual cases where moral choices had to be made and then sought out what principles could be applied in making such decisions. By beginning with experience, the methodology might be more acceptable to the modern American mind, its educational presuppositions and cultural pre-dispositions.

*   *   *

Attending the hearings was not all I had to do. Between November 1984 and the summer of 1987, I gave over sixty lectures on the Economic Pastoral all over the United States and in Europe. As examples of lectures given or panel discussions on which I participated, I could name many Catholic colleges and universities everywhere in the nation. But many secular schools were also interested. For example, such lectures took me from Texas A&M to Pace University in New York (that lecture usually called "The Wall-Street Lecture"), from the University of Pennsylvania and the Wharton School of Business in Philadelphia to Penn State University in my home state of Pennsylvania. I spoke at many gatherings of union leaders and business corporations. On Capitol Hill, I appeared before the U.S. Congress/Joint Economic Committee and before the Subcommittee on Foreign Relations of the House Appropriations Committee. I was asked in 1986 to preach at the Baccalaureate Service at Stanford University in California and give the Third Harry Emerson Fosdick Lecture at Riverside Church in New York. Many bishops invited me to talk in their dioceses to both priests and lay people. I accepted as many of these opportunities as I could without neglecting the people of my own diocese.

*   *   *

Two questions of special interest remain. How was the letter received outside the country, e.g., in Europe and in South America? How it was received in my own city of Milwaukee?

Of special importance to me were the talks I gave in Europe between 1984 and the fall of 1987. In all, I made four trips to Europe, speaking on the letter in Rome, Venice, Praglia, Ivrea, and Milan in Italy. In Switzerland I lectured at the University of Fribourg, then in Austria at Graz and Linz (June, 1986), and finally returning to Italy after the final draft of the letter had been voted on and published (October 1987). The first draft of the letter had been translated into German, French, Spanish, Portuguese, and Italian and had appeared in whole or in part in various European and South American periodicals. The final document of November 1986 was published in all those languages in book form.

Europeans were, first of all, fascinated by the process, namely, that the Catholic bishops would expose their work to all the members of the Church and to the society at large for a critique in order to make the letter better. They were pleased that the drafting committee held hearings on the points involved in order to obtain the best advice possible and that it would be willing to be a part of symposia at Catholic and non-Catholic universities on the subject. Finally, they were full of praise that the drafting committee felt free to work with the Jewish and Protestant communities on the topics treated. Many European bishops privately warned me this process would not be well accepted in Rome. First, they judged that the curia would never engage in such a lengthy and open process and would not want to feel pressed to do so by public opinion. Second, they knew that the curia had a fear of the American "democratic" way of doing things, seeing these processes as a way of trying to introduce such thinking into other aspects of church life.

The most significant and patent difference between these talks and those in the United States was that in Europe I could presuppose among the listeners an intimate acquaintance with Catholic social teaching and its history. Many of them had grown up on this material. It was the basis of much of the thinking in the Catholic Democratic Parties that had come into being after World War II. Political leaders like Alcide De Gasperi, Konrad Adenauer, Robert Schuman, and others were well versed in this teaching. But, in all these countries, I found the younger generation a bit disillusioned with the current leadership. The older, post–World War II leaders had died off and the leadership had now passed to a new generation, more pragmatic and less articulate of Catholic values. The younger generation realized that it had to take now a new course. Often, after talks, especially in Italy, members of groups like the Comunione e Liberazione (CL) would stay behind to talk to me privately and sound me out on the changes they saw coming in Europe and ask how they should react. They talked about their disillusionment with the current leadership and how they were seeking a rejuvenation of Catholic influence in their political roles. Here they were finding Pope John Paul's social teaching most helpful because it was fresh and demanding and a way of revitalizing Catholic social teaching.

Most memorable for me was the talk at the University of Fribourg in Switzerland. In the room where I spoke, a plaque was attached to the wall stating that the Fribourg Union, a group of scholars interested in social issues, had held meetings in that very room in the 1880s. They prepared there material for Pope Leo XIII's encyclical on the rights of labor, *Rerum novarum* (1891). The university was rightly proud of the role its scholars had played a hundred years before and how their work led up to the first truly significant papal social encyclical.

I can honestly say that in Europe the document was well accepted, giving hope to a younger generation of politically involved youth and stimulating interest in the universities and Catholic associations.

*   *   *

How did the letter play out in Milwaukee? It received mixed reviews. Naturally, the labor community and those engaged in social action were most supportive. Members of religious orders of men and women, like the Jesuits, the Capuchins, the Racine Dominicans, and the many groups of Franciscans, had members personally involved in social action projects and were enthusiastic about the thrust of the letter. The Jewish and Protestant leaders were encouraging and highly sympathetic toward the contents of the letter. It also received strong public support from economists at the University of Wisconsin in Milwaukee (UWM). The financial community, for the most part, was thoughtful and open-minded about the questions asked. On the other hand, the Catholic business community and the leadership at Marquette University were overwhelmingly negative.

The Catholic business leaders in the community immediately distanced themselves from the letter. I was surprised how personally they took any criticism of the market economy and how defensive and thin-skinned they were, as if every criticism was aimed at them. I was told that, because of my involvement in the writing of the Economic Pastoral Letter, contributions to the archdiocese from more affluent Catholics were greatly reduced with a loss of income to the archdiocese. That may well be true, but the archdiocese had never depended on big contributions from the more wealthy Catholics in the community. Personally I was glad this was so since it permitted the diocese to be as straightforward and prophetic as it thought it should be. In this attitude I had followed Archbishop Cousins's example.

Marquette University, except for the School of Business which organized opportunities for me to speak to students and alumni, was not helpful; in fact, in some respects it was openly antagonistic. Dr. Quentin Quade, vice-president for Academic Affairs at Marquette — seen as the real power with regard to the inner workings of the university — had already taken a strong negative stance against bishops interfering in political questions. In

May of 1982, when the Peace Pastoral was in progress and shortly after I had been named chairman of the drafting committee of the Economic Pastoral, Quade submitted an op-ed piece to the *Catholic Herald,* the archdiocesan newspaper, on the relationship between bishops and politics. I will quote from this essay since it is indicative of an attitude found occasionally in the United States, but seldom expressed with such florid rhetoric:

> How does [the bishop] hope to be an uncluttered beacon calling all to the Good News if he is, at the same time, pretending that the Good News contains a clear indication of precisely how many nuclear warheads we should have (if any); the exactly right amount and kind of aid to give to El Salvador (if any); the certain knowledge of the correct level for a minimum wage (if any); and so on infinitely through the infinity of practical questions which equally good people quarrel and separate? . . . To the extent the Gospel is made known to people, and to the extent the call for integral response to Gospel values is insisted on by credible witnesses, there is a chance for the Church to be vibrant and at the same time for Church people to be benevolent, humanly-productive contributors to the political process. To the extent these obligations are preempted by a presumptuous and unwarranted hierarchical politization, the great potential of the flock as a leaven in the polity will be diminished or obliterated.

It did not surprise me when Dr. Quade was listed as one of the first to appear before the Simon-Novak committee. The idea he proposed there about bishops staying out of any issue that had political ramifications was discussed by that committee, but rejected. In fact, we all are still embarrassed by the slowness of the Church to take stands in Germany on the Nazi agenda (one had heard the same rhetoric there, namely, that the role of the Church was to preach Good News and not interfere in political issues). We heard about the slowness of the German bishops to condemn the Holocaust. We heard about the slowness of the American bishops to protest the Vietnam War. And on and on. There are many issues about which the Church has and should have no position, but there are also others where the moral aspects are so important that the Church cannot keep silent.

As I look back — with a bit of nostalgia — on the writing of *Economic Justice for All* and the many events that surrounded it, I consider it one of the most important and formative periods of my life. If I have seemed a bit too effusive in talking about it and if I seem to have gone into much detail about my involvement in the process, it is because of the importance I attach to the letter as such and to the role it played in my life. I also do so since in so many ways I grieve. It was a moment that cannot be repeated.

CHAPTER 13

Sorting Out Positions

Milwaukee-Rome (1983-1988)

Throughout 1984, I found myself juggling several responsibilities — family concerns as well as archdiocesan and national church activities. In this, I was doing what most people in the United States constantly are asked to do. In 1982, my oldest sister Betty was diagnosed with lung cancer. She had been in Rome during my years of schooling there, and, living with an Italian family, was able to introduce me to many parts of Italian life I would never have seen from Sant'Anselmo. Having left the little town of Patton right after high school, she went to Washington and joined the State Department. Her first assignment was Panama and then Rome. In 1951 she was due for another move, this time to Hungary. At first I thought she would marry and stay in Italy. This was without doubt the wish of the man she was dating, but, instead, she resigned from the State Department and returned to the States with me in 1951, a move prompted by a concern that my mother be well taken care of. After she had acquired an excellent job with US Steel and my sister Barbara was well settled as a nurse in one of the bigger hospitals in Pittsburgh, Mother moved there from Patton to be with them. Betty came back to Rome on vacation many times between 1967 and 1977 when I was abbot primate. We always had experiences to share and talk about. It was painful now to see "Bettina," as her Italian friends affectionately called her, slowly waste away from lung cancer. She was heroic in the last months of her illness, never uttering a word of complaint, never seeking any pity, and showing signs of a deep personal and sustaining faith. Sometimes when I would be traveling from

Milwaukee to the East Coast for a hearing or to Washington for a meeting, I would go by way of Pittsburgh to spend a day with her. During the first half of 1984, this routine became a regular part of my journeys. She died on July 26 and was buried in Carrolltown, near our mother.

The Economic Pastoral that I have described fully in the last chapter was with the Peace Pastoral an unprecedented effort on the part of the U.S. Bishops' Conference. What brought it about? First, the American bishops of that period were the product of the Depression and the reaction to the Depression that formed the New Deal. Most of them came from working-class backgrounds and understood the problems of those striving to move ahead in American society, still a formidable WASP stronghold. They knew what economic hardship was because they had experienced it.

That age has since passed. Newer bishops are from a different generation of Americans; they have other concerns. In addition, Pope John Paul had begun his quiet but relentless campaign to reduce the importance of bishops' conferences all over the world and pushed for a higher degree of centralization. The Revised Code of Canon Law, which he approved in 1983, had made it clear that bishops' conferences would not play a significant role, but would be increasingly restricted by Roman interference. It would be impossible for the conference to issue another document of the same caliber using the same open process. As I move through the ensuing years in this account of my life, that dynamic of Roman control will become clearer.

I had been a member of the bishops' conference now for almost ten years and had begun to understand the dynamics of the group and the unarticulated divisions within it. At first I saw this division as between the "Jadot" bishops and the rest. The "Jadot" bishops, including myself, were appointed during the period Archbishop Jean Jadot was apostolic delegate to the United States, 1974 to 1981. Jadot, after undertaking an extensive analysis of what a vacant diocese needed and performing a thorough consultation among priests and laity of the diocese, sent to Rome the names of three candidates for the post. He usually selected men who were open-minded, independent thinkers, and popular among their fellow priests and the laity. By historians of the period, they were often described as "pastoral" bishops, their predecessors being more usually described as administrators.

Somehow this explanation never seemed to tell the whole story. Something else was working itself out. We "Jadot" bishops fit comfortably with those bishops who had come under the influence of Cardinal John Dearden and who agreed with his concepts of how a conference of bishops should function. In terms of this influence, we were all "Dearden bishops," as were most of our immediate predecessors. When I was appointed a bishop in 1977, this Dearden group was the majority in the conference.

What characterized the "Dearden bishops"? To describe that stance, one has to understand the spirit of "ultramontanism" (beyond the mountains) that arose in the European Catholic Church in the middle of the nineteenth century. Some bishops then looked to Rome for validation of, and support for, what they were doing — especially in the areas of education and formation of faith — as they sought ways of preserving their Catholic identity after the French Revolution, the Napoleonic period, and the national movements that wanted state control over the Catholic Church (like Gallicanism in France or Febronianism and Josephinism in the German-speaking countries). Ultramontanism culminated in a heightening of the position of the pope in all matters, including those governing the local churches.

Although historically related to each other, ultramontanism is not totally synonymous with papal infallibility. Infallibility is restricted to doctrine, ultramontanism to the centralization of church governance. The long pontificate of Pope Pius IX (1846-1878) marked an almost irreversible victory for papal dominance and control and thus of the ultramontane movement. The person, prestige, and power of the pope became a part of Catholic identity in a way unknown in previous centuries. When the bishops looked to Rome to solve their problems, Rome willingly did so and created among the bishops stronger bonds of dependency on the curia and its offices.

Historians of the phenomenon often cite two other manifestations of ultramontanism in the United States. First, a separate Catholic school system was created so that the young would not imbibe Protestant ideas that dominated American culture. Second, post–Council of Trent devotionalism — such as Eucharistic adoration, Corpus Christi processions, May crownings, and public recitation of the rosary — was encouraged to differentiate Catholics from their Protestant neighbors and strengthen their identity. On the positive side, both the schools and the devotionalism helped break down ethnic rivalries among new immigrants and insert them into a Catholic subculture, a safe haven for their faith. Experience showed that at its best, especially in times of distress and need, ultramontanism did assure unity, if not uniformity; at its worst, it evolved into a closed mentality where loyalty was prized above honesty and where American Catholics remained second-class citizens.

Before and for decades after the Revolutionary War, the American bishops tended to be independent and governed the Church through their frequent national councils, the results of which they would send to Rome for confirmation and then vigorously fight for their approval. But that spirit began to change with the large Catholic immigration in the nineteenth century. Some Irish bishops, who dominated the U.S. Catholic Church, picked up the spirit of ultramontanism from their contacts with the hierarchy in Ireland and imitated it in the new world. The enemy here, however, was no longer England, but the dominant Protestant WASP culture. During the nineteenth and the twentieth centuries, ultramontanism continued to divide the bishops, there always being a few who were favorites with the pope and the curia, acting as conduits to Rome for all that was happening in the United States, and, through their Roman connections, having a strong influence on the naming of new bishops.

Before Vatican II, Cardinal Dearden may have been ambivalent about his attitude toward ultramontanism, but he came away from the council with a strong conviction of the need for decentralization. At Vatican II, he had been a member of the committee that wrote the Dogmatic Constitution on the Church, *Lumen gentium,* and had wrestled with the question of the relationship between the local churches and Rome. He could not help but notice during the council how often bishops, wanting to respect cultural differences, could not, or did not want to, impose uniform solutions, and thus found themselves delegating the working out of problems to the local churches. This was especially true in the field of liturgy. As the first president of the bishops' conference in the States, Dearden sought to keep it independent of Roman influence and control. Although appointed archbishop of Detroit in 1959, he was not named a cardinal till 1969. Probably he had displeased Rome with his positions.

Dearden retired in 1980, but occasionally came to the bishops' meetings. I recall, in particular, a relaxed and informal meeting we held in 1982 in Collegeville, Minnesota, where he presented a paper entitled "Collegial Sharing in Ministry." I can still remember his pale, aging face, his soft melodious accent, and his tired-looking demeanor, but age and ill health had not brought any loss of mental acumen. This is how I recall the content of the talk and how I would sum it up.

He began with the premise that Vatican II had affirmed the importance of the local churches and that the college of bishops was related to a bonding or sharing among those local churches. He remarked — I recall well — that the conferences of bishops, in the document on the Church, were treated in the same paragraph that talked of patriarchates and the synodal structures of the early Church. If bishops are members of a college of bishops, then collegiality is more than just an attitude. It must take some kind of continuous structural form for sharing — one that is actuated more than just once every few centuries through an ecumenical council. He refuted the argument that the conferences came between the pope and the individual bishops. He saw them as an aid to both the pope as a member of the college of bishops and to the individual bishop who shares the care, with and under the pope, for the universal Church as well as for his own diocese. In performing its respective tasks, the conference is an auxiliary instrument at the side of both. Conferences provided the possibility among the bishops of sharing on a more continuous basis. He added: "And sharing does not come easy to a person in a position of authority."

Cardinal Krol succeeded Dearden as president of the conference (1971 to 1974); its method of operation did not change. In fact, since I was in Rome at the time, I would hear members of the curia say they wished the president was still Dearden, since Krol felt he came to Rome with a mandate from the American bishops and would not go home until he obtained what they wanted. Krol was followed by a succession of bishops of the Dearden school, each elected for three years: Joseph Bernardin (1974-1977), John Quinn (1977-1980), John Roach (1980-1983), James Malone (1983-1986), John May (1986-1989), and so on.

But a change took place in the spirit of the conference when in 1981 Pope John Paul II appointed Archbishop Pio Laghi as apostolic delegate to succeed Archbishop Jadot. His candidates for bishop were rather different than Jadot's. First came the rising to prominence of two "ultramontane" archbishops, both named cardinals in 1985, Archbishop John O'Connor of New York and Archbishop Bernard Law of Boston. The change in the makeup of the bishops' conference was noted by Archbishop Laghi himself in his opening remarks to the bishops in the November meeting in 1986, the meeting at which the Economic Pastoral was approved. He observed, with evident pleasure, that during his five years as apostolic delegate, he was responsible for the appointment of almost a hundred new bishops, thus changing the character of the conference. Later during the bishops' meeting, this statement became embarrassing when Cardinal Law's name appeared over and over again on the ballot for different positions, first to be president of the conference, then vice-president of the conference, then to be an elected member to the synod of bishops on the laity the next year and each time to be defeated. Although he received about a hundred votes, it was never enough to obtain the majority needed for election, but it was enough to make everyone take note that the spirit of the conference would be changing. Bishops who were strong supporters of the conference as a needed entity in church structure understood that it would be useful only if it could maintain its freedom and integrity. They saw in these votes a sign portending future changes for the conference — at least that was the talk in the corridors among older bishops.

*　　*　　*

Although the vote on the final draft of *Economic Justice for All* and the election of officers were the main action items on the agenda at the November 1986 meeting, another drama was playing itself out behind closed doors. I was very disturbed about it, for it was creating a new level of tension between the U.S. Conference of Bishops and the pope. With apprehension, we all looked forward to the presentation that Bishop Raymond Hunthausen, whom we affectionately called "Dutch," was to make during the executive session, i.e., with no TV cameras or members of the press present. Accusations of bad management in the archdiocese of Seattle where he was archbishop had reached Rome and provoked an investigation. Rome appointed Cardinal James Hickey of Washington, D.C., to make a trip to Seattle, interview some people (it was not clear how they were selected), and write up a report (not to be given to Dutch). Then an auxiliary bishop, Bishop Donald Wuerl, was assigned to Seattle as an auxiliary bishop to take over certain areas of the archbishop's pastoral ministry. It was never clear who, Rome or Hunthausen, was to make the decision about what powers were to be delegated to the new auxiliary bishop. From a practical and theological point of view, such a situation was intolerable — as was soon evident. It would be like saying that someone would be governor of a state but have no say in how the prisons were run, the state parks maintained, or the universities financed.

The Hunthausen case followed upon that of Father Charles Curran, professor of moral theology at the Catholic University of America, who had been deprived of his professorship and declared unfit to teach Catholic theology. These cases were much talked about in the American press, since they touched a vital concern for justice and fairness, virtues that were deeply rooted in the history of our nation.

Dutch was a person totally without guile, strongly principled, and profoundly pastoral. His fellow bishops respected him highly; he was a real *mensch*. He gained prominence first by his refusal to pay, since 1982, half of his federal income taxes in protest against U.S. military policy. Then he joined protests in his own area of Washington State against the Trident nuclear submarines based there. A cloud hung over the disciplinary action against him because, shortly before the investigation, President Reagan had moved to name a U.S. ambassador to the Holy See, and Rome had raised the rank of the papal delegate in the United States to that of nuncio, the equivalent of ambassador. Many in the country were asking if, through this new mechanism, some secret political pressures had been put on the Church to silence Hunthausen. Most of us wondered and could never totally suppress that suspicion.

The situation of a bishop in the Catholic Church is a unique one. His legal rights within the Church are not spelled out; the pope personally is the arbiter of each case. With regard to the accusations brought against Archbishop Hunthausen, the procedures taken and the solutions decided upon seemed improvised and ineffective. It was also evident to the bishops gathered at this meeting that any one of them could be the next bishop so judged, since complaints to Rome were a common aspect of American Catholic culture.

The gathered bishops in Washington that November of 1986 wanted to be of support to one of their own; many saw him as being treated unfairly and without proper procedures, but they could not come to any consensus on how to be of help. It would have been unthinkable in that climate for the bishops to pass a resolution that in any way appeared to place themselves between Rome and a local bishop. It was not clear to me what Dutch was asking of us, but, after his long passionate talk and plea for help, the bishops felt their hands were tied. At the meeting I lamented the conference's impotence. We could only offer moral support and state our willingness to be of help if needed. Ultimately, Rome appointed Cardinal Bernardin, Cardinal O'Connor, and Archbishop John Quinn to work out a solution — which they did.

*　　*　　*

For months before this November bishops' meeting, I had been mulling over both the Hunthausen saga and the case of Charles Curran. These instances seemed to be clear signs that the atmosphere of openness and respect for each person in the Church, created by Pope John XXIII's talk at the opening of Vatican II, was being reversed. I brooded over this situation and asked myself what response I, as an archbishop, should take. Thus, in September, i.e., two months before the bishops' meeting, I wrote two short reflections for the archdiocesan weekly newspaper, the *Catholic Herald,* entitled "The Price of Orthodoxy." (Later I was to learn that some people in Milwaukee faxed the articles immediately to officials in the curia in Rome.) The *New York Times* picked up the articles and wrote about them (September 24, 1986) under the headline: "Leading Archbishop Challenges Vatican on Silencing Dissent." As could be expected, many other newspapers followed suit.

In the beginning, I made reference to St. Paul and his concern about false doctrines. False doctrines, I knew and admitted, easily led to bad pastoral practices that could be harmful. For me it was not a question of concern for truth but the method of approaching such questions.

In those articles, I referred to the opening talk of Pope John XXIII at Vatican II (1962) which was my inspiration. Pope John said that in the past the Church had condemned, often with greatest severity, ideas considered false. He contrasted that with the present day where the Church preferred to make use of the "medicine of mercy rather than that of severity." He continued: "She considers that she meets the needs of the present day by demonstrating the validity of the teaching rather than by condemnations."

In addition, I spoke of those historical periods when heretics were hunted down and brutally treated. I went on to write: "Unfortunately, such periods also produced, in addition to the cruelty mentioned, fear. In such an atmosphere, amateurs — turned theologians — easily became headhunters, and leaders were picked, not by their ability to work toward a synthesis of the new knowledge and the tradition, but by the rigidity of their orthodoxy, so that often second-rate and repressive minds, riding on the waves of that fear, took over." I cited the period of Pope Pius X when organized "informers" in each diocese reported to Rome any semblance of heresy as they saw it. I lamented the number of theologians who had suffered in the past from this atmosphere, naming thinkers in the 1940s and 1950s who were silenced — Yves Congar, Henri du Lubac, Teilhard de Chardin, and John Courtney Murray — all of them rehabilitated by Vatican II. The price of orthodoxy one could see was a Church that lived in fear.

I could feel myself inwardly rebelling against having to live and function in such a repressive atmosphere. I had accepted that I would be a part of a "loyal minority" during the pontificate of Pope John Paul II, but I had not anticipated how such isolation would feel. There were certainly bishops among us who felt like I did, but we had to talk about it in the corridors and not in public.

Occasionally at the meeting that November bishop friends would come up to me and warn me that I would be next on the list of those to be silenced. Conservative Catholic papers were pressing Rome to bring some action against me. Although I did not know it at the time, I must have been on a short list of U.S. bishops to be "brought into line," as preparations for my *ad limina* visit planned for 1988 would point out.

Around the country there was some reaction to my articles, especially among Catholic commentators. One response in particular tied together many threads of the situation in which I found myself. In a syndicated column for October 14, 1986, William F. Buckley, Jr., founder and editor of the *National Review,* wrote an article on my reflections to the Hunthausen and Curran situations.

Buckley commented: "The problem there, if you want to put it so, is that Catholic theology is, so to speak, copyrighted in the Vatican and although it retains the liberty — and has in the past — to change here and there the construction of this or that doctrine, it is the Vatican that does this, not a local bottling plant. Right now, Pope John Paul II is opting for Classic Coke, etc." At the end of the column, Buckley noted: "If Archbishop Weakland runs out of energy, there are those who hope that lack of energy will also enervate his desire to introduce socialism to the United States. Let us hope that before that happens, there will still be enough church-attending Christians to pray efficaciously that he will fail."

The story grew more complicated. Since this was the moment when the American bishops' Economic Pastoral Letter was in the public eye, there was interest in it in many circles. In May of 1985 I was invited to speak about its contents at the North Shore Congregation Israel in Glencoe, Illinois. I talked to a full house and a very supportive audience. Often at my speeches I would be confronted by members of Lyndon LaRouche's party. They had a special animosity toward Jews but also toward Benedictines. (The source of that antipathy eluded me.) I was thus not surprised when, after the talk and before the question and answer period, a woman, later identified as Janice Hart of the Lyndon LaRouche Party, came rushing up to the bema, and, ripping open a wrapped package containing a piece of bloody liver, threw it at me. After she was apprehended by the security guard and I had regained my cool, I asked the audience to reflect with me on how historical this evening was: here was a Catholic archbishop speaking in a Jewish synagogue and both of us together were being treated to this ignominy. That event was important and has remained with me because it happened in a synagogue, a place where I had been invited to speak for the first time in my life.

The congregation brought charges against her. Buckley's *National Review* (September 28, 1986) took note of the case, observing that her throwing of the liver "probably isn't nice, but what so many have longed to do can hardly be much of a crime. The target is a gentleman [that was me!] who desires to consign the country to socialism on the basis of his own, admittedly horrifying, experience of childhood penury and only getting chocolate ice cream once a week (that's close — we don't always understand him), wherefore, it follows everybody should suffer the same misery in the name of justice. Or something. We assume Mrs. Hart missed — the wire reporters would have blared a bit if she'd connected with the liver. She faces a $500 fine, which is utterly ridiculous. Forty hours of community service is more like it, especially if she can spend it in target practice."

It was evident to me that Mr. Buckley was not so much interested in the two articles I had written on "The Price of Orthodoxy." Rather, his concern was the Economic Pastoral. I had to learn shortly after becoming a bishop not to answer such attacks in kind; the over-simplification, the ridicule, the demeaning attitudes — all were part of the worst aspects of the American political culture.

*   *   *

Working on the Economic Pastoral, no doubt, had taken me away too much from archdiocesan work and tensions were becoming visible. We needed a process to bring together clergy and lay people, religious men and women, the professional lay staffs and the people in the pews. Newer ethnic groups — Asians, Latinos, and the last influx of blacks during World War II — had their own aspirations. It was time we all sat around the same table. Consulting all the members of the local church now seemed possible with newer technological means, such as computers. We already had some experience in the participatory entities to try this on a broader scale. I was excited about this opportunity to see what the Spirit was saying to the Church of Milwaukee.

In order to set priorities for the future of the archdiocese, we needed a diocesan synod that would bring all the disparate groups together to listen and to discern. In the past, synods were ways of creating particular legislation for the local church, especially for the clergy, but modern technology made it possible to use them for strategic planning in ways that would involve the faithful of the entire diocese. The first synod of the Archdiocese of Milwaukee had been held in 1847 and the second in 1891. No more were ever held. But Milwaukee was ready now for one. The *Renew* program had just finished successfully; we had in place an Archdiocesan Council of Priests, an Archdiocesan Pastoral Council, and a Finance Council. We were ready to plan in earnest. After consulting those councils, I decided to move ahead, and so in August 1984 published a pastoral letter called "Walking Together," convoking the synod for 1987.

The leadership for organizing this gigantic project fell to Father Don Thimm and Dr. Maureen Gallagher. With these two skilled professionals to guide us, we had the knowledge and the courage to move ahead. In retrospect, I can say with pride that the process, as complicated as it was, ran smoothly and accomplished its goal to a degree I could never have expected.

Our computers listed 215,000 households, or units, in the archdiocese. How does one consult that many people in a significant way? We began by sending out 215,000 questionnaires to these families or households and added to them the priests, deacons, religious men and women, and a few thousand teens between the ages of fourteen and eighteen. The questionnaire raised sixty-four different issues that a focus group had prepared. What was the interest of the faithful in these, or in any other they wanted to discuss? Over 50,000 questionnaires were returned, most of them the composite response of a whole family.

Even if we had stopped the process there, I would have been happy, since I learned a good deal from these first responses. For example, no differences in opinion could be found between rural and urban Catholics: they all sought the same kind of vital church life. There were fascinating differences, however, between, say, the priests' priorities and the lay people's. Priests, for example, put a high value on the salaries of professional lay people working full time for the Church, but the same concern, *pro dolor,* was not yet shared by the laity. The role of women was a high priority among priests and women religious, but not among the laity. I will not go into all the details of the synod. We tried to bring as many people as possible into the process, having synods in each parish first to talk about the issues, then regional meetings, and finally a meeting of representatives of the whole local Church.

As we began the process I had to ask myself how I would deal with issues that might contradict church doctrine or discipline. I knew that themes such as the ordination of married men, the ordination of women, changes in the Church's teachings on contraception, and others would arise. And they did. I was frank with the people and said we could not vote on such issues, but that, in my *ad limina* report to Rome, I would mention that they were brought up so that Rome would be informed. Themes of this sort went beyond our competency as members of a universal church, but others should know that we did raise them. This seemed to satisfy the desires of those who felt strongly about each of these issues.

The final convocation was held in the large conference center in Milwaukee from Friday evening to Sunday evening the last weekend of August 1987. Each parish elected six delegates, and a teen between the ages of fourteen and eighteen was elected by the young people of the parish. A number of priests and deacons were elected by their peers; a similar election took place among men and women religious. According to Canon Law, all the members of the archdiocesan pastoral council and priests' council were invited. I was asked to appoint some from the Asian, African American, and Native American communities so that there would be no imbalance. The total number came to over 2,000. So that those living far away did not have to travel back and forth, people in Milwaukee opened their homes to those wishing to stay over.

I thought trying to work out a process with so many people would be a nightmare, but it ran smoothly and every member had a chance to meet other Catholics from a variety of backgrounds. I recall one woman from a farming area telling me it was the first time she had ever discussed with an African American woman her anxieties about raising a family in the Central City. The black woman, in turn, had no idea how difficult life on the farm could be and how financially precarious such work was.

I spent the time going from group to group, listening to the discussion, taking time out to answer questions, and just enjoying so many people enthusiastic about their faith and their Church. It is impossible to sum up the wealth of suggestions that came from the synod; it took me years to see the implications of all the propositions that the members voted on.

When they were asked to select the five top issues for the diocese to work on, they placed them in the following order: (1) stewardship of time, talent, and treasure (involvement or participation); (2) life-long Christian formation; (3) meeting educational and other needs of families; (4) creating a sense of community; and (5) acknowledging and responding to racism.

The archdiocesan synod ended that Sunday afternoon with a festive Mass in the big arena called Mecca. Since there was space for only 5,000 people, we had to limit the number of tickets available for each parish. It was one of the most memorable Masses I have ever celebrated. There was electricity in the air. The singing was magnificent. I teased the crowd that people passing by might think we were Lutherans we had sung so well! As we returned to the vesting area, Archbishop Cousins, who was then eighty-five and in ill health, had tears in his eyes and said how thankful he was that God permitted him to be a part of the occasion. As I recall my own feelings, they were ones of pride in Milwaukee's Catholic faith community. Wherever I went in the archdiocese for the next decade, people would come up to me and tell me they had been members of the synod and how powerful and influential that event had been in their lives as Catholics.

If I have gone into detail about the synod, it is because it affected decisions in the archdiocese for the next fifteen years. We held meeting after meeting of the APC and the ACP to discuss the points and how they should be implemented. I reorganized the whole structure of the central offices in the light of the results to provide more of the support parishes wanted, reducing the staff considerably. But then I created eight new positions called "parish consultants." Each consultant had two districts to work with, maintaining an office out in those districts to help keep the parishes in touch with the resources available according to their needs. The consultants came into the central offices one day each week, and so in that way I could hear from them how things were going in their districts. A preaching institute was founded and many other programs embarked on — all inspired by synod resolutions.

When the faithful at the synod spoke of wanting to belong to a vital parish, they meant one that had good liturgies where the preaching and the music had quality and where there were outlets for involvement in social justice programs.

*   *   *

But nothing stopped. Shortly after our synod, Pope John Paul II was making his second trip to the United States, September 10 to 19. He was holding a meeting with all the American bishops in Los Angeles and I felt it was important for me to participate. After that, I had to be on my way to Rome; I had been elected one of the four American delegates to the synod of bishops from October 1 to October 30. The subject was the role of the laity, a theme in which I had a special interest and certainly wanted to probe more deeply.

In 1979, the pope had visited the northern cities on the East Coast and the trip had gone smoothly. This second trip was to begin on September 10 in Miami, followed by a tour of cities in the South and Southwest, visit to Los Angeles and San Francisco on the West Coast, and end with a stop in Detroit. The press predicted that there would be large protests along the way, especially in San Francisco, that would harass the pope, as similar groups had done shortly before in Holland and Belgium.

This trip was to be seen as a form of dialogue between the Church in the United States and the pope; this would appear as an adaptation to American culture. Each stop was dedicated to a theme with someone from the Church in the States named to speak before the pope. His remarks, then, were booked as a response to the speaker in question. But, contrary to American custom, the designated speakers were to send their prepared talks to Rome before the trip took place so the pope could prepare his response to them. Since his actual responses in city after city sometimes seemed to ignore what the selected speaker said, it was never clear to me whether the procedure had really been followed. One could not tell whether he understood what they had said or not. He was always gracious to those who spoke.

In Los Angeles, for the "dialogue" with the bishops, four of us had been selected to present speeches on different topics to which he would then respond. The setting in the old San Fernando Mission was perfect, a quaint but relaxed atmosphere. In this case, as demanded by Rome, we bishops had written our speeches, shared them with one another for peer criticism, and then sent them to Rome a few months in advance. No changes in the text were then permitted. Thus, the pope's response worked off the text given him and his staff. Four talks were too many and, since his responses were also substantial in length, the meeting seemed interminable. For some inexplicable reason the press was not allowed to be present, but they received ahead of time copies of the prepared talks and the pope's response to each.

Cardinal Joseph Bernardin of Chicago spoke first on U.S. culture and the relationship between the Church in the United States and Rome. Archbishop John Quinn of San Francisco spoke on the moral teaching of the Church and the need for dialogue with the American Catholic faithful since that teaching was not always accepted — a delicate topic. I had been chosen to give the third talk about the role of the laity, especially of women, in the Church. Finally, Arhchbishop Pilarczyk of Cincinnati spoke of the priest shortage and the question of ministry in the Church, emphasizing that laity wished to be able to participate fully in the inner life of the Church.

Then came the pope's lengthy response. As I listened to the first part in which he touched on the paper delivered by Cardinal Bernardin, I had the feeling I was watching a professor correct a less-than-gifted student; his tone and demeanor seemed to me to be condescending. It was painful to see a cardinal treated this way so publicly. His response to Archbishop Quinn's paper was sharper in tone with a strong emphasis on obedience to the magisterium and squelching of all dissent. "Dissent from church doctrine remains what it is, dissent; as such it may not be proposed or received on an equal footing with the Church's authentic teaching."

One can see why I was shivering a bit as I waited to hear his response to my contribution. The pope picked up on my statement about the Church in the States having the largest number of educated and formed Catholics in history and then somewhat snidely asked rhetorically what influence, however, they were having on the U.S. culture today. Since I had a sentence on family life and strengthening families, he took advantage of that sentence to stress the teaching of *Humanae vitae* and the "intrinsic relationship between the unitive and procreative dimensions of the marriage act." Then he spoke at length on abortion before responding to what I had said about women, carefully outlining his position in two points: "the equal dignity of women and their true feminine humanity." He made clear what he meant by this phrase when he said: "The Church proclaims the personal dignity of women as women — a dignity equal to that of men's dignity. This dignity must be affirmed in its ontological character even before consideration is given to any of the special and exalted roles fulfilled by women as wives, mothers or consecrated women." The rest, he said, would have to be left for the synod on the laity that would take place in Rome during the month of October.

His response to the presentation of Archbishop Pilarczyk was good and encouraging. He accepted as a positive evolution that the laity were more and more involved in the inner life of the Church and accepted this change as the product of Vatican II. But he then spent most of his time talking about vocations of celibate men to the priesthood and the need to avoid prophecies of doom and pessimism.

To conclude his talk, he added other points that had not been brought up by any of us but that he wanted to mention. He talked of the need to emphasize among the faithful again the frequent reception of the sacrament of penance; he spoke of the abuse of the use of general absolution; he stressed the need for a type of pastoral care for homosexuals that did not weaken the Church's teaching in this regard; he cited the need of re-examining the role and content of sex education in Catholic schools and the rights of parents to determine what their children would hear; and, finally, he stressed the need for more chaplains in the military service — an addition that caused a perplexed reaction as it seemed out of keeping with the other points raised. (Was it added under the influence of Cardinal O'Connor?)

When the talk was finished, I said to myself that this experiment of a "dialogue" seemed more like a classroom lesson where the students read their papers and the professor gave his criticisms. I was not sure it would be seen as a sign of the way collegiality should work among bishops or between the pope and the bishops. After the pope's presentation, probably every bishop present would have liked to have engaged him in a free-for-all discussion on many of the points raised, but that was not on the agenda.

After the trip was over, the press talked more about the speeches given in the presence of the pope than about his replies. Two stood out and were later frequently commented on: Father Frank McNulty's talk delivered in Miami on the role of priests in the United States and the speech given by Donna Hanson in San Francisco on the role of the laity. They were honest, frank, and respectful, but spoken from the heart. For example, Donna Hanson said: "Not to question, not to challenge, not to have authorities involve me in a process of understanding is to deny my dignity as a person and the rights granted to me both by Church and society." The pope's response gave the impression of two ships passing in the dark. Some of the other talks were just as impressive, e.g., those by Father Stephen Tutas and Sister Helen Garvey on the role of religious life today or the fine talk by Father Thomas Harvey about the Catholic Church's work for charity and justice in the United States. Many had hoped the pope would say something positive about the Peace Pastoral or the Economic Pastoral during his trip, but it was as if they did not exist.

The pope's staff had feared more than any other his stay in San Francisco. But from that stopover came one of the most memorable images of the whole trip. At Mission Dolores outside of San Francisco his visit with victims of AIDS was poignant and moving. As I watched on TV, I noted that he entered the congregation with his usual assurance and then immediately mingled among those present, blessing them on the forehead, touching them affectionately. His white garment stood out among the darker surroundings. With the sick he was gentle and compassionate, unafraid to embrace them. Later in his talk he refused to support the thesis of some Evangelicals that AIDS was a punishment from God. His statement that "God loves you all, without distinction, without limit" echoed in the minds of those present for some time to come.

When I was in Rome during the month of October, I heard from many members of the curia how pleased the pope was with his visit. According to these sources he explicitly said that those who had prognosticated that it would be an unpleasant ten days for him were simply wrong.

*   *   *

Next, I was scheduled to attend the synod on the laity in Rome from October 1 to 30. It turned out to be a long month. Four bishops were elected by the U.S. conference to represent them at that synod: Cardinal Bernardin of Chicago; Archbishop John May, archbishop of St. Louis and president of the conference; Bishop Stanley Ott of Baton Rouge, chair of the bishops' committee on the laity; and me. It pleased me to have been elected a member of this group. In preparation, the bishops' office for the laity, under the capable guidance of Dolores Leckey, a vibrant, cultured, and intelligent director, held hearings with lay people all around the country.

Earlier that year, I had been invited to Milan for a meeting of the European bishops who were to attend that same synod in October. The conferences of bishops of Europe, in keeping with the general spirit of the nations of Europe at that time, sought to create more and more ties to each other and thus had formed a European Council of Conferences of Bishops. Cardinal Basil Hume, my old friend from London, was chair. I accepted the invitation to attend because it could provide a preliminary view of how the European countries saw the coming synod. The European conferences had one important concern that had no American counterpart. It is important to understand this concern for two reasons: first, one could not penetrate the dynamics of the coming synod and some of its debates without knowing of it; and second, without this knowledge one could not appreciate the direction the pontificate of Pope John Paul II was taking.

During his pontificate there was a sharp rise in lay movements in Europe, both in numbers and in influence. Since the pope saw these movements as the means for a spiritual revitalization of Catholicism in Europe, he gave them his full support. Hundreds of thousands of their members would flock to the annual gatherings in the Square of St. Peter's for the encounter between the pope and members of these movements. He took those occasions to give them their marching orders. They supplied much of the pope's work-force. Wherever one went among the offices of the curia, one found members of these groups employed there. They also were responsible for doing most of the work behind the scenes needed to organize the synods of bishops. They organized the gatherings for the pope with youth from all over the world every few years. In the summers, these groups would be found spending evenings out at Castel Gondolfo, singing with the pope and hanging on his every word.

He put his hopes on them as the leaven to change European culture from its secular tendencies to a renewed Christianity. He saw these groups as his military units, his "green berets" always at his command. These new groups often had curious canonical arrangements, but their basic allegiance was directly to the pope; they were regarded as coming directly under the pope functioning in his role as pastor of the universal church. Pope John Paul II liked to describe his role in those terms. The tension the European bishops were feeling was the relationship, then, between these movements and the local dioceses with their diocesan bishops.

The most significant of them was Opus Dei. Pope John Paul II formed it into a separate diocese under their own bishop, a super-diocese that covered the whole world. Opus Dei became a sort of "church within a church." Another group, the Focolare Movement, had been founded by Chiara Lubich in Northern Italy in the 1950s as a way of deepening the spiritual life of its members. Her writings were clear and plain, not marked by conservatism, but taking a more modern spiritual bent that I found inspiring to lay people. I liked her as a person, too, since she was unaffected and sincere.

In the late 1960s in Rome I became involved with the Comunitá di Sant'Egidio, a lay initiative that combined daily prayer with works of charity. Their spirituality was lay-oriented, marked by an identification with the poorest of the poor and a strong emphasis on daily community prayer, especially in the evenings. On Saturday they had a full meeting of members to examine their lives and work, followed by a Saturday evening Mass. On Sundays they could be found among the poorest suburbs of Rome helping with the liturgy and engaged in teaching catechism and other projects.

I have already mentioned Comunione e Liberazione, founded in Milan by Monsignor Luigi Giussani. They were the most clearly political of all the movements. Their annual conventions in Italy attracted many of the leading cardinals of the curia and an array of Italian politicians. The writings of Giussani, elegant, thoughtful, challenging, and demanding, were especially noteworthy. He was able to uncover the best in contemporary thought, especially the literary, and leave the rest behind.

A newer group called the Neocatechumenate had arisen in Spain and was popular in some sections of Europe. It seemed to be one of the pope's favorites. It was based on the model of the Rite of Christian Initiation of Adults into the Church. Difficulties arose with this group because they never integrated into the parishes in question and were accused of forming a church apart.

Lastly, there was the Legionaries of Christ and their lay component, Regnum Christi. Founded in Mexico over fifty years ago by Father Marcial Marciel, they were, strictly speaking, a clerical group with abundant vocations, but with a very active lay appendix. All their priesthood candidates had to study at their headquarters in Rome. As a result, their presence on the Roman scene was more significant than that of any other group. They, too, were often invited to Castel Gondolfo on summer evenings for songfests. We often smiled as we observed their clerical students going off to the Roman Catholic universities each day for class, all sporting the same neat traditional haircut, carrying the same briefcases, and wearing their Roman collars with pride. We called them "the Catholic Mormons," as they looked so much like the young Mormons seen in groups on the streets of Rome.

Sometimes I heard these movements compared to societies like the Knights of Columbus in the United States. The comparison limps because the Knights are much more integrated into the local churches, very close to the bishops, and not as spiritually or as politically oriented. It would be more helpful for an understanding of them to compare them to the Cursillo or the Charismatic Renewal movements.

The question to which the European bishops constantly returned could be framed thus: What is the relationship between these groups and the local Church? That question was debated long and hard before the pope at the October synod with Cardinal Martini of Milan as the most insistent on the rights of the local bishop.

The theme most pressed by the American delegation differed. We in the States, as Archbishop May pointed out in his talk at the synod, saw the renewal of Catholicism among us as taking place through a renewed vitality in the parishes. The parish was for us the place where the spiritual lives of our Catholics were formed. I could well attest to that statement from the synod we had just held in Milwaukee.

*   *   *

While I should have gone over to the archives to look up my box of information from this synod, I realized that I kept putting it off. I knew that reading through all the material would just evoke depressing feelings about that month and that meeting. But I finally went to the archives and asked for the big box. When it came, I blew the dust from the top and gingerly opened it. There I found everything from the synod, including my pass, my nametag, printed documents sent to the members before and during the meeting, my hand-scribbled notes, and other accumulated material.

What caught my attention at once, however, were not the official documents but the glossy covers of 30 Giorni, the magazine published by the Comunione e Liberazione (CL) movement. The one from September of that year, with its negative prognosis of the papal trip, I had thrown into the box, too, since it had been passed out to all the members of the synod. Beside it was the issue for the month of October with articles on the synod itself. Archbishop Schotte, the director of the synod office, forbade all the other groups who wanted to pass out literature in the aula to do so, but made an exception for this group. Again the material was very anti-American. Specifically Cardinal Bernardin and Archbishop Weakland were named as the "dissenters."

This issue also carried an interview with Jean-Loup Dherse, a prominent Catholic lay man who had been vice president of the World Bank, then director of the channel project between England and the coast of France, and now appointed as a lay adjunct secretary to the synod. He was a distinguished French Catholic lay man and certainly merited being invited to the synod. In that interview he was asked what he thought of the Economic Pastoral Letter of the American bishops, and answered, snidely to say the least, that it was the kind of trivia-pursuit that Americans engaged in occasionally. He also added that it was the work of only a few American bishops who then forced it on the rest of them.

Bernardin and I protested to Schotte that this kind of material had been officially circulated. The Canadian bishops, very upset, complained even more vigorously to Schotte about the way in which the synod was doing everything possible to disgrace the Americans. I spoke personally to Monsignor Giussani, founder of the CL and still its spiritual guide, about the anti-American attitude of 30 Giorni, but he answered that he had no control over the magazine. Archbishop May, very angry about the Dherse interview, called a public press conference and totally denied the remark that the Economic Pastoral was only the wish of a few bishops who inflicted it on the others.

Dherse himself the very next morning looked for me at the coffee break to tell me that he was deeply disturbed by the published interview. He asserted that he had not said any of the things attributed to him, that they were the words of the interviewer from CL, and that he held just the opposite view of the letter. But the damage was done. I felt that Bernardin and I had been listed among the "untouchables," and during the whole meetings had to wear our scarlet letters — "D" for dissenter.

The synod began, as I have noted before, with each bishop — all two hundred and some — delivering an eight-minute talk. Some of the guests and observers were also given time to speak. This procedure lasted for about two weeks and was a brutal discipline of having to listen to scattered thoughts that often contradicted each other. We four delegates from the United States had agreed among ourselves on the topics each would address. Archbishop May spoke eloquently of the need for vital parish life if there is to be any kind of renewal of the laity in the Church after Vatican II. Cardinal Bernardin confronted the delicate issue of the role of the U.S. Catholic laity in politics. It was a positive approach that ended with more questions than answers. Bishop Stanley Ott gave a much appreciated plea for a distinct lay spirituality that was related to their work. I had been selected by the bishops to talk in particular about the role of women in church and society. As I re-read that intervention, I know that I would not change a word of it twenty years later.

I opened my talk with a quote from Pope John XXIII's encyclical *Pacem in terris* (1963) about the rights of women, who, he said, no longer will be "treated as mere material instruments, but demand rights befitting a human person both in domestic and public life." Then I added: "Many women, it is true, are satisfied with the present situation. But it is difficult, if not impossible, for us bishops gathered here to realize the pain and frustration that so many other women feel toward the Church. Women who are loyal to and love the Church express dismay and discouragement if their talents and contributions to church life are stifled or rejected. They want to be heard and consulted on issues that affect them deeply." The talk ended with a list of recommendations that would permit women to function in all liturgical roles that do not demand priestly ordination and to assume decision-making roles on all levels of church life. I called for more sensitivity to language in liturgical and official church texts so that it would not seem to exclude women.

The Canadian bishops and many of the European bishops were delighted with the clarity of the talk and thanked me for "putting my neck on the block." There was, however, one exception. A bishop from India who spoke after me, one of the members appointed by the pope, lamented that the participants at the synod were being forced to listen to speeches from bishops of rich countries about the role of women in church and society when the real problems facing women were different. In his country, he said, women were worried about solving the basic needs of feeding their children and educating them, not about taking power from the clergy. When I saw him at the bar during the break, I reminded him that in his city in India the previous year the number of fetuses that had been aborted because they were female was over 30,000! I stated that perhaps in his country there was an even greater problem with the lack of respect for the dignity of women than in my own. He was a bit taken aback by my rebuttal, thanked me, and then slid away to the other end of the bar. The next day he sought me out before the sessions to thank me profusely for the frank remarks, since he now realized the depth of the problem the Church in his country faced. Several times before the end of the synod he again took me aside to thank me for talking with him. I cannot say we became friends, but at least there was some common bonding at the end.

After all the speeches were finished, we broke up into various language groups to discuss the material and questions proposed by the directors of the synod. I was assigned to English Group-3. The first item of business was to elect a chairman of the group. I can use that election as an example of the negative atmosphere toward me in the synod. Archbishop Derek Worlock of Liverpool, an old friend of mine from earlier synods when I was abbot primate of the Benedictines, was also a member of this group and immediately nominated me. Archbishop Simon Pimenta from Bombay, India, was also nominated. On the first ballot the vote was a tie: 11 to 11. On the second ballot the Indian bishop won by a vote of 12 to 10. One of the participants said he had been informed, but he would not say by whom, not to vote for Weakland because Weakland is a "dissenter." Worlock was astonished by all of this talk and a bit angry as well. But all of the name-calling did not inhibit me from speaking my mind during the meeting. Admittedly, I felt awkward at times, as if some of the others were scrutinizing everything I said to find some heresy.

At the end of the synod, the items I was most interested in did not make it into the final propositions to be given to the pope, but were lost along the way. All in all, as I wrote at the end of the synod, we Americans did not lose ground on the role of the laity in church and society, but we also did not gain much.

Yet, as expected, much of the debate on the floor centered on the role of the movements and their relationship to the local bishop. It was not a point that brought much unanimity. In the propositions voted on to be handed on to the pope, the neat division that kept the clergy in the Church and the laity in the world did not get any emphasis. The proposals on women did not break any new ground, but at least we did not go backward. Best of all, the renewal demanded by Vatican II was seen first as implying the creation of vibrant parishes, as the American delegates had emphasized.

The spirit of a synod had changed radically between 1974 and 1987. In the previous synods there were frank exchanges and great excitement about the many diversified cultural points of view on any topic. Moreover, there was frankness and sincerity in the speeches. At this synod, slowly but inexorably it was dawning on me that during the present pontificate I would remain out of step. It was very evident at the synod that all bishops there fell into two classes, those that enjoyed papal, and thus curial, favor and those who did not. All the cardinals and bishops appointed by the pope to this synod were in the first category; they formed a bloc of their own. After a bit, their expressions of loyalty and fealty became very trying. There was a division between those who expressed ecclesiastical politically correct ideas, laden with current papal quotes, and the others.

That synod left a bitter taste in my mouth. Thanks to people like Dolores Leckey, Cardinal Hume, the Sant'Egidio community, and a few others, I survived the month, so that it now is only a vague, but still distasteful, memory. What also kept my spirits alive during that month was the consoling recollection of the archdiocesan synod a few weeks before. It was the source of hope for me.

Now, after taking from the big archival box what notes I needed about that synod on the laity of 1987, I closed it without much hesitation, handed it back to the archivist, and consigned it to the dust I knew it would soon accumulate.

*   *   *

1987 was an eventful year with many ups and downs, highs and lows. I hoped that 1988 would be a quieter period. I was flattered that the bishops were electing me to so many public roles. It was a sign of their confidence.

Every three years the bishops elected a new president and vice-president of the conference. Each bishop was to suggest candidates for the two positions and from that list the first ten would constitute the ballot. It had become customary that the vice-president, after serving for three years, would be elected president.

Every three years my name was among the top ten suggested, and I would be asked if I wished to stand for election or withdraw my name. I always withdrew, since I could not see myself serving as vice-president for three years and then president for three more. It would have hampered my ability to say what I really thought. But it did bolster my self-esteem and helped me get through some of the difficult times. I liked my fellow bishops and enjoyed working with them, never missing a meeting, always doing my homework by reading every document to be voted on, sending in amendments where it seemed appropriate, sitting on committees when asked, and, as was evident with the Economic Pastoral, taking up the tasks delegated to me with all my energy. I whole-heartedly believed in the importance of the conference and saw it as a vehicle for expressing collegiality with the other bishops.

The role of a bishops' conference may seem to some an abstract question of no consequence, but it remains important for an understanding of the Second Vatican Council and its implementation. In some ways, working out the relationship between the local churches and Rome could be compared in the history of the United States to the balance of power between states' rights and those of the federal government. The First Vatican Council (1869-1870) had dealt with the role of the pope, but, because of the Franco-Prussian War, had to be suddenly terminated before that council could take up the role of the bishops. The Second Vatican Council's solution on what structural form collegiality among the bishops *cum et sub Petro* would take was tentative and inadequate, probably in the hope that the post-conciliar period could articulate in practice the proper balance.

So, e.g., before leaving Rome at the end of the council in 1965, the bishops, afraid that the situation might easily revert to the way it was before the council when the power of the curia seemed unlimited, stated: "Bishops, as legitimate successors of the apostles and members of the Episcopal college, should appreciate that they are closely united to each other and should be solicitous for all the churches. By divine institution and by virtue of their apostolic office, they all share joint responsibility for the Church" *(Christus Dominus)*. Using words like "by divine institution," the bishops were making as strong an argument as a council could make for some form of structural participation.

Since the role of the conferences of bishops was central to what was happening in the Church in the United States during the mid-1980s, a summary of the state of the question at that time would be helpful. The debate about the role of a bishops' conference is important because it explains the inability of the conference of bishops in the United States to respond forcefully as a body to the sex-abuse problems among the clergy — problems that began to be revealed in their enormity between 1985 and 1995 and which I will to take up in the next chapter.

The general and most popular perception in the press and among the people in the pews about the role and power of a conference of bishops presupposed that it possessed legislative power for its own region. Thus, most people expected that the U.S. Conference of Bishops would initiate a unified, coordinated response to any given problem, agreed upon by all the bishops of the nation and valid for the whole country. They presupposed a conference of bishops had the power to do so. Rome and many bishops simply did not agree with that perception. They resisted such an assumption since it infringed on their rights as diocesan bishops and placed an authority, i.e., the conference of bishops, between them and the pope. Pope Paul VI mandated the formation of conferences of bishops throughout the world without giving them a clear portfolio.

Pope John Paul II clarified his position on the conferences of bishops. When the Revised Code of Canon Law appeared in 1983, Canon 455 stated specifically that conferences could only legislate in those cases in which common law prescribes it or a special mandate of the Vatican permits it. In all these cases, however, a two-thirds vote of the bishops would be required and Rome's *recognitio* (approval) would have to be obtained before the decree could be promulgated. In this way, the pope saw to it that the legislative power of the bishops' conferences was limited.

But what about the more delicate question of the teaching role of a conference? This issue had not yet been solved. Theologically it was posed in these terms: Does a conference of bishops have a mandate to teach? That question arose at the meeting of bishops in the Vatican on the Peace Pastoral in 1983 and again at the extraordinary synod of bishops of 1985. Since that synod was composed of the presidents of all the bishops' conferences from around the world, the members were reluctant to accept the curial position. The debate ended by asking the pope to appoint a committee to study the issue. Sometime in late January of 1988, we bishops received from the conference of bishops in Washington a draft statement on the teaching authority of bishops' conferences, sutured together by five congregations in Rome under the chair of Cardinal Ratzinger. All the conferences of the world were to send back their evaluation by the end of the year.

It was a curious trial-balloon. Conferences of bishops were seen as pastoral aides to individual bishops to assist them in the governance of their dioceses, but no teaching authority could come between the individual bishop and the pope. On the question of the teaching authority of a bishops' conference, the document stated that "the Episcopal conferences do not, as such, properly speaking possess the *munus magisteri* (teaching office)" (#V). In the final observations, the Roman document stated that any document of a conference must have a two-thirds vote and receive the *recognitio* (approval) from the Holy See before publication. In other words, this document sought to limit the ability of conferences to publish in their own name documents of a theological or moral nature just as the code had limited the conferences in the legislative area.

The American bishops, when they assembled in November 1988, voted to reject the document, and their vote was sent on to Rome. Almost every conference of bishops throughout the world did likewise. The results of the consultation were never published, and the document was placed in some pigeonhole in an office in the curia, only to be resurrected some ten years later, i.e., 1998, when Pope John Paul II published a slightly modified version as his own document *(motu proprio)* under the title *Apostolos suos*. As a compromise, this final version stated that conferences of bishops could publish doctrinal statements provided they were voted on unanimously by all the bishops — a practice with no past history in the Church. If that was impossible, then a two-thirds vote would be required and the document would have to have Rome's approval.

Through these documents and the discussions that surrounded them, it became ever more evident that the vitality of the conferences of bishops would be destroyed and they would take less and less initiative. As I watched all this happen, I was dejected. Many of the statements from the conciliar documents that spoke of a more active engagement on the part of the bishops in the decisions that affected the life of the Church became meaningless. Rome's control over the local churches was now total. Some bishops, especially those newly appointed, seemed to accept without thought this centralization. Others of us regretted it. If we were expected as bishops to model for the whole Church a sense of co-responsibility, it became more and more difficult to do so effectively.

But the trend toward centralization during the pontificate of Pope John Paul II was now clear and unrelenting. Everything would have to be referred to Rome. Although the curia had many bright and capable people working there, they would continue to be overwhelmed by the volume of material sent to them from around the world for their approval. I did not hesitate to attribute to the pope himself the heightened centralization that occurred during his papacy and the attempt to silence contrary voices. Because of the length of his pontificate, this attitude caused a heaviness in the Church, a sense of uneasiness and alienation on the part of some, especially among those theologians and bishops not in his favor, and consequently sharp divisions. As he grew older and more sickly, he could no longer personally control the centralization he had set in motion, and lesser minds in the curia began to show the inadequacies of the system.

*   *   *

If 1988 began on an ominous note with this draft document on the role of conferences of bishops, Milwaukee was still a safe haven for me. It had truly become my home and I always returned there after meetings elsewhere in the country with joy and a sense of relief. I knew I would always find waiting for me questions about the implementation of the resolutions of the archdiocesan synod. The enthusiasm and energy with which the archdiocesan pastoral council and the priests' council tackled this renewal was contagious. The most illusive of the resolutions spoke about the need to combat racism, and it was difficult to sort out what could be done about the negative attitudes that produced it. We stumbled a bit in sorting out our response to this issue, although the mere fact that it was voted a priority was itself illuminating and consoling.

Another important task awaited me. Since 1988 was the year for the *ad limina* visits of the American bishops to Rome, I knew I had to prepare my report and submit it well in advance. Our region would be the last to make this trip, our visit being scheduled for December. Having been a bishop now for ten years, I felt more secure in writing up what I felt the curial offices in Rome should know about this archdiocese.

As would be expected in this report of 1988, I wrote much about the archdiocesan synod that had taken place the year before, its lengthy preparation, the participation of so many, and, of course, what I had learned from it. My enthusiasm shines through. I was honest and kept my promise

319

by mentioning that every region brought up the questions of the possible ordination of married men because of the impending priest shortage and the wish that the question of the ordination of women would be opened for discussion.

At the end of the questionnaire for the *ad limina* report one was given the possibility of listing special concerns the bishop might have at that moment. I took advantage of that possibility to talk of many things. I spoke at greater length about the cases of sexual abuse of minors by clergy, noting that I sensed it was a sign of the lack of psychological and sexual development of candidates to the priesthood and this experience should bring about a renewed examination of formation in the seminaries. I wrote effusively about all the ecumenical and interfaith events happening in the diocese and outlined some of the older and new social justice issues. I also admitted in all honesty that there was some disillusionment creeping in among the older clergy, those who had made the transition required by Vatican Council II, who now feared such efforts may have been in vain. I was encouraged by the vitality of the archdiocese and thought I caught that adequately in my account of the last five years and especially in the description of the archdiocesan synod.

Having sent the report off to Rome in ample time for the visit there, buoyed up by the results of the synod in the archdiocese and with new energy directed toward its implementation, I went off to the meeting of the bishops' conference at St. John's Abbey in Collegeville in June of 1988 in high spirits.

The *ad limina* visit of 1988 was far more serious than I had anticipated and took place in a very different atmosphere. I had naively expected that I might be singled out for some praise for the drafting of the Economic Pastoral Letter, approved so overwhelmingly by the American bishops in 1986. Or I even thought that perhaps the pope might want to discuss further the talk I gave in his presence in Los Angeles on the Catholic laity in the States in 1987.

On the contrary, before this 1988 visit, I was met with an unpleasant and ominous surprise. At the spring meeting of the U.S. bishops that year, I was approached by another archbishop of the bishops' conference who had already been to Rome for his *ad limina*. He wished to inform me that he was designated by the Congregation for Bishops to meet with me privately and confidentially before my visit. I was to be the new Hunthausen! If I had had to pick an archbishop for this kind of distasteful meeting, it would not have differed from the one chosen by the Congregation. He was someone I highly respected. I knew his opinions would be unbiased, frank but fair.

Curiously, the designated archbishop had been instructed by Rome not to come to Milwaukee for this discussion in order to keep it absolutely secret and to avoid critical reactions in the American press. Rome wanted to avoid the negative publicity that had surrounded the visit of Cardinal Hickey to Seattle during the administration of Archbishop Hunthausen. Thus, we were instructed to meet elsewhere, and I agreed to make the trip to his archdiocese.

This time I was told that the issues to be discussed would be sent to me beforehand and would not just be given to me when I met with the officials in Rome. To prepare for the *ad limina* visit in December I was to answer points that were troubling to Rome.

The only person I confided in about the coming investigation was Cardinal Bernardin. Although I did not see much of Joe (as we all called him), in spite of the proximity of our archdioceses, I still considered him a friend and knew he would understand what was happening. While still at the meeting of bishops in Collegeville in June, I caught him after one of the sessions and mentioned I had something serious I wanted to bring up with him. We went outside and sat on a bench out of earshot of the other bishops. I told him as much as I, at the time, knew. He was not surprised, in fact almost expecting it, although he said he had not been informed about it. For the first time in many years, I broke down, crying a bit. I guess I was tired, sad, and frustrated. I had worked so hard on the Economic Pastoral and had stretched myself to the limit to do so and at the same time carry on a heavy load back in Milwaukee. The archdiocesan synod was a view of a local church at its best, and I felt I had every reason to be proud of its success. Instead, I seemed to be bombarded with complaints by a few ultra-conservative people who had Rome's ear.

Joe told me he knew there were American cardinals and bishops who wanted Rome to force me to "clam up," and we both knew there were cardinals and bishops in the curia who felt the same way. He said he was willing to be of help, but his own weight among the curial officials was very limited. Joe agreed the archbishop assigned the task of doing the "investigation" was a decent and honest person and expressed the hope his wisdom would prevail.

It was fortuitous that this happened at the Benedictine monastery of St. John in Collegeville, since I was able to take a few long walks in the gardens and on the isolated roads that surround this abbey and school, just reflecting and praying about the course I should take. I also spent some quiet time in the abbey church asking myself pointed questions about my own stubbornness, my own fragility, and my own ideals. The strength of that edifice seemed to give me strength. I decided that I would stand tall, not succumb to the fear tactics being used, and continue to be true to the image of bishop I thought was needed in our day.

Some few days later I received from the archbishop-interrogator the documentation I would be asked to respond to, namely, an unsigned list called *Notes* that began with: "There are a number of areas in the pastoral government of the Archdiocese that require attention." These were classified into six sections: (1) Dissent from Church Teaching; (2) The Ordination of Women; (3) Archdiocesan Personnel; (4) Homosexuality; (5) Seminary; (6) Sacraments and Liturgy.

Before meeting with the designated archbishop at his home, I personally prepared in writing responses to the questions raised, being careful not to answer statements that seemed to want to draw me out rather than present objective facts. For example, under "Sacraments and Liturgy" there appeared the sentence: "There are occasional reports of liturgical abuses in the Archdiocese. Female altar servers are commonplace." I did not answer that kind of sentence.

When I met with the designated archbishop, he showed me first his letter of appointment by the Congregation for Bishops that mentioned explicitly that this was an official mandate and that the Holy Father had been informed that it was taking place.

What struck me at once was the large number of Xerox copies of articles from the *Milwaukee Journal* and *Milwaukee Sentinel.* In the section on "Dissent from Church Teaching" the articles I had written for the diocesan Catholic paper called "The Price of Orthodoxy" were the subject of a lengthy critique, but more about "the tone of the articles" than their content. Most of the other issues raised I had already been dealing with in the Congregation for the Doctrine of the Faith or for Liturgy. (Naturally I am amused today in noticing that among the criticisms raised against me then was the affirmation that I had said the Vatican should recognize the State of Israel!) On the issue of homosexuality they wanted to discuss the group called "Dignity" and the fact that this group was attending a Sunday evening Mass in one of the churches. I smiled that I was being criticized because people were attending Mass on Sunday.

However, I was impressed by how thorough the monitoring was and by the amount of time it must have taken to prepare all this material. It had to have been done by someone living in Milwaukee. For example, I was presented with the transcript of a call-in radio program where I had been asked about the ordination of women and where I had stated my willingness to be surprised by the Holy Spirit in this regard. (Here I had in mind an interview Cardinal O'Connor had given to *The New Yorker* when he was asked the same question. He had answered: "This Pope will never change that decision. But a future Pope *could* announce that he is going to do something unexpected." Later in the article the interviewer again remarked: "So it is conceivable that sometime in the future women may be ordained? The cardinal nodded, cleared his throat, and said, 'Yes, it is conceivable. But, I remind you, not in the lifetime of this Pope.'" *The New Yorker,* March 23, 1987, 63-65). One must remember that we were back then in 1987 and 1988 before the present pope declared his position definitive.

For about five hours the archbishop permitted me to talk about the issues presented and other aspects of my episcopal ministry. This kind, but shrewd, archbishop, at the end of the interview sought to give me some prudent advice, namely, that I should become less visible, stop writing and speaking in public, and "wait it out." I certainly wanted to take seriously his wisdom, but must admit that I would have found it almost impossible to be a bishop and limit myself to administration and sacramental services. It just did not seem to fit my concept of what was needed in today's church and world.

The report the archbishop wrote and sent to Rome after our day together must have been a positive and sympathetic one, although I never received a copy of it from Rome or any comments about it.

*   *   *

I set out, then, for the *ad limina* trip to Rome in December of 1988 with some preoccupation. On arrival I found the usual phone call awaiting me setting an appointment to meet with Cardinal Bernard Gantin in the Congregation of Bishops at his request the next day. My dealings with the Congregation for Bishops on this and subsequent visits became more complicated. Cardinal Gantin had been appointed to succeed Cardinal Baggio in April 1984. I had always admired Gantin, having known him since he was archbishop of Cotounou in Benin, West Africa, and I was abbot primate of the Benedictines. He was a fine example of the best of the young Catholicism of Africa and demonstrated what that continent would contribute to the life of the Church.

Because of our previous friendship he seemed embarrassed in having to deal with any complaints that came in about me. He avoided direct confrontation by sending me over to see Cardinal Ratzinger and adding that he would have the archbishop who was his second-in-command draw up something in writing. Cardinal Gantin strained to be overly friendly during this visit, when in reality he seemed to be ill-at-ease. None of the issues in the document entitled *Notes* that had been sent to me via the archbishop-interrogator were brought up and even the visit itself was not mentioned. Finally he suggested that, to obtain more clarity, I make an appointment to see Cardinal Ratzinger, a meeting that was set up for the next day.

After leaving Gantin's office, I decided to stop in at the Signatura Apostolica (the highest court of appeal in the Vatican setup) to speak with its prefect, Cardinal Achille Silvestrini, about what rights a bishop might have in a case such as this. I had known him for years and always trusted his judgment. He was friendly, but did not know how to reply, not being sure of the existence of any legal procedures that a bishop could employ, especially if the pope would authorize an apostolic visitation of his diocese. He insisted the wisest route would be to try to solve the problem "diplomatically."

The next day Cardinal Ratzinger received me warmly. It was also good having just the two of us together without secretaries or note-takers. I gave him a copy of the unsigned *Notes* from the Congregation for Bishops with the points to which I had to respond. He stated explicitly that this document had not been prepared by his congregation, that he had never seen these points, and that he and I had already discussed most of the items in previous meetings. It struck me as strange that Cardinal Ratzinger's office was not the originator of the whole process and that the cardinal himself seemed in the dark about it. I had received the definite impression from Cardinal Gantin that he truly believed the questions in the *Notes* came from Ratzinger.

On this occasion I looked forward with some hesitation to the quarter of an hour alone with the pope as I was eager to see if he would bring up the naming of an archbishop-interrogator and my visit to that archbishop's home. During the audience he did not allude to any of the items in the *Notes* or anything about the unusual interrogation. In general, he seemed relaxed, but it was clear he did not want to engage in any discussions at all. Not even the Economic Pastoral was brought up. It was a short meeting.

After this trip I wrote the following remark in my notebook: "From these interviews I came away perplexed. They [the cardinals] all seemed to back away from the initial points in the *Notes* and tried to downplay the whole affair. It is hard to say what will be the next step."

Fear, I know, is engendered through secrecy. For example, all the documents cited above were marked at the time *sub secreto pontificio* (under pontifical secrecy) so I never shared them with anyone else. (I remembered the old saying I had heard many times during my years in Rome: "A pontifical secret is one that everyone in Rome knows except the pope.") I preferred to keep their contents to myself — not always a wise procedure if one seeks to maintain one's own equilibrium and self-esteem. I did not discuss these negative and belittling reviews of my work as an archbishop with anyone, but buried them deep within me. I tried to reflect on them frequently and seriously *coram Domino* ("before the Lord," i.e., in the depth of one's own conscience).

Through it all, I retained a deep respect for the Holy Father as pope, but found little to love and admire in his style of treating people who disagreed with him. I was convinced he was indeed a very holy man, but not one without flaws. At the same time, in the midst of this negativity on the part of pope and curia in my regard, I tried to maintain my own dignity as person and bishop. God alone would be the judge of my life and my work.

What conflicting emotions of fear, anger, and gratitude I felt in these months! One cause for gratitude that I had was the reassuring memory of Archbishop Cousins who had passed away on September 14 at the age of eighty-six. He had suffered from a serious cancer that had spread through his whole body. I probably never thanked him enough for all he had done for the archdiocese during the difficult upheavals of the 1960s — a time often called in Milwaukee "the Groppi" period. Cousins believed in people and their innate goodness. Never having studied in the Eternal City and not speaking Italian, he always feared Rome and the curia. The priests rightly loved him as a father figure, and I came to learn that I could always count on his support. His funeral was glorious, a soaring liturgy to celebrate a kind and lovable leader. From then on I started to pray to him that I might have the stamina to face my future as a bishop with dignity and inner assurance, as he had done in his day.

CHAPTER 14

Managing Conflicting Models of Church

Milwaukee (1989-1996)

B y the end of the 1980s, the divisions within U.S. Catholicism and tensions between the bishops and the curia were becoming more pronounced. At the beginning of 1989, the pope, becoming uneasy about this
situation, called the U.S. archbishops to Rome for a meeting in March with
curial officials. Most curial officials were not very clear as to the scope of
our meetings or enthusiastic about its usefulness. This Roman meeting
was an inverse-image of the one held in Los Angeles in October 1987 on the
occasion of the pope's trip, except in 1989, Vatican officials were totally in
charge and the "dialogue" was carried out according to the Roman definition of collegiality. They selected the speakers and spoke first. No resolutions were to be formulated at the end.

The meeting was held in the hall of the "Broken Skulls," deep in the
bowels of the Vatican. I had been there only once in 1969 at the special
bishops' synod on collegial bodies in the Church and had sparred with Cardinal Wright. In twenty years, much had changed in the Church and, although the faces were different, the underlying agenda, namely, the role of
the curia versus the outlying "provinces," never varied.

John Paul II, the secretary of state, thirty-five American archbishops,
and twenty-five top officials of the curia were present. The theme selected
by the pope was: "Evangelization in the Context of the Culture and Society
of the United States." The cardinal prefect of each Roman congregation
was designated to explain how his department viewed the United States
and its culture, and then an American cardinal or archbishop was to talk

on the same topic, there having been no exchange of papers beforehand. At the end of each day there was an open mike. The meeting was not organized to come to any resolutions or conclusions.

I do not know who selected the American speakers, but presupposed this choice had been made by the curia. That selection highlighted the roles of the recently appointed American cardinals, John O'Connor and Bernard Law named in 1985, and James Hickey and Edmund Szoka named in 1988. The most intriguing assignment was given to Cardinal Joseph Bernardin, who was appointed special secretary and charged with making a summary at the end of the meeting. At first it seemed a useless even demeaning task, but the choice later proved providential. The Bernardin summary is the only place where there are references to remarks from the floor: What, if any, limits on compromises should be recommended to Catholics in debates about public issues with moral implications? How could one develop a better understanding of conscience-formation? What might be the influence of feminism in the States? What are the repercussions of the lack of a sense of tradition as a value in U.S. Catholic culture? And so on.

Since I had not been assigned to give a talk, I just relaxed and listened, sometimes amused by the difference between the American and Roman perspectives. For example, Cardinal Martinez Somalo of the Congregation for Liturgy spoke on the egregious liturgical abuses in the States, emphasizing the bishop's duty to correct them. Archbishop Daniel Kucera of Dubuque, the American respondent, pointed out that there were some abuses on the left (committed by those seeking too many unauthorized changes at once) and some on the right (committed by those not willing to make any changes, even those promulgated by the bishops), with most priests and people relatively content in the middle.

Only the talk by Cardinal O'Connor sounded a chord that began to resonate more and more in Catholic Church circles, and was worth remembering. Toward the end of his speech, an evident pessimism took over: he commented negatively on the American judicial system and its tendency to create an atmosphere of moral relativism; he spoke critically about the media, especially its portrayal of violence and its cynicism toward all forms of authority; he complained that the public educational system had become almost totally secularized. All of these influences in recent years, he claimed, had altered dramatically the values that had underpinned American culture. His concluding words were: "In response, I see the church more and more becoming a counterculture, a voice crying in the wilderness."

Cardinal O'Connor had an enormous influence in Rome and the pope listened attentively to his every word. I knew I should ponder those words carefully because they would have a continuing effect on how the Vatican would view and treat the Church in the States in years to come.

The other talks progressed in pairs with alternating points of view but no in-depth discussion. The meeting completed, there were no obvious winners or losers; no resolutions were agreed upon and thus no visible tensions.

We concelebrated the final Mass with Pope John Paul II in the crypt of St. Peter's Basilica at the tomb of St. Peter. It was an intimate setting, thankfully without the pomp surrounding the large nave above us. It was easy to sing in that more confined space, our voices — slightly off pitch — resonating as they bounced off the low ceiling and marble tombs of the many popes buried there. There was the sarcophagus of Pope John Paul I, hurriedly put together because of his unexpected and untimely death; the marble small chapel that held the tomb of Pope John XXIII; and the simple, but raised and slanted, elegant marble slab in the burial chamber selected for Pope Paul VI. I saw our Mass as a vivid symbol of dedication and struggle amid continuity and contrast; I prayed to all three popes.

*   *   *

Back home in Milwaukee there was plenty to do: I continued to work on implementation of the archdiocesan synod and met regularly with the elected councils and with the ecumenical and interfaith communities. To these, were added meetings with some special groups. Several times a year I began to meet with the superiors of the religious orders of men and women. Then, I began a monthly meeting with a rotating group working in healthcare, such as administrators, doctors, nurses, chaplains, and professors of moral theology from the seminaries, to discuss some of the frequent moral questions arising in the hospitals. There were periodic luncheon meetings with a group of theologians and scripture scholars from the seminaries and universities to keep abreast in those fields and to know those scholars better.

Between my *ad limina* visits of 1988 and 1993 two of my special concerns increased the irritation of the curia and the pope. One was my insistence that the role of women in the church be broadened and, specifically, sessions I held in the archdiocese for women on the topic of abortion. The second was my search for solutions to the impending priest shortage; I publicly opened the question of ordaining married men. Both of these topics were very important, and I gave them a great deal of thought and energy.

At their fall 1989 meeting, the bishops of the United States passed a resolution condemning abortion, a statement that I supported. After the meeting, as I nestled down in my seat and buckled up for the flight from Washington to Milwaukee, something about the meeting began to disturb me. Lingering in my mind was the image of the bishops, 280 gray-haired men, passing a resolution that they expected all American Catholics to embrace. My uneasiness grew: other than the conference staff, no lay people, especially no women, were a part of the discussion on a topic vital to all, but especially to women in the Church. It occurred to me that, from a pastoral point of view, it would be helpful to listen to women in my own archdiocese as they expressed their feelings on this difficult subject. A passage from Pope Paul VI's first encyclical, *Ecclesiam suam,* came to mind: "Before speaking, we must take great care to listen not only to what people say, but more especially to what they have it in their hearts to say" (#87).

I did not foresee that conducting these local sessions could become a sensational event. But it did: just planning to listen brought my name to the front page of the *New York Times* and catapulted me into enormous conflict with conservative Catholics, some fellow bishops, and the Roman authorities.

For months, I had been under pressure from political pro-life groups to have priests preach more often and more forcefully against abortion. The Milwaukee priests were solidly anti-abortion in their attitudes, but felt that some groups were making this issue so prominent that all the other social justice concerns were being minimized or neglected. The priests wanted no part of the rising violence against clinic workers. The pro-life groups also expected me to attend public rallies and protests at abortion clinics and to lead them in reciting the rosary. They were upset when I would not. Some Catholic pro-life women opposed Cardinal Bernardin's consistent life ethic, the so-called "seamless garment approach," which tried to hold together all the life issues as important to Catholics. These women felt this approach diminished the emphasis that should be given to the abortion issue and that it was a betrayal of their work over many decades. This group represented a small portion of the women in the archdiocese, and there seemed to be a silent majority that was not often heard from. It was those voices that I wanted to encourage and listen to. The mail began to pour in. I was surprised by the eagerness with which women from around the country wanted to join in the discussion. Men wrote too; they wanted a series of meetings to discuss their feelings and responsibilities. All women invited to the sessions knew that our purpose had nothing to do with changing the Catholic Church's teaching on abortion, but the majority felt we bishops had much to learn from them and appreciated the opportunity to have their say.

How would I go about hearing that voice? At first, I had no idea. My staff was not daunted by the project. They helped me think through the logistics of obtaining the feedback I was looking for. Six sessions were planned in March of 1990, three by invitation and three as open sessions. The three invitational sessions were aimed at hearing from women with highly specialized ministries: first, professional women working in church ministries; second, women in health care and social ministries; and, third, women from college and university faculties. The three open sessions were to be held around the diocese.

At each session, the women sat around tables, eight or ten in a group with a trained facilitator and secretary. I made an opening statement reiterating the Church's position, but inviting their frank discussion of the issues as they saw them. At the end of the meeting the secretaries presented to the body a summary of what was said at each table. If anyone felt an important point had been omitted or incorrectly stated, she could come to the microphone. The process tried in this way to avoid longwinded and repetitive prepared statements. During the discussions I wandered from table to table, trying to absorb the tenor of the remarks and answer any questions, if needed.

For the entire process I had asked Mary Feeley, a theologian, to join the sessions and help me work out a final synthesis of the material. Mary had a solid Benedictine background and I felt comfortable working closely with her. She was intelligent, sensitive, and unafraid to correct me when she thought I was misinterpreting a point of view. Calm and serene, nothing seemed to crack her composure.

The first sessions were tense but went well. I appreciated the frank comments and the depth of emotions, sometimes raw, but there was palpable energy in the air. I had sensed this would happen because many women, not able to attend a meeting or feeling inhibited, wrote me beforehand. Some having had abortions felt this was their first opportunity to talk about their state of mind at the time, how distraught they were, and about their lingering sense of guilt. (That is why I supported so strongly Vicki Thorn and her "Project Rachel," for reconciliation of women who had had abortions.) As I moved from table to table, I sensed many women had come because this was their only chance to speak to the Church. It became a sign to them of a different kind of church, one that would listen to all voices, especially of the wounded. A few women came with prepared texts, sometimes of great length, and were unhappy that they were not permitted to deliver their speeches. They found it difficult to listen to opposing views.

The public sessions, held last, were the more difficult; by that time reporters and TV cameras were swarming around the hall, hoping to grab a woman who would talk about what she and others were saying. Expecting that some women did not want to speak in front of cameras, we had to establish ground-rules that permitted the press to interview participants only after the sessions and only if the person consented.

My hopes had been to continue the sessions to hear from women in the Latino and black communities who were underrepresented in the six sessions. Eventually I heard from them in writing since they did not want to be involved in sessions now so heavily publicized. To complete the picture, I also had hoped to coordinate sessions with men only, but these, too, had to be cancelled. Some women voiced the opinion that the Church did not emphasize sufficiently men's responsibility, especially for children born out of wedlock, but, inconsistently, felt men should not be a part of a decision to abort or not abort. We ended the process. Frankly, after six sessions and the publicity they generated, I was emotionally exhausted. I could not have absorbed any more. I knew that listening was an art, but I did not know that it could be so draining. Even so, would I still have held the hearings? Decidedly yes.

Through the next months I sat with Mary Feeley in my conference room, all this material spread before us, as we reflected on what was said, recalled the general atmosphere, and tried to assimilate all the spoken and written material. Finally, in a written essay I summed up my reactions and had it published in the local Catholic paper. Re-reading it after a decade-and-a-half evokes the same emotions of trust and confidence in the voices of women in the Church. At no time did any women say that abortion was a moral good: they all found it a moral evil. But their fears about a future in which it could again become a criminal act were evident. The majority of the women applauded the consistent ethic of life as proposed by Cardinal Bernardin. They were supportive of the Church's teaching on protecting life and its sanctity at all stages, but emphasized that the Church had to be more consistent in its actions in support of life from birth till death. I put this in my report.

I could not refrain from mentioning in the report my surprise at the number of women — some members of pro-life groups — who did not accept the Church's teaching prohibiting birth control. That was not the subject of the hearings, but, to be truthful to what I heard, I reported this fact. Their attitude would often be articulated by phrases like, "We want our choice before conception, not after." I also tried to answer those in the pro-life movement who felt priests were not supportive of their groups and their aims, would not publicly associate with them in their cause, and did not preach often enough about the evils of abortion. I pointed out some characteristics of their groups and their approaches about which priests felt uncomfortable — lack of compassion, narrowness of vision, ugly and demeaning rhetoric, questionable tactics, and lack of interest in other life issues. I was very surprised, even disturbed, by the strong influence of Protestant evangelical and fundamentalist positions among some pro-life Catholic women. They arrived clutching their bibles, opened to show specific texts underlined in red, and carrying tightly in their fists imitation rubber fetuses that they then placed on the tables for public display. They did not seem to understand that proof-texting, taking quotations out of contest to prove a point, was not the Catholic approach to scripture and not part of our tradition. Many women who had been politically active in the pro-life cause for years were frustrated, their efforts having shown no clear results. I felt sympathy for them. Nonetheless, I had to ask if at times they were not their own worst enemies. At the end I called for more civility in this debate.

These suggestions were not taken to heart, but seen as another indication that I was not supportive of their cause. From then on, a small but vociferous segment of Milwaukee's Catholic population saw me as an enemy, not friend, and opposed almost any program I proposed. They denounced me as an enemy of their cause. Their criticisms reached Rome where, for the next decade, the hearing sessions were taken as a sign that I advocated abortion-on-demand.

At the time of the Milwaukee hearings, Cardinal John O'Connor was the chair of the bishops' Pro-Life Committee. He was upset by this initiative. Though he never expressed his criticisms to me directly, some American bishops and old friends in Rome reported his anger to me. I have always defended my decision by pointing out that a good teacher has to listen; teaching does not take place in a vacuum. In fact, if I have any regret, it would be that more bishops did not have the same experience of listening to these women. Because of the national publicity the hearings generated, I sent all the documentation and my printed remarks to Cardinal Ratzinger, knowing that there would be complaints and it would be wise for him to have a complete narrative of events. I received no immediate response.

In mid-summer, I received a letter from the University of Fribourg in Switzerland asking me if I would accept an honorary degree on November 15. I had been chosen by the theological faculty because of my involvement in the Economic Pastoral Letter. Given their historical connection to Pope Leo XIII's *Rerum novarum* and my earlier visit for a symposium on Catholic social teaching, I accepted. The Fribourg theological faculty had the power to award pontifical degrees but had to submit the names of the recipients to the Congregation for Education in Rome for approval. They saw this request as a matter of protocol. The new prefect of that Roman congregation was Archbishop Pio Laghi, formerly papal nuncio to the States. He had just been three weeks in office when the request from the University of Fribourg arrived on his desk. His response was to deny the conferring of the degree, stating the hearings on abortion that I conducted were "not without doctrinal importance" and they caused "a great deal of confusion among the faithful." Later, an official from his congregation told the press that Laghi had consulted "some American bishops" before making this decision. As a result, the members of the theological faculty at Fribourg University decided not to award any honorary degrees that year. As could be expected, all of this was reported in the press, secular and Catholic.

When I went to the bishops' meeting in Washington that November, there were many questions from the media. At the meeting, I was grateful that Bishop James Malone presented to all the bishops a resolution of personal support for me that was approved by a solid voice vote. Probably that irritated the Roman curia even more.

The week after the bishops' meeting, Archbishop Laghi wrote me a letter expressing his regrets if his refusal had caused me any distress, "I apologize for not having talked to you before nixing the degree." There being some ambiguity about how to interpret the listening sessions, Rome did not want to be seen as giving public approval to anything that may have come out of those hearings. I never heard from Cardinal Ratzinger's office and naturally let the matter drop.

*   *   *

Rome was concerned about maintaining a common front on the battle against abortion. But more than that, I sensed in its reaction to the hearings a fear of the feminist movement then so prominent in American culture. The abortion hearings and the reactions to them should then be seen in the larger question about women's role in the Catholic Church as it was playing itself out in those decades.

I was uneasy with the current church structures in which all authority was in the hands of the ordained and leadership positions were not open to women. The official reply that women had always played a prominent role in the history of the Church, especially by their holiness, their educational endeavors, and their care for the poor, was not an adequate response to the question of why their leadership talents found no outlet in church structure. I knew any church about to enter the twenty-first century had to find a credible middle ground between male dominance, on one side, and a kind of feminism that demeaned men, on the other. I became more and more uneasy with the image of the hierarchy as a male "club" where the leadership gifts of women were dismissed. The quip that women were only seeking power could be turned against men as well; the male dominance in Catholicism was increasingly visible in the ever-growing number of religious ceremonies on TV. My hope was that the Church would use this moment of history to create between men and women in the Church a sense of partnership of equals, an atmosphere where everyone could contribute his or her gifts to build up the one Church of Christ.

It was impossible to avoid the question of the non-ordination of women to the priesthood. In 1976 the Congregation for the Doctrine of the Faith had published *Inter insigniores* in response to that question. Pope Paul VI specifically approved the document, giving it the greatest weight a document from a Roman congregation can have without being a papal pronouncement. The oft-quoted sentence in that document is: "The Church, in fidelity to the example of the Lord, does not consider herself authorized to admit women to priestly ordination." The strongest argument proposed is that an all-male priesthood was "willed by the Lord Jesus Christ and carefully maintained by the apostles." An iconic argument, based on Paul's letter to the Ephesians, followed in which the relationship between man and woman in marriage, a spousal relationship based on love, was seen as a mirror of the relationship between Christ and the Church. This iconic argument was given as an argument *ex convenientia*, i.e., of fittingness, but not an apodictic proof. This carefully written document traces the history of the question, admits to some of the yet unsolved historical evidence, and alludes to the negative attitudes toward women in the first centuries of the Church that lasted into the Middle Ages, but sees no possibility of any change in the tradition. An argument from tradition is a weighty one in the Catholic Church.

When asked in a public forum about the ordination of women, I would reiterate the points found in *Inter insigniores,* a document that I knew almost by heart, and was never surprised when those listening, especially younger women, would simply say they did not agree, and found the arguments unconvincing and even discriminatory. I did not think that the topic had been discussed sufficiently among theologians and historians; thus it was not "ripe" for a definitive decision. I agreed that the document of the Congregation for the Doctrine of the Faith certainly held pride of place, but that the teaching had not been declared a dogma that must be believed by all. Most of all, I was reluctant to accept the idea that the Church did not have total power over the sacraments and its ministers and felt I could show many examples from history — especially in reacting to the Protestant Reformers — where the church claimed that power with regard to the evolution of the form, matter, content, and even minister of the sacraments.

The bishops' conference had appointed a committee to begin a pastoral letter on the role of women in church and society. Though I was not involved in that effort, I watched how it marked a turning point in how bishops wrote pastoral letters. The process began with many listening sessions around the United States, following the process of the letters on nuclear proliferation and economic justice. This theme turned out to be just as contentious as they. A first draft appeared in April of 1988.

In September of that year, the pope published an apostolic letter called *Mulieris dignitatem.* This letter was a treatise on Christian anthropology based on his exegesis of the opening chapters of the book of Genesis. His letter proved very divisive among Catholic women. In spite of its many beautiful and moving passages, I did not find it convincing. In addition, his biblical analysis of Genesis and his philosophical and anthropological description of gender roles and characteristics did not seem to be traditional in Catholicism.

John Paul II says in this letter that the priest, when celebrating the Eucharist, acts in the person of Christ and assumes the role of Christ (male) as the spouse of the Church (female) in the iconic image from Ephesians. Thus, the celebrant had to be a man. What had been presented in 1976 in *Inter insigniores* as an argument *ex convenientia* (of fittingness) was now elevated to a confirmation of the priesthood as restricted to those of the masculine gender. Theologians had pointed out that in the analogy "Christ-is-to-Church" as "husband-is-to-wife," the *res analogata,* or the basis of the analogy, was not gender difference but the same kind of unselfish love to be found in both relationships.

In any case, this new document and the ensuing debates among women forced the drafting committee working on the bishops' pastoral letter to totally re-do its work. At first they had decided not to talk about the ordination of women, but now felt they could not avoid accepting the pope's letter as their own position. In the end, the attempt to write a pastoral letter on women failed; it did not receive a positive vote of two-thirds of the bishops.

The practice of the bishops' conference that no document would be presented to Rome before it had been voted on by the American bishops no longer was to exist in practice. The curia simply felt free to intervene in the writing process of a document by American bishops anywhere along the line. In this way, once again, the teaching role of a bishops' conference was undermined. Rome's argument was that the subject matter touched the whole Catholic Church, not just the Church in the United States.

*   *   *

The *New York Times* asked me to write an op-ed piece on women in the Church; it appeared December 6, 1992. In it, I express my deepest anxieties: I had been involved in this question since my time as abbot primate of the Benedictine Order, and it was not a topic about which I could easily accept the status quo. The editors gave it the provocative title: "Out of the Kitchen, Into the Vatican."

My piece was simply a cry to keep the door open to further developments and to weigh carefully what the exclusion of women from ordination might entail. I was especially concerned about the next generation of women in the Church. What if it became unacceptable to capable women who had leadership qualities? In what I thought was prophetic style, I predicted that, if the issue was closed, some men and many women would attempt to redefine the nature of priesthood and begin to minimize its role and importance, becoming a purely cultic role. Or women would just leave and go to other Christian denominations where they would have the opportunity to accept leadership roles. I called for the naming of women to all the offices in the Vatican and to the diplomatic corps and for using the insights of women theologians in the formation of church documents. Per-

336

haps it was not discreet on my part to mention that in the past there had been in the Church a tradition of considering women as inferior to men and this impression had to be changed. I called this our contemporary Galileo-challenge.

Cardinal O'Connor entered the fray by responding in his diocesan paper, reminding me that the *New York Times* was his hometown newspaper. I was pleased that he agreed with most, but not all, of my points. His first disagreement focused on the leadership roles in the curia to which women could be appointed; he objected that this would send the wrong signal, because if women were to take the place of some of the cardinals and archbishops in the curia, "would the perception not be created that the church is abandoning the hierarchical structure, not only in Rome but throughout the world? . . . Would it not be speculated that if a woman could head the Congregation for Bishops or the Congregation for the Doctrine of the Faith that a woman could be pope?"

His final paragraph was of special interest to me: I was too optimistic about the future of any cultural harmony between church and world. He stated his view directly: "I tend toward believing we are in for years and years of confrontation. . . . I sincerely believe that the church is today, and must continue to be, countercultural."

The day after a summary of Cardinal O'Connor's response appeared in Milwaukee's local newspaper, an elderly gentleman at the cathedral came up to me after Mass and remarked: "Remember, Bishop, he is a four-star general and you have only two stars." Without necessarily reflecting on it, this gentleman pointed to the difference in our ecclesiologies. O'Connor's was a military man: the pope is the commander-in-chief giving the orders, we bishops are the generals (the cardinals being those with four stars), the priests are the minor officers, lay people are the combat troops. My model of the Church was much more like the United States of America with a federal government and states' rights.

As I re-read the two pieces, I see that the cardinal and I were not that far apart. Theoretically, I was more driven to involvement, without fear, in the world's problems; I saw much to be reconciled between the Church and our American contemporary culture.

*　　　*　　　*

When I went to Rome in March 1993 for the *ad limina* visit, the shortage of priests was certainly on my mind. Milwaukee had begun to feel the effects

337

of their diminishing numbers and I knew that it was only the beginning of many adjustments. The archdiocese had tried one vocational program after another with meager results. Some of the conservative Catholic periodicals were convinced that conservative dioceses had many vocations, those with a "liberal" bishop none. Over and over again I heard that refrain. But I knew many very conservative bishops whose dioceses had no vocations at all. The "official" line was that Jesus promised there would be sufficient laborers for the harvest; if these were lacking, the fault must be in us. (I never recalled that Jesus said that there would be sufficient candidates for the priesthood among those willing to accept a celibate commitment.) My view was that a larger pool of candidates with the intellectual, spiritual, and leadership qualities required for priesthood was needed. Taking candidates only from those declaring themselves willing and able to accept a celibate commitment did not provide such a pool. And because so few candidates were applying, there was the fear of taking inferior or risky candidates — liberal and conservative.

Reflecting on this shortage, I recall a conversation that was to repeat itself, with slight variations, many times over the next decades. During the late 1980s on a visit to a parish on the south side of Milwaukee, I sat next to an elderly, pensive, and troubled parishioner. He was distraught about the possibility that the parish where he had worshiped for over seventy years, where he had been baptized, made his first communion, and been married, might close. I asked him how many children he had had, and he sheepishly and with a chuckle responded ten. When I asked if any ever thought of becoming a priest, he replied no. Then when I asked if any of his children had married and settled in the neighborhood, he again responded no; some lived in the suburbs, some had moved to other cities, especially to southern states. Finally, he conceded the point: "I guess I see why the parish is closing."

Between 1966 when the Second Vatican Council had ended and 1984, e.g., the number of priests in the United States had fallen by almost 20 percent with no end in sight. What organization can afford to lose that percentage of its trained personnel and not feel the effects deeply? The reasons for these departures were many, but I feel sure that the desire to marry was the most common one, probably accompanied by the realization that leaving and marrying was the only way for them to be totally honest as human beings. Perhaps many hoped — even expected — the Church would eventually change its discipline and they would be permitted to return to active priestly ministry as married priests. That desire was intensified when they saw the Church admitting married clergy from Protestant denominations and permitting them to function as married priests.

The post-conciliar period must have been a moment of abrupt awakening for most priests, including about sexuality. The mood in the Church forced priests to examine their own commitments, especially in the light of the new positive appraisal of the vocation of the laity and the positive assessment of human sexuality and new understandings of human development and maturity.

When the great exodus came, fewer priests with a homosexual orientation left the priesthood. Thus, the proportion of gays in the priesthood became larger than that found in the general male population, creating in some places signs of a visible gay clerical culture. As experience has shown, large numbers of gays exhibit deeply spiritual sensitivities that have made them effective priests. Moreover — I give here a personal opinion — many gay clergy were key players in keeping the Catholic Church in the United States alive and vital in that difficult period of transition. They carried the burden of overwork while they confronted the challenges stemming from the dramatic changes that the Church was undergoing. For all of this — I am sure — they will receive no praise, only the admonition to remain closeted.

Many other factors might have influenced the shortage of vocations to the priesthood, like the possibility that young Catholics could choose from many secular vocations and had the means to pursue their goals. Even so, I still believe the fear of not being able to live celibate lives seriously affected many who thought about priesthood and then, reluctantly, gave up that dream.

*   *   *

It was difficult to discuss the question of the priest shortage and the whole celibacy issue on the floor of the bishops' conference without the session turning into a pledge of loyalty to the pope, or without the accusation that our very discussion of the shortage was bringing on a self-fulfilling prophecy. As a result, the bishops gave the impression that maintaining a celibate clergy was a higher value than providing sacraments to our people. What pope would want to go down in history as having changed the requirement of celibacy for diocesan clergy in the West?

What solutions were open, then, for us in Milwaukee? Supporting the program for the Permanent Diaconate was an important aid. These men assisted priests in many roles and took a portion of the burden of the priests' work off their backs. But they were not full time in their ministries and we soon learned that their priorities had to be family first, then work, and finally the volunteer contributions they could make to the parish.

Importing priests from foreign cultures, not uncommon in some dioceses, had its drawbacks. Rome frowned on this practice, arguing that these young churches were in greater need of priests than we were. Some saw this as a form of "ecclesiastical imperialism." There were also many serious issues of cultural adaptation that had to be faced, language being only one of them. Expanding the use of lay ministers was helpful, but the limitations to this solution were evident: lay people could not celebrate Eucharist, confer the anointing of the sick, or hear confessions. All of these solutions simply limped and could be nothing but stopgap measures.

An idea came to me from a trip to Russia in March 1990 for a dialogue with the Orthodox Church. It was sponsored by Pax Christi International and led by Cardinal Franz Koenig of Vienna. On Sunday during the week of the dialogue, I accompanied Russian Orthodox Bishop Elia of Kaluga to his diocese since he was taking possession of a church being given back to the Orthodox by the government. It was the chapel of the convent where Brother Zosima in the *Brothers Karamazov* had lived. The bishop told me that many of the original icons suddenly reappeared, people having hidden them for decades under the floors of their modest homes. As frequently happened in those days, the Gorbachev government was handing back to the Orthodox bishops many church structures for which no priests were immediately available. In such cases, Bishop Elia explained to me, he would gather the parishioners together, talk about the qualities needed for a priest to serve their parish, surface from among them the name of a qualified man, married or single, gain his consent, and then ordain him while he was still in training — mostly through a kind of correspondence course — a procedure that seemed sensible and logical, and that answered the needs of these Orthodox communities.

After listening to the advice of the priests' council and the archdiocesan pastoral council, in the summer of 1990, I wrote the first draft of a pastoral letter to the people explaining the seriousness of the situation and how we might begin to remedy it. I put that first draft out for discussion and feedback, intending to write a final version later in the year. I wrote that, if it became evident that no resident priest would be available for a parish and that there was no prospect of getting one in the near future, "I would be willing to help the community surface a qualified candidate for ordained priesthood — even if a married man — and, without raising false expectations or unfounded hopes for him or the community, present such a candidate to the Pastor of the Universal Church for light and guidance." In the light of what I had heard from the faithful and believing they too possessed the fullness of the Spirit, I felt an inner compulsion to write that sentence — even though I knew it would fall on deaf ears.

The secretary of state in Rome responded to the first draft of my pastoral letter in February 1991, informing me that he was writing in the name of the Holy Father. He stated that an "appropriate Apostolic Exhortation was under preparation in which the Supreme Pontiff will offer the Universal church orientations and directives to face adequately the same delicate question [namely, the shortage of priests]." He then said that my "intervention cannot but appear to be out of place and, objectively, a sort of provocation." I guess it was, but I could see no other realistic solution. When this exchange was over, curiously I felt a sense of relief: I had relayed my concerns in the most striking way possible. I had suggested what seemed like a real remedy, but knew in my heart from the icy response that nothing would change.

To prepare the people for the shortage to come, I spoke at every opportunity about collaboration, tried to make sure that every parish was working with others, seeing this as stage one of the process of reducing the number of parishes so that they could be more easily administered by the diminishing number of priests.

All of that was the easy part. The hard part was to move ahead when the time came toward merging or closing parishes. I did so reluctantly. It was a no-win situation. Moreover, I knew that people's allegiance was primarily to their parish; their Catholicism was identified with it. The closing or merging parishes would almost certainly reduce the number of practicing Catholics. I was right to have that worry. When the time came, many stopped going to church rather than switch to a new parish.

For the priests, it was a question of morale. They had seen their own co-workers leave to marry; they had to adjust their ministry to all the challenges after Vatican II; their reputations had been negatively affected by the sex-abuse scandals; they had to minister to a more educated and sophisticated Catholic population than before, some of whom were constantly criticizing them for not being conservative enough or for being too conservative. The priests were not trained to be the lightning rod for so much unhappiness; they had to keep peace among many divergent points of view, political and ecclesiastical; they feared being turned into sacramental machines or overburdened administrators. Yet, it was clear that these mergers and closings could only go so far. How many people could a single priest effectively minister to? Were we creatively constructing a new and vibrant concept of church life, or were we in a holding pattern just covering the bases?

I did the best I could to keep hope alive, but I continued to have many ambivalent feelings about those efforts to consolidate. I did my best under the strictures of having only a celibate male clergy, but at times, I felt we were being asked to run a marathon with our legs tied in a sack.

The merger of parishes was an event made for television. It was easy to find disgruntled people who were unhappy and ready to vent their anger when they saw a microphone. But it was nothing compared to the merging or closing of schools, which often preceded the merger of the parishes. If closing parishes was the hardest part of my job, closing schools was a close second. We simply did not have the money available nor could we annually raise sufficient funds to subsidize all our failing schools. I am now very glad that we did not try to do so. Those dioceses that subsidized schools, especially grade-schools, often came to regret it. When they could no longer raise sufficient funds and found themselves piling up debts, they often had to close large numbers at once. Archbishop Cousins had established the policy that every parish and every school had to be self-sufficient; it was a wise one and I followed it.

But several factors became a blessing in helping us maintain a solid Catholic school system. In 1992, the former DeRance Foundation was totally restructured to become the Archdiocese of Milwaukee Supporting Fund. The income from that fund was used to help many of the schools with special projects. We could not have kept many of the poorest schools functioning well without it. During the next ten years, i.e., till my retirement in 2002, that fund provided thirty-five million dollars for archdiocesan projects, many of them involving the schools. I will forever be grateful to Erica John and the John family for their generosity and support that never wavered.

The second blessing came through the establishment of a group called PAVE (Partners Advancing Values in Education). It was a body of lay men and women, not all Catholic, organized to find funds to support the Catholic school system and other private religious schools. This group, headed by Don Schuenke and John Stollenwerk, set about raising millions of dollars each year, convinced of the value of the Catholic schools for educating the kind of students who would make a mark in our society. After some years of remarkable success, the group began to broker money for the county and federal sources and so it ceased to be a corporation under the archdiocese.

At the same time its members became convinced of the need for a voucher system so that parents, especially the poorest, could have more control over where they sent their children to school. With these prominent Catholic lay men taking the lead and with the mayor, the governor, and the state legislature in favor of the program, the city of Milwaukee began an experimental voucher program with 15,000 students. It has continued to grow through the years and now includes many more students.

I had to think through the voucher program and the effect it might have on the Catholic identity of our schools. It became apparent that from now on most of the students attending parish schools would not be members of that parish or, for that matter, even Catholic. As I weighed all the pro's and con's, I knew that the voucher program was not a perfect system, but that it could be effective and important if done right. To maintain Catholic identity would require constant vigilance and probably continual political battles.

Since over 50 percent of Catholic students were attending public schools, it also meant that Catholics had to have a significant interest in what was happening in those schools to make them better. It also meant strengthening religious education programs for those students.

*   *   *

The hearings with women about abortion and the shortage of priests were on my mind when I arrived in Rome for the *ad limina* visit in March of 1993. I was not surprised when I was informed of a call from Cardinal Gantin telling me to be in his office the next morning. This time the conversation was very general as he tried to impress on me the many criticisms brought against me in Rome. I said I appreciated his concern and certainly knew of these complaints. I do not recall any meeting during this trip with Cardinal Ratzinger.

The private audience with the Holy Father began on a very different tone. I brought up my involvement in the dialogues with the Eastern Orthodox Churches in the States. He plied me with questions about the Orthodox Churches, especially the Russian and Ukrainian; he was well informed. The fifteen minutes went fast and I did not have time to bring up other issues. In fact, at the beginning of the meal that the bishops shared with him in his apartments, he again started to ask me questions on the dialogue with the Orthodox and, only after a time, noticed the others were not being brought into the conversation so he changed the topic to include them.

At the end of the audience, however, the Holy Father took a piece of paper that was lying on the side of his desk and glanced at it. He said it was a reminder from his staff to mention something special to me. Some of my fellow bishops, he informed me, wanted him to say they thought I was too soft on contemporary American culture and should be more explicit that the Church here in this world is the *ecclesia militans* (the fighting church). He said those same bishops felt I conceded too much to contemporary culture. Although he never brought up the hearings with women about abortion, I felt sure he must have been referring to them. (I was not surprised when one of the pope's secretaries after the visit supplied me with the information that Cardinal O'Connor had seen the pope the previous week.)

This visit was frustrating only in that I did not have the opportunity to talk to him about issues, especially the shortage of priests and the sex-abuse cases, that seemed so important not only in the Archdiocese of Milwaukee. He noticed my frustration and, in terminating the audience, again mentioned he only brought up the issue of the *ecclesia militans* at the insistence of some American bishops.

Since nothing serious had been brought up by Cardinal Gantin and the meeting with the pope had gone as well as could be expected, it surprised me when, a few days later and while still in Rome, I received the following hand-delivered letter signed by Cardinal Gantin. I present it in its entirety since it is a clear example of the ambiguity I was dealing with.

> Because of my office as Prefect of this Congregation, I find it necessary to bring to your attention certain matters that we have alluded to and that affect your pastoral government as an Archbishop of the Catholic Church.
>
> In this regard I wish to mention the lack of esteem for "the Vatican" that, on more than one occasion, you are perceived to have shown. Your attitude toward the Holy See is perceived as negative. As Prefect of the Congregation I have the duty to remind you of your responsibility as a pastor of the Church and member of the Episcopal College to promote love for the Holy See, above all by effective example.

Among the requirements of Catholic unity there is the need to accept the tradition of the Church. According to ecclesial practice, reinforced recently by a Synod of Bishops, it is not possible to present married men for ordination to the priesthood. The ready acceptance of this discipline in a spirit of faith and ecclesial obedience precedes and facilitates making efforts toward truly effective solutions to the problem of the lack of priests.

On the question of the ordination of women, your position is perceived to be in opposition to the teaching of the Church. Moreover, the charge of "intransigency" — a word used by Your Excellency — on the part of the Church in this matter, can seriously damage Church authority and Church government.

It is further perceived that you attribute to the Holy See unwillingness to accept fully the Second Vatican Council.

Consequently, on the occasion of your *ad limina* visit, I wish to ask you to reflect "coram Domino" on your general attitude toward the Holy See, and to change whatever there is in it that goes contrary to promoting respect for the Holy See, love for the Holy Father and total communion between the local Church and the universal Church.

As was his custom in the past, the cardinal added a hand-written note to me in French, the language we always spoke together, to soften somewhat the tone of the typed letter, so different from the tone of our conversation in his office.

*   *   *

My struggles over the role of women in the church were not to end with the public exchange between me and Cardinal O'Connor on the church's treatment of women or the indirect approach admonishing me to be more countercultural in this regard. My desire to keep the question open in Rome fell on deaf ears. In May 1993, two months after my *ad limina* visit, the pope published a new document on the non-ordination of women, *Ordinatio sacerdotalis,* again labeled an apostolic letter addressed to the bishops of the world, in which he unequivocally stated:

Wherefore, in order that all doubt may be removed regarding a matter of great importance, a matter which pertains to the church's divine constitution itself, in virtue of my ministry of confirming the brethren (cf. Luke 22:32) I declare that the church has no authority whatsoever to confer priestly ordination on women and that this judgment is to be definitively held by all the church's faithful.

I can still recall how difficult it was when I received this document. I knew I had no choice but to be obedient to the pope's command, even though I wanted him to leave the door open to more theological dialogue and development. It seemed obvious that the Holy Father was coming as close as possible to pronouncing something *ex cathedra* without using the word "infallible."

What did the word "definitive" mean in this context? *Lumen gentium* of the Second Vatican Council stated that such statements were to be given *religiosum voluntatis et intellectus obsequium* (#25). Authors have translated the phrase *religiosum obsequium* in different ways: "religious assent," or "loyal submission," or "religious docility." I feel sure this expression means that the teaching proposed acquires primacy of place as the official teaching of the papal magisterium and must be accepted as enjoying the presumption of truth.

I had to wrestle with that presumption and accept it, not just as a bishop, but as a Catholic. The Holy Father was pinning me — and many others — against the wall with no room to squirm. I had hoped it would be otherwise. I could have continued to try publicly to oppose this decision, but knew it would not be in the spirit of the *obsequium religiosum* that was being asked of me by the text of Vatican II. I felt I could not publicly fight it, regardless of the weaknesses I found in the pope's arguments and explanations. I lamented the loss of so many women's talents if leadership positions in the Church were denied them.

I have continued to reflect on the consequences for the Church this decision could cause. Women had been important in the formation of my own vocation to be a priest; many other priests have told me the same story. To have women alienated from the Church would bring about a further diminution of vocations. Whatever the consequences, I felt I had done my best, in all loyalty, to voice my concerns and that I would have to leave the Church and its future in Christ's hands. But as I reflect back now some decades later, I feel that this document should be counted as one of the major factors in alienating a younger generation of competent women from the Church. How often I would give talks to high-school boys and girls and to groups of young men and women of college age and would find that this question of the non-ordination of women was the first they would ask! After listening to a lengthy description of the official Church's position as enunciated by Pope John Paul II, they would simply make it clear that they were dismissing the Catholic Church as having nothing convincing and meaningful to say to them about their lives and their future.

When historians, decades from now, talk about the lack of vocations to the priesthood in the Catholic Church at the end of the twentieth and beginning of the twenty-first century, or when they try to analyze the reasons for the falling off of active church participation, I hope they do not forget to include as a contributing factor this silent group that left the Church — or at best stood on the sidelines — not because of the sexual abuse by 4 percent of its priests, but because of closing the discussion on the inclusion of women at all levels. From generation to generation, women have always been the most significant bearers of the Church's life and tradition; to lose them was tantamount to losing the future.

Yet, in working at that moment through the intellectual difficulties the pope's document posed to me, I came to realize how profoundly Catholic I was in the depth of my being. Obedience to the magisterium, the teaching authority in the Church, was the most difficult part of being a Catholic, but also the rock of security. I observed too many squabbles among Christian churches because there was no ultimate authority that could break through the disputes with the final word. But I acknowledge that what is for us Catholics our strongest asset, namely, the hierarchical teaching authority, is also, at times, our most burdensome and most confounding belief. My problem in this case was partially with the decision itself, partially with its timing.

I wonder how many times in our lives we Catholics find ourselves at odds with some teaching in the Church. Most of the time, I think, we reserve judgment for the time being and move ahead in the midst of our doubts. Seldom are these so momentous that they totally disrupt the whole of our Catholic baptismal covenant. As a bishop, I did not have the luxury of reserving judgment and had to accept that Peter remains Peter, even if his impetuous nature shows itself over and over again over the centuries.

*   *   *

During this period, the most serious issue facing the Catholic Church in the United States was the sexual abuse of minors by some clergy. Most historians looking at the subject mark 1985 as an important dividing point. By the time the bishops assembled that spring at St. John's Abbey in College-ville, Minnesota, articles had appeared everywhere in the press, Catholic and secular, about cases of sexual abuse of minors by priests, especially the case of Father Gauthe in Lafayette, Louisiana. As difficult as it was to read these stories, their publication aired the problem and required the bishops to address it.

At that first discussion in 1985, psychologists and other experts spoke to the bishops and answered our questions. I do not see how any bishop after that meeting could have maintained that he was ignorant of the severity of the damage to the victims or that he did not know of the likely possibility of recidivism among the perpetrators. Even if some bishops thought the number of potential victims was being exaggerated, the number was still staggering. Some may have been lulled into thinking that we would find a new program to deal with this addictive behavior, just as Alcoholics Anonymous had dealt successfully with alcoholism. From these expert presentations, it was evident that the possibility of such a remedy was out of the question, given the deep-seated nature of the behavior. In addition, no one could now say that young victims would not remember the abuse or that they would "grow out of it." The wounds were too evident and visible — thanks to the descriptions from the victims themselves.

It became evident at that meeting that the bishops would not come up with a common program or approach. Many were reluctant to talk about incidents in their own dioceses and did not want to see a nation-wide solution emerge. They held to the idea that each diocese was a separate entity responsible only to Rome. We bishops could exchange views but not impose anything on one another. By that time it was clear, too, that the powers of a bishops' conference in the Revised Code of Canon Law of 1983 were very limited and that there was no way the conference could impose a uniform procedure.

This led to a growing gap in perception between the reality of the situation and the expectations of the press and the public. The press took it for granted that the conference could and would come up with general policies for the whole country. I knew after that meeting that such a solution was not forthcoming because each diocese would claim its independence and adhere to its own policies. Two additional factors were also evident: an attitude of secrecy was still very strong among the bishops, and Rome had not yet grasped the seriousness of the situation.

Later that year, I received in the mail a document written by three authors discussing the sexual abuse of minors in the U.S. Catholic Church. I raise it here because over the years it has been frequently cited as evidence of how the bishops were responding to the crisis. The document was titled, "The Problem of Sexual Molestation by Roman Catholic Clergy: Meeting the Problem in a Comprehensive and Responsible Manner." In it Father Michael Peterson of St. Luke's Institute elaborated on the psychological aspects of the situation; Father Thomas Doyle, OP, wrote a canonical opinion; and Mr. Ray Mouton, the attorney for the Lafayette, Louisiana, victims, contributed a legal appraisal. A short time after I had read the document, Father Peterson was passing through Milwaukee and came to see me. Although I had never met him, I knew of him through a relative he had helped face a difficult grieving period. We spent about an hour-and-a-half discussing his contribution to the document.

At that time psychologists were making a clear distinction between pedophilia (sexual attraction to pre-pubescent children) and ephebophilia (sexual attraction toward adolescent minors), as he had in his paper. We discussed in depth the question of recidivism, especially with regard to predatory ephebophilia, and if there were any real cures for any of these so-called paraphilias. He was very skeptical about the results of any such claims. (With time I noticed the distinction between pedophilia and ephebophilia, helpful to psychologists but of no importance in the legal field, seemed to drop out of the discussion.)

I read the section by Father Doyle, which simply repeated the relevant canons from the Code of Canon Law. Moreover, because Father Doyle was considered "light weight" as a canonist by his colleagues, I was reluctant to attach too much importance to it. Mouton's section was interesting, but since the laws of each state varied so extensively, I did not spend much time on it.

One way for a bishop to respond to an accusation of sex abuse was to convoke a canonical trial in the diocese and to dismiss a priest found guilty. But at the time, Rome, already critical of the U.S. marriage tribunals, did not look favorably on local tribunals aimed at the dismissal of a priest. Moreover, were such trials possible, the priest would certainly appeal a decision for dismissal from the priesthood to the Roman ecclesiastical courts. As marriage cases indicated, there was a wait of several years before these courts pronounced on cases. I could easily imagine the years a sensitive case such as asking for the dismissal of a priest would have taken! (A few years later, when I presented to Rome the results of such a local trial that is exactly what happened.) We bishops discussed the possibility of a national tribunal since many dioceses did not have sufficient personnel trained and qualified to conduct such trials. Given the atmosphere of restricting the powers of conferences, many bishops did not favor any solution on the national level. It seemed that each bishop had to work out the solution he felt best for his own diocese.

Since so much of the reporting on this issue in the Archdiocese of Milwaukee happened on my watch, I have spent hours searching my own mind and heart as to what I saw happening and how I reacted to it. These reflections leave me troubled and questioning; I feel very vulnerable even as I try to relate those thoughts with as much objectivity as I can. I write not to justify my reactions or those around me, nor to blame anyone, including myself. What I want to do is describe the learning process I, with many other bishops, was going through and how we responded to the crisis as it continued to grow. Of course those responses seem inadequate in light of what we know today.

If I have learned one important point in this process, it is not to judge the past by standards or knowledge that we have today. Thirty years from now, with more knowledge about sexuality and addictions, our successors will wonder how we knew so little at the beginning of this new century. I can only describe what I knew in the 1970s and then how that knowledge grew, how it changed and altered through the next decades.

My experience with sexual abuse of minors before 1985 has already been alluded to — a skimpy knowledge of the existence among some adults of a sexual attraction toward youngsters; but, not having been abused myself, that knowledge was abstract. I had no idea of the prevalence of such attractions, especially among the clergy. It was simply not on my radar screen. When I first had to confront it as a bishop in 1979 in dealing with the case of Father Bill Effinger, I now know that what I did was inadequate, even though it was what any bishop in the United States would have done at the time. The "cure" proposed for any moral evil, including this one, was to strengthen one's will-power, develop a deeper spiritual life, and avoid the occasion of sin. A bishop could also threaten suspension from any priestly activity if the problem persisted, but not dismissal from priesthood. It was not bad advice, just inadequate for the power of the addiction.

It would not have even occurred to me that such a cleric could be dismissed from the priesthood, as I had never heard of a case of dismissal except when a priest had contracted a marriage. Seminarians learned that they were to become priests forever. They would belong to a particular diocese or religious order, and the diocese and religious order assumed the obligation to look after them till death. This was called incardination. Cases of errant priests, whatever the evil might be, were treated as members of a family. It would have been contrary to our church culture to think that the bishop, a father-figure, had the responsibility of reporting the priest to the police. If the family of a victim wished to do so, I never would have tried to convince them otherwise, but my first experiences showed that parents were reluctant to report such cases to civil authorities. They did not want to put their children through the strain of the publicity and the exposure that would ensue.

Perhaps it is true that we bishops became protective by thinking we were acting like the father of the family, but that is the way we thought then. Some now say we were concerned about protecting the Church, its assets, and its good name. (The question of assets did not arise until much later.) We probably were worried about the good name of the Church, but also about the good name of the priest and his family. We had all been imbued with the idea that everyone had a right to his or her good name and that it was wrong to take it away from anyone. Thus, we were hesitant to make information, especially before it was proven correct, more public than necessary. The idea of monitoring predators was not a common practice. We could not see the danger that lay ahead by not adopting a monitoring policy and were oblivious to the possibility of recidivism. In those early years, I knew nothing of law suits, especially civil ones, and they did not play a role in my thinking.

In our confessional practice in the Catholic Church at that time, we presupposed two things. First, we taught that any one would not be tempted beyond their power to control their urges. We believed that people received graces sufficient to resist such temptation. Second, our practice seemed to deal largely, if not exclusively, with the offender without much reference to those offended against. Only in the case of theft did we talk of restitution, but even there we did not reflect on any psychological harm done to another, only material harm.

Looking back on these first cases that came to me before 1985, namely, William Effinger, Richard Nichols, and then Siegfried Widera, I wish I had known more about the nature of sexual molesters and, especially in these cases, the risk of recidivism. Slowly it dawned on me that our methods, mostly spiritual and psychological, were inadequate to the problem. No one then spoke of "sexual addiction." Do I regret not having had this knowledge then? Yes, very much.

In handling these cases, I had accepted naively the common view that

351

it was not necessary to worry about the effects on the youngsters: either they would not remember or would "grow out of it." Later I often asked myself if I really believed that. In the first cases, the parents usually said they would take care of their child if I got the priest out of the area. My general reasoning was that there were probably some kids who "grew out of it" and then some who were deeply disturbed for life. I had never talked in depth with anyone who had been abused to ask them what, if any, were the lasting effects. In my high school days when a situation of abuse arose, it was dealt with by the superior and the students heard nothing more about it. But I did recall a conversation with Cardinal Hume when he was still abbot of Ampleforth. He mentioned knowing someone his own age who had been abused as a child and had carried a deep psychological wound.

At that time there also was a growing spate of literature, mostly in non-professional journals, about "repressed memory syndrome"; unfortunately this did not bring clarity. Not being a psychologist, I had to leave that phenomenon to the professionals, but I came to see that quite clearly psychologists and therapists were going through the same learning curve we all were. Probably they knew little more than we bishops. Therapists tell me that standard textbooks in their field in those years did not treat in depth — if at all — sexual addiction, or outline the effects abuse could have on minors. The depth of searing wounds that such victims can carry through life became apparent to me over the next decade as I listened to case after case. My lack of insight at that time is my greatest regret.

As I think back, I wonder if I had not also been taken in by the way in which the judicial system handled cases where the perpetrator was a professional person. The legal system seemed then to treat doctors, lawyers, teachers, judges, and also clergy in a lenient manner, as if they would have the inner personal strengths to avoid the evil in the future — just as the bishops assumed. One seldom if ever read newspaper stories about these cases. It is the only way I can explain the attitude of the judge in Ozaukee County. In 1975, he had reviewed the many accusations brought against Father Siegfried Widera. Yet having reflected on their severity, he sentenced him to only two years of probation, with the proviso that Archbishop Cousins move Widera from Ozaukee County. The general indifference to these crimes also explains how many cases brought against Father Lawrence Murphy by members of the deaf community in 1975, again during Archbishop Cousins' time, were thrown out of court by the judge without any serious investigation. We all considered sexual abuse of minors as a moral evil, but had no understanding of its criminal nature.

If judges required that the priest be moved, it implied that such a move would give the priest a chance to start over, and before 1985 this was the common practice. Thus, when Father Widera went out to Orange County, California, in 1976 to live with his brother, this would have been seen as giving him "a chance to start over." (How often that phrase recurred in those days!) Archbishop Cousins talked to Bishop William Johnson of the Diocese of Orange by phone and then, since the bishop was leaving the diocese for some time, wrote to the chancellor about Widera, saying that "in his earlier years there was a moral problem having to do with a boy in school" that was "adequately confronted." "More recently," he continued, "there has been a repetition and that according to State laws further psychiatric treatment is mandated with the strong recommendation that no immediate assignment be made in the environs of the Archdiocese." Cousins' assessment was then worded as follows: "From all the professional information I can gather there would seem no great risk in allowing this man to return to pastoral work, but there are legal complications at present writing. Incidentally, these legal technicalities would permit Father's going to another State as long as treatment is continued." Cousins advised a temporary assignment with some part-time work and residence with other priests. He ended by saying: "Though I anticipate no recurrence of this past aberration, I would certainly want to be informed if the slightest suspicion were to develop. I would like to show fraternal charity to a fellow priest but I cannot be virtuous at the expense of a fellow Bishop." It seemed perfectly evident to me that the bishop of Orange was being accurately informed of the problem he would be dealing with. Since Archbishop Cousins and Bishop Johnson would have been seeing each other at least twice a year at the bishops' meetings, it was also an invitation to "talk to me at the coffee break."

Although I had seen Widera's name among the 500 priests who belonged to the Archdiocese of Milwaukee, I first learned in 1981 of his trial for sexual abuse of several minors in Ozaukee County, the probation period imposed on him of two years, and the circumstances that took him to Orange. In 1981 the chancellor of the Diocese of Orange wrote me asking if I would excardinate (release) Widera from the Archdiocese of Milwaukee so that they could incardinate (insert) him into the Diocese of Orange. The letter said that he had been assigned to a parish in Buena Park and then transferred four months later "due to the fact that the parish was given over to the Irish Augustinian Fathers." He was assigned to another parish and then moved after four years "due to the diocesan policy of rotating associate pastors approximately every four years." I took these two explanations as an indirect way of informing me that Widera was not moved because of any recidivism. The chancellor also noted in the letter that Widera had been assigned to work with the Naim conference and served as spiritual moderator for all the Naim conferences of the diocese. The Naim conferences, named after the widow of Naim whose son Jesus had raised from the dead (Luke 7:11-17), had as their scope a pastoral ministry to widows, a relatively safe pastoral task for someone with Widera's inclinations. In the light of this letter, I signed the document of excardination.

I was surprised to read in about 2006, some thirty years later, in the newspapers the claim that Archbishop Cousins had hidden Widera's problem from the bishop of Orange. Bishops in those days put very little in writing about problems of this sort so I was surprised that Cousins had talked to Bishop Johnson on the phone and written to the chancellor as much as he did. About such matters, a bishop would have been very discrete; Cousins seemed to have gone out of his way to relay the facts and raise a warning flag. Moreover, the case was no secret in Milwaukee; there had been a public trial with pictures in the local papers.

Since bishops or superiors of religious orders generally put little in writing, it was not unusual for the files of priests and religious to contain only the official documents of ordination and their assignments. As far back as the French Revolution, a siege mentality had invaded the Catholic Church in most of Europe. As the years passed, especially in those countries where the Catholic Church was no longer a dominant force, that secretive mentality grew stronger. Though it varied from nation to nation, there was always a fear of leaving evidence that could be used against the Church. As abbot primate, I had found that mentality in Germany where personnel files of monasteries and convents had been taken by the Nazis. Lurid parts were published as a way of closing the institutions. Among the Irish it was the fear of the English overlords, a fear they brought to the United States but where the enemy was controlling WASP leadership and the growing number of Nativists. This fear often extended to the press, which was seen as being in the hands of the Church's enemies. Some of the older bishops still exhibited this chronic Catholic paranoia, and the tendency toward secrecy was evident in the very first discussions of the sexual-abuse problem we bishops engaged in. This tendency was shared by the older generation of Catholic laity as well.

Finally, in describing the atmosphere before 1985, I would have to mention the lack of clarity about the supervisory role of the bishop with regard to the personal lives of the priests in his diocese. During those years I struggled to understand in practice what that supervisory role meant in civil law and how it might differ from church law. Civil lawyers kept talking about *respondeat superior* as the way of expressing the bishop's role. Did that mean that the bishop was responsible for everything a priest did twenty-four hours a day? How could anyone logically be held to such a responsibility? When I arrived in Milwaukee, there were over 500 diocesan priests and over 500 priests belonging to the Jesuits, Capuchins, Salvatorians, Pallotines, Carmelites, and so on, each group having its own superior, not to mention the over 2,500 sisters belonging to numerous religious congregations of women. It was easy to say that the superiors of religious orders should be responsible for their own members, but that did not correspond to the common perception, especially if the religious were working in an archdiocesan apostolate. Nevertheless, I took the position that the religious superior should be the one to respond if the accused was a member of their order.

I wrote an article for the *Catholic Herald* (May 28, 1988) summing up my thoughts on what I had learned to that date about sexual abuse among the clergy. As I re-read it now, I see that it was honest in assessing the situation current then. So, e.g., I wrote that little had been done to help victims in the past but that the old attitudes had changed radically. The negative feelings toward psychology and psychiatry in society-at-large and in the Church in particular no longer existed. I admitted that I now believed that the deep-seated cases of pedophilia involving pre-pubescent children "do not seem curable and are rarely totally containable." I also saw the priestly status as a hindrance rather than a help for the pedophile and that the return to the lay state seemed the best course for the priest, society, and the Church, but I added that "it is not always easy to convince the person of this [return to the lay state] nor to obtain from Rome such a laicization if it is against the priest's will."

I reflected on the difficulty of detecting these tendencies, especially during seminary training. Although the profile of the pedophile was emerging more clearly, analyzing the causes and recognizing the signs had not produced convincing indicators. I then approached the cases of ephebophilia, i.e., sexual abuse of post-pubescent victims. I wrote that "this [age] does not reduce the seriousness of the matter, but it does make a difference when one is looking for causes or studying social conditions and environments." This was followed by a paragraph expressing my concern about the lack of psychosexual development, a study in its infancy at that time. But the following paragraph became the only one from the total article ever quoted by the press:

> In these twenty-five years I have learned one very important thing: No two cases are alike — each is different from the other. Frequently, for example, the abuser was also abused as a child, but often not. Sometimes not all adolescent victims are so "innocent"; some can be sexually very active and aggressive and often quite streetwise. (We frequently try such adolescents for crimes as adults at that age.) Pastorally, such cases are difficult to treat: we must not imply that the abuser is not guilty of serious crime, but we could easily give a false impression that any adolescent who becomes sexually involved with an older person does so without any degree of personal responsibility. But each case is different, we must remember.

I was massacred in the press for that paragraph. Every explanation I gave seemed to make matters worse. I was accused of "blaming the victim," making excuses for the priests, and all kinds of other manifestations of insensitivity. As a bishop I was worried, as I tried to explain later, that the Church might be sending out a false message to teens if it even suggested that older teens had no moral responsibilities for their acts if they found a sexual partner over eighteen. I admitted readily that such responsibility might be greatly diminished, or even could be made non-existent, by circumstances, especially if the abuser was a person of confidence and trust like a priest.

There is no doubt that I held less sympathy at that time for some victims between sixteen and eighteen years of age. Where did that come from? I believed then, and still do, that it grew out of my experience in Europe and my travels around the world. Canon law was, in its own way, also an influence as it reflected the more general European practice. In that code sixteen was the age of consent, and this was mirrored in the laws determining the legal age of marriage in most European nations — sixteen for men and fourteen for women. The concept of a long adolescence, so characteristic of American society, was not common among other nations. I certainly was not arguing in favor of reducing the legal age in the United States; I accepted the American law of eighteen. I note that it was only in 1994, years later, that the pope — contrary to the advice of many of his canonists — changed the canonical age for minors in the United States in the sexual abuse cases from under sixteen to under eighteen to conform to civil law here.

My explanation certainly never satisfied the press. But, as sometimes happens, good came come out of a mess. Some time earlier, the Common Council of the City of Milwaukee had appointed a task force on sexual abuse and domestic violence with a very sensitive and effective chair, Terry Perry. As I reflect back on those days, I see her as a kind and wise person. She spoke animatedly but gently in words that were always insightful and to the point. What drew me to her was the breadth of her vision. She was not fixated on only one social injustice in our society, but seemed to care about all those treated unfairly. I highly respected her and her knowledge and came to trust her. That task force asked to meet with me and the collaboration that followed was, at that moment of history, the beginning of a change in my own way of thinking. Through the witness of the members of this board, I began to see some of the harm done even to these older teens because the abuse happened in a delicate period in their lives when they were seeking their own sexual identity.

With the advice of this task force, I created a permanent group (called Project Benjamin) with members from the community to aid the archdiocese in assisting in our response to victim-survivors of clergy sexual abuse. On that board were professional psychologists and therapists, victim advocates, and experts in dealing with both victims and perpetrators, although these experts reviewed and critiqued in particular our responses to victims. I found them insightful and convincing; certainly I was out of my depth in dealing with the complexities of these issues, which had never been part of my training. As events unfolded I had to learn the hard way.

The first contact person and coordinator in the archdiocesan offices was one of the most caring people one could imagine, Mary Kay Balchunas, associate director of family and parenting programs. A hot-line to contact her was put in place so victims could reach her directly, the number being publicized wherever we thought it would be helpful.

1985 was a real dividing line in the awareness of clerical sexual abuse and the severity of the problem; it was the beginning of the bishops' discussion on possible ways of handling the situations. For me a second dividing line was 1992 with the public admission by Father William Effinger at Holy Family parish in Sheboygan of abusing a boy in the late 1970s, a case I had not known about; I did know of two cases involving him in 1979 and had been observing him closely since then. I was always concerned that the surveillance in place was not satisfactory, especially after hearing the discussions among the bishops and the experts in 1985. I had sent Effinger away again in the mid-1980s for alcohol treatment and asked the clinicians also to investigate carefully if there were any signs of recidivism in the abuse of minors; they had seen none. There was also an incident in the parish brought to my attention by a group of concerned parents; alcohol had been given to eighth-grade students seemingly by Father Effinger. I checked carefully with the parents to see if anything else was reported by the students and was told that nothing had been. Effinger personally assured me that everything was fine, but still I worried. Unfortunately I too readily believed him. Because he was so conservative in his theology, I assumed his conservatism carried over into his private life.

After his public admission of abuse in 1992, I went to the parish for an open meeting with the parishioners. Project Benjamin was already in place so that the members could assist me that evening and in subsequent meetings. On Sunday I returned to celebrate all the Masses at that parish and to meet with concerned parishioners. Experts were available if anyone wished to consult them. In the school and religious education classes, personnel from Catholic Social Services trained in dealing with child abuse began programs to help the kids talk about any problems they may have experienced in the hope of surfacing other victims. A similar program took place with high-school students. The one area of pastoral concern we had not anticipated involved the older and more traditional shut-ins to whom Father Effinger had been ministering. They simply would not believe the newspaper stories, were grieving, and had no one to talk to.

A few days later other victims from the Sheboygan area began to come forward, and I met with them and their families. For the first time, I realized that I represented the Church in these cases and had to take the blame for all that had happened. I never did understand why the priest involved was not the primary object of this anger, but the feeling was that the Church had deceived them. It was not an easy situation, and I realized in a very graphic way the harm done, not just to the young persons, but to their families and others as well. I knew that I had not done enough in this case and realized again how difficult it was to monitor another's behavior. I also had to admit that a conservative theology was not an indication of correct moral behavior. I had to become more astute and skeptical in sifting through and dealing with the excuses and promises of perpetrators. Those days will live forever in my memory. If anyone were to ask me what case has given me the most lasting grief and which I wish I could do over, it would be the Effinger case.

One salutary effect of dealing with individual cases was the close attention I paid to discussions among the bishops, which now occurred at almost every meeting. I recognized the need for a more sophisticated response in handling perpetrators. At the invitation of a therapist, Lloyd Sinclair from Madison, I joined the Wisconsin Sex Offender Treatment Network. This group of therapists dealt with child sex abuse in Wisconsin's criminal justice system. I needed to learn more about how they handled perpetrators and what their professional thinking was on recidivism and monitoring.

The burning topic of discussion was the possibility of eventual reassignment of perpetrators in the archdiocese. The question was not pertinent when the cases were recent, since the district attorney took over, and the perpetrators usually ended up with prison sentences. That solution made the decisions of the archbishop much easier, as there was no talk of reassignment. The problem arose in dealing with those who had abused in the past; they were especially difficult if there had been only one reported incident or the statute of limitation had expired.

In 1985, during the first open discussion among the bishops of the problem, Dr. Fred Berlin, MD, PhD, a recognized expert from the Department of Psychiatry and Behavioral Sciences at Johns Hopkins University School of Medicine, urged us not to be too swift in seeking dismissal from the priesthood, arguing that the Church was better organized for monitoring priest abusers than the larger society. But if the cases were old and the statute of limitation was passed and if they had never been convicted of any crime, it was not clear whose responsibility they were. If these men were no longer the responsibility of the Church, Berlin believed they would have no effective supervision at all. Given my experience with Father Effinger and the inadequate monitoring he received, I wasn't sure I wanted, or any bishop could accept, such a responsibility.

The treatment centers that had grown up to deal with clergy problems, usually alcoholism, now entered the picture more vigorously, offering their services for evaluation and treatment. In general, they were more optimistic about reassignment than most of us bishops. My experience made me more negative. As the profile of a pedophile became clearer, examples of recidivism more commonplace, the chance of rehabilitating any perpetrator seemed very unlikely. But what alternatives existed?

At that time there was discussion among the bishops about asking Rome for changes in church law, at least for the United States, which would permit swifter canonical trials so that predators could be returned more rapidly to the lay state. The pope, with good reason, feared speedy administrative trials, citing as proof the corruption and lack of true justice that he had experienced in Poland during the Communist period through administrative tribunals. This being the case, many bishops placed men on administrative leave, withdrew their priestly faculties, and gave them jobs usually held by lay people. That, too, turned out to be an unsatisfactory solution as it deprived lay people of work rightly theirs; it could only be seen as a temporary holding-pattern. We tried this in Milwaukee for a short time, but soon gave it up as not very helpful; no one could possibly monitor such men twenty-four hours a day, seven days a week.

While a committee of the bishops' conference tried to devise canonical solutions acceptable to Rome, most bishops continued to improvise local solutions. Historically, Rome had almost always sided with priests in cases against their bishops; this was certainly true in the history of the American Church. Perhaps Rome had seen too many occasions when bishops tried to rid themselves of difficult and tiresome priests by dismissing them and saw their task as defending the priests' rights. I knew of this history and was not surprised when the first response from Roman canonists focused on the rights of the priests in these cases. They were seen as innocent till proven guilty; leniency rather than severity was recommended.

This created a noticeable tension between the bishops' urgent need to immediately dismiss offenders and Rome's more measured response. Perhaps years from now when the history of those years is more fully written, the Roman response will be seen as wiser. But, in the meantime, bishops were left with strictly limited possibilities. If an offending priest would not voluntarily seek a return to the lay state, the bishop was limited in what he could do. Short of dismissal though a lengthy canonical trial, most of the solutions proved inadequate. If a perpetrator had spent some time at a clinic and if the prognosis by the clinicians was hopeful, bishops sometimes ended up giving the perpetrator limited pastoral work under strict supervision. The priest had to promise to work and live under a monitoring system that would assure there would be no danger to children.

In working out these half-solutions, most bishops followed the five principles for effective response to sexual abuse by clergy issued publicly after their June 1992 meeting: (1) respond promptly to the allegation of abuse; (2) if the allegation seems plausible, remove the alleged offender from ministry and get him help; (3) comply with the obligation of civil law about reporting; (4) reach out to victims and their families; (5) deal as openly as possible with the incident. Gradually these aims were changed so that the healing of the victims was placed first, and the emphasis shifted from putting all one's energy into dealing with the perpetrators to making the victims the primary concern. Later that emphasis gave way to taking preventative measures, placing the care and concern on protecting children. But thus far, there was no test to uncover the tendency to pedophilipa that allowed screening during the seminary years.

Like most other dioceses, Milwaukee began, with the help of the sexual abuse response team from Project Benjamin, to work out concrete procedures for treating each case that was reported to us. Since the numbers of reported cases were increasing in the early 1990s and the number of victims was rising, the members of Project Benjamin advised me to hire a trained psychologist who could spend more time and follow up on all the cases. I hired Dr. Liz Piasecki, whose good work helping the victims cannot be overemphasized. She also worked with the committee assigned by the bishops' conference to draw up recommendations for the bishops. These appeared regularly in manuals called *Restoring Trust* (vol. 1, 1994; vol. 2, 1995; and vol. 3, 1996). We were doing our best to get help for all victims who presented themselves and to respond rapidly and compassionately. Our primary goal was to help the healing of the victims.

At the same time I knew there was a good deal of work to do in dealing with the perpetrators, especially when the incidents were beyond the statute of limitation. Expert advice encouraged me to separate the task of caring for victims from that of dealing with the perpetrators. Thus, these cases were left primarily in the hands of the vicar for clergy. Critics complained that this was like appointing the fox to protect the chicken-coop. Cardinal Bernardin in Chicago took a different approach: he appointed a committee composed predominantly of lay people to deal with the perpetrators. We bishops were told that Rome frowned on this solution, as it seemed bishops were abdicating their authority in a way that was not proper or even legal. In 1993, as an intermediate solution, I asked Judge Leander Foley, a retired circuit-court judge, to look at all of our cases, note what we were doing wrong, and give his frank and honest assessment. Although this was personally helpful to me and to the vicars for clergy, it did not allay all fears and criticism, especially among members of the press. Though I later followed Bernardin's example, regardless of Rome's displeasure, I wish I had done so earlier.

In this atmosphere, the morale of priests was sinking fast and no one in the country or in Rome seemed to worry about it. The priests came through the late 1960s and 1970s still positive about their own ministry, even as many of their classmates resigned to marry. They were now confronting an acute shortage of their numbers as the Catholic population continued to grow and the amount of work increased. Add to that those problems that followed the sex-abuse scandal in their ranks. Some of them felt that the press was singling them out and overlooking other professions and institutions where the number of sexual abuse cases was high.

The complexity of this situation was almost overwhelming. There were cases where it was necessary to work with five different groups of lawyers on a single case. First, there was the lawyer representing the archdiocesan interests; second, a lawyer was appointed for the accused priest since his concerns might not be those of the archdiocese, and I felt strongly he should have his own legal representation; third and fourth, were the canonical lawyer of the archdiocese and the canonical lawyer advising the priest so that his canonical rights were not violated; fifth and finally, were the insurance companies' lawyers. Once or twice an accused priest immediately hired without my knowledge his personal lawyer who stepped in, refused to let me talk to his client, and worked out on his own a settlement with the victim.

Slowly we began to work out the procedures so that all sides could feel they were being treated fairly. The early 1990s were the years of refining procedures on how to deal legally and canonically with each case; I thought every diocese was doing the same thing. We bishops exchanged documents and shared them with the bishops' conference. Sometimes it is said that the lawyers, especially those of the insurance companies, were dictating to the bishops and not vice versa. This was not my experience. The lawyers for the archdiocese never told me I could not do something that I felt, for pastoral reasons, I should do. Just the opposite happened: I was told to do pastorally what I felt I should do; they would pick up from there.

While I waited for Rome to decide what procedures would be put in place on how to handle the perpetrators, I tried to work out a monitoring system that could be as effective as possible under the circumstances. I was not totally at ease with this; I had been duped once and feared a second occurrence. The priest was given a limited pastoral ministry under the supervision of a pastor and parish council who knew about the accusations against the priest. It meant reporting to a permanent deacon who, before becoming a deacon in our diocese, had taught such monitoring to the police force in one of the major cities of our nation and whose expertise I found very useful.

But none of this proved wholly satisfactory. The practice of the civic judicial system was evolving with pressure from the public to reveal the names and residences of the perpetrators. I hesitated to disclose such information, judging that this would mean the priest-perpetrator probably would have no remunerative work at all; the diocese would be responsible for someone who would be on his own all day and not be adequately supervised and, finally, whose salary we had to pay. Though I was very uneasy with partial but supervised ministry, like most U.S. bishops, I did not know how else to proceed. I was as frustrated as the press and the public. In hindsight, I wish I had had other options, but this holding-pattern seemed to work at the time, and to my knowledge, no new incidents were reported of those priests under supervision.

After Dr. Piasecki was on board taking care of victims, making sure they were getting good therapy, and keeping track of their needs, she came to me asking that we sponsor a few of them to go with her to a meeting of SNAP (Survivors Network of those Abused by Priests) at Collegeville, Minnesota. I agreed. The group returned appalled by the level of anger that dominated the proceedings and the dictatorial way in which the meeting was handled. For example, no one who reported a positive experience in the way a diocese treated them was given a chance to share their story. Members of the Milwaukee group felt "victimized" again. Our aim as a church, to try to bring peace and reconciliation to victims, did not fit into SNAP's agenda. Having SNAP as an adversary was a tactical mistake for me, since the press constantly listened to SNAP's voice and gave it extraordinary credibility. Bishop Sklba and I were always ready to talk with victims and their families, but I admit I found there was no common agenda between what I thought should be the aims of a church that followed the precepts of the gospel and SNAP's displays of anger and personal vindictiveness.

During the 1990s I truly felt that I was doing the best I could under the circumstances, certainly as well as, if not better than, bishops of other dioceses with whom I spoke. I also knew that in this acrimonious atmosphere a more positive story would never be accepted. History will have to make the ultimate judgment.

After my retirement, excellent national studies revealed that the number of incidents of abuse by priests in the country peaked in the 1970s and 1980s. Naturally everyone asks: Why then? What caused this? Most of the answers do not seem to tell the full story. I cannot say the abusers I had to deal with morally defended their actions; perhaps there were national

cases when this happened. Some blamed the sexual revolution that flourished in those decades. Perhaps the culture catered to and encouraged
certain narcissistic traits. Some blamed Pope John XXIII for opening of the
windows of the church at Vatican II. That opening was more evident in the
area of pastoral approaches, liturgy, and relationships with other churches
and faiths. I do not remember it brought a major shift in moral theology,
although it did bring a change in the attitudes toward sexuality, especially
among the clergy, from negative taboos to more positive considerations.
Certainly it did not condone sexual acts with minors.

Some blamed the sexual abuse crisis on the larger proportion of homosexual priests in the priesthood during that period. Of itself, that was
unlikely to be the source of the problem unless it was accompanied by a
lack of sexual maturity. I continue to think that the major factor was the
poor formation of candidates in the 1950s and early 1960s that did not
foster social and sexual maturity. Seminary classes were very large and
the major seminaries self-contained so that a candidate with unresolved moral and sexual issues could easily hide behind the outward appearances of conformity in discipline. A young man who kept the prescribed discipline of the minor and major seminary, who passed all his
exams, and who seemed docile and obedient would be passed on from
year to year. Although most seminaries used the usual psychological
tests for their candidates, there were no specific tests to screen potential molesters.

Since I will have more to say in the next chapter about how the question of dealing with sexual abuse of minors was handled in my final years
as archbishop, I end the description of this period by recalling the reconciliation service held in 1995 at St. John's Cathedral. I presided and asked
Archbishop Harry Flynn of Minneapolis to preach. Archbishop Flynn was
chairing the bishops' special committee on this issue, having done superb
work with victims in Lafayette, Louisiana. A large number of victims and
their counselors gathered to pray together that afternoon; I was grateful to
them for coming. The staff made private rooms available for counselors to
meet with a victim if they wished. The police, taking seriously death
threats against Archbishop Flynn, Bishop Sklba, and me, insisted that we
wear bulletproof vests for the ceremony. This saddened me but emphasized ever more vividly the anger that existed in the Catholic community. I
tried not to take this anger personally, but to see myself as a symbol of the
Catholic Church and the Church's lack of care for these particular victims.
It did not prevent all of us from praying for those who had been abused by

members of the Church, in the hope that we could begin with them a path of healing, inner peace, and reconciliation.

*   *   *

Sometime in the late 1980s or early 1990s a group of us bishops — probably about fifteen in all — who were unhappy with the inability of the conference to face some of the neuralgic issues we had to deal with in our dioceses (like the priests' shortage, the role of women, liturgical matters, and so on) began to come together during the annual meetings. We would go out one evening, usually on Monday, to a restaurant near the hotel where the bishops' meeting was held. At the restaurant we reserved a private room and spent the evening in discussion and mutual support. These meetings became more and more important to those of us who found the formal meetings of the bishops lagging in their ability to tackle the major issues of our day.

For some years — I could not say precisely when the idea began — some members of this same group would fly into Milwaukee on the day after Easter for a few days. Again, without a rigid agenda, we just talked together with openness and frankness about our concerns. I prized those occasions as they were the kind of mutual support so many of us bishops felt we needed.

Periodically the leadership of the conference, knowing there was some discontent, would propose that we rethink how we functioned at our meetings or how we should change or streamline how we worked. Committees would then be appointed to review what we were doing and suggest how to proceed in a better fashion. In 1995 we were again in such a mood for change. The "rump" group at our dinner meeting decided to respond as a group to the request of the *ad hoc* committee for restructuring by writing a document that would express all of our concerns. Several of us worked on drafts during the summer, and eleven of us were able to meet and sign off on it. Since the "rump" group contained a larger number of bishops, our group drew up a list of the bishops we felt would be willing to sign the document; the number came to forty. But we hesitated to seek those signatures, knowing it might look as if a "palace coup" were being planned. Instead, eleven of us signed it, my name being first of the list. The document was then submitted to the committee working on restructuring the conference. The document reached the press and was usually referred to, a bit improperly, as the Document of the Forty. In many ways it was the last hurrah of the "Dearden bishops" and an open plea for a return to some of the ideas abandoned after Vatican II. (The document was published in *Origins,* vol. 25, no. 8, July 13, 1995.)

We bishops could not avoid discussing collegiality and the relationship of the conferences of bishops to the curia in Rome. Many of the themes that I have had to deal with in my life as a bishop were mentioned in the paper — Rome's intervention in the workings of the conference, the lack of consultation, the true meaning of Vatican II as it affected the work of the bishops, and so on. It called for more openness and more collaboration between the bishops and Rome, with a more evident respect for the role of bishops in the Church. It also touched on the reasons why there is so little honest discussion among the bishops and emphasized the exaggerated concept of loyalty "interpreted to mean a strict and undifferentiated application of all Roman norms." It stated that, when a bishop speaks out openly at this time, it is looked upon as disloyal and dangerous to the faith of the community. In reflecting on the need for more trust between Rome and the local bishops, the document ended by stating: "The issue of pedophilia among priests continues to create a very serious credibility problem for the U.S. bishops because of our perceived unwillingness fully to address and explore the reasons for this terrible tragedy."

The document was an internal one sent to the proper committee working on the restructuring of the conference and its procedures, but then somehow was leaked to the press. Several Catholic periodicals took up a few of the points in the document and so it engendered for a short time some public discussion.

During the next trip I made to Rome, I had a chance to meet informally with Cardinal Ratzinger. He wanted to bring up the Document of the Forty Bishops. First of all, he wished to make it clear that he was not of the same mind as the editors of some of the conservative newspapers and periodicals and did not want to be seen as supporting their position. His comments centered on the need for consultation on the part of the pope before issuing a statement. After discussing incidents where the conference received documents from Rome to be implemented and where there had been no previous consultation, the document also had stated:

> Likewise, the recent apostolic letter *Ordinatio sacerdotalis* was issued without any prior discussion and consultation with our conference. In an environment of serious question about a teaching that many Catholic people believe needs further study, the bishops

are faced with many pastoral problems in their response to the letter. The questions now being raised by women, theologians, ecumenists, and many of the faithful as a result of this new apostolic letter present an immense pastoral problem that might have been prevented had there been more regular and open communication from us to Rome.

The cardinal wanted simply to state that in his official position he had to defend the pope's prerogatives in the light of the First Vatican Council, especially that the pope could exercise his teaching authority alone without the previous consultation or consent of the bishops — the wisdom of doing so being another matter. Otherwise, he did not want to make any observations about the document, leaving us bishops to discuss the matter as we pleased.

As I re-read the document now, I am struck again at its urgency and frankness, its brashness and forthrightness, and though I was not its principal drafter, it accurately expressed my views at the time. Though it contained important historical insights, it is never cited by historians of the period; nonetheless it remains an important witness to the unease many American bishops were experiencing with the centralizing procedures in place during the pontificate of Pope John Paul II. Nothing much came of the statement, however, and, as usually happens in the Catholic Church, it was appropriately filed. The tensions, however, did not disappear.

During these years I still remained very active in the bishops' conference, having been elected to chair the ecumenical committee in 1991. My esteem for the staff of that department of the conference was boundless. If I might brag about one decision I lobbied for in those years, it was to begin a dialogue with the Muslim community in the States — a decision I never regretted.

My ecumenical work took me to Russia twice in 1991 for a dialogue with the Russian Orthodox Church under the auspices of Pax Christi International and led by Cardinal Franz König of Vienna. In September of 1993, I went to Milan to participate in an interfaith gathering. Then, in 1995, I led a group of Orthodox and Catholic bishops to Rome for meetings in the secretariat of state and an audience with Pope John Paul II. Within twenty-four hours of being received by the Holy Father, we were being warmly welcomed by the Ecumenical Patriarch Bartholomew in Istanbul.

Because of my involvement in the drafting of the bishops' Economic

Pastoral Letter and my writings on liturgical issues, my name was familiar abroad. In 1990 I headed a delegation to El Salvador as support for the archbishop of San Salvador, Arturo Ribera y Damas, who was under death threats from forces within the military. In March of 1992, I was invited to deliver the Von Hügel lecture at St. Edmund's College in Cambridge on the economic letter. In March 1993, I flew to Melbourne, Australia, to deliver the opening address at a huge congress on church music. A group of ultra-conservative Catholics there had tried to keep me from coming by sending a dis-invitation on a piece of the archbishop's stationery mechanically reproduced and bearing his forged signature. Since this story was in all the press before my arrival, my talk gained even more publicity. When I rose to speak to the 5,000 assembled, I received a standing applause and a very warm and enthusiastic Aussie reception. In late summer of 1995, I was in England for a talk at the annual meeting of the priests of England and Wales. I found our problems in the States, especially the shortage of priests, closely resembled theirs.

I end this busy period of my life with mention of what was the highlight: the 150th anniversary of the founding of the Archdiocese of Milwaukee in 1843. To mark this event, Bishop Sklba and I visited all the parishes and major institutions within the diocese. We would go to a cluster of two or three parishes on Sunday morning and return late on Monday night with many events planned in between. In addition, we participated in many projects and events with the Jewish community, since they too were celebrating the 150th anniversary of their arrival in Milwaukee. Most of all, I remember, admittedly with a tinge of nostalgia, the final Mass in 1994 with about 9,000 present. One could only marvel at the prayerful and festive liturgy, the exuberant singing of the faithful, and, most of all, their Spirit-filled hope about the future of the Church here.

CHAPTER 15

Struggling toward the Finish Line

Milwaukee (1996-2002)

*I*t was a chilly fall day as I started outlining the events of my last years as
archbishop of Milwaukee. Sitting on the patio was out of the question. So I
*spread out my papers on the dining-room table. From there my eyes could
take in the dead flowers that hadn't been trimmed. I could watch the Canada
geese waddling on the lawn. After a while I became hypnotized by the green,
turbulent water of Lake Michigan beyond. It would be a difficult chapter to
write since many events were racing through my mind and I was trying to sort
out my emotional reactions to them. On the yellow pad in front of me, I jotted
down words like: sabbatical, Common Ground Initiative, prostate cancer,
synod for America, my 1998 and last* ad limina *visit, a new millennium, ecumenical endeavors, talk at the synagogue in 1999, cathedral renovation, my
thoughts on the pontificate of Pope John Paul II, the Eisenberg Commission,
sexual-abuse cases, and my last months as bishop.*

In the early 1990s a few American bishops petitioned Rome for personal sabbaticals — an unknown phenomenon for Catholic bishops. Some
bishops supported the idea of sabbaticals for priests and sought funds to
help them finance a semester away, especially for updating in preaching,
counseling, biblical studies, and moral issues stemming from contemporary advances in medicine after Vatican II. People were asking more of
their priests and they needed to deepen their knowledge and sharpen
their communication skills. If this was true of priests, it was more so for
bishops who had to engage all these issues in the public forum.

That a bishop himself might need or could profit from a sabbatical brought an amusing reaction from some Roman officials: they feared the practice would weaken the image of the teaching authority of a bishop. One official in Rome, with evident sincerity, put it to me this way: "Sabbaticals for bishops could give the faithful the false impression that a bishop needed periodic re-tooling in theology, as if he did not already possess, by his ordination, the full knowledge necessary." Turning the grace of office itself into a new and continuing source of knowledge seemed a dangerous theology to me!

From my notes I see that I had been thinking of a sabbatical as early as 1993. My primary purpose was to finish a doctoral dissertation on medieval Milanese chant begun in 1956 at Columbia University. To finish I needed all the mental acumen I could muster. Years had elapsed since I seriously delved into the extensive research I had done in the mid-1950s. I did not want to wait till I was seventy-five, retirement age for bishops, before trying to complete this complicated project.

In January 1995, I was in Rome with a group of Catholic and Orthodox bishops and used the occasion to present to Cardinal Bernardin Gantin of the Congregation for Bishops a formal letter requesting a six-month sabbatical beginning one year later, January 1996. As I sat in his modest office, I thought of the many times our paths had crossed and I had interacted with him. It was easy for us to reminisce together about those years when he was a young bishop of Cotonou in Benin and gave his ancestral property for two monasteries, one for Benedictine monks and one for sisters. This time I was again relaxed and pointed out to him I had been a superior in the Catholic Church for thirty-three difficult years. I not only needed a period for research, but deserved a temporary respite from the constant grind. My primary purpose was to finish the doctoral dissertation, but I also needed time for personal renewal. Cardinal Gantin listened sympathetically.

In addition, I pointed out that Bishop Sklba was capable of handling the diocese without difficulty for six months. Gantin, however, noted that the requests from other bishops had been for just three or four months. If I were to ask to be absent for a longer period of time, he feared the pope might want to appoint an administrator from outside the archdiocese — one who could have ideas different than mine on how to run a diocese. Gantin proposed I ask for a four-month sabbatical and then take a month before and after as vacation. He meant well, but my response was a strong no: I did not want to employ such legalisms and feared they could later be used against me with the accusation that I had turned a four-month leave into a six-month one. He finally agreed to submit my request for a six-month sabbatical to the pope and to support it.

In addition to completing the thesis, I knew that I needed some time away; being a bishop was taking its toll and some aspects of my work had become burdensome. In previous conversation, the cardinal and I had talked about the many complaints he received about me, especially from Polish pastors in Milwaukee and some of the conservative church groups. He also knew that these negative evaluations had reached the pope, although the latter never brought them up to me. In addition there were the perennial and more serious problems of the decline in vocations to the priesthood and the consequent need to consolidate parishes. The sex-abuse cases were also weighing heavily on me: I felt trapped between the lengthy canonical procedures for the dismissal of priests and the reality a bishop had to face in American culture.

I waited anxiously for four months for a response from Gantin's office. It finally arrived in late May. The cardinal wrote that the pope granted the six-month sabbatical — no question of appointing an administrator was raised — and that he wanted me to spend that time in a monastery, not only working on Milanese chant, but reflecting on my "relationship as Bishop with the Archdiocese, with the Church Universal, with the Magisterium, and with the Successor of Peter" — a typical Roman way of saying he was displeased with my work as a bishop. The letter also stated that before my departure the Congregation of Bishops would supply me with points which the Holy Father wished me to reflect on and pray about. I was asked to make a response to these points after the sabbatical was over. Finally, Cardinal Gantin requested that I send to his office my intended calendar and program. He added: "I take this opportunity to remind you that, while the fact that you have been granted the sabbatical will be public knowledge, the contents of this letter should better remain confidential." Why? I was not sure.

It took me a month to work out new plans in the light of this letter. I sent my program to the cardinal on June 29, stating that I planned to make St. Mary's Abbey in Morristown, New Jersey, my temporary home because it was situated between Princeton and Columbia in New York. (Princeton and Yale had invited me to spend the sabbatical time as a visiting scholar on their campuses, but I turned down those offers.) I wrote to the cardinal that I wanted to go to Milan for three weeks after Easter to check books and manuscripts not found elsewhere. I added that I looked forward to receiving the assigned reflections, writing: "I am very concerned about the erosion in the last decades of the concept, role, and rights of the local bishop in the church and would be more than willing to reflect on this concept and its relationship to the universal church, especially in the light of writings of the patristic period and *Lumen gentium* of Vatican Council II." On the secrecy issue imposed on me, I answered that, of course, I would consult theological, spiritual, and canonical experts as necessary, but I also pointed out that "such secrecy, as you well know, in the American culture is often seen as manipulative and a condition that in society has so often led to the abuse of human rights." Strangely enough, no points from the congregation for bishops were ever sent me and thus no further mention of a written response. As I re-read all this correspondence with Rome, I feel a certain annoyance: the pope had no understanding of what it would take to finish the dissertation, especially one where the primary sources were in Milan. My request for a sabbatical had been turned into an imposed penitential period to be spent in a monastery.

Nonetheless, my sabbatical plan otherwise went well. Columbia University readily re-admitted me. I had begun my work before time-limits on completing dissertations had been imposed. Having no specialist in medieval music on the faculty there, they appointed Professor Leeman Perkins, a distinguished scholar in Renaissance music, to be moderator of the thesis and asked Professor Peter Jeffery of Princeton, a renowned specialist in medieval chant, to be the first reader. It turned out to be a pleasure to live at the abbey in Morristown. The prayer-life was exemplary and the working conditions fine. The monastic community was gracious, welcoming, and accommodating. When I went to Milan to work for three weeks as planned, Cardinal Carlo Martini insisted I stay at his residence in the heart of the city since it was close to my sources. He arranged visits for me to work in the libraries and parishes possessing the manuscripts, periodicals, and books I needed. I returned to Milwaukee only for Holy Week, the priests' overnight in May, and ordinations.

In the six months allotted me I was able to immerse myself in the material needed for the dissertation and to rewrite what I had started back in the 1950s. In December 1999 I defended the thesis *cum distinctione* — a rarity I was told in the department of music — and received the doctorate at Columbia's 2000 commencement. This earned degree, of course, meant a great deal to me. Even so, the thirty-five honorary degrees I received as primate of the Benedictines and archbishop of Milwaukee I always saw as a validation that I must have been doing something right. Of course, the merely ceremonial nature of such awards was often apparent. For example, at Yale in 1993, we recipients walked from the president's office to the outdoor pavilion for the ceremony. I marched in front of another honoree, Alistair Cooke. Students were lined up along the walk; as Cooke passed, one of them pointed to him and said loudly: "That must be the archbishop!" He looked the part; we both chuckled.

*   *   *

During the months I spent at St. Mary's Abbey in Morristown in 1996, I followed as closely as I could the news about Cardinal Joseph Bernardin, archbishop of Chicago, who had announced the year before that he was suffering from pancreatic cancer. I would not say that Joe — as everyone called him — and I were close, but we were friends and thought alike on most issues. We did not socialize much, nor did I call him regularly to exchange pleasantries. An exception was April 2, since we shared the same birthday. On that day we would phone to express best wishes to one another. Although he had much more experience than I in being a bishop, I was a year older.

We worked on many committees together and had frequent occasions to exchange ideas. I often took advantage of such meetings to confide about my run-ins with the curia. He was always supportive and would fill out the picture for me, supplying me with information of what was happening behind the scenes in Rome. He was frank in reporting that Rome had "written me off," and that he did not want to fall into the same position. Though his relationship with Rome is not a subject I could write about authoritatively, he hinted enough about his skirmishes for me to understand that his relations with Rome were difficult. It seemed to me that he too had been "written off," but it was harder for Rome to do so definitively since he was a cardinal. Rome also had come to rely on him to resolve tricky situations in the United States where his skills of bringing people together and working out an acceptable solution were needed — as he did with Archbishop Hunthausen and the Archdiocese of Seattle.

Joe's role in the bishops' conference was pivotal. He was president of the conference when I was named a bishop and subsequently chaired many of its committees. Whenever there were conflicting views on a document or on how to proceed, his advice would carry the day. He had gained the trust of all as a consensus builder and the reputation among the bishops as a centrist. I soon found that Joe was every bishop's friend, always available to those who sought his advice and support. Most of all, he was a

373

"Dearden" bishop, having worked closely with Cardinal Dearden when the latter was president of the bishops' conference right after Vatican II. He was, in effect, the successor of Dearden in providing leadership among the bishops.

Among the more agreeable meetings we both attended between 1993 and 1996 were those initiated by Monsignor Philip Murnion of the National Pastoral Life Center in New York. Phil, endowed with a keen theological sensitivity, had a doctorate in sociology from Columbia University and kept abreast of all that was happening in the Church and world. A few times a year he gathered together a group that acted as a think-tank or a sounding-board for issues he felt the Catholic Church had to face on the American scene. With Bernardin as the key person in the group, he invited a mixed group of bishops, priests, and prominent lay Catholic scholars. There was only one rule: no one was to be quoted afterwards. We spoke freely of our concerns for the Church. These gatherings acted as a strong support group for Bernardin — as they were for all of us — since he could speak frankly and personally there about the pressures on him.

Out of those gatherings came the idea of the Common Ground Initiative. During the last meetings of 1995 and then into 1996, we discussed the possibility of forming a new group that would bring together people with opposing views in the U.S. Church to reflect seriously and prayerfully on their differences. I see by my calendar that early in 1996 I attended a meeting of the group at a hotel near Dulles Airport and then another at the end of July in Ypsilanti, Michigan, where we worked on that idea and on a document to accompany its announcement. It meant our unstructured pick-up group would have to be abandoned in favor of the new one because of time constraints on each one of us and the financial burden on the National Pastoral Life Center, but we all seemed to see the value of doing this. We all agreed that polarization was the most serious problem the U.S. Catholic Church had to face — the traditionalists had been more realistic in calling it "the battle for the American Church." Sitting down with the protagonists of the various positions seemed to be the only way to confront the differences. During the discussions the pick-up group had on how to proceed, Joe made it clear that he did not want it to become a project of the conference of bishops, probably since disagreement on the precise role and image of authority in the Church at that time was seen as among the major, if not the most serious, obstacles. We all agreed with him.

When I saw Joe after the announcement of his cancer in June of 1995 and his press statement on August 12 forming the Common Ground Initiative, it was clear that he was failing and seemed unwell. Frequently he had to change his sitting position to seek relief from pain; he fell asleep frequently when others were talking; he was rapidly losing weight and not eating. But there was a growing aura of peace about him, a calm resignation, and a renewed zeal for the betterment of the Church. This new project he realized would be his last, and he put all his effort into it. It summed up what his whole life had been about — reconciling different positions so the group could move forward. In this, he resembled Pope Paul VI.

The title given to the document announcing this initiative was *Call to Be Catholic: Church in a Time of Peril.* Perhaps its assessment of the Catholic Church in the United States in the 1990s was too negative, but, by opening with such an alarm, the group thought it would alert people to the problem by shocking them out of their lethargy. The document presupposed that all would agree on the benefits of dialogue as a positive way of reaching mutual respect and understanding, since no one group had a monopoly on truth. The document also presupposed good will on the part of all and an openness to listen to those with whom they disagreed. The document did not go into the theories of dialogue. Perhaps that was a mistake, but that term had been used so often by Pope Paul VI from his very first encyclical that we presupposed people would interpret the term in the way Pope Paul had used it. We were to find out that the very word "dialogue" was open to many interpretations. Some cardinals feared Bernardin, by using that word, was advocating a consensus approach to determining church teaching.

I was pleased when Joe asked me to be a member of the Common Ground Initiative as I truly believed in it and what it had to offer. Cardinal Roger Mahony from Los Angeles also joined us in the effort.

The immediate reaction to the news conference in the Catholic and secular press was very positive, and the response among the laity even more so. The Initiative did create, however, high expectations among clergy and laity that would be hard to fulfill. They were eager for some mechanism to confront the divisions affecting the life of their parishes and projects. But a set of unexpected responses shook all of us. The first to throw down the gauntlet was Cardinal Bernard Law of Boston, followed by Cardinals James Hickey of Washington, Anthony Bevilacqua of Philadelphia, and Adam Maida of Detroit. As all of their negative responses to the Initiative appeared in the media, one had the distinct impression that each cardinal had the same talking points before him, and all their responses became variations on given themes. They saw dissent from church teaching as the major problem, and, thus, immediately spoke about the need to squelch it in the Church through obedience to the magisterium, especially the papal magisterium. They further emphasized that dissent should never be permitted an equal place at the table with the magisterium. There were other criticisms of the document, but most of them were insignificant compared to this one.

Cardinals publicly airing their differences before the whole world, believers and non-believers alike, was a rare historic moment, not seen for over a century in the U.S. Catholic Church. Joe took this public reprimand from his fellow cardinals personally. It grieved him greatly, even though their public, often harsh, statements acted as proof of the Initiatives thesis that polarization reached to the highest levels in the Church.

What could have provoked so many of the other cardinals to express this public disagreement with the Bernardin Initiative? I am convinced the cardinals considered it their duty to defend the untramontane position — namely, the need to refer all matters to the pope for resolution as the only way to maintain unity in the contemporary Catholic Church.

Some cardinals, including Cardinal John O'Connor of New York, had responded a few months earlier to a sensitive but theologically subtle and astute lecture Archbishop John Quinn of San Francisco delivered at Oxford entitled "The Claims of the Primacy and the Costly Call to Unity." Archbishop Quinn was responding to the pope's encyclical *Ut unum sint* in which the pope asked how he could exercise his role of primacy in a way that would be more acceptable to the Orthodox Churches, but keeping his prerogatives laid down in the First Vatican Council. In response to Quinn, O'Connor wrote a lengthy and rambling defense of the curia and of papal power. He took up all the issues Quinn had raised — appointment of bishops, collegiality, the curia — and answered them in an ultramontane framework.

Undoubtedly Quinn's lecture followed by the Common Ground Initiative made the cardinals nervous. It was clear to any astute observer that the cardinals felt the ultramontane position of referring everything to the pope was being challenged by both Archbishop Quinn's lecture and now Bernardin's Common Ground Initiative — a solution that did not even seem to bring Rome into the picture.

For the next years I attended the sessions sponsored by the Initiative and found that the process worked effectively, but perhaps not in the way I would have expected. As the group of scholars and proponents of differing views on a given subject met for the first time — it was usually on a Friday evening — I could sense there was tension in the air. I felt it personally many times as I met for the first time people who had written negative appraisals of my own writings. But the unifying factor came from the first Mass celebrated on Saturday morning. I often had the privilege of presiding at it. At that moment, we realized we had more in common that united us than differences of ideas that divided us. In fact, I came to esteem highly people about whom, before that experience, I had been very dubious.

On the other hand, it was difficult to persuade people with extreme positions on the right or left to participate, since they were not interested in dialoguing but in issuing manifestoes. We also had to learn that the Latino and black communities had issues that did not coincide with those of the older Catholic mainstream and that we had to find space to include them on every subject.

On October 24, 1996, Joe announced that the pancreatic cancer was no longer in remission and that he had a limited time to live. He died on November 14. On November 20, I made the trip by car to Chicago for his funeral. Almost all the U.S. cardinals and bishops formed at the entrance of the cathedral what seemed like an unending line of swaying miters. It was a brisk day. We archbishops, coming at the end of the line, had to stand outside for a long time and were shivering from the damp cold. Once inside, I had a panoramic view of the service from my chair against the wall at the back of the apse. From there I could see the backs of all the bishops lined up in front of me and observe all the cardinals in the first row near the main altar. The gigantic nave of the church was filled with dignitaries, priests, religious, and the people of the archdiocese.

Cardinal Mahony celebrated the Mass at Bernardin's request. The homily was preached by Bernardin's secretary, Monsignor Ken Velo. History will continue to point out the most telling moment in that homily. Velo spoke affectionately, at times also humorously, about his old "boss," but also mentioned that Bernardin was not afraid to take initiatives. When he said the words: "He wanted people to come around the table to see not what divides us but what brings us together. He wanted to make common ground holy ground," applause broke out in the body of the church and then enveloped all of us. As those in the body of the church rose to their feet, we in the apse joined them. Finally the cardinals — Law, Hickey, Bevilacqua, and Maida being the only ones sitting — had to rise as well. I was grinning from ear to ear. The *vox populi* had spoken! They understood who their beloved bishop was and what he had been trying to accomplish, even if the illustrious cardinals did not.

*   *   *

The week after Bernardin's funeral I went into the hospital with an enlarged prostate that required surgery. During my sabbatical, although I was mentally agile, I felt my body beginning to show signs of aging. I had had a persistent problem of an enlarged prostate. About two years before, a urological specialist, Dr. Jack Pope, had performed biopsies on the prostate and found no cancer. Since the medication I was taking during those two years was not reducing its size, the doctor decided to perform a TURP operation (trans-urethral re-sectioning of the prostate).

Before long the whole town knew that Dr. Pope had written a prescription for a few antibiotics that I should take before the operation! When I went to pick them up at the pharmacy, I learned the pharmacists had not filled the prescription because they thought it was a practical joke — the pope prescribing a few antibiotics for Archbishop Weakland!

The results of the operation showed that six chips from over ninety removed were cancerous. This information disturbed me more than I expected. I was old-fashioned enough to react very strongly to the news of having the big "C." But my reaction was stronger because I knew that both of my grandfathers had died of prostate cancer. How vividly I recalled the stench of urine that filled their rooms and the frightening tubes coming from their bodies that gathered the bronze liquid into containers by the bed. I remembered their discomfort and, finally, their painful and protracted deaths. My doctors assured me progress had been made since the 1930s and there were many new ways of treating prostate cancer. I read everything I could about possible ways of proceeding and decided on radiation therapy in the event not all cancer had been removed.

This was my first major illness so I reflected on how much I had to be thankful for. But I knew I also had much yet to learn. As a person accustomed to being always in control (a control freak!), I had to learn to put my trust totally in God — not easy for anyone — and then in the physicians and those around me. It was a salutary experience. For the first time in my life I was anointed by Bishop Sklba in the chapel in the archbishop's residence before I left for the hospital. I was deeply moved by the experience. I realized now what the bishops at Vatican II meant in their renewal of the sacrament in emphasizing that it was meant for the sick, and not reserved for the moment of dying. For me to come into contact with my own mortality and humanness in this way was an unexpected blessing.

During my illness I found how hard it was to pray as I wanted. Whenever I had visited sick people confined to their beds, I would offer the common platitude that God was giving them more time to pray. I learned now that I had time on my hands and little to do, but I was too woozy and distracted for concentration and for extended praying. The most I could do was to utter short petitions from the heart, frequently of resignation. I had to leave the praying, as with so many other things, to others. I also learned that it is easier and more glamorous to serve than to be served. We all love to be the hero and to be independent. It was good for me to admit that I needed others to care for me. I wrote in the Catholic weekly paper: "Sickness teaches us that holiness does not consist in some abstract, mystical goals, but in contending with the moment at hand, its earthiness, its realness, its demands. It is in the midst of sickness that we must find God and his son Jesus Christ. Somewhere the Spirit is at work in the middle of what seems to be so human, so fragile, so weak, so expendable."

In the midst of this, I was more tense than usual, especially with the gruesome visions of my tormented grandfathers that I could not get out of my head. Right after the operation I had difficulty urinating and the doctor frequently had to insert a catheter. Over several days he would take the catheter out for some time, but, when there still were no results, he put it back in — a process that happened over and over again. Finally — I recall it was late Saturday afternoon — he explained to me that a nurse would come in early Sunday morning to take out the catheter and that it simply had to work this time or he might be forced to do something more invasive to check if there was some blockage.

At 10:00 on Saturday evening a petite young nurse with a huge smile entered the room to assure me she would be in at six o'clock the next morning to take out the catheter, that she was well practiced in doing so, and that I should sleep well and have no worries. It seemed like just a few minutes later when she woke me saying it was 6:00 a.m., time for the catheter to be removed. In two seconds, with me being very groggy, she was dangling the catheter in front of my sleepy eyes. As she did so, I recall, she chirped up: "And you, Bishop, confirmed me." I remember all I could do was break out into a hearty laugh at the incongruity of it all. But this relaxing seemed to do the trick and the doctor was pleased with the results.

The operation took place in November 1996, and I had to wait till the following March before radiation could begin, thirty-five sessions spread over seven weeks. Each morning during March and April at 9:00, Monday through Friday, I would sit in the nondescript waiting area in the oncology section of St. Joseph's Hospital covered only by an awkward ill-fitting hospital gown. The TV was always set at an insipid talk show. As I looked at the other patients, I realized how lucky and blest I was. We patients soon got to know each other, even if only superficially. We learned only the first names of those being radiated; that seemed to be enough. As usual, I was always called "Rembrandt." I recall we celebrated someone's birthday with a cake. We watched some faces shine with elation when they announced this was their last day of radiation, or noticed that others, without any announcement, suddenly ceased coming. Someone might say they were in "hospice care." Some recognized me, most did not. Sickness is a powerful social equalizer; the ashes that year at the beginning of Lent were more meaningful than ever to me.

During the first weeks of radiation I carried on my usual schedule, going to my office after the morning session at the hospital, taking some appointments and meetings, returning home for lunch, profiting by a long siesta under the covers, and then celebrating a confirmation in the evening. After about three weeks of this routine, I did not have the energy for any evening sessions. Even before noon I was depleted. Nor did I have the energy to play much serious music on the piano, no Beethoven, no Liszt for sure. But, after a light supper, I would take out stacks of music saved from when I was growing up, that is, from the 1940s and the 1950s, the Big Band era. Over and over again I would play *Star Dust, Sentimental Journey, Deep Purple, Serenade in Blue, This Love of Mine, To Each His Own, Mood Indigo, I'll Never Smile Again,* and on and on till I was tired and could fall asleep.

By mid-May I was back at work with full energy and probably changed a bit from all these new experiences; I was less in a rush now to prove something. Perhaps, too, I began to value and savor each moment of the day more than I had before my illness. As strange at it might sound, from a spiritual point of view I could sense a mellowing taking place within me and a growing empathy for others that I had not experienced before. What I had perhaps known theoretically I now knew from personally passing through the emotions involved in being a cancer patient. The sabbatical at the beginning of 1996 had been good for the brain, but the prostate illness at the end of that year and into 1997 was good for the soul.

*   *   *

A new millennium was coming; newspapers, magazines, television were full of information about the approaching year 2000. Some religious fanatics predictably were expecting the end of the world and preparing for it. Other people were more concerned about the malfunctioning of computer systems in the United States, especially for air travel and commerce. My sabbatical and bout with prostrate cancer were my remote preparation for the celebration of the new millennium and my approach was one of gratitude. I expected to reach that new millennium and experience the excitement it would bring. I was also planning for the future, for the Church, for the archdiocese, and for myself; the millennium would not be a singular event to be lived through, after which life would resume its normal trajectory. Living into a new millennium offered a singular opportunity for reflection and spiritual growth.

In these preparations I found myself in tune with the pope who, for the Catholic Church, wisely tried to place the emphasis on spiritual renewal. As early as 1994, he had sent out a document, *Tertio millennio adveniente,* to begin preparations for the year 2000. Publishing this document early could forestall the predictions of some religious groups that the world would end in 2000. It placed the emphasis instead on positive planning for the new century. The pope also announced special synods of bishops for each continent as one way to prepare for moving the Church into the future. These synods were to emphasize local needs and not just those of the Universal Church. Such special synods had been held in 1991 on the Church in Europe and in 1994 on the Church in Africa; these were to continue with synods for all the continents.

I was especially intrigued by his idea of a synod among bishops of North and South America planned for the fall of 1997. He spoke of a New Evangelization for both hemispheres, even though their Christian origins and history were very different. The pope emphasized two specific issues under the broader label of evangelization: "justice and international economic relations, in view of the enormous gap between the North and the South" (#38). According to the statutes drawn up for this special meeting, the U.S. Conference of Bishops was permitted to send fifteen delegates. When I was elected by the U.S. bishops to be a part of that group, I broke my firm resolution never to attend another synod and accepted the invitation.

Rather than reside on the Janiculum Hill at the North American College with most of the U.S. bishops, I chose to stay at the Domus Sanctae Marthae, a newly constructed "hotel" built within the Vatican walls for the conclaves of cardinals who would be electing future popes. It lies on the left-hand side of St. Peter's as one faces the basilica, a short distance behind the papal audience hall constructed during the pontificate of Pope Paul VI according to a design by Pier Luigi Nervi. Nervi included a smaller auditorium on the second floor specifically for such meetings as synods and furnished it with the latest equipment for simultaneous translations. That building, in turn, opened onto a small square formed by the walls of the Holy Office on one side and Vatican offices on the other. That square is easily accessible and now forms one of the busiest entrances to the Vatican.

Domus Sanctae Marthae provided a convenient place to stay for meetings in the Nervi hall. Moreover, most of the bishops staying there were from Central and South America, from Haiti and the Caribbean. The food was exceptionally good and I made a point of eating with different bishops each lunch to get a better feel for the national groups. I especially gravitated to the shy bishops from Haiti who lived and worked under such difficult circumstances and who felt most at ease speaking in French rather than Spanish or English. Living there also gave me a chance to talk with Bishop Grullón of San Juan de la Maguana, the diocese in the Dominican Republic where priests from Milwaukee served. A few other American bishops had made the same choice so I was not isolated from them.

The chapel in which we concelebrated each morning was modern and well designed. That Mass was always in Latin to accommodate so many different languages and cultures. But only a few of us older bishops were able to be the principal celebrant in Latin. I was especially surprised that the new and younger South American bishops were the least comfortable, many saying they had never studied Latin and had never celebrated Mass in that language. One day a younger bishop tried to do so, but he had no idea what he was saying, pronouncing each word as if it were Spanish and missing the proper phrasing of the words. It was painful for him and for us.

The synod of 1997 began on November 17 and ended on December 13 — not the best season for Rome, and we had more than the usual amount of cold rain. I was glad to have only a short walk to and from each morning and again each afternoon. But evenings out presented a challenge that I had not expected.

A few days after I arrived I went out to dinner in Trastevere with two priests from Milwaukee who were staying at the North American College during their sabbatical. No one begins a meal in Rome before 8:00 p.m., and it always goes on for a few hours. We finished after 10:00. It had started to rain heavily and we hailed a cab. The plan was to drop me off first at the entrance near the Holy Office on the left of the basilica and then for the cab to continue up the hill to the North American College.

When I got out of the cab, I realized there were no lights, no guard, and the gate was tightly locked. The cab had left. I tried to find shelter under the Bernini columns that encircled the square, but found the entrance to them was also barricaded. At first I was going to climb over the lowest section of the barricade to the colonnade, but after a fruitless try, changed my mind. I made my way around the colonnade, being continually splashed by the fast moving traffic, till I came to the end of the colonnade only to find the entrance to the whole square in front of St. Peter's blockaded with high wooden trestles tied together. I continued walking along the barricades that closed off the square till I came to Bernini's colonnade on the right-hand side of St. Peter's Square. The colonnade there being blocked I walked on along the wall of the Swiss guards' building for a hundred yards or so till I reached another entrance to the Vatican, the Porta Sant'Anna.

There the Swiss guard on duty took pity on me. First, he explained that the Italian police had taken over responsibility for security of the whole Vatican property at night. At 10:00 p.m. they put up barricades to prevent anyone from entering. Then, he instructed me how to break in! I had to return to the square of St. Peter's and there I would find, toward the middle, a spot where two trestles met, one of which I could move and slide through sideways. Since I was already soaked, more walking in the rain did not matter much.

I returned the way I came, testing each link in the barricade until I found the one that was not tied, and slid in. My shoes now soaked had leather soles and presented a new problem. I struggled to walk up the cobblestone square, slipping and staggering like a drunk, hoping and praying I would not fall. Twice I glanced to the right at the façade of the papal palace to see if there were still lights in the pope's rooms on the top floor (could I call out?), but saw none. When I finally arrived at the Arco delle Campane, a Swiss guard suddenly emerged having received a phone call from his confrere on the other side. He led me through an underground passage that I did not know existed for the short distance to the Domus Sanctae Marthae.

When I asked how, in the future, I should enter the Vatican at night, he patiently explained that it was best to tell the cabbie to enter by the Porta Sant'Anna. There the guards are accustomed to showing the drivers how to circle behind St. Peter's and reach the Domus. The guards know approximately how many minutes that trip will take by cab and thus when to expect the cabbie's return. I entered that way a few times in the following weeks, and it worked. Fortunately the cardinals gathered for a conclave are sequestered and not allowed out for evening meals; they'd never have to figure out how to "break into" the Vatican. I should have seen that disadvantage in staying at the Domus. More significantly, I realized how long it had been since I lived in Rome. Once I had been more of an "insider" and would have known how to get into the Vatican — even at night. Now, I was an "outsider."

*　　*　　*

The synod for America received little notice, even in U.S. Catholic newspapers. It was overshadowed by another event. The evening before the opening session, several cardinals of the curia and their staffs held a press conference presenting a new document signed by eight cardinals, prefects of different curial offices. No precedent existed for such a large number of signatures, and the purpose was certainly to give as much weight as possible to the document. Although it had been signed August 15, it had not been promulgated till the day before the synod opened. The message bore the complex title: "Instruction on Certain Questions Regarding the Collaboration of the Non-Ordained Faithful in the Sacred Ministry of Priests." The substance of the document was to reiterate the essential difference between the priesthood of the faithful and the ordained priesthood and to draw clearly demarcated boundaries for lay ministry in the Church so that it would not encroach on the role of priests.

Among the members of the bishops gathered at the synod the question was asked: Why now? How will this document influence our deliberations? In many ways, it was a greater challenge to some of the South American bishops who had few priests and had divided their parishes into barrios with lay leaders in charge of each. They also relied very heavily on lay catechists. It was too soon for the U.S. bishops to understand the import of the document, but it was clear that no one would dare rise on the floor of the synod to propose expanding lay ministry as a solution to the shortage of priests, even as a temporary, emergency solution. This press conference made the headlines of every Catholic newspaper and periodical and little was said about the opening of the synod.

At first I was disturbed by the title given the synod, *Ecclesia in America,* since the use of the singular presupposed that North and South America formed one continent. For us Americans this is not the way we count the continents, but some Europeans, including Italians, do consider the two Americas as one continent. The pope had noted this discrepancy in his 1994 document when he first mentioned the possibility of this synod, saying it was a synod for the Americas (in the plural) and also noting that the Christian origins of the two hemispheres were different.

I had hoped this synod would be a smaller and thus allow for more in-depth discussion; I was wrong. There were 300 total participants, 236 bishops with the right to speak and vote. As usual, for several weeks we had to listen to an eight-minute talk from each bishop and from chosen observers, bringing the number or speeches to 253, and once again the preparatory material was poor. Rome has an allergy toward any kind of sociological survey of the Church and the issues it faces. Thus, no thorough scientific studies were made beforehand.

One of the short talks that held my attention was given by then Archbishop Francis George of Chicago. The first part of it could easily have been the basis for a lengthy in-depth discussion, but it passed by without much attention. Working with the notes I took and now re-reading his intervention, I see that Archbishop George — in eight minutes — succinctly pointed out the differences between the first evangelization of the northern hemisphere compared to that of the southern. The Catholic immigrants to the United States in the nineteenth century, he observed, came into a religious culture that was predominantly Calvinist, one in which they were a minority and never felt totally at home, but one that has left a lasting impression on the whole of U.S. culture. (His words that the U.S. citizens are "culturally Calvinist" continued to run through my head for days. I made a note to seek out authors who may have studied how much Calvinism remains in American civil religion.) George admitted that the religious origins of Canada were more diversified, giving it a unique set of traditions.

The evangelization in the southern hemisphere, he reminded us, was done by the European colonial powers, especially Spain and Portugal, which created a culture that till some decades ago seemed solidly Catholic. Today it is experiencing changes that come from Pentecostal and other recently founded Protestant Evangelical groups that have made their way from the United States to the South. At the same time, the many immigrants from South to North, legal and illegal, are changing the face of Catholicism in the States. He noted the difficulties Latinos must confront in this new U.S. culture where they are a minority (Hispanics) within a minority (Catholics) and the temptation among the Latino professionals toward secularization.

I found his analysis fascinating and wished we could have analyzed these differences to understand in greater detail what was really happening at the grass roots. His intervention changed my way of thinking. At first, I doubted if there would be much to talk about between the two hemispheres because of the differences in our historical roots. I now realized that our future as churches was totally intertwined, a mixture that would be something new. The Latino culture had much to bring to us at this point while we had a duty to help them think out in their own countries how to relate to the newly created American religious phenomena entering their previously Catholic cultures.

My own eight-minute intervention was a plea for a vision. I saw globalization as a positive moment for the Church, a *kairos,* given that we already, by being Catholic (with a large or small "c"), had a sense of a universal church and an organizational structure that was itself global. I outlined certain values I thought the Catholic Church could bring to that emerging global culture, but without having the time to elaborate on any of them. These included such basic concepts as the dignity of every human person on this planet at all stages of life; action for the stability of the family in the light of the divorce rate and the frequency of cohabitation; a plea for the rightful role of women in all aspects of social, political, and ecclesial life; opportunities for remunerative work for all that went beyond national boundaries; greater emphasis on human development through education; and concern for ecology and care for this earth.

I listened carefully to the interventions from South American bishops. Naturally the whole issue of liberation theology, having been severely criticized by Cardinal Ratzinger in two separate instructions (1984 and 1986), was avoided with just passing references to the value of the "comunidades de base." Although several proponents of American neoconservative economic theories and the positive values of capitalism tried to get their opinions accepted, they were rejected by South Americans as being "neoliberal." Much to my dismay there was almost no mention of the drug-trafficking problems in both hemispheres and no in-depth analyses of the social issues, especially violence, that drug-trafficking provokes.

Pope John Paul II came to most sessions but did not seem engaged. As often happened with him in those years, his head would nod as if sleeping, but then be raised again as if he had heard something that interested him. Though he usually had a book, I seldom saw him turn a page.

After a summary of all the speeches, we were put into language groups for discussions on the major points. I was elected to chair one of the three English-speaking groups. For the first time at a synod there was no group for the Latin language! After these discussions were synthesized, we returned to the language groups to work on propositions we wanted in the final draft of the document to be produced by the pope and his staff. The propositions from all the groups were brought together and voted on by the body, an indication of how much support each one received. Finally, in January 1999, over a year later, the pope's reflections on that synod and the discussions appeared in a rambling and repetitive document entitled *Ecclesia in America* that broke no new ground and satisfied very few.

As much as I was engaged in the workings of this synod and as interested as I was in the issues, I was regularly distracted by phone calls from Milwaukee's archdiocesan lawyer. He had to call me frequently about the Marcoux matter: the demands for money, encounters with Marcoux's lawyers, meeting with the district attorney, and so on. The letter I had written to Marcoux in 1979 (see Chapter 1) was back in play: he wanted to sell it to me for a million dollars. As a result, I was not sleeping well, and at one point, the diocesan lawyer was sufficiently concerned that he suggested Bishop Sklba fly over to be with me. This seemed unnecessary. But it is true that I was distraught; it was as close as I had ever come at any time in my life to cracking physically and emotionally. Fortunately I had to chair one of the groups, and that forced me to concentrate on the material and issues at hand.

Needing someone to talk to, I went to see an old, retired, highly-respected Italian priest-canonist in Rome who had worked in the curia his whole life and whom I knew casually from my years there. He was living now in a house of his order surrounded by his books and supportive confreres. Naturally we had to talk a bit about "the good old days" before more serious topics could be broached. I presented to him the outline of my problem. At the time, I was weighing whether I should resign as archbishop and fight Marcoux's accusations in the open or stay on and try to resolve the situation quietly. I knew a public fight would damage my reputation, but it seemed the only way to put an end to it. This old priest disagreed. He felt the "Roman" way of handling such matters, "for preserving the good name of the Church," was to take the more discreet option of reaching an agreement with Marcoux.

*   *   *

In May 1998, just five months later, I was back in Rome again, this time for the customary *ad limina* visit. As requested, six months before making the trip, even before I had gone over for the synod for America, I had responded in writing to a detailed questionnaire from the curia. Most of my remarks centered on the shortage of priests and I ended my observations by saying: "As can be gathered from what I have written here, I feel that this is an important moment for the church in the United States. . . . I expect that the moment will be lost in arguing over unimportant matters and that the future does not look bright. I fear, most of all, that the vitality of the church in the United States — that I now see diminishing — will disappear (as it did in the Dutch church) and give place to a greater indifferentism and personalism, so that the church will be more and more marginalized in American culture."

What I wrote at the end of 1997 still rings true to me. As I re-read it, I sense that it was a cry from the heart, stemming both from frustration and anxiety. I had no idea which Vatican offices would read this section of the report, but I felt better having written it, even if it sounded alarming and pessimistic. During the visits to the various curial offices during my *ad limina* visit, not one person in any office brought up my report to discuss the points raised or even to refute them.

This was my last *ad limina* visit, and I had few expectations. There was the usual phone call from Cardinal Gantin asking that I come the next day to see him. He said that Cardinal Ratzinger would be with him for the meeting; this surprised me since I had done little to provoke Rome. I had been engaged in dialogues with the Orthodox and in my local church and I had not to my knowledge provoked the curia in any major way. At the meeting Cardinal Ratzinger did most of the talking. He stated that, for the most part, the difficulties raised in Rome about me were not primarily questions concerning my teaching as such — thus not a matter that pertained to his congregation — but were rather a question of my attitude. In fact, he said, since 1992 little if anything new had been added to my file in his office.

I tried to explain to the cardinals my concept of collegiality, of the role of a local bishop, and of the conferences of bishops. I expressed concern over the urgency of certain problems that we were facing in our country and that we were not being given adequate freedom as a local Church to solve, for example, the sex-abuse cases, the shortage of priests, the role of women, the language of our liturgy, and so on. It was clear to me that both were uneasy with the vagueness of the accusations against me. What it boiled down to, as Cardinal Ratzinger said, was my lack of "docility."

As I entered the papal library for my private audience, the archbishop exiting mentioned that he was not sure the pope had really understood anything he said. The pope's health had deteriorated perceptibly. There were very few points I wanted to make and did so rather rapidly, spending only a short time with him. I was not sure he had understood what I was saying. Among other things, I mentioned having had prostate cancer two years before. There was no reaction from him.

As I was leaving, he suddenly asked me out of thin air: "How old are you now?" When I replied: "Seventy-one," he did not look me in the eye but, with bowed head and expressionless face (caused by his medication for Parkinson's disease), just gave a low, indistinct grumble. I interpreted it — rightly or wrongly — as a way of saying, "I guess I still have to tolerate you for four more years." Later he mentioned to a priest from Milwaukee who worked in the papal offices that, till my visit that morning, he had not known of my cancer. He had heard more than I assumed!

On my way home from this trip, I confess that I was still very confused. Again, the pope did not want to deal personally with any complaints. Yet, I asked myself: Who had initiated the meeting with the two cardinals?

There had been a curious happening three days before this *ad limina* visit. The pope had signed a document called *Apostolos suos* on the teaching authority enjoyed by bishops' conferences. That document had been shelved ten years earlier (see pages 317-18) and now it had been revived. The conditions under which a conference could produce a teaching document were so impossible to fulfill that it became clear that Rome would decide everything that seriously affected the Catholic Church in the United States and around the world. The centralization process was complete.

*   *   *

The documents concerning the millennium coming from Rome made it a jubilee year of reconciliation. I appreciated this attitude and made it my own. Jubilee years, based on the concept in Hebrew scripture of letting the land lie fallow every fifty years and then returning it to its original owner, had been celebrated in the Church since 1300. It was a way — patently artificial, I knew — of pointing out the need people have at special times in their lives of being able to begin again on a level playing field. Even though this idealistic idea of a jubilee year was never consistently practiced even among the Jews of old, the concept behind it still has a universal appeal. I

felt attitudes like forgiveness, reconciliation, and restoration should belong in every religious body.

In Milwaukee, it was proposed that we make the Eucharist the focal
point around which the local faith communities would gather. We planned
to end the year with an archdiocesan Eucharistic Congress. With this in
mind, I asked Bishop Sklba to help me write a pastoral letter called *Eucharist without Walls*. (As I re-read this now, I think the title is probably the
best part of it.) One of the perennial temptations for the Church — and unfortunately most religious bodies — is to become inward-looking. The emphasis on social justice is an antidote against such a sectarian tendency.
At a mini-Eucharistic congress with 7,500 participants from all over the
archdiocese in October 2000, I explained the phrase "Eucharist without
Walls." It meant the Eucharist without boundaries, without the walls of
time, without the walls of space, without the walls of specific persons,
races, or nations. It meant that Jesus was present, is present, will be present to the faithful until the end of time.

The jubilee year presented two specific tasks. The first involved emphasizing the importance of pilgrimages, and I made two, one with the
priests of the archdiocese to the holy places of France in 1999, and one with
Catholic and Orthodox bishops to Mount Athos in Greece in the year 2000.
The second task was to seek reconciliation with those religious groups
from which we were estranged. The most important event in that effort
was a meeting with the Jewish community of Milwaukee, an event of importance to me and, as it turned out, to all those who attended.

Making a pilgrimage has been an important part of the jubilee year in
the Catholic tradition. Centuries ago, it meant a long journey with many
physical sacrifices to popular shrines, but especially to Rome and its four
major basilicas. Though we Americans readily run marathons, we never
seem to grasp the religious aspect of a pilgrimage. A pilgrimage was the
church in miniature: all the pilgrims strove together for a common goal,
making many sacrifices on the way, suffering for and with one another,
praying together and individually along the way, yearning for places of re-
freshment and repose, all the while telling stories and sharing wisdom.
Life itself has often been called our earthly pilgrimage on our way to the
dwelling place Christ said he had prepared for us.

The pilgrimage with forty some priests of the archdiocese was
planned for September 29, 1999, around the fiftieth anniversary of my solemn profession as a Benedictine monk. Since I had pronounced those
vows at the abbey of Solesmes in France, the possibility of renewing them

in the very same place appealed to me. Our first stop was Annecy near the border of Switzerland and the diocesan see of St. Francis De Sales, patron of our seminary. Then to Avignon, Arles, Tours, Solesmes, Mont Saint Michel, Omaha Beach, Lisieux, Rouen, and Paris, ending the trip with a Mass at the tomb of St. Vincent de Paul. We were graciously received at Solesmes and the ritual of renewing my vows had special meaning. In addition to Solesmes, one of the more touching visits was to the cemetery at Omaha Beach. Some priests were in tears as they recalled friends and relatives who were buried there. I felt that I was in a gigantic open-air cathedral where people I had never known but respected and loved were buried, it evoked my Catholic instinct to see the Communion of Saints everywhere.

This pilgrimage was wonderfully satisfying; I now understood how pilgrimages helped people to bond in their sharing a common experience. I came to know some of the priests better, and I am sure, they had a few new insights into me. Afterwards each of us had many stories to tell. (My love for pilgrimages might explain why I love Chaucer so much and find his writings so "catholic.") After returning home, I felt renewed in spirit and ready to face the future with equanimity.

*   *   *

The second pilgrimage took place during the jubilee year itself: I led a small group of six Orthodox and Roman Catholic bishops to visit some of the monasteries on Mount Athos. Athos is a rugged peninsula jutting out from Northern Greece; it is thirty-five miles long and, as the bird flies, about four miles wide. The mountain rises to 7,000 feet and looks like an arthritic finger. About 2,000 Orthodox monks live on the mountain in twenty independent monasteries and many priories (sketes). After I had been sent to Istanbul in 1975 by Pope Paul VI, my desire to visit these monasteries had intensified. The last thing Patriarch Dimitrios said to me when I left Istanbul was he hoped that I would be able some day to visit the monks on Mount Athos, and, perhaps, God willing, begin a dialogue among monks of the East and the West. I had never been able to fulfill that desire, but I never forgot it.

In 2000 much was happening on that Holy Mountain because of the millions of dollars being poured into its development by the European Union. The many chapels were being renovated, the icons cleaned and repaired, the libraries catalogued and properly humidified, the guest-rooms redone and modernized. Though the peninsula is only accessible by boat, roads between the monasteries were being constructed. Previously one traveled from monastery to monastery on foot or took a small boat to the base of the hill. On my visit it was a noisy and busy place; the many small harbors were full of mainland workmen coming and going, mixed in with a few traveling monks. (I noticed one with a cell phone!)

We did not have the time to visit all twenty monasteries, but were fortunate in visiting seven of the independent houses, namely, Iviron, Koutloumousiou, Dionysiou, Stavronikita, Pantokrator, Vatopedi, and Panteleimon. Several priories were also on our list.

At first I thought I would not be physically fit enough for the ruggedness of the trip, but I fared as well as some of the others. I dreaded the thought of the steep climbs, and was glad when other solutions were at hand. For example, we arrived by boat at the harbor below the monastery of Dionysiou; to reach the building perched high above us on the cliff the monks provided a tractor that pulled a large wagon. It was a Fellini-esque, sight with the feet of all these men in long black robes and strange headgear dangling over the edge of the wagon as we were hauled up the steep road. If it had broken loose, we would have landed somewhere on the cliff or in the water.

At each stopover we were treated graciously and greeted with raki, something sweet, and a glass of cold water, and each monastery gave us a gift as we departed. Since the monks consider us Catholics *barbari,* or pagans, we were not permitted to pray with them but were kept in the outer narthex where we could hear the singing, interrupted occasionally by the tinkling of the silver chains of the thuribles and the sweet smell of the incense. After a few hours as I would sit there, I began to fall asleep only to be wakened again by the censer-bearers. At least we could sit while our Orthodox brothers had to stand throughout the long ceremonies.

Although the trip was too short to engage in any real dialogue, I was satisfied to have fulfilled one of my deepest desires. And yet, this form of monasticism raised more questions than it answered. Is this what "flight from the world" really means? There were many holy monks there and many saints, but still I was troubled by their isolation. What was its meaning and witness in the contemporary world?

After this pilgrimage to Mount Athos, I would be resigning as co-chair of the dialogues with the Orthodox. They had been a significant part of my life and formative in my thinking about the nature of the Church. In 1979 I had been asked by the president of the bishops' conference to co-chair with Archbishop Iakovos, the Greek Orthodox archbishop of North and South America, the theological dialogue between the Eastern Orthodox Churches in the United States and the Catholic Church. Monasticism, having its origin in the early Church and thus before the split of 1054, was a phenomenon we held in common. I felt a special affinity to the Orthodox: their liturgical tradition was embedded in their identity; their theology was rooted in the "Golden Age" of the patristic period; and their clergy were wholesome and mature. And then, given so many national and ethnic expressions, they were able to maintain the basic unifying characteristics of Orthodoxy itself, and their esteem for the monastic tradition.

Each year, I attended three dialogue sessions with the Orthodox, two with Catholic and Orthodox theologians and scholars and one with Catholic and Orthodox bishops. At first the dialogues touched on practical and pastoral points, but then took up the two most divisive issues, papal primacy and the *filioque* question. We bishops, six to eight on each side, met yearly for an overnight to become acquainted with the theological debates taking place nationally and internationally, but especially to discuss the pastoral implications that any kind of unity among us might imply. It was evident that the major pastoral concern centered on maintaining our distinctive identities in a pluralistic society like the United States.

The pilgrimage to Mount Athos with the Orthodox bishops was a fitting ending to my official involvement with this ecumenical dialogue. I had done my best to heal the century-old wounds, and hoped and prayed that in the new millennium this work would come to fruition. I certainly did not expect to be alive when a basis for a unified church would be accepted by both Catholics and Orthodox.

*   *   *

In March of 2000, Pope John Paul set the tone for reconciliation during the jubilee year by presiding at a ceremony begging forgiveness for the wrongs the Catholic Church had committed through history — from supporting slavery to the practices of the Inquisition. Some officials in Rome thought he was unwise to admit that the Church had been wrong in so many cases, but it was refreshing to hear him apologize, and I applauded his decision.

In the archdiocese of Milwaukee, we also worked on reconciliation with the Jewish community. On November 7, 1999, the Milwaukee Catholic-Jewish conference sponsored a joint prayer service in Congregation Shalom Synagogue to mark the twenty-fifth anniversary of our dialogues. I had

393

the honor of preaching. As I looked out from the bema over all the Jews and Catholics present, I realized that I knew almost all of them personally, had interacted with them over the past twenty some years, and felt totally "at home." I explained our Catholic interpretation of a jubilee year, the conversion we hoped the year would bring in our hearts, the importance of asking for forgiveness and seeking reconciliation so that we would be different people to begin a new millennium.

I apologized for the hurtful and harmful statements against the Jewish people throughout the centuries — statements that implied that they were no longer loved by God, that God had abandoned them, that they were guilty of deicide, and that they were being punished by God. I asked forgiveness for all the teaching and preaching that may have led to the holocaust and may have indirectly contributed to the horrors of genocide. I was thinking in particular of St. Augustine's "theology of contempt," namely, that the Jews, for refusing to accept Christ, were constantly being punished by God as an example to all of us were we to follow in their path. Finally, I asked for forgiveness if Catholics in any way in the city of Milwaukee contributed in the past to those movements that denigrate Jews and threatened their well-being in our midst. To all these statements the Catholics present answered "Amen."

As I looked out into the congregation, I noticed tears in many eyes — of Jews and Catholics alike. I summed up our hopes, saying I believed that the God we both worship would not be divided by our human hatreds; that God will not go back on his word and reject a covenant; that we have to change our attitudes toward one another because we are all created in the image and likeness of the one God; that we must not see each other as rivals before the one God but as brothers and sisters in that one God's unique and living love. Again the "Amens" roared.

Finally I urged all those present to move forward together to try to heal the world, to seek the intrinsic worth of all people on this globe independent of their race or religious beliefs. We had to work together to reverse the Cain-syndrome that has haunted the human race from time immemorial, accepting that we are responsible for one another's well-being on this planet, that we are willing to be the voice of the voiceless, that we would strive to reach out to others in need through works of charity, so that when anyone hurts we all hurt. After these statements the "Amens" truly filled the hall as one voice. From my vantage point I could see many of the people hug each other, Catholic and Jews alike — a kiss of peace.

The office of the bishops' conference for dialogue with the Jews sent this talk to all the U.S. bishops advising that it could serve as a model for those who had a desire to organize such a reconciliation service. Many bishops wrote to say they had used it. Tears well up in my eyes, as I write about this service and its aftermath. I feel that God used me on that occasion; I spoke from my heart and went beyond my rhetorical abilities. I understood that such a deeply prayerful gathering was only possible after twenty-five years of dialogue in which we have come to know and trust each other as friends.

We closed the jubilee year in November 2000 before the Advent liturgies began. Was the jubilee year a success? Certainly a partial one. But many groups alienated from the Church did not find reconciliation. Some voices were raised asking that Rome, in the spirit of the jubilee year, grant a dispensation for all marriages that needed to be regularized; that permission be given to all dioceses to have a general absolution granted to whomever wished it; that there be a gathering with gay and lesbian Catholics; and so on. None of these took place. But for those who found themselves inspired to enter into the jubilee year with faith, even with its limitations, it was a rewarding experience and a way of starting the millennium with a positive attitude.

*   *   *

At the beginning of 2002, the archdiocesan Catholic newspaper reported that the renovation of the Cathedral of St. John the Evangelist received more press notice during 2001 than any other event. And so it did.

Sometime toward the end of the 1990s, Father John Endejan, the amiable and well-loved cathedral rector, came to discuss the state of the cathedral building and its needs, from painting the inside and redoing all the wiring, heating and air-conditioning, to cleaning the soft cream-city brick and painting the outside. My instinctive sense was that the old church needed more than cosmetic changes, and suggested that perhaps it was time to look at all the cathedral buildings. The old grade-school and high-school buildings were in moth balls; the large gym and the nuns' convent had been rented out, but those leases were soon to terminate. Three-quarters of the cathedral block would soon be empty, just boarded-up buildings.

There was another reason to look at the whole block. Downtown Milwaukee was undergoing a vital renaissance. New apartment houses and condos were going up. The art museum was attracting national attention.

395

The expansion of the lakeshore frontage and other projects meant a renewed interest in the downtown area and its revitalization. We had to think about the cathedral and its historical importance in the heart of the city. The cathedral could still boast of being a vital parish with a specific downtown outreach. The poor came there each day at noon for something to eat, but, even in the coldest weather, found no place to sit down and get warm. They received their sandwich at the door and went back into the cold.

The original cathedral, built around 1855, had suffered a disastrous fire in 1935 and the whole roof had caved in. The archbishop at the time, Samuel Stritch, decided to work out plans for restoring it, but did not have the money because of the Depression. His successor, Archbishop Moses Elias Kiley, rebuilt the cathedral and rededicated it in 1942. In that renovation, two rows of steel pillars were inserted, cutting the broad expanse of the original church into a main aisle with two darkened side aisles. A new apse with nine steps to reach the main altar was added. Over that main altar, Bishop Kiley had placed a large baldachin imported from Italy. Some of its supportive marble columns had been damaged in shipping and steel bands were applied to hold the pieces of the columns together. The back of the baldachin facing the wall had been left unfinished.

The building remained that way until another renovation was undertaken in 1975. A second marble altar was installed in front of the altar of reservation; this arrangement meant that the priest was always saying Mass with his back to the Blessed Sacrament. Moreover, the renovation of 1975 used many different colors of paint on the walls and ceiling, some twenty in all. The renovations of 1942 had diminished the seating capacity of the cathedral; it could hold only 750 people. One of my hopes was to enlarge that capacity.

The cathedral parish council agreed that we should think in bigger terms and organized many committees. Father Richard Vosko was brought in as liturgical consultant, Jim Shields was selected as the architect, and fund-raising begun in earnest. All kinds of creative ideas were explored. Some rubbings were made and the original colors emerged: the tops of the columns had been gilded and the vaulting had been a rust color that contrasted with the gold. We decided to return to those colors. Not all the parishioners liked the idea of making changes, feeling a paint job would have been just fine. Once the planning started in earnest, however, more and more people came to see the wisdom of renovating both the cathedral building and the whole cathedral block. The engineers told us that the newer high-school building was the least solid, but the older grade-school building was worth retaining. We tore down the high school, made a little meditation park where the buildings had stood, and, retaining the original idea of a nineteenth-century European square, built a garden wall perforated with large openings so that the garden inside could be seen from the street. The old grade-school building became the parish offices, the center for feeding the poor, and the meeting rooms for AA and other social concerns groups. The former convent was turned into an assessment center for homeless women and children.

My profoundest wish was that the worship space would be adjacent to a gathering area and that there would be room for feeding the poor in a proper setting. By adding an atrium to the side of the church that connected the cathedral to the new outreach center, that purpose was worked out to perfection. Worship flowed naturally into outreach.

The entire design was presented to the public in August of 2000. A few protest letters came in, especially from people who were not cathedral parishioners. Moving the altar forward was one concern in the complaint letters, though it was just a few feet from the placement in the original church. The greatest disagreement centered on placing the altar of repose in the elegant domed area originally built for the baptistery but no longer used as such. I answered all letters with patience. The total costs were estimated to be about eleven million dollars, five million for the cathedral building and the rest for the remaining demolition and reconstruction. Twice I presented the project and plans to the archdiocesan council of priests for a vote and each time the result was twenty-four yes and one no. I presented them to the finance council and the archdiocesan consultors for their okay. In January, 2001, I announced that the cathedral would be closed from May 20, after ordinations, till February of 2002. In mid-April, 2001, I signed the contracts and the construction company began to buy the materials.

Two days after we had closed the cathedral and work had begun, Mr. Alan Kershaw, an American canon lawyer resident in Rome hired by Catholics United for the Faith, presented to four offices of the curia denunciations against me and petitioned that work on the cathedral renovation be halted. The congregation for bishops sent the letter they received on to the congregation for worship stating that the latter was the competent office for handling this matter. I never saw a copy of that denunciation. Another was sent to the congregation for the clergy, which immediately sent me a copy and asked for my response. I was being accused of closing parishes to get money to finance this project. It was easy to prove the contrary and

397

that congregation wrote to Mr. Kershaw stating that, after examining the case, they saw no signs of any illegal actions.

A third denunciation was sent by Mr. Kershaw to the pontifical commission for the cultural heritage of the church, which sent me a copy of the denunciation and asked for all the pertinent material. The major complaint to that office centered on the destruction of the baldachin. This office sided with me in stating that the baldachin had no artistic value and that I had acted perfectly within my jurisdiction in deciding that it could be taken down.

Finally, a copy was also sent to the congregation for worship. I have never seen that copy since they refused to share it with me. Without consulting me, they wrote to Mr. Kershaw saying that, at first glance, it looked as if canonical and liturgical norms had been broken. To my surprise I read that letter in the local press since Mr. Kershaw had e-mailed a copy to the local CUF leaders. The congregation for worship also sent to Mr. Kershaw a copy of a letter they were sending me asking for detailed information and requesting me to stop the work. Again, before receiving the congregation's letter, I read it in the local press. This was a curious way of proceeding, since Rome, even if it disagrees with someone, always follows the proper formalities. I refused to stop the work without a hearing; with the project that far along, this would have involved breaking the contract with the loss of several million dollars.

At the advice of Archbishop Gabriel Montalvo, the papal nuncio in Washington, I went to Rome at once to speak personally with Cardinal Jorge Medina, prefect of that congregation. In these last years as bishop, I was often in touch often with Archbishop Montalvo. He was a consummate diplomat, always gracious and helpful. I could not have handled this matter without his quiet advice and support. The meeting with Cardinal Medina in Rome took place in his formal conference room; many members of his staff were present. Bishop Sklba came with me. I arrived with a binder for the cardinal containing all the information he could ever have wished for, together with all supporting canonical and liturgical backup. He seemed oblivious to the lack of proper protocol in having sent letters addressed to me first to Mr. Kershaw so that they appeared in public before I saw them; he was also insensitive, almost flippant, to any financial losses the archdiocese might suffer. I reminded him that the Vatican norms for building and renovating churches state clearly that the local bishop was the ultimate authority and that none of the issues he raised had any canonical or liturgical import but were matters of taste.

During that meeting I had the feeling he had pronounced me guilty and was now looking for the reasons, given that those he had at first proposed held no weight. As the meeting dragged on, I knew I was getting nowhere. I am not a poker player, but I had the feeling that he wanted to impress me with the fact that he held cards I did not know about. Or perhaps it was just a bullying technique to keep me guessing where he would strike next. I realized that we had come to no understanding when, as I was leaving, he stated that I could expect further word from him.

Having found the meeting unsatisfactory, I went to see a canonist who was accredited to try cases before all the Roman ecclesiastical tribunals, Doctor Martha Wegan, an astute Austrian woman who had lived many years in Rome. After looking over all the material, she assured me I could well bring a case against the cardinal and his office, especially if there was a loss of money should he press his effort to halt work on the cathedral. She expressed her willingness to take the case to the Signatura Apostolica (the highest ecclesiastical court in the Catholic Church). She even prepared the recourse papers in the event I wanted to start the case. I told her I would let her know after returning home and receiving the cardinal's letter. When she tried to obtain copies of the denouncement received by the cardinal from Mr. Kershaw and the minutes of the meeting held in the congregation, she was denied them — contrary to all procedural rules.

Several weeks after returning to Milwaukee I received the awaited letter from Cardinal Medina indicating four points in our plans that contradicted canonical and liturgical law (but not the original ones he had first mentioned). Again a copy had been sent to Mr. Kershaw and appeared in the local press before I received it. The four points the cardinal raised were: (1) the Blessed Sacrament chapel was too small; (2) there were only two confessionals; (3) the organ encasement was too big; and (4) artwork was being destroyed. Several canonists around the country who on my request examined the letter said it had no force in law, so I called Archbishop Montalvo, the papal nuncio, to state that I would not halt the work and that it would continue. He simply stated he understood and would inform Rome of my decision.

To this day I am not sure I understand what the real problem was. It could not have been the fact that the Blessed Sacrament was to be kept in a side-chapel, since Medina knew as well as I that this was the custom in almost all cathedrals, including the cathedral of Valparaiso, Chile, where he had been bishop before coming to Rome. The more difficult question was why the cardinal chose to play this scenario out in public. Finally, I came to see it as a show of power. Whenever I met in Rome with Cardinals Gantin or Ratzinger, I always felt I was talking to other bishops and was treated by them with respect as a bishop. This time I had the feeling I was simply being taught, like a schoolboy, a lesson about who really held authority in the Church. Certainly it was not going to be me — a bishop from the hinterland.

I heard from no higher authority in Rome, but, a few months later, sent to the secretary of state a resume of the whole case. In that letter I also said that I had not proceeded with a court case to the Signatura Apostolica, although the project had lost inestimable amounts of money because of the cardinal's public action. His actions made it nearly impossible to raise the rest of the money needed to finish the whole project. Many of those who had pledged donations and many prospective new donors refused to give, saying that "the project did not meet the pope's approval." I chose not to seek legal recourse, even if the Roman canon lawyer and others canonists said the case was a solid one; I knew that the Roman ecclesiastical courts take years to come to a decision. It seems they never learned the proverb: "Justice delayed is justice denied." Before the case would be brought to a conclusion, both Cardinal Medina and I would be retired and concerned about other matters. Instead I simply moved ahead with the project.

Miraculously, the cathedral renovations and the adjacent atrium and office building were completed on time and paid for. Money still had to be raised for the women's assessment center. The cathedral could be rededicated on February 9, 2002. Conrad Schmitt Studios in Milwaukee did all the gilding required and finished on schedule. The construction company, Grunau and Co., worked without delays and with close control of the costs. The corona above the altar was done by a famous Italian sculptor, Arnoldo Pomodoro, and the corpus by Giuseppe Maraniello. These pieces, too, arrived before the re-dedication. At the end we placed in the vestibule of the newly renovated space an inscription that read: "This Cathedral was renovated not without difficulty, exactly according to the norms of liturgical renewal established by Vatican Council II and solemnly and joyously inaugurated and rededicated on Feb. 9, 2002, by the Archbishop and Ordinary Rembert G. Weakland, OSB." Under the high altar we placed the relics of St. John Vianney and St. Francis Xavier to remind us of serving the parish and then going beyond it. One of the most satisfying outcomes was that the capacity had been increased and the cathedral could seat over a 1000 people.

During the months the cathedral was closed for renovation, I celebrated the 8:00 a.m. Sunday Mass in the cafeteria of the gym, which had been altered for temporary usage. At first I thought it would be a sacrifice for the people, but the intimacy of the place had an effect on all of us. I caught myself changing my preaching style to a more conversational one. It also helped to weld the cathedral parishioners into a more unified group. That feeling carried over when they moved back to the larger, but still warm and aesthetically pleasing, atmosphere of the renovated cathedral.

It was a privilege to celebrate Holy Week for the first time in this newly renovated space. After those ceremonies in particular, I knew the renovation fulfilled my deepest expectations. It provided a beautiful space for worship; now one gathers around a glistening white altar and no longer has the impression of praying in a long tunnel. In addition, one experiences the space in the fullness of its width, like the pre-1942 church, from stained-glass windows to stained-glass windows. The removal of the old high-school buildings permits the light to shine through the bluish hues of the windows in all its intensity. Everything — the baptismal font at the entrance, the pulpit, and the central altar with crucifix above that seems to rise through the thorns to the Father like the sacrifice from the altar — seemed right and proper; we had a magnificent, prayerful, and beautiful space in which to experience, as a worshipping community, God's transcendence.

*   *   *

Most of my bishop friends thought I should have gone directly to the pope with the problem of the cathedral renovation and complained about the way I was treated. I decided not to do so, since I was unsure that he was alert enough to handle such matters. It was sad to see him physically deteriorate before the public eye and I did not want to add to his concerns. I also feared he might hand the matter over to someone else and the discussions would be further protracted. Given the publicity in the newspapers, I did not want to put him, or whomever he would have appointed, in a position of having to countermand openly the work of a senior member of his staff.

Because Pope John Paul II's pontificate was such a long one, he had the opportunity of imposing his vision on the Catholic Church as it entered the twenty-first century. He did so forcefully and without flinching. Even in his weakened condition, he continued to give the appearance of being in charge and taking the Church in the direction he wanted. As an outsider, I was never certain how effective his personal involvement was in his last years. I have reflected long about the difficulties under which I labored as a bishop during his pontificate. I have tried to analyze, as best I can, how, as the bishop of a local church, I related to him. Just as I spent ten years in Rome as abbot primate of the Benedictines during the pontificate of Pope Paul VI, so twenty-four of the twenty-five years I was bishop took place during the pontificate of Pope John Paul II. From the very beginning of his pontificate, I found myself increasingly at odds with his highly centralized government, while trying to remain true to myself and honest in my dealings with him and the curia. My stance could not have been called one of loyal opposition; that was a concept totally foreign to the Roman scene. In writing about his pontificate, I realize the delicacy of the subject; I do not want to commit an injustice to his memory, but I cannot tell my story without expressing my attitudes and convictions, positive and negative, toward that overly long and, at times, burdensome pontificate.

My first reaction to the election of Cardinal Wojtyła was enthusiastic. Having met him many times when I was abbot primate of the Benedictines, I had come to hold him in great esteem. I felt that he would bring a healing attitude to the Church because of his personal sufferings and hardships during oppressive times. I never lessened in my esteem for his talents and gifts, even if, through the years, I felt his style and his way of handling a global Church of a billion people was oppressive itself and far too centered on his own person. As the years flowed on, I became more and more disappointed; many of the hopes I held at the beginning of his pontificate were never fulfilled.

He was, beyond doubt, a very holy man, worthy of being officially recognized by the Church. He was filled with the capacity for world leadership. While it seemed that the Catholic Church was becoming less and less meaningful on the world stage, he was able to carve out a niche that showed his personal magnetism and strength of will. His election came at just the right moment in history. He understood Communism and knew how to combat it. One can truly say that the positive events leading to freedom in his native Poland could never have happened without him. That such a revolution happened without bloodshed was a miracle.

In addition, he furthered the development of Catholic social teaching through his encyclicals and novel approaches — from the creative and innovative *Laborem exercens* (1981) to the less confrontational *Centesimus*

annus (1991). His critiques of capitalism will remain one of his lasting lega-
cies. I was disappointed only with the realization that he did not write a
letter on the 110th anniversary of Pope Leo XIII's *Rerum novarum* in 2001 as
an attempt to apply his teaching to a whole new international and
intercultural world. The globalization foreseen by Pope John XXIII was
now a reality and in need of a solid set of governing ethical principles.

In addition, his support for ecumenism and interfaith dialogue was
unbending and genuine. In the spirit of Vatican II and its documents, he
sought to work toward the healing of the wounds of the Reformation and
especially the ruptures with the Orthodox Churches that dated back to the
eleventh century. In such dialogues he seemed to be able to leave many issues unresolved and still seek to move ahead toward some kind of unity.
For example, in the dialogue with the Orthodox Churches he never raised
the question of their practice of tolerating second and third marriages.
Nor did he ask what their teachings were — if any — regarding contraception, issues on which, within the Catholic Church, he maintained a rigid
position. He also opened up new directions in our relationship to the Jewish community by his recognition that God's first covenant with the Jewish
people was never abrogated, since God never goes back on His word, but
he did this without resolving the Catholic position that all salvation comes
through Jesus Christ. In all of this he was most faithful to the wishes of the
bishops at Vatican II and was not swayed by the criticism of many in the
Church who saw ecumenism and interfaith dialogue as weakening Catholic identity.

With incredible energy and zeal he kept alive a sense that the Catholic
Church should embrace every area and culture of the world. In this respect
he continued the policies of Pope Paul toward internationalization with the
appointment of more and more indigenous clergy as bishops. His trips and
their many speeches remain historical records of an expanding Church that
left Western civilization and the Carolingian Empire behind. On those trips
he seemed to accept the need for the inculturation the Church required to
be global, setting an example by the introduction of native and indigenous
elements into his liturgies. For this we must all be grateful. On the other
hand, he could never give the Church in those nations full liberty to
inculturate the faith the way they might have wished because it would have
led to a married clergy and other changes of discipline.

In my opinion, the negative aspects of his pontificate outweigh the
positive. Although I admired his handling of the Communist menace, he
never seemed to be able to bring the same forceful dynamism to confront

dictatorships on the political right, especially in Central and South America. There, I would hear bishops and people lament that the only place where the Church was allowed to openly confront political injustices was Poland.

Moreover, his rigidity on the question of a married clergy made it almost impossible to take care of the needs of the large Catholic populations of Latin America, thus opening the way for the entrance and rapid expansion of more lay-oriented Pentecostal and Evangelical religious movements from the United States.

My hope that there would be a renewal of theological investigation and a flowering of theological and philosophical inquiry in the Catholic Church, as there had been at Vatican II, never came about. On the contrary, tensions within the body of theologians and between them and the Holy See increased. After a period of time, it became evident that only certain theologians were favored, namely, those who supported a particular, narrower point of view like his own; the rest were shunted aside. It was noticeable that at synods of bishops, e.g., he invited to attend and speak only theologians and observers whose thinking never challenged his own. Dialogue was acceptable outside the Church, but not within it.

Another deeper disappointment was his concept of and approach to human sexuality. Many would say his views were Victorian. It was always surprising, however, how often sexuality came up in his writings. In fact, lay people during his pontificate often complained they were tired of hearing so much about sex and sexual issues from the pulpit, especially from celibate clergy. Because his concept of sexuality was more like that of a stream of water that could be turned on and off at will, he never touched the hearts of those finding life more difficult, psychologically more complicated, and sexually more ambiguous.

Probably the most serious negative aspect of his pontificate was its continually centralizing tendency and distrust of the rest of the Church. In his talks he never denied the collegial role of bishops, but in practice his style went back to that of Pope Pius IX with an exaggerated emphasis on the person of the pope and papal teaching, almost to the exclusion of ideas other than his own. His appointments to leadership positions showed this ultramontanism at work. In fact, the acceptance of his every word as official church doctrine created an unusual atmosphere, not traditionally Catholic if one looks at the long history of the Church, where allegiance to his person and teaching on all levels became synonymous to many with what it meant to be Catholic.

The traditional degrees of certitude that the theological manuals of the past attached to each doctrine — from *de fide definita* through several lesser degrees like *proxima fidei* and *theologice certa* to *pia opinion* — were forgotten, and with the publication of the Catechism of the Catholic Church, they all seemed to be homogenized and became part of official Catholic teaching. I noticed a tendency in the Vatican to call all views contrary to the accepted papal teaching at that time "ideological." That term became ubiquitous as a put-down of any opposing position.

In his administration, John Paul especially emphasized the role of the College of Cardinals. Although it did not exist for the first millennium of the Church, and although it had no roots in scripture or theology, in practice, he gave the college greater importance than the whole body of bishops. He gave it a prominence and influence that did serious damage to the concept of collegiality. Several times when the U.S. Conference of Bishops found itself at an impasse with a curial congregation and the officers of the conference were not able to resolve the difficulty, the U.S. cardinals were asked to make a trip to Rome since "only they would be listened to." If a bishop wanted to be promoted to a new diocese or have someone he was "grooming" moved up, he naturally would go to a cardinal-patron for help. I am afraid that the pope never realized how strange and incongruous it seemed to the contemporary Western mind to appoint as cardinals those who agreed with his positions and then make them into his chief counselors and advisors. In that way, he deprived himself of hearing different points of view that may have been helpful to him and the Church. The curia quickly realized this situation and acted accordingly, treating cardinals with deference.

In addition, I was disappointed that the pope and the curia under him did not base their pastoral decisions on thorough research. With his scholarly background, I had hoped he would see the need to be sure that his analysis of a situation was correct before proposing a pastoral solution. I always had the impression that more credence was given to letters reaffirming preconceived notions than to valid sociological studies. Over and over again I felt his decisions and those of his collaborators were made on the basis of anecdote, hearsay, complaint letters, and unverified press reports.

For example, whenever I would visit Rome, especially on *ad limina* trips, I noticed it was taken for granted that the decline in vocations to the priesthood was due to the blurred lines between the roles of the clergy and that of the laity with the usurpation by the laity of powers reserved to the priests. In accepting this explanation, it was not necessary to consider if perhaps the real problem was celibacy and the fear of young people in accepting such a life-long commitment. Or perhaps the reason went even deeper. How much has Catholic tradition in the States been tainted by the common American religious virus that religion is a private matter "between me and God" and there is no need for intermediaries? Has the Catholic tradition that God works through people, especially through specific signs and symbolic acts performed by the ordained with the gathered community, been totally eroded through the privatization of religion? Is that why there has been a drop in confessions and Sunday Mass participation? Investigation at these deeper levels just does not take place.

In the issuing of new liturgical norms there was an unwritten presumption that there had been a loss of belief in the Real Presence, even though the results of the polls had been mixed and confusing, both in the way questions were formulated and in the responses. As a result, a return to older devotional practices of adoration was encouraged. On the other hand, no one asked why the Orthodox Churches, which have never possessed visible tabernacles in their churches or any adoration practices, never experienced a problem of belief in the Real Presence. I could go on and on about the need for deeper analyses, but these examples suffice. I felt in so many instances the pastoral remedy to be applied did not correspond to the causes of the illness.

I was disappointed that Pope John Paul II did not distinguish the essentials of the Church's spiritual life, i.e., scriptures and the sacraments, from the many devotions that arose from private revelations. While Pope Paul VI was careful not to impose on the whole Catholic Church his personal choices for private devotions, Pope John Paul II had no such inhibitions. Catholics always had enjoyed a freedom of selection with regard to private revelation. The approval of a specific one did not signify that anyone would be less Catholic by not accepting it or by accepting it with a bit of skepticism.

His appointments to the offices of the curia remain a mystery to me. Some were people of the highest caliber who took their role seriously and performed well; others were less than competent — almost disgracefully so. His choice for bishops was clearer: Absolute loyalty to his person and to his position on certain key issues was a requirement. In fact, if one wanted to look for the most glaring weakness of his pontificate, it would be the careerism it engendered. It would not take a genius like Machiavelli to write the handbook for advancement in the Church during his pontificate. Leadership qualities were secondary; loyalty was first. This was especially worrisome since he left much in the hands of curial officials, creating a major barrier between himself and the local bishops. This interference of the curia grew progressively more intolerable as he grew weaker and less involved.

I was never sure of the theological and philosophical underpinnings of his writings and speeches. They did not seem to be based on scripture, even if scripture was used as a launching pad for lengthy discourses that went way beyond the meaning of the original text. I never totally understood the phenomenological roots of his teaching — if phenomenology created those roots. His writings were not easy to assimilate. I would read each new encyclical pacing the room to keep my attention level high, but it was not always easy to sum up the substance of what he had written.

What surprised me most was his intolerance of views opposed to his own, especially among theologians, the force with which he reacted to suppress them, and the secrecy of the procedures. He never seemed to be able to create just and fair processes within the Church or create tribunals and courts in Rome that were examples for the rest of the Church. Cases would drag on and on for years with constant changes of personnel and procedures. I had hoped that with his background of having lived under Nazi and Communist regimes, he would have been more sensitive to justice and the need for clear and open trials, even in the area of theological discourse. Personally, he seemed to make the decisions himself in many cases, like those involving bishops, but would never discuss the problem directly with the bishop in question.

Unlike Pope John XXIII, Pope John Paul II failed to recognize the signs of the times. Pope John had noted as one of the signs of our times a desire of all people to have a say on the decisions that affected their lives. John Paul II had many misgivings about democratic processes, even for nations, and only later in life reluctantly accepted democracy as the best form of civil government. He saw democracy as weak, indecisive, compromising in attempting to please the majority, and as having no place in the Church — even though his own election as pope had been a democratic one. His model of the papacy was that of a benign monarch. He tolerated no disagreement with his policies, rewarded those who were loyal to his person and views, and sought to silence any voice that could lead to disunity as he defined it.

He did not read the signs of the times, namely, the openings of Vatican II toward more participatory government on all levels of church life, and as it had been in the early centuries of the Church. Discerning the action of the Spirit in the whole Church was not on his agenda. This failure was probably the most important lost opportunity in the post-conciliar period.

I realize now that being a bishop during the pontificate of such a forceful and unbending pope was not an easy task for me. I was too much of a free spirit, intellectually too restless, and not able to acquiesce to his thought with peace of mind. Nor was I able to do nothing but carry out the externals of my job. Most of all, my fear of authoritarianism grew stronger and stronger. It was not a matter of grave import during the pontificate of Pope Paul VI since I had easy access to him and accepted that he was truly concerned about me as a person. I never felt that way about Pope John Paul II. In my encounters with him, I was always cautious, wondering what he really meant and why he asked me the (few) questions he did.

*   *   *

I soon found out that as retirement approached there were many anniversaries to be celebrated. June 24, 2001, was the fiftieth anniversary of my ordination to the priesthood. Most of my near relatives came to Milwaukee to celebrate. Since the cathedral was closed for renovation, we held a more intimate ceremony in the seminary chapel. I appreciated a low-key event. At the priests' overnight in May, I had celebrated with the other jubilarians. 2001 was also the twentieth anniversary of the founding of the parish at Sabana Yegua in the Dominican Republic and so at the beginning of September, at the request of the parishioners, I made a trip there for the festivities. In fact, I was there when I heard the news of 9/11. At first, the information that came over the radio was very garbled. I went with some of the other people from Milwaukee visiting the parish to a near-by hotel to watch CNN on TV. After a day or so I was able to arrange a flight to Milwaukee, as I wanted to be home and participate in whatever interfaith prayer services might be planned.

Before leaving, I was deeply touched by how many parishioners came to the rectory to give me the traditional *abrazo* and words of sympathy. It felt like a reversal of roles this time and I appreciated their personal and sincere concern. We Americans were the ones who were now vulnerable. Later I was told that about a hundred people working in the towers who perished were from Baní, a small city we always passed through to go from Santo Domingo to Sabana Yegua. I have often asked myself how the world might have been different if we had used this moment for bonding and mutual grieving among all of us who were suffering losses. Back home in Milwaukee I participated in ecumenical and interfaith events marking the losses of 9/11, but I found it difficult to keep before the public eye the other nations who were also grieving.

*   *   *

But this grieving and reflective atmosphere over 9/11 was soon to end in the archdiocese as we entered 2002. The first half of that year remains in my mind as an uncontrollable whirlwind of events that I could not totally absorb but had to react to. They remain a blur in my mind.

In early January, the *Boston Globe* printed article after article about the sex-abuse cases in the archdiocese of Boston. Soon dioceses adjacent to Boston were also the objects of investigations that continued to fill the papers. The effects of all these articles began slowly to reach the Midwest and the Milwaukee Archdiocese. As the national secular press reprinted the Boston articles, many of those reports began to appear in our own papers. Before that time our own Catholic weekly carried very few articles on the sex-abuse cases in the archdiocese, covering mostly those that were the subject of public trials. That picture now changed. Naturally our own practices became the object of intense scrutiny by the local press.

My first reaction to the Boston situation was one of anger. I could not believe that the Church in Boston had done so little to uncover and then take steps to prevent these abuses of defenseless children. It seemed to me and to other bishops in the Midwest that the East Coast dioceses had not taken seriously our many discussions as bishops going back to 1985. They had not followed the guidelines we had put in place, even if we had no authority to enforce them. I simply could not believe this neglect. There was no way to defend it.

I was angry also at the East Coast reporters. It seemed to me they equated the Church there with the whole U.S. Catholic Church and did a great injustice to other parts of the Church, especially in the Midwest. They neglected the journey we had made, the struggles we had undergone to try to understand the enormity of the situation, the money we had spent on therapy, on hot-lines and offices where one could report such abuses, the increasingly professional help we were using, and so on. Certainly, one could say we had made mistakes of judgment, especially before 1985, and we may not have listened to the best psychological advice, but we had tried to grasp the situation and its gravity within the limits in which we had to work. In the reporting, there was no chronological perspective; all cases, old or new, were treated alike. I resented this lack of professionalism. It is true we had shifted our emphasis. Now we came to see our main task as care for the victims, especially after seeing the disastrous effects of abuse in so many cases. We had less confidence in the help therapists could give perpetrators: Was it effective? What assurances did we have in returning priests to ministry? It was as if we had done nothing. Old cases were dragged up; the same information, not always accurate, was repeated over and over again. I learned how much reporters borrow from each other and how seldom they find the time to go back and check each other's work. How I wished that Cardinal Bernardin or someone of his stature were alive to put in perspective what had already been done in parts of the country beyond the East Coast revelations of inertia.

Right away some began to interpret this barrage from the *Boston Globe,* the *New York Times,* and affiliated papers as the old Nativist anti-Catholicism, but I did not think that was an accurate judgment. There may have been some truth in the remarks that everyone who had a gripe against the Catholic Church or a pet theory was jumping on the band-wagon, but I knew in my heart that there was too much truth in the reports to "shoot the messengers," even if their motives at times may have been mixed. The Church, especially its hierarchy, was viewed as arrogant and judgmental, acting as if it were omniscient and above criticism. Who could deny this? The hierarchy too often acted as if it was responsible to no one and no one had a right to hold it accountable. Now we were being humbled and brought to our knees. Although I was, at times, upset with the inaccuracies of the reporting, especially when no distinctions were made between diocesan priests and religious order priests and when no attention was given to the way these cases were handled in the whole of society in previous decades, I knew the problem was grave and we had to accept the devastating nature of it and its repercussions. The priests, too, were upset, especially that the Catholic Church was being singled out, that other groups where there had been many cases of sexual abuse of minors were not being investigated nor lawsuits brought against them. It is a shame that this question of money, with the implication that the Church was wealthy and should pay exorbitant sums, negatively affected the attitudes of many of the clergy and created toward the press, especially toward the local press, a bitterness that, I fear, remains unchanged after many years.

It seemed to me that the peak of this relentless criticism, first directed toward Cardinal Law as the primary example of these insensitive attitudes, shifted then to the Catholic Church at large and its bishops in general. If I am correct, this happened in Milwaukee after an article on Cardinal Law in *Newsweek* on March 7. Pressures then began to mount rapidly.

The greatest rightful concern on the part of the faithful was that a few priests with credible allegations against them that were beyond the statues of limitation were in limited, supervised, but active ministry. After two fruitless attempts, I had come to the conclusion that it would be impossible to have a priest returned to the lay state. Each case went to Rome and the long delays began. Second, I was convinced that it was not fair to give such men jobs that belonged to the laity. Like many other bishops, when the institutes that dealt with predators assured me that a priest could be put in pastoral ministry with proper supervision, I set up such a system. In addition, invited by a therapist in Madison, Lloyd Sinclair, I became a member in 1994 for at least six years of a group called Wisconsin Sex Offender Treatment Network. It was composed of therapists working primarily in the prison system. I did so to obtain a realistic picture of what an array of experts thought about recidivism and how they handled it. I also came to know how much we all had to learn about sexual predators and how rampant sexual child abuse was in our society.

However, pressures to name these priests and where they were working increased. I realized the fears of the parents, and, although I had every reason to believe the system we had in place was as effective as anywhere in the States, I knew that the credibility of any bishop at that point was zero and there were indeed grave risks.

I also was not totally convinced of zero tolerance, i.e., if there had been only one accusation against a priest in the past, he should be returned to the lay state. I readily admitted that this should be the penalty, however, for any case in the future. It just seemed too sweeping and lacking in specificity to be helpful.

The best result of all the publicity, however, was that many cases of those victimized in the past came to light and we were able to offer help with therapy. But the problem of what to do with the perpetrators remained. In mid-March I announced the formation of a special commission called the Eisenberg Commission, taking its name from its chair, Howard Eisenberg, dean of Marquette Law School. I handed all the files over to the commission and the members quickly agreed to list publicly the names of any priest with verifiable allegations in even limited supervised ministry. I accepted their decision.

Around April 9, the president of the conference of bishops went to Rome to discuss the problem of Boston and the Church in the United States with the pope and his consultors. The result was that the pope called a meeting of all the officials of the conference and all the cardinals of the United States in Rome for April 23-24. I was not impressed with this procedure, since, again, I did not believe that the knowledge and wisdom of the cardinals on this issue was in any way superior to that of other bishops. It seemed more like a gathering in which the East Coast members of the hierarchy could defend themselves. Understandably, it was not an effective meeting.

In the meantime, on April 2, to be precise, I mailed my letter of resignation as archbishop with the plea that I be able to retire immediately. The response was that my retirement was accepted but would be effective only when they informed me. (This was called in Latin a *nunc pro tunc*.) On April 21 a group of twenty-one bishops and abbots and my siblings came to Milwaukee for a Mass in the newly renovated cathedral (it was the Sunday of the Good Shepherd) to celebrate my retirement and the twenty-fifth anniversary of my being named a bishop — although that anniversary was some six months in the distance.

Some members of my family were worried about me as I seemed to them under exceptional pressure. They were especially displeased with the *Milwaukee Journal/Sentinel* and its edition that day. The anniversary was hidden away in the middle and a case of a pedophilia was on the front page. Afterwards they noted I did not seem to be myself. They were correct. For the first time in my life as a superior, I felt helpless. Even resigning did not seem to be an option since that was now in the hands of Rome. I did not know what more I could do.

On May 16, I attended a gathering organized by my staff to hear the mind of the people on this issue. Six of these were scheduled and I attended the one in Brookfield at St. John Vianney Parish. The picture the following day in the paper told the whole story. No one was interested in a structured meeting. At the same time no one by now really trusted any of us bishops. It was a hopeless situation. The picture showed a woman screaming at me. The priest she was talking about was deceased; I had never met him and only vaguely knew about the case. What could I say? No words could take away her pain. No action of mine could rectify the past. All I could say was that we were doing our best, knowing it would not be seen as enough.

During those weeks I was also receiving many e-mails, most unsigned, some from members of the press warning me of things to come, some from very angry people, some with scathing insults. Most were full of rumors that I would soon be brought low. Rumors were also repeated to me that conservative people were paying private detectives to investigate my life, that money was passing hands to pay Marcoux for a big exposé, and so on.

A new pressure came from the press; they wanted access to all the settlement agreements. What I thought had been standard legal practice (certainly used, I had noted, by the newspapers in handling their own labor settlements with individuals) was now seen as secrecy. I wasn't sure I understood from a legal point of view the difference between secrecy and confidentiality, which, to my way of thinking, was an important part of both the ecclesial and legal systems. I finally agreed that if a victim wished to release to the press a settlement, he or she could do so. The secrecy after all was there to protect the victims.

Marcoux's lawyers interpreted this release to include the settlement with him. I could not contradict that interpretation since they acted immediately. I was also tired of the whole mess. Knowing it would not go away without full revelation, but hoping that such revelation would also bring a sense of freedom to me, I accepted the inevitable results. I presupposed, however, that the press would not include my case with all the pedophilia cases, as they were totally different. The contrary happened. Most papers just tossed it into the hopper with the others, no distinctions being made. Even the *New York Times* did the same. The pitch of anti-bishop fervor was so high at the time that I realized there would be no way this settlement could be played out in the press as I had understood it and as I talked about it in my apology. As the lawyers had explained it to me, I was being accused of having tried to keep Marcoux from earning wages from his Christodrama by my criticism of it. When the lawyers advised me to accept the settlement, the hope was to avoid more expenses by trying to prove the contrary.

Now I simply resigned myself to the inevitable.

It was difficult to grieve over something that transpired twenty-some years before — less so for something four years ago. But I did grieve and I was angry at myself for being so lax, stupid, and foolish. I knew, though, it was time now to look toward the future. I decided to hold no animosity toward anyone, certainly not toward Paul Marcoux. Without trying to excuse or minimize the negative aspects of my relationship with him, I had put that issue to rest many years before. Toward the press, at first, I held some anger, but with time that, too, has mitigated. They are human, too, and have their own weaknesses and prejudices. Unfortunately, they seem to create among themselves an inner culture that reminds me far too much of the clerical church culture. The legal system and the psychological community were also in a process of growth that I respected. I came to blame no one, including myself, for not having had sufficient knowledge previously when it was needed.

If I have any sadness, it is that we have made too little progress in understanding and helping victims regain a full life. Too many seem to be left in anger. I also regret that, although we have made much headway in delineating the profile of the perpetrators, we have made little progress in detecting this addiction early on and then seeking some sort of cure or humane control. We all are, in that sense, victims of the times we live in and have to accept those limitations, hoping and praying that the next generation will do better than we did. For these reasons, I am at peace with my God, with my Church, and with myself.

What may I conclude of this longe serye,
But after wo I rede us to be merye,
And thanken Juppiter of al his grace?
And er that we departen from this place
I rede that we make of sorwes two
O parfit joye, lastynge everemo.
And looketh now, wher moost sorwe is herinne,
Ther wol we first amenden and bigynne.

Chaucer: The Knight's Tale,
The Canterbury Tales

(What conclusion may I draw from this long train of argument but advise
that joy should follow our grief, while thanking Jupiter for all his goodness? And before we leave this place I suggest we make of two griefs one
perfect joy that shall last for ever. Now watch: there where we find the
deepest grief, there shall we begin the cure.)

Final Reflections

O n Monday, May 7, 2007, with the priests of the Archdiocese of Milwaukee, I went to Lake Delavan for the twenty-third annual priests' retreat. Five years had passed since my retirement; I was now over eighty .
years old. This annual retreat was the one opportunity we had each year to
come together in a relaxed way to pray; to celebrate ordination anniversaries; to reflect on our ministry; and to listen and respond to inspirational
and challenging talks. I was happy to be with them once again.

Outside my room was a patio with an old-fashioned rocking chair
where I could watch the lake. On Tuesday, early morning the only visible
motion was a lone fisherman standing in his boat out on the lake, its surface without a ripple. The resort was almost empty except for 275 priests; it
was a quiet and peaceful setting. During the next two days I sat rocking, reflecting and outlining my ideas for this last chapter. My only official "duty"
that week was to preside and preach at Morning Prayer on Wednesday, the
last day of the overnight. In my ruminations, the sermon and the epilogue
played off one another.

In jotting down my thoughts about this final chapter, I asked myself
why I was writing these memoirs. In the beginning, these reflections were
primarily for my own benefit, to see the whole at once and to try to make
sense of all that had happened to me, the comfortable and the stressful,
the lapses and the successes.

But why publish them? Why share them with others? There are many
reasons not to do so. One aspect of contemporary culture that I have al-

ways intensely disliked is the temptation to make someone's weaknesses, especially sexual, into a demeaning form of public entertainment. I do not want my life to be used in such a way. Nor would I want to expose my life to others' prurient curiosity.

But finally, there are positive reasons to tell my story. I have lived from the Depression and Second World War to the economic and cultural globalization of the United States and the whole world. The U.S. Catholic Church has passed from being an immigrant, predominantly working-class community to a well-educated, professional, and affluent one (albeit with a very large and new population of immigrants). The U.S. Church has had to adjust to the changes brought about by Vatican II, with all the excitement, fervor, and expectations the council engendered — but also the divisions and anxiety that followed. For all of us it meant opening the windows, as Pope John XXIII proposed, to the culture around us and accepting the challenges that brought. My story has meant recalling and recounting my efforts at implementation under two very different visions of what the council intended — that of Pope Paul VI and that of Pope John Paul II. Furthermore, because of the devastating sexual-abuse cases that have come to light, it has also meant examining, even questioning, the strength of the Church's own moral fiber.

Looking back on my life, I realize I have often had a front seat in that history, even at times playing a minor role as a minor actor. More than a quarter century later, reading what others are writing about that period, especially the years of Pope Paul VI, I detect a good amount of revisionism. I have thought it important to say how I, as one individual, saw what was happening then. True, it is only one believer's experience, but, I hope, one worth sharing and saving for posterity.

This reflection reminds me of one of my favorite stories from the Talmud: The sages of the Jewish community, reassembling after the destruction of Jerusalem, worried that subsequent generations might seek a word from Torah and not find it. They set out, then, to collect the results of all the discussions in an attempt to preserve them, together with the names of those who had handed them down. Since the majority of these were binding decisions, some asked why they should preserve the minority voices, especially if it be the voice of a single sage. Someone proposed that in that way those voices could be recalled and refuted and thus deprived of their influence. But Rabbi Yehuda said: "They are preserved so that one may be able to rely on them when their hour has come." Thus, I record my story "for when the hour may come."

Why in my work and interests was I so concerned about church structure and the role of authority? For many Americans, religion is all about the individual's relationship with God; for them, structures become an obstacle to be removed or ignored. That is not my life-long conviction. In reciting the Creed, I continue with faith — if not always with fervor — to affirm: "I believe in one, holy, Catholic, and apostolic Church." For me religion is not just personal but also communal. In addition to my relationship with a merciful, loving, Triune God, I must relate to this planet and everyone on it. I also believe that God uses humans, with all our foibles and warts, to bring about a kingdom of mutual love and service. I believe we are a communion of saints, but also, in the here and now, a communion of sinners. When the organizational structure does not serve and facilitate these relationships but instead becomes an end in itself, it needs to be reformed, not abandoned.

What have I learned in looking over these eighty years that I would want to pass on to my fellow Catholic believers? The answer to that question melded with the themes of the homily I had prepared for the final day of the priests' retreat.

*   *   *

On Wednesday morning, with alb and stole under my arm, I took the outside path from the distant lodge-house where I was staying to the room, transformed into a chapel, where we would be reciting Morning Prayer. The few early-birds among the other guests at the resort were on their way to the golf-course. The gift shop had just opened and some were picking up the morning paper — usually the *Chicago Tribune* or the *Wall Street Journal*. It was a beautiful day.

The text for the Morning Office on that Wednesday in the Easter Season was taken from St. Paul's Letter to the Romans 6:8-11. The full text is the first reading during the Easter Vigil, reminding us that baptism is a participation in the dying and rising, the paschal mystery, of Jesus Christ. I had been meditating for weeks on that text and what I might say to the priests. I was haunted by the fact that, deep within me, I believed the Catholic Church I loved and had served for so many years was in denial. I hesitated saying this so bluntly — even to myself. I realized the Church had to do more dying before it could fulfill the mission given it by Christ. I was distressed that church leaders, myself included, tended always to blame everyone but themselves for the crisis in which the Church finds itself —

419

the dearth of vocations to priesthood and religious life, the rise of secularism in countries once Christian, the shifting of many in countries once Catholic to other Christian groups, the deaf ear given to the Church's teachings on moral issues by many practicing Catholics, and the inability to deal adequately and in a gospel fashion with problems like sexual abuse. All this had been floating in my mind as I prepared the homily.

Our provisional chapel had a makeshift altar and pulpit, a bowl of incense on a high stand, and a few candles. The priests were gathering as I arrived. While vesting in a nearby room, I could hear the organist at the electronic organ practicing. Like other such occasions the singing was good, and I felt I was back in the monastery. The all-male voices, the low ceilings, and the roughly hewed wooden beams added to the sonority.

When it came time to preach, I admit I was more nervous than usual, and my heart was pounding a bit. It is never easy to preach before fellow priests; one fears they have already taken out their little notebooks to write their critique. I decided long ago not to be intimidated by them, but to rely on their good will and desire to hear something that would be helpful. But I was emotional about what I had to say since it also involved me very personally. With a story or so to set the context, I began to search the meaning of the passage from St. Paul: what our participation in the dying and rising of the Lord Jesus might be, first as a Church, then as individuals.

I knew that dying and rising was a long and on-going process for the Church and for our whole life. Being incorporated into the Body of Christ, as Paul put it, was not incorporation into a static entity but a constantly growing spiritual search to become more Christ-like through dying and rising to new life. We had to die to our old selves as church and as individuals in that Church. Our conversion is a slow, life-long process.

To what should the Church be dying today? I cited the example of Pope John Paul II who, during the Holy Year of 2000 — against the advice of his staff and close advisors — apologized over fifty times for past injustices committed by the Church throughout history.

But there were and are many faults. From my experience I felt the first and most serious fault the Church should die to in our day is its arrogance, to which I personally — especially as a bishop — had contributed. When I browsed through the newspaper articles on the sexual abuse cases in the East Coast dioceses, I could not help but sense that the most frequently cited negative trait of the current Church was its arrogance. Although this is usually said of the hierarchy, I would have to say that I also find it among many lay people, both traditionalists and progressives. That was the same adjective used about me by some talk-radio hosts in Milwaukee. Yes, I tended to be too arrogant, too cocky, too dismissive of other points of view.

The Church must also die to its claims on perfectionism. Cardinal Ottaviani was the exponent of the Church as the *societas perfecta* (the perfect society) but that view was rejected by the bishops at Vatican II. Christ did not come to found a perfect society here on this earth, but a society of struggling sinners. Again I recalled to the priests the phrase used by Cardinal Francis George at the synod for America in 1997 that we American Catholics are, from a religious point of view, culturally Calvinists. We tend to confuse the ideal with the reality; we like to give to the world the appearance of being the perfect model. In this, we deny the sinful reality that lies beneath and that in our day has become ever more visible. Priests and bishops are also sinful and need the same kind of spiritual supports as the laity.

Is this confusion of the ideal with real also the source of a growing fear, especially prevalent among secular voices in American society, that, in the long run, the Catholic hierarchy would like to create a situation in which all laws governing our nation would mirror Catholic moral positions? Does the Catholic Church want to create in the United States a Catholic confessional state and impose a Catholic moral law on all, like the *sharia* in Muslim states?

As church we must also die to our judgmentalism. We Catholics, perhaps because of the defensiveness inherited from the period when we were a minority in the United States, have become a judgmental people, too readily blaming someone else when we have an internal problem. I recognize this judgmental quality in myself and still have much to die to.

Finally, I mentioned that the Church must die to its omniscience. For some reason, the Church feels it must hurry to join in every controversy and give an authoritative solution. I yearn for the days when the hierarchy would do in our day what it did in the past regarding many squabbles between theologians, especially from the competitive religious orders: just saying the equivalent of "Cool it, Boys." There is a story — probably apocryphal — that Pope Paul VI once commented in jest: "I never knew it would be so difficult to be infallible." Many in the Church find that "creeping infallibility," i.e., the growing tendency to claim to have the final answer, is far too common among us. It would be wise for all of us to read again the Grand Inquisitor's dialogue in Dostoevsky's *Brothers Karamazov,* reflecting especially on how we priests and bishops think the faithful are so ignorant that we must give them all the answers, that they really want to be led and not take responsibility for their own spiritual lives, and that we are competent to lead simply by the weight of our office and authority.

If the Church has lost so many among the American intelligentsia, artists, musicians, and even theologians, it is because it gives the impression that it does not need them — being self-sufficient in creating and judging what it feels best for its faithful to live the gospel message. Because we have alienated all these groups and they do not feel at home in our midst, we no longer are able to create a Catholic culture that is the expression of our faith, that describes our journey as Christian disciples facing contemporary struggles with the modern world, and that can help sustain all of us on pilgrimage.

We must die as a Church to all these temptations. We all are the Church and so we must personally die to them too. And then, there are other personal sins, attachments, and handicaps we must die to, some of them not of our choosing. In this last category, I cited the infirmities that come with age, loss of memory, loss of dear ones in death, loss of friends from whom we have become estranged, and, in my case in particular, loss of one's good name. Each person has to die to personal losses.

At this point in my homily I said: "You are probably waiting for me to finish this section so I can name the ways in which I see us rising with Christ, enumerating the positive signs of hope. I am sure I could do so, but I choose not to do so. I do not want to fall into the neo-Pelagianism of our American culture, i.e., the belief that we can solve any problem with our own ingenuity and skill. Instead, I want to present a different kind of example that avoids the search for a programmatic solution outside ourselves."

That example I selected was a gift from Vietnamese Benedictine nuns when I visited their monastery in 1968 right after the Tet offensive. It was an elegantly carved, small wooden vase about six inches tall and a small circular wooden tray that were meant to be used as a chalice and paten for Mass. At first these beautiful objects looked to be nothing but fine specimens of lacquer-ware. Although I never used them for Mass, I kept them on my shelf, dusted them frequently and just held them or ran my hands over them. Wherever I moved, they came with me. Slowly, through the years, from the oil of human fingers touching them, mine and those I showed them to, and from the rags that dusted them, the black lacquer has begun to wear thin and one can see that underneath had been painted iridescent, shimmering tropical fish, especially gold fish. Together with the gold, the silver, red, and blue hues were now coming through.

Our dying does not of itself create new life, but the wearing away that comes from our dying to our corroding attitudes and actions permits the image of Jesus Christ to shine through. If this is true of us personally, will it not be true of the Church as well? I hope that it will be true of me. My daily prayer now in my old age is that I can continue to die to self to rise to new life.

The whole body of priests rose to applaud that homily, and I felt their continued support for the last stage of my earthly journey.

My story now comes to an end. Since texts from Chaucer's *Canterbury Tales* have accompanied my narrative, I wonder what Chaucer would have thought about it and where he would have placed it. He may have added it to the vignettes told by the Monk when his turn came — to be one more example of those who through stupidity have fallen from high places. Or perhaps he would have included it in the Parson's tale at the very end, that long and long-winded sermon on penitence, for that is the spiritual way we are told for arriving at the celestial Jerusalem. Or perhaps he would have just left it as it is, a sign of human folly, laced with some good things and some not so good, that mixture which every one carries into old age and ultimately to the grave. Like all the other tales of human pilgrimage it must end with a fervent prayer for God's gracious love and mercy on such a flawed but grateful pilgrim.

Acknowledgments

I n the first version of this book, I included long lists of people who had
been influential in the various periods of my life, e.g., the monks who
were significant in the early years at St. Vincent Archabbey, professors at
Juilliard and Columbia University who took an interest in my work and
reached out to me, Benedictine superiors and monks from around the
world who encouraged and supported me, and finally lists of priests and laity in Milwaukee, especially women, who were a part of my staff or leaders
in the many Catholic societies. There were also the many leaders in the ecumenical and interfaith community of Milwaukee from whom I learned
much and whose leadership I both enjoyed and found supportive. Realizing
how heavy such enumerations of names made the memoirs, I selected out
only a few in each period to represent the many. Here, however, I want to
thank all those whom I failed to list and simply say that I am grateful to you.

But my conscience would bother me if I did not name several people
who were especially helpful in the task of writing my tale. At St. Vincent
Archabbey in Latrobe, Pennsylvania, the archivist, my confrere, Father
Omer Kline, OSB, in his habitual gracious way, found everything I asked for
without difficulty. The archivists at Archbishop Cousins Catholic Center,
both Timothy Cary and Shelly Solberg, should bill me for shoe-leather
worn through by the many trips they made searching for the documents I
was looking for. I want to thank Ethel Gintoft, the outstanding retired editor of the *Catholic Herald,* whose brochure, *A Shepherd's Watch,* told the
story of what happened during the twenty-five years I was archbishop. It

served as an invaluable starting point for the last chapters of my work. For knowledge of the past I always referred to the monumental work by a priest of the Archdiocese of Milwaukee, Father Steve Avella, *In the Richness of the Earth: The History of the Archdiocese of Milwaukee 1843-1958* (Milwaukee: Marquette University Press, 2002).

Most especially, I would like to acknowledge those who were willing to read what I wrote chapter by chapter. They not only offered wise advice but encouraged me to continue when I thought that writing such a long and complicated story was too arduous. Their persistence became a sign of hope that I should share the work with an even larger readership. I mention Professors John Goulet and James Liddy (now deceased) of the English Department of the University of Wisconsin–Milwaukee. They could not have been more frank in their comments, but they always remained positive, even enthusiastic, about the work and urged me on.

I thank Doctor Anthony Meyer, MD, Psych., medical director of the Milwaukee Psych Hospital, not only for reading everything I wrote, but for kind and astute remarks as I tried in these last five years to make sense out of my life. Without his gentle but persuasive probing this book could not have been written. I would also like to acknowledge Father James Schroeder, SCJ, Dr. of Clinical Psychology, who read each chapter for me, annotated them with most helpful comments, and was always available to talk about his reactions to what I wrote. His supportive friendship goes back many years. For her professional help in compiling the index and for her wise suggestions during the writing of the manuscript, I would like to express my thankfulness to Ms. Jean Mullooly.

I would be remiss if I did not mention in gratitude my two sisters, Barbara Weakland and Marian Weber, who read the entire work while it was in progress. It was good being able to talk over with them the early years of growing up in Patton, Pennsylvania, sharing stories about relatives and the town. Much of what I wrote was done on my laptop at Barbara's condo in Hollidaysburg, Pennsylvania, while she provided the relaxed atmosphere needed for concentration and reflection.

How can I express my gratitude to William and Samuel Eerdmans, who felt the book was worth publishing and were willing to make sure that happened? And the publisher's wisdom in asking Margaret O'Brien Steinfels to be the special editor was an indication of their desire to make it as accurate and compelling as possible. Her help was inestimable and I am much indebted to her wisdom and insights, her queries and suggestions.

Acknowledgments

I gratefully acknowledge those who willingly contributed photographs for the book. Photographs supplied by the Archdiocese of Milwaukee Archives are used with permission; those supplied by *The Catholic Herald* are used with permission; photographs copyright 2008 by The Benedictine Monks of St. Vincent Archabbey, Latrobe, Pennsylvania, are used with permission; all others are from my personal collection.

Lastly, I would like to thank all those Milwaukeeans who remained close to me during these last six years, especially the group that used to attend the 8:00 Mass at the Cathedral of St. John the Evangelist and whose friendship encouraged me to continue making Milwaukee my home. Yet, with age, the yearning to return to my monastic roots grows ever stronger.

Index

Abortion, hearings with women on, 329-33

Ad limina visits: in 1983, 264-65; in 1988, 319-25; in 1993, 343-45; in 1998, 388-89

Antoniutti, Card. Ildebrando, 128, 150, 200; first encounter with, 131-33; opposition to courses for nuns, 148-49; opposition to liturgical changes at Sant'Anselmo, 141-42

Archbishops, American, and dialogue with Roman curia (1989), 326-28

Archdiocesan Council of Priests (ACP), 256, 305; on renovation of St. John's Cathedral, 397; on shortage of priests, 346

Archdiocesan Pastoral Council (APC): formation and topics treated, 244-58, 305; on shortage of priests, 346

Archdiocese of Milwaukee: 150th anniversary of, 368

Arrupe, Pedro, S.J., 151, 152; and farewell gathering, 227; as president of Union of Superiors General, 193

Authoritarian rulers, fear of, 33, 43-44, 105-6

Baggio, Card. Sebastiano, 224, 239-40

Benedict XVI. *See* Ratzinger, Card. Josef

Benedictine nuns and sisters, 135-36

Benedictine spirituality, 55-60

Bernardin, Card. Joseph: advice on *ad limina* visit (1988), 321; chairing Peace Pastoral, 273, 275, 278; Common Ground Initiative, 374; last illness and death, 377-78; role in dialog with curia (1989), 327-28; at synod on the laity, 309-10; talk before pope (1987), 306-7

Bitgers, Jeanne, 256-57

Brasó, Abbot Gabriel, 120, 128, 190

Buckley, William F., Jr., 301-2

Bugnini, Archbp. Annibale, 127-28, 141, 203, 206

Butler, Bp. Christopher, 121, 133

Cancer, operation for prostate, 378-81

Casaroli, Card. Agostino, 217; and Benedictines in Hungary, 168-72; on Church in U.S.A., 240; and economic pastoral letter, 279; and ordination of auxiliary bishop, 247

Cicognani, Card. Amleto: as secretary

of state, 113-14; and image of Church in U.S.A., 211-13

Collegiality and bishops' conferences: *apostolos suos,* 389; National Conference of bishops, 263, 296-98, 316-18, 366-67; in Vatican Council II, 230, 250-53

Common Ground Initiative, 374-77

Comunitá di Sant'Egidio, 228

Consilium ad exequendam, 118, 203-4

Costello, Maurice, O.S.B., 47-48

Cousins, Archbp. William, 225, 251, 255, 325

Dearden, Card. John, 118, 156, 280; "Dearden bishops," 295

Economic Justice for All, 263, 273-92

Ecumenism and Interfaith dialogues: among Benedictines, 220-22; apology in Milwaukee synagogue in year 2000, 393-95; as bishop in local church, Muslim/Catholic dialog, 262; chairing committee of bishops' conference, 367; with Jewish and Catholic scholars, St. Vincent Archabbey, 116; with the Orthodox churches, 391-93

Eisenberg Commission, 411

Eucharist without Walls, pastoral letter, 390

Faith crisis, personal, 49-51

Forty bishops, group of, 365-67

Gantin, Card. Bernardin, 323-24, 344; sabbatical request, 370-72

George, Card. Francis, 385-86

Gnassi, Mother Ildegardo, 147-48

Greenberg, Noah, 86

Guardini, Romano, 73

Hertzmann, Prof. Erich, 84, 85

Hlavcak, Michael, O.S.B., 48

Homosexuality, 17-19, 44-45

Hume, Card. Basil: as abbot of Ampleforth, 127, 173, 192, 200; as archbishop of Westminster, 223-24, 230, 238, 242-43, 352

Hunthausen, Archbp Raymond, 298-99

Jadot, Archbp. Jean, 165, 218, 281; "Jadot bishops," 294

John XXIII (Card. Angelo Giuseppe Roncalli), 70, 418

John Paul I (Card. Albino Luciani), 6, 236

John Paul II (Card. Karol Wojtyła), 6, 179, 207, 237, 241; apologies, 420; assessment of pontificate, 402-8; on ordination of women, 335, 345-46

Koch, Archabbot Alfred, 3, 42-43, 53, 61, 62, 70

Krellner, Justin, O.S.B., 49, 60, 61

Laghi, Card. Pio: and degree from Fribourg in Switzerland, 333

Lang, Prof. Paul Henry, 85

Law, Card. Bernard, 297-98; and sexual abuse cases, 411

Lay commission and economic pastoral letter, 281-82

Lay movements in the church, 308-11

Lefèbvre, Archbp. Marcel, 220

Leonilla (Connors), Sister, 35, 36, 39

Liberation theology, 176

Marcoux, Paul, 4, 7-10, 13, 385, 413

Mayer, Card. Augustin: as Benedictine, 65, 71, 126; as curial official, 200-202

Medina, Card. Jorge, 398-400

Merton, Thomas, O.C.S.O., 94, 107; death of, 166-67

Milroy, Dominic, O.S.B., 192

Montalvo, Archbp. Gabriel, 13; renovation of St. John's Cathedral, 398

Newman, Card. John Henry, 58, 251

Novak, Michael, 281, 283

O'Connor, Card. John, 297; assessment

of American culture, 327-28, 332; on role of women in church, 337
Ordination of married men, 337-41
Ordination of women, 334-37, 345-47
O'Reilly, Msgr. James, 77, 79-81

Pannonhalma, abbey of, 136, 167-72, 173
Paul VI (Giovanni Battista Montini), 3, 6, 89, 237, 317; assessment of pontificate, 215-20; on ordination of women, 334
Pius XII, 72, 74
Play of Daniel, 86-88
Polish misunderstanding, 6, 238-39
Priests, shortage of, 338-42
Project Benjamin, 397

Quade, Prof. Quentin, 257-58

Ratzinger, Card. Josef (Benedict XVI), 264-65, 280, 318, 324
Renew Program, 258-59
Rigali, Card. Justin, 240
Rule of St. Benedict, 114, 162-63

Sabbatical for doctoral degree, 369-73
Sacrificium laudis, 121, 123, 130-31, 134
St. John's Cathedral, renovation of, 395-401
St. Malachy's Parish, N.Y., 77-79
Schaut, Quentin, O.S.B., 56-57
Sexual abuse of minors by clergy, 40, 45-47, 268-71, 347-65; Boston and national news 409-12

Simon, William, 281
Sklba, Bp. Richard, 246-47, 254
Solesmes, abbey of, 55, 62, 68, 69, 390-91
Strittmatter, Archabbot Denis, 70, 94-95, 99-101, 112
Strunk, Prof. Oliver, 85, 86
Synod of bishops: in 1969, 153-56; in 1971, 156-58; in 1974, 206-9; in 1987, 309, 311-15; in 1997, 384-87
Synod of the Archdiocese of Milwaukee, 302-5

Thesaurus for Benedictine Office, 202

Ultramontanism, 295-96
Union of Superiors General (USG), 150-53

Vagaggini, Cyprian, O.S.B., 65-67, 71, 193
Vatican Council II, effects of, 103-9
Villot, Card. Jean, 142-43, 149

Ward, Barbara, 158, 273
Watelet, Ambrose, O.S.B., 139, 141, 192
Weakland, Basil, 24-26
Weakland, Mary (Kane), 27-29, 32, 46-47, 236-37
Wisconsin Catholic Conference, 261
Wortnam, Ildephonse, O.S.B., 49, 53, 116
Wright, Card. John, 155, 223
Wyszinski, Card. Stephan, 178